The Companion to Roses

The
Companion
to
Roses

JOHN FISHER

VIKING

Front cover: *This hand-finished colour mezzotint and engraving (dated 1805) from R. Thornton's* Temple of Flora *was the seventh in the series and the only one to have been designed by Thornton himself. The flowers shown comprise: pink centifolia roses; the white centifolia sport 'Unique Blanche' ('White Provence'); a striped sport of 'Unique';* Rosa hemisphaerica, *the double-yellow sulphur rose; and a wild rose of the Synstylae group.*

VIKING
Penguin Books Ltd, Harmondsworth, Middlesex, England
Viking Penguin Inc., 40 West 23rd Street, New York, New York 10010, U.S.A.
Penguin Books Australia Ltd, Ringwood, Victoria, Australia
Penguin Books Canada Ltd, 2801 John Street, Markham, Ontario, Canada L3R 1B4
Penguin Books (N.Z.) Ltd, 182–190 Wairau Road, Auckland 10, New Zealand

First published 1986

Designed and produced by
Bellew Publishing Company Limited
7 Southampton Place, London WC1A 2DR

Typeset in Plantin light

Printed in Great Britain by W. S. Cowells Ltd

British Library Cataloguing in Publication Data
Fisher, John, *1909-*
    The companion to roses.
    1. Roses
    I. Title
    635.9'33372   SB411

ISBN 0-670-80811-3

Acknowledgements

I am grateful to the officers and members of the Royal National Rose Society – in particular to Michael Gibson, E. F. Allen, R. D. Squires, R. C. Balfour and Lieutenant-Colonel K. J. Grapes for their encouragement and help, and also to the Society's magazine *The Rose* over the years, and to its present editor, Janet Browne.

My thanks are also due to Anne Cocker for notes on the history of the family nursery; to Patrick Dickson and L. Stewart of Dickson Nurseries Ltd, as well as to members of the Harkness family, for recounting incidents in their star-studded careers; to the officers of the British Association of Rose Breeders (BARB); to Sam McGredy, now of Castor Bay, Auckland, New Zealand, for keeping in touch; for Di Sawday of Apuldram Nurseries for information on the running of a successful retail rose nursery; to Mr T. Kenwright of Sealand Nurseries for background to *in vitro* cultivation of roses; to Angela Pawsey for notes on the (British) Rose Growers' Association and on the history of Cant's of Colchester; to Robert Wharton of Wharton Nurseries, Harleston, Norfolk, for an insight into large-scale production methods in a wholesale rose nursery; and to Tony Corlett, manager of the rose unit of Southdown Flowers and Vice-Chairman of the British Cut-Rose Growers' Association.

Others to whom thanks must be given are: M. L. Evans of Hoopers of Chichester for giving me a florist's views on roses; David Welch, City of Aberdeen Leisure and Recreation Department, for telling me about his work with amenity roses; J. Craig Wallace, Director of Parks, Belfast City Council; and the Clontarf Horticultural Society and the Dublin Corporation Parks Department for notes on the roses in St Anne's Park.

In France, I have to thank Guy Surand, Directeur des Parcs Jardins et Espaces Verts for his invitation to join the horticultural writers, artists, perfumers and others, comprising one section of the international jury at the Bagatelle rose judging. I am grateful to Bernard Mando, the head gardener at the Bagatelle, and André Brunel who occupies the same position at La Roseraie de l'Hay-les-Roses, for showing me the particular treasures under their charge. I am also very grateful to Mlle A. M. Saget for guidance on the methods used to process rose petals in the international perfumery industry and for introducing me to a number of French technical and artistic works on roses. I am also grateful to Alain Meilland for the pedigree of 'Pareo', his gold-prize-winning rose at the Bagatelle in 1985; to Georges Delbard for sending details of his *in vitro* cultivation methods; and to Jean Gaujard of Roseraies Gaujard for information on his family and on the Pernets.

I am indebted to Hanni Bartetzko of the Verein Deutscher Rosenfreunde and to Mathias Tantau for information on the roses of the Federal Republic of Germany, and to Herr Zimmerman, Senior Director of the Archives and Library of the City of Hildesheim, for information on the centuries of rose-growing at the cathedral; to Tessa Goody of the Flower Council of Holland for material on the Verenigde Bloemenveilingen, Aalsmeer; to Pernille and Mogens Olesen for their up-to-date account of the Poulsen Roses Company.

It was a pleasure to receive from David E. Gilad, Past President of the World Federation of Rose Societies, notes on the rose in Israel. My thanks go to Elizabeth Cooper of the Bermuda Rose Society for a delightful survey of the growing of old roses on the islands. Patricia Harney of the Ontario Agricultural College, Guelph, Ontario was kind enough to explain the trends in Canadian rose-breeding.

My thanks are also due to David R. Burton, President of the National Rose Society of New Zealand; to Victor J. Cowley of the US Federation of Rose Exhibitors; to Harold S. Goldstein of the American Rose Society; to George E. Rose, Executive Director of All-America Rose Selections, for his valuable comments; to Susan Funk of Jackson & Perkins; to Joyce Demits and her sister Virginia Hooper of Heritage Rose Gardens, Fort Bragg, California and to Patricia Stemler Wiley of Roses of Yesterday and Today of Watsonville, California, for information on 'old' roses now being grown in that state.

Details of miniature roses have come from Ralph S. Moore's Sequoia Nursery at Visalia, California, from Nor'east Miniature Roses, Rowley, Minnestoa, and from Miniature Roses, Beaverton, and Justice Miniature Roses, Wilsonville, both in Oregon. Ken Strobeck of the Portland, Oregon Rose Festival Association has provided a programme of the 1985 celebrations, and the Dallas Area Historical Rose Group and Bobby Fagg, Supervisor of the Samuell-Grand Rose Garden, have aided my search for the original Yellow Rose of Texas.

I am glad to acknowledge the help of Archbishop Bruno B. Heim, formerly Apostolic Pro-Nuncio in London, in tracing the history of the Golden Rose, and of the Officium Caeremoniarum Pontificalium in providing further information. I am grateful to Raife Wellsted, Curator of the National Postal Museum, for information on the philatelic rose. The Performing Rights Society has helped to trace titles, composers and lyricists of songs about roses. I am also grateful to Iona Opie; to G. D. Rowley, Department of Botany, Reading University, for his views on the status of *Rosa dumalis*; and to Paul W. Patton, Plant Protection Division of Imperial Chemical Industries. I was delighted to receive from Dr Th. Zwygart, President of the Gesellschaft Schweizerischer Rosenfreunde,the delightful book that the Association published on the occasion of its 25th anniversary.

I owe thanks to Dr Brent Elliott and Miss Barbara Collecott of the Lindley Library, for their unfailing patience; to the staff of the London Library; to the reference and music libraries of the West Sussex County Council; to Mrs Aquilina and Ms Rosemary Clarkson of the archives section of the Hammersmith Public Library for information regarding the plants dispatched by Lee & Kennedy to Redouté's patron M. Heritier and those sent to the *ci-devant* Empress Josephine.

Ib Bellew of the Bellew Publishing Company provided the inspirational idea for this book; Nancy Duin the meticulous editing; and Gabrielle Allen the picture research.

Mrs Pat Onions succeeded in pathfinding her way unerringly through a jungle of mistyping and corrections to make copy fit for a printer.

Messrs Faber & Faber were kind enough to allow me to use material on Ellen Willmott and on the Meilland family from books published by them to which further detailed reference is made in the text.

Aalsmeer

The flower auction at Aalsmeer, 10 miles (16 km) south-west of Amsterdam, where 900 million roses in 80 varieties are sold each year, is the world's greatest, and the premises on which it takes place – covering an area equivalent to fifty-five football pitches – is probably the world's largest commercial building. The VBA (Verenigde Bloemenveilingen Aalsmeer) is a growers' cooperative with more than 4000 members, which was established in 1968 on a site where flower auctions had been held since 1912.

Sales take place on the Dutch auction system – that is, the price falls until a buyer indicates that he is ready to pay it. Each consignment is introduced by the auctioneer, who quotes from an inspector's report on the quality of the flowers – for example, roses – on offer and the grower's name. The flowers themselves are displayed on trolleys carried before the buyers' eyes on a moving bandway.

The price on offer for a consignment at any given moment is shown by a counter moving round a vast dial. The dial shows not only the moving offer price but also the units (cents, guilders, etc.) in which the pointer is operating, the number of flowers per bunch, bucket, box, etc., the number of units on offer, the minimum purchase quantity and, when the transaction is concluded, the registered number of the buyer who has made the purchase. The buyer who stops the dial has the right to buy the whole of the lot on offer, or he can take a portion, in which case the dial indicates the balance still available.

Each buyer, whether he is a street-vendor or a big wholesaler, has a registered number and is provided with a plastic card that activates the keyboard at which he will sit during the auction. By pressing the keys, the buyer indicates to the computer his registered number and bid, making it possible for him to be given almost immediately a full record of the transaction, and for a trolley to be loaded at once with his purchases and sent off to his own centre in the building for packing and dispatch. All accounts are settled on the spot by cash or credit card.

Abyssinia, Holy Rose of

The Holy Rose of Abyssinia, originally known as *Rosa sancta*, has been planted in Christian sanctuaries in Ethi-opia for, in all probability, more than 1500 years. It is a low-growing shrub rose – about 3 feet (1 m) high – with large, blush-pink flowers.

It has some of the characteristics of *R. gallica* and *R. phoenicia*, which suggests that it may be a wild hybrid that originated not in Ethiopia but in western Asia, the natural home of these species. If, however, it were a hybrid between *R. gallica* and *R. phoenicia* it would be a triploid (*see* MEIOSIS) and therefore barren, which means that reports of it growing wild should be treated with caution.

Graham Thomas, an established authority on shrub roses, has speculated that the Holy Rose could well have reached Abyssinia with St Frumentius, who converted the population of the Tigre province to Christianity and in AD 326 was consecrated Bishop of Aksum, the city that, through the centuries, has remained the spiritual centre of the Christian church in Ethiopia. Some experts claim to have recognized the petals of *Rosa sancta* in Egyptian tombs of the Ptolemaic era – that is, from the 4th to the 1st century BC. If so, the Holy Rose would have been known in Egypt, and perhaps in other parts of the Mediterranean basin some six centuries before it reached Abyssinia. Until quite recently it was referred to as *Rosa richardii* in honour of the botanist Achille Richard who accompanied the French government's mission of exploration to Abyssinia of 1839–43; his description of the rose, written in orthodox botanical Latin, appeared in his *Tentamen florae abyssinicae*, published in 1848. Nowadays, however, there has been a move to treat it as a form of *Rosa damascena*.

The Holy Rose was first cultivated in Britain by the nurseryman William Paul in 1902. It is still grown on both sides of the Atlantic and appeared in the American *Modern Roses 8*. In catalogues, it is to be found sometimes as *Rosa sancta*, sometimes as *R. richardii* and occasionally as *R. x richardii*, to indicate its suspected hybrid origin.

An Ethiopian horticultural pretender – 'The Yellow Rose of Abyssinia' – appeared towards the end of the last century. This was the title mistakenly given in more than one standard work – including Gertrude Jekyll's – to *Rosa ecae*. This is a native of Afghanistan, and has enough distinction without borrowing from elsewhere. The flowers of *Rosa ecae* are deep orange yellow, and the plant, with noticeably small leaves, long upright reddish-brown branches, and dense prickles and bristles of the same reddish colour, make it easily distinguishable. Its Latin name is the result of the arguably deplorable practice of naming a species after an individual instead of after the essential characteristics of the plant itself. The person concerned – Eleanor Carmichael Aitchison (initials E.C.A.) was the wife of an army surgeon and botanist, Dr J. E. T. Aitchison, who served under Lord Roberts in the Second Afghan War of 1879, and discovered and named the plant. No doubt he felt that his wife deserved something special for having accompanied him on most of his botanical expeditions.

Advertisement for William Paul & Son, who first cultivated the Holy Rose of Abyssinia, Rosa sancta.

Alba roses

These are magnificent healthy shrubs with grey-green leaves and flowers that are either pure white, clear pink or pink-tinged, and are good for a solus position or as a backdrop to smaller bushes. They are regarded as hybrids of *Rosa canina* x *R. damascena*.

Officially, *Rosa alba semi-plena* is the White Rose of York and *R. alba maxima* is the 'Jacobite Rose'. Many have

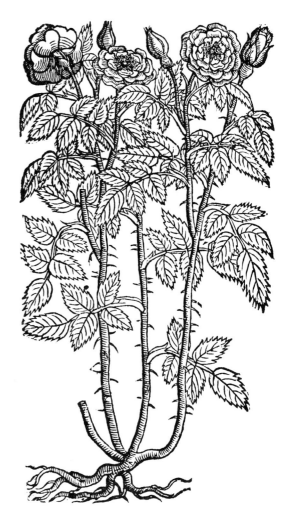

Rosa alba *from the 1597 edition of the* Herball *of John Gerrard.*

French names because of the effort made by French nurserymen to develop them.

Favourite varieties include:

'Maiden's Blush' and the (larger) *'Greater Maiden's Blush'*, both respectively pink with deeper pink centres and a strong fragrance. Also known as 'Cuisse de Nymphe' ('Nymph's Thigh') and 'Cuisse de Nymphe Emue' (more formally, *Rosa alba incarnata*).

'Celeste', one of the oldest varieties of alba, with soft pink semi-double flowers contrasting with foliage described as the colour of lead.

'Könegin von Dänemarck' ('Queen of Denmark'), a later arrival (probably 1826), has somewhat paler leaves and QUARTERED flowers; an elegant and still popular variety.

'Félicité Parmentier' and *'Amelia'*, both more compact, the former showing reflexed petals and the latter bright gold anthers.

Alexandra Rose Day

Usually held on the third Tuesday of June, Alexandra Rose Day was established in 1912 by Queen Alexandra, widow of

King Edward VII, to raise money for charity. The project was conceived by the Queen during a brief stay in her native Denmark when she visited a priest who had turned his house into a home for crippled children. His garden, full of the most beautiful roses, provided the resources to pay for their upkeep: he sold the roses and used the proceeds to help in feeding and clothing his 'family'.

Today, HRH Princess Alexandra is President of Alexandra Rose Day (headquarters: 1 Castlenau, Barnes, London SW13 9RP). The small pink and white wild roses are assembled out of linen by disabled people at the John Grooms Craft Centre, Edgware, near London, and sold to the public. An annual revenue of around £250,000 is looked for.

All-America Rose Selections

All-America Rose Selections (AARS) was founded in 1938 to provide a trials system leading to a seal of approval for roses of quality that could be grown anywhere in the United States with a reasonable expectancy of top performance. Membership includes almost all the major US rose-producing organizations. The AARS headquarters is at 513 West Sheridan Avenue, Shenendoah, Iowa 51601.

Since 1938 more than 2600 varieties have been tested by the AARS, and 121 – a little over 4 per cent – have been chosen as AARS award winners. These award winners, comprising less than 1 per cent of the known named varieties of roses, now account for 40 per cent of the 45 million rose plants sold annually in the United States.

The AARS controls twenty-one official test gardens in nineteen states scattered over the US. Most of these are located at universities or in large public rose gardens and are under the supervision of the AARS Test Garden Committee, with one judge allotted to each trial garden. Instructions regarding the layout of the trial garden, planting, care, time and manner of judging, etc. are prescribed and enforced, and AARS members are encouraged to visit the gardens and work with the judges whenever possible.

Candidate judges are called on to serve what amounts to a two-year apprenticeship, although that period of time may be extended if the judge needs additional experience. Once every five years, all judges and others associated with the testing programme meet at a central location for an intensive seminar on the judging of roses.

At the AARS trial grounds, the roses are scored on vigour, habit, disease resistance, foliage, flower production, bud and flower form, opening and finishing colour, fragrance and stem as well as on overall value, under the direction of the AARS scoring schedule committee. Roses on trial are assigned a code number that is their only identification during the two-year trial period. At the end of the trials, the AARS compiles the scores sent in by each judge for each entry. These are compared with other roses of the same period and with the standards set by previous roses and by the AARS. Sometimes as many as four varieties in a year qualify as award winners, sometimes none at all.

Roses that are submitted to the All-America Rose Selection trials will already have undergone four years of trials in their breeder's nursery (*see* HYBRIDZING ROSES), and only after the variety has gained high enough scores to indicate that it could be a potential award winner is the variety patented. The awards of the AARS are made and the entrants so notified in the year following the two-year trials. From then on, preparations are made for supplying the market with plants in the year following that in which the awards will have been publicly announced. The AARS award winner for 1985 was 'Showbiz', a scarlet floribunda, and the winners for 1986 were all hybrid teas: 'Broadway', orange-and-white bicolour; 'Touch of Class', coral-pink; and 'Voodoo', orange-red.

The AARS has test or demonstration gardens in: California, Colorada, Connecticut, Florida, Georgia, Illinois, Iowa, Kansas, Louisiana, Massachusetts, Michigan, Minnesota, Missouri, New Jersey, New York, Ohio, Oklahoma, Oregon, Pennsylvania, South Carolina and Texas. Practically all of them are open to the public. Award-winning roses to be launched the following year can also be seen in 132 AARS-accredited public gardens in forty-one states (and the District of Columbia) – thus allowing prospective buyers to assess how each rose performs under local conditions. These are:

Alabama: Battleship Memorial Park, Battleship Memorial Parkway, Mobile; Springdale Plaza Park, Airport Blvd, Mobile; Bellingrath Garden, Theodore.

Arizona: Valley Garden Center Rose Garden, Phoenix; Gene C. Reid Park, 900 S Randolph Way, Tucson.

Arkansas: Arkansas State Capitol Garden, Capitol Grounds, Little Rock.

California: Fountain Square Garden, 7115 Greenback Lane, Citrus Heights; Descanso Gardens, 1418 Descanso Dr., LaCanada; Exposition Park, 701 State Dr., Los Angeles; Morcom Amphitheatre of Roses, head of Jean St, 1 block off Grand Ave, Oakland; Wrigley Gardens, 391 S Orange Grove Blvd, Pasadena; Capitol Park, 15th St & Capitol Ave, Sacramento; Parker Garden at Balboa Park, Park Blvd & Plaza de Balboa, San Diego; Golden Gate Park, J. F. Kennedy Dr., San Francisco; San Jose Municipal Garden, Naglee & Dana Ave, San Jose; City Rose Garden, Los Olivos & Laguna, Santa Barbara; Civic Center, 8200 Westminster Ave, Westminster; Rose Hills Memorial Park, 3900 Workman Mill Rd, Whittier.

Colorado: War Memorial Garden, 5804 S Bemis St, Littleton; Lions Club Memorial Garden, 700 Long's Peak Rd, Longmont.

Connecticut: Norwich Memorial Garden, 200 Rockwell St, Norwich; Elizabeth Park Garden, 150 Walbridge Rd, West Hartford.

Florida: Florida Cypress Gardens, Cypress Gardens; Walt Disney World, Lake Buena Vista.

Georgia: Elizabeth Turner Rose Garden, University of Georgia, Athens; Greater Atlanta Garden, Piedmont Park, Atlanta; Rose Test Garden, 1840 Smith Ave, Thomasville.

Hawaii: University of Hawaii Maui Agricultural Research Center, Kula.

Illinois: Nan Elliott Memorial Garden, Moore Community Park, Alton; Merrick Garden, SW corner of Lake Ave & Oak St, Evanston; Cook Memorial Park, 413 N Milwaukee Ave, Libertyville; Glen Oak Botanical Garden, 2218 N Prospect, Peoria; Sinnissippi Garden, 1300 N Second, Rockford;

Washington Park Garden, Washington Park, Springfield; Cantigny, 1 South 151 Winfield Rd, Wheaton.

Indiana: Lakeside Garden, 1500 Lake Ave, Fort Wayne.

Iowa: Iowa State University, Horticultural Gardens, Ames; Bettendorf Park Board Municipal Garden, 2204 Grant St, Bettendorf; Noelridge Park Garden, 4900 Council St NE, Cedar Rapids; VanderVeer Park Municipal Garden, 214 W Central Park Ave, Davenport; Greenwood Park Garden, Grand Ave, 45–49 Sts, Des Moines; Weed Park Memorial Garden, Muscatine; State Center Garden, 300 block of Third St, State Center.

Kansas: E. F. A. Reinisch Rose Garden, 4320 W 10th, Topeka.

Kentucky: Kentucky Memorial Rose Garden, Kentucky Exposition Center, Louisville.

Louisiana: LSU Rose Test Garden, South Campus Dr., Baton Rouge; Burden Research Garden, LSU Annex Garden, Baton Rouge; Hodges Gardens, Highway 171 S, Many; American Rose Center, Jefferson-Paige Rd, Shreveport.

Maine: Deerings Oaks Park Rose Circle, Portland.

Maryland: Brookside Gardens, 1500 Glenallan Ave, Wheaton.

Massachusetts: James P. Kelleher Rose Garden, Park Dr., Boston; Stanley Park of Westfield, 400 Western Ave., Westfield.

Michigan: Michigan State University, Horticultural Gardens, East Lansing; Frances Park Memorial Garden, 2600 Moores River Dr., Lansing; Wayne County Coop Extension Garden, 5454 Venoy Rd, Wayne.

Minnesota: Lake Harriet Garden, Roseway Rd & Lake Harriet Parkway, Minneapolis.

Mississippi: Hattiesburg Area Garden, Campus of University of Southern Mississippi, Hattiesburg.

Missouri: Rose Display Garden, Capaha Park, Parkdale & Perry Ave, Cape Girardeau; Laura Conyers Smith Rose Garden, 5200 Pennsylvania Ave, Kansas City; Missouri Botanical Gardens, 2345 Tower Grove Ave, St Louis.

Montana: Missoula Memorial Rose Garden, 700–800 Brooks St, Missoula.

Nebraska: Lincoln Municipal Rose Garden, Antelope Park, Lincoln; Memorial Park Rose Garden, 57th & Underwood Ave, Omaha; Boys Town Rose Garden, Dodge St, West Omaha.

Nevada: Reno Municipal Rose Garden, 2055 Idlewild Dr., Reno.

New Jersey: Brookdale Park Rose Garden, Bloomfield; Rudolf W. van der Goot Rose Garden, Mettler's Rd, East Millstone; Lambertus C. Bobbink Memorial Garden, Thompson Park, Lincroft; Jack D. Lissemore Rose Garden, Davis Johnson Park, Tenafly.

New Mexico: Prospect Park Rose Garden, 8205 Apache Ave NE, Albuquerque.

New York: Edwin de T. Bechtel Memorial Rose Garden, New York Botanical Garden, Bronx; Cranford Memorial Rose Garden, Brooklyn Botanic Gardens, 1000 Washington Ave, Brooklyn; Sonnenberg Gardens, 151 Charlotte St, Canandaigua; Queens Botanical Garden, 43–50 Main St, Flushing; United Nations Rose Garden, New York; Old Westbury Gardens, Old Westbury; Maplewood Park Garden, 100 Maplewood Ave, Rochester; Central Park Rose Garden, Schenectady; Dr Edmund B. Mills Rose Garden, Thorndon Park, Syracuse.

North Carolina: Biltmore House & Gardens, 1 Biltmore Plaza, Asheville; Tanglewood Park Rose Garden, Highway 158, Clemmons; Fayetteville Rose Garden, Fayetteville Technical Institute, Hull Rd, Fayetteville; Raleigh Municipal Garden, 301

Pogue St, Raleigh; Reynolda Rose Gardens of Wake Forest University, 100 Reynolds Village, Winston-Salem.

Ohio: Stan Hywett Hall & Gardens, 714 N Portage Path, Akron; Columbus Park of Roses, 4015 Olentangy Blvd, Columbus; Charles Edwin Nail Memorial Garden, Kingwood Center, 900 Park Ave W, Mansfield.

Oklahoma: J.E. Conard Municipal Garden, Honor Heights Park, Muskogee; Municipal Rose Garden, Will Rogers Park, 3500 NW 36th St, Oklahoma City; Tulsa Municipal Rose Garden, Woodward Park, 1370 E 24th Place, Tulsa.

Oregon: Shore Acres State Park, 13030 Cape Arago Highway, Coos Bay; Corvallis Rose Garden, Avery Park, Corvallis; George E. Owen Municipal Garden, 310 N Jefferson, Eugene; International Rose Test Garden, 400 SW Kingston Ave, Portland.

Pennsylvania: Malcolm W. Gross Memorial Garden, 2700 Parkway Blvd, Allentown; Hershey Rose Gardens, 621 Park Ave, Hershey; Longwood Gardens Inc., Kennett Square; Marion W. Rivinus Rose Garden, 9414 Meadowbrook Ave, Philadelphia; Robert Pyle Memorial Rose Garden, West Grove.

South Carolina; Edisto Memorial Gardens, Riverside Dr., Orangeburg.

Tennessee: Warner Park Rose Garden, 1101 McCallie Ave, Chattanooga.

Texas: Samuell-Grand Municipal Garden, 6200 E Grand Blvd, Dallas; El Paso Municipal Garden, 1702 Copia St, El Paso; Fort Worth Botanic Garden, 3220 Botanic Garden Dr., Fort Worth; Houston Municipal Garden, 1500 Hermann Dr, Houston; Brown Center Rose Garden of Lamar University, Orange; Tyler Municipal Rose Garden, corner of Front & Boone Sts, Tyler; Victoria Rose Garden, Riverside Park, Victoria.

Utah: Territorial Statehouse Rose Garden, 50 W Capitol Ave, Fillmore; Nephi Memorial Rose Garden, 100 East 100 North, Nephi; Salt Lake City Municipal Garden, Sugar House Park, 1602 E 21st S, Salt Lake.

Virginia: Arlington Memorial Rose Garden, Bon Air Park, Wilson Blvd & Lexington St, Arlington; American Horticultural Society, River Farm Garden, 7931 E Boulevard Dr., Alexandria; Bicentennial Rose Garden, Norfolk Botanical Gardens, Norfolk.

Washington DC: George Washington University, between G & H, 20th & 21st Sts.

Washington State: Fairhaven Park Rose Garden, 107 Chuckanut Dr., Bellingham; Chehalis Municipal Garden, 80 NE Cascade Ave, Chehalis; Woodland Park Rose Garden, 700 N 50th St, Seattle; Manito Park, Rosehill, W 4–21st Ave, Spokane; Point Defiance Park Rose Garden, 5402 N Shirley, Tacoma.

West Virginia: Ritter Park Garden, 800 McCoy Rd, Huntington.

Wisconsin: Boerner Botanical Gardens, Whitnall Park, 5879 S 92nd St, Hales Corners.

Amateur Rose Breeders Association

This British association, founded in 1975, participates in the trials held by the ROYAL NATIONAL ROSE SOCIETY at St Albans, and roses bred by its members have regularly secured trial ground certificates there. The Association has its own trial ground at Cheadle, Stoke-on-Trent, and has published some useful research papers, including a review by F. C. Buckley on *The Germination of Rose Achenes.* Secretary: D. Everitt, 48 Shrewsbury Fields, Shifnal, Shropshire TF11 8AN.

Amenity roses

Amenity roses are those planted for public display in municipal gardens, squares, terraces, around road furniture, on roundabouts and on central reservation areas of dual carriageways.

It has been shown that, in temperate areas, roses are cheaper to maintain than grass in any area that has to be mowed by hand-propelled machines. In a paper read in 1981 to the World Federation of Rose Societies meeting in Jerusalem, David Welch, representing the City of Aberdeen (Scotland), explained that, in his experience, the additional cost of preparing ground and planting roses can be recovered in three or four years. Once established, roses need to receive attention only once a year in a single operation, which includes pruning, lightly forking the surface of the ground and applying fertilizer and, where necessary, weedkiller. Grass, on the other hand, may need cutting up to twenty-four times a year, and the edging must be attended to two or three times, in addition to an occasional treatment with weedkiller.

The rose bushes are close-planted to give the plantation a healthy and vigorous look from the start. Close-planting also minimizes the need for dead-heading as the growth of new shoots conceals the spent blooms. Weeds are only a minor problem if the ground has been prepared in advance.

Dense barriers of prickly stemmed roses along the central reservations of dual carriageways help to prevent pedestrians from breaking through and crossing busy roads at unauthorized crossing points. At the roadside, the roses perform the same function and, in addition, help to define the edge of the road in snowy weather. They must, however, be able to stand up to the spray from salt that is strewn on roads in winter to de-ice them.

Large splashes of closely planted roses, known as *massifs*, have become specially popular as landscape decorations in France. For this purpose, purplish roses such as 'Manou Meilland' look at their best against the contrasting green of a grassy slope. A competition for landscape roses (*Roses de paysage*) has been organized for 1986 onwards by the Direction des Parcs Jardins et Espaces Verts de la Mairie de Paris, which is especially interested in *paysage urbain* (*see* BAGATELLE, CHÂTEAU DE).

The (British) Rose Growers' Association's suggested list of amenity roses is pragmatically arranged in groups according to height, with each of these groups being divided into colour (e.g. pale yellow, golden yellow, clear yellow, gold, golden copper, apricot, copper, orange, etc.), with notes in each case on the habit (such as bushy-upright, spreading, etc.) and the structure, shape and size of the blooms. Bedding roses are treated separately from park (shrub) roses and climbers. The Association's suggestions for roses suitable for planting along trunk roads is of interest to those with gardens fringing any kind of highway. In this section, their recommended roses include:

Height: 36–48 inches (0.9–1.2 m)

Pink, flesh	'Frau Dagmar Hastrup' (*Rosa rugosa* cultivar)
Pink, rose	*R. virginiana*
Magenta	'Yesterday' (modern shrub by HARKNESS)

Height: 48–72 inches (1.2–1.8 m)

White	*R. spinosissima* (botanically *R. pimpinellifolia*)
Pink, flesh	*R. x dupontii* (possibly *R. moschata* hybrid)
Pink, deep rose	'Scabrosa' (*R. rugosa* cultivar)

Height: over 72 inches (1.8 m)

White	*R. sericea pteracantha*
	R. rugosa alba
	R. multiflora
Creamy	'Nevada' (*R. moyesii* hybrid)
Clear yellow	*R. hugonis*
Pink, flesh	*R. rubiginosa* (*Rosa eglanteria*)
	R. woodsii 'Fendleri'
Pink, rose	'Highdownensis' (*R. moyesii* cultivar)
	R. rugosa rubra
Red	*R. moyesii* 'Geranium'
Crimson scarlet	*R. moyesii*
Purple	'Roseraie de l'Hay' (*R. rugosa* cultivar)
Magenta	'Hansa' (*R. rugosa* cultivar)

American Rose Foundation

The American Rose Foundation, closely linked with the AMERICAN ROSE SOCIETY and contactable at the same address, was established in 1952 to promote research for the benefit of all rose growers. Its work includes field studies of rose diseases and pests, the development of thornless UNDERSTOCKS, genetic experimentation, biochemical soil analysis and finding solutions to the problems of maintaining and increasing vigour in garden rose plants. Since it is non-profit-making, it qualifies as an educational establishment under Section 501/c/3 of the US Internal Revenue Code, and gifts made to it are therefore tax deductible. The results of its investigations are published in the *American Rose Annual* of the American Rose Society, or in the *American Rose* magazine.

American Rose Society

The American Rose Society with some 20,000 members, the majority of whom are amateur rose growers, is the largest specialized plant society in the United States. Founded in 1899, it is currently organized into eighteen districts:

Buckeye (Ohio)
Carolina (North and South Carolina)
Central (Iowa, Kansas, Missouri, Nebraska)
Colonial (Virginia, West Virginia, Maryland, Delaware, Washington DC)
Deep South (Georgia, Florida, Alabama)
Great Lakes (Michigan)
Gulf (Louisiana, Mississippi)
Illinois–Indiana
Yankee (Maine, Massachusetts, New Hampshire, Rhode Island, Vermont, Connecticut)
New York
North Central (Wisconsin, Minnesota, North and South Dakota)
North California (Nevada [excluding Las Vegas], Hawaii, northern California)
Pacific Northwest (Washington, Oregon, Montana [part], Idaho [part], Alaska)

Pacific Southwest (Arizona, New Mexico, Las Vegas [Nevada], El Paso [Texas], southern California)

Pennsylvania–New Jersey

Rocky Mountains (Colorado, Utah, Wyoming, Idaho [part], Montana [part])

South-Central (Texas [excluding El Paso], Oklahoma)

Tenarky (Tennessee, Arkansas, Kentucky)

The Society also has more than 350 chapter and affiliated societies in the US. It publishes the *American Rose Annual* and the monthly *American Rose* magazine, maintains an extensive postal lending library, and sponsors two national meetings and rose shows each year.

The ARS also organizes the annual survey known as the 'Proof of the Pudding', in which rosarians throughout the country assess the worth of newly introduced varieties – and of some of the old. Ten points are awarded for a really exceptional rose; 9–9.9 for outstanding roses; 8–8.9 for excellent roses; 7–7.9 for good roses; and 6–6.9 for roses of fair quality. Those averaging below this mark are classed as being of doubtful value. The findings are sent to the district branches of the ARS and the final results are assembled by the 'Proof of the Pudding' Committee.

The ratings and prizes awarded to the varieties assessed by the 'Proof of the Pudding' judges are recorded in the ARS's annual publication *Handbook for Selecting Roses*, which includes some 2000 rose varieties – most with numbered ratings. The ARS also cooperates with its district branches in conducting schools for training rose-show judges and sets the qualifying standards for JUDGING.

The ARS has been delegated by the International Horticultural Congress as the International Registration Authority for Roses (*see* REGISTRATION OF ROSES), and publishes monthly and annual lists of all new roses registered with the IRAR. (*See also* AMERICAN ROSE FOUNDATION.)

Anatomy of the rose

Rosarians worshipped the rose for some 2000 years before paying close attention to its anatomy. Thus John Gerard, whose *Herball* was published in 1597, still referred to rose petals as 'leaves' and lumped styles and stamens together as 'threads' or 'chives'. Today we cannot be so insouciant, and some knowledge of the main features of the rose plant is mandatory for anyone wishing to find his or her way about a rose catalogue or to distinguish one rose from another in the flowerbed.

Starting at ground level, the *surculi* are first noticeable. These are new growths that appear after the main flowering season, and from these, next year's flowers will, it is hoped, be derived. (These growths should, of course, not be cut away.) The hardier-looking shoots on the plant will be growths of earlier years, and from spring onwards, they will develop shorter lateral branches, on which, in most cases, the flowers are displayed. The BRIER ROSES, however, are an exception: their flowers are carried on still smaller branchlets that grow from the laterals – one way of distinguishing these ornamental members of the rose family. In MOSS ROSES, both the stems and the leaves are endowed

with glands – small roundish vessels containing a distinctive perfume.

The 'THORNS', though obnoxious, can often serve to identify the plant on which they have grown. Some are straight, others hooked; some grow in pairs, others are scattered irregularly. Some are white, others red or brown. There may be bristles between them, or there may be no 'thorns' at all.

The surfaces of the wood and the leaves may also proclaim the identity of a particular rose. Both may be *glabrous* – that is, having no hair – or they may be *pubescent* – in other words, thinly covered with short, soft hairs. If the covering of hairs is denser, it is said to be *tomentose;* if the hairs are soft but longer, the covering is called *pilose* or *hirsute* or, if shaggy, *villous.* A covering of coarse stiff hairs is said to be *hispid.*

The shape and disposition of the foliage also varies greatly. The leaves of the rose are characteristically *pinnate* – that is, composed of more than three leaflets arranged in two rows along a common 'stalk'. Some rose leaflets are *ovate* (broadest in the lower half), others are *obovate* (broader in the upper half), and the surface may be wrinkled or smooth. The edges of the leaves may be *serrate* (with points directed forward), *crenate* (scalloped), blunt at the tip, *mucronate* (with a short narrow point) or *revolute* (with the edges turned under).

In additional, scale-like or leaf-like attachments are to be seen growing at the base of the leaf stalk. These are the *stipules,* and their shape and especially the manner in which they are attached to the leaf stalk varies from one species to another. Stipules may be toothed, fringed, comb-like or slashed. They are called *adnate* when they grow along the leaf stalk.

Closely associated with the stem are leafy growths known as *bracts.* It is from the *axil,* or upper angle between the bract and the lateral or branchlet, that the flower stems normally grow (though not in the case of *Rosa pimpinellifolia* because it has no bracts).

Coming to the flower itself, there are the petals and, in the midst of them, the stamens, topped by anthers, from which the pollen is discharged, and the styles, the columns bearing the stigmas that will receive the pollen. In some roses – *Rosa arvensis*, the field rose, the MUSK ROSES and others – the styles are united in a single column.

The wild species normally have five petals. The exception to this is *Rosa sericea* and its close relations, which have but four. The bloom of the garden rose may be globe-shaped, cupped or tazza-shaped (i.e. like a shallow bowl). The petals may be *imbricated* (with the edges overlapping like tiles) or *reflexed* (turned back at the edges).

Beneath the petals is the calyx, or cup, that protects the petals in the bud stage and may to some extent (but not always) support them after the flower has opened. In the case of the rose, the calyx is made up of five sepals that are sometimes joined but are usually distinct from each other. Some sepals are long, narrow and upright; others have crests. Some persist until the 'fruit' is ripe, but others fall

Anatomy of the rose: Rosa clinophylla (R. lyelli) *from J. Lindley's* Rosarum monographia *(1820).*
A. 'thorns'   B. pubescence   C. stipules   D. bracts   E. calyx
F. petals   G. stamens   H. flower stalk   I. seven leaflets.

away earlier, and roses that have this characteristic can be distinguished from those without it.

The stamens, styles, petals and calyx are all attached to what is known as the *receptacle*, the thickened tip of the flower stalk. In roses, the receptacle takes the form of a flask: the calyx, petals and stamens are attached near to its rim, and the ovules develop near its floor. Thus the styles, which are the connecting link between the ovules and the stigma, have to pass through the narrow neck of the flask to take their place among the petals in the body of the flower. It has been suggested that this arrangement protects the ovules from the jaws of beetles visiting the rose for pollen.

The flowers may be solitary as in the Pimpinellifoliae, or few as in some of the Caninae. They may appear in flat-topped *corymbs* as in some of the Synstylae, Caninae and Cinnamomeae, in *panicles* (branched inflorescences) or in apparent *umbels* with flower stalks arising like the spokes of an umbrella from the top of the main stem.

See also HIPS and SINGLE ROSES AND DOUBLE ROSES.

Aphid

A horrifyingly enlarged drawing of the rose aphid *(Siphonophora rosae)* appears in the 1920 edition of the Revd Joseph Pemberton's classic work *Roses: Their History, Development and Cultivation.* The creature is magnified ten times, to some two inches (5 cm) long, and is spindle-shaped. It has the normal complement of six legs and long curved antennae, but it is also equipped with a hollow elephant-like trunk about half as long as its body. This trunk has three needle-shaped pincers at the end with which the aphid (also correctly spelled 'aphis' with the plural 'aphides') pierces the soft parts of rose shoots to suck up the life juices of the plant. From the other end of its body, two club-shaped excrescences project, from which a gummy solution known as 'honey dew' is excreted. This may be attractive to ants but is disastrous for the rose shoot, since it blocks the breathing pores of the plant. In all, there are about ten different varieties to be feared by the rose grower, by no means all answering to the name 'greenfly' usually used by gardeners for the whole tribe.

The aphid is able to produce live offspring without having to mate first, and each of the colonies to be seen on rose shoots will have come from a single wingless 'female' that has given birth to others equally wingless and fecund, and equally independent of the male. Towards the end of the season, however, a change occurs. Instead of incomplete mass-produced wingless females, male and female aphids are born, each with wings. They mate, and the females then produce eggs which can overwinter on the rose bush. The intermediate-stage sexless 'females' emerge early in the spring to complete the life cycle.

The wise rose grower tackles the aphid problem while the rose is still dormant – when it is safe to spray the plant with a solution such as Mortegg (which contains tar-oil) that kills the aphid eggs, remembering that they are often laid on the lower branches of the bush. However, 'systemics' such as Benlate and Nimrod, which are absorbed through the leaves into the plant's system, are the most effective deterrents to sap-sucking insects such as aphids. It is also important to burn all early prunings in case there are any unhatched aphid eggs on them, and to keep a sharp look-out for any early aphids that may have escaped the attentions of the spray gun.

The rose aphid (magnified × 10), from the Revd Joseph Pemberton's Roses.

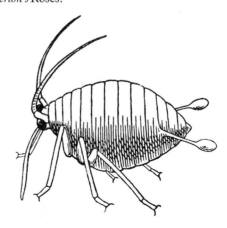

As well as the rose aphid, other equally undesirable aphids are: the rose-grain aphid *(Metopolophium dirhodum)*, which divides its attentions between roses and cereal crops; the small green aphid *(Pentatrichopus tetrahodus)*, whose visits to gardens are unpredictable; and the rose-root aphid *(Cinara rosae)*, which can be detected at the base of stems.

See also ENEMIES OF THE ROSE.

Art, the rose in

The rose has been glorified in almost every branch of art – sometimes in its own right, sometimes as part of a design and often in a symbolic representation. It is to be seen and admired on ceramic tiles, in the sculpture of the Della Robbias, in illuminated manuscripts, in metalwork, on engraved drinking glasses (particularly in the period of the Jacobite rebellions), in Honiton lace, on Chinese fans, embroidery and textiles (for just as JOSEPHINE advanced the rose in gardens, so Napoleon commended it to the silk factories of Lyon). The rose also appears on jewellery, carpets and wallpaper, on Sèvres soft-paste porcelain where the 'Rose Pompadour' (sometimes wrongly called the 'Rose du Barry') was introduced in 1757, and in many other art forms to be seen, for instance, at the Victoria & Albert Museum in London, and in similar richly endowed depositories across the world.

However, it is on paper, canvas, silk or vellum that the rose comes most vividly to life, in portraits recalling not only the plant itself but the artist who painted it and the period in which he or she lived.

The 15th century to the French Revolution

In Europe, artists from the 15th century onwards began to paint the rose as an object of beauty in itself. Sandro Botticelli chose *Rosa alba* as the most suitable model for the shower of blossom that fell from the sky as Venus was born, rising from the sea on a scallop shell. The work, painted in about 1482, is to be seen in Room VI of the Palazzo degli Uffizi in Florence in which Botticelli's best-known works are displayed. Similar roses were used to edge the cloud in Botticelli's *Coronation of the virgin and the saints* in the same gallery. In his painting *Primavera* ('Spring'), executed between 1475 and 1478, in which we see Flora strewing flowers while Mercury chases away the clouds, a red rose akin to *Rosa gallica* is visible. His *Madonna and child* of 1468 to be seen at the Louvre shows a double red gallica in fairly close detail and what appears to be a flattish double yellow rose.

As a SYMBOL, the rose was closely associated with the Virgin Mary, and an outstanding example of this is the painting by Bernardino Luini to be seen in the Palazzo di Brera, Milan, known as the *Madonna in the rose arbour*. Here, too, we see the saucer-flat flowers and long feathered sepals of *Rosa alba* climbing up a trellis of squarely aligned canes. The same subject, with the same roses, painted about 1440 by Stefan Lochner, can be seen in the Wallraf–Richartz Museum in Cologne. Albrecht Dürer's *Feast of the roses* (also called *Madonna of the rose garlands*), which established the

artist's reputation as a painter as well as an engraver and master of the woodcut, was commissioned by the German community in Venice to be one of the side panels of the altar of the church of San Bartolommeo which they frequented. It was painted during Dürer's visit to Venice in 1505–7 and shows the Madonna crowning a kneeling emperor with a coronet of roses, while the Christ-child offers a similar chaplet to a cardinal.

A number of Spanish painters also used the rose in their compositions. Bartolomé Murillo liked to strew roses here and there in his paintings, and his love for the flower is nowhere better shown than in the portrait now to be seen at the Dulwich College Picture Gallery, London, executed about 1670. Known as the *Flower girl*, it shows a young strong-armed peasant girl seated with, in her lap, centifolia roses for sale. She wears an Andalusian-style headband decorated with another large pink rose. Velázquez also featured the rose, particularly in his *Coronation of the Virgin*, painted about 1642 and now in the Museo del Prado in Madrid. The Madonna's crown is a modest single-tier chaplet of roses, and Velázquez was criticized for not having endowed his model with a more spiritual look and a less worldly dress and scarf.

It is, however, to the Dutch school that we must turn for portraits of the rose during the late 16th and 17th centuries. Jan Brueghel (1568–1625), known as 'Velvet' Brueghel because of his ability to convey the texture of silks and petals, was first and foremost a flower painter and among the first to produce set-flower pieces. Nevertheless, his paintings do not include the rose that was to become so familiar as time went on – namely ROSA CENTIFOLIA, the so-called cabbage rose – a fact that has led rose historians to conclude that this rose, which made its first appearance in Holland, had not yet reached that country or at least was still scarce at the time that Jan Brueghel painted most of his pictures. Those who followed him – including Jan Davidsz de Heem (1606–84), Rachel Ruysch (1664–1750), Jan van Huysum (1682–1749) and (in Flanders) Daniel Seghers (sometimes Seeghers, 1590–1661) – made use of not only *Rosa centifolia*, but also *Rosa foetida*, the 'Austrian' brier and *Rosa hemisphaerica*, the double-yellow rose.

In France, in the pre-Napoleonic era, the rose remained an adjunct of the Baroque and the Rococo styles, despite Madame de Pompadour's interest in the rose (well displayed on the lady's bosom in the 1759 portrait by François Boucher in the Wallace Collection, London). One should not, however, overlook the charming watercolour by Jean-Baptiste Huet, painted in 1786 and entitled *Lovers' meeting*, which shows two fashionably dressed young people showing a surprising interest in sprinkling water over a tub of *Rosa centifolia*. This painting, though in a private collection, is reproduced in *French Watercolours of the Eighteenth Century* by Philippe Huisman (Thames & Hudson, 1969).

After the Revolution

The place of the rose in art could not but be affected by the political upheavals of the French Revolution, which altered both the place of the artist in society and his conception of what subjects were significant, as well as his views on how they could best be portrayed. No longer were the wishes of the patron paramount, or the views of the Church decisive. The artist was free to go his own way, even if that led – as it often did – to starvation. Scenes of realism replaced flower still-lifes, and the discovery that the hues of everyday objects could be intensified by juxtaposing complementary colours made it unnecessary to borrow any from the rose.

There were nevertheless some romantics who rebelled against the 18th-century Age of Reason and the logic of Descartes, and the philosophy that led Gauguin to seek paradise in Tahiti and Delacroix to 'discover' Morocco survived at home in Henri Fantin-Latour whose evocative paintings of the rose have seldom been surpassed. Fantin-Latour was a contemporary of Manet, Monet and Degas and, along with that of Cézanne and Pissarro, his work was exhibited at the Salon des Refusés held in 1863 at the instigation of the Emperor Napoleon III, where works were shown that had been rejected that year from the Salon supervised by the French Royal Academy. There, the most sensational painting was probably Manet's *Déjeuner sur l'herbe*, which showed a nude woman, not in the permitted form of Venus or a nymph, but sitting beside two prosaically dressed men.

Renoir was also an admirer of the rose. His four-year stint as a decorator of porcelain in the Paris workshop of the Lévy brothers later stood him in good stead. When Ambroise Vollard, the dealer who bought so many of Renoir's paintings, visited the artist one day in the late 1890s, he was surprised to see that Renoir had been painting a vase of moss roses (now in the Louvre in Paris). Renoir explained that he had done so in order to carry out some research into the flesh tints he needed for his nudes. He had, however, already painted *Roses in a vase* in 1876 and was to execute another in 1910. In the last three years of his life, between 1917 and 1919, he painted many groups of them, though they remained much as before: luxuriant, dishevelled, beautifully lit and without a trace of self-importance. Many would indeed prefer to see the outdoor study of red standard ('tree') roses in his *Rose garden and château of Wargemont* (now in a private collection) near Dieppe in Normandy where, in the 1880s, he was a frequent guest of Alfred Berard the art collector and his family.

Other French artists also found inspiration in the rose. Two months before he committed suicide in 1890, Van Gogh painted an attractive vase of white cluster-flowered roses, now in the collection of Mrs Albert D. Lasker in New York. Manet painted roses in a glass of champagne – showing the good sense to put them in a tall glass and not the wide chalice in which the wine so quickly loses its sparkle – one of many small studies of flowers painted by the artist during the last summer of his life. The main rose in the champagne glass is yellow and of the modern high-peaked type, and the prismatic blue lights of the glass are reflected both in the leaves and in the petals of the flower itself. This portrait was painted in 1882 and is part of the Burrell Collection in Glasgow.

Today, if fewer studies of significance are made of the rose, one explanation is perhaps to be sought in the types of roses most often publicized and consequently grown now. These display colours of such intensity and arrogance that the sensitive artist might well hesitate to add any interpretation of his or her own.

See also REDOUTÉ, PIERRE-JOSEPH.

Attar of roses

Attar of roses is the ultimate essential oil of roses obtained by distillation, and a number of legends link it with the MOGUL EMPERORS of central Asia.

Mohammed Hâchem, in his *History of the Mogul Emperors*, wrote that, in 1612, during the course of a fête given by the Persian princess Nour-Djihan in honour of her husband the Emperor Djihânguir, the mother of the princess noticed that some strongly scented foam had formed on the surface of the rivulets of rosewater that ran through the garden. The foam was collected and the Emperor rewarded his mother-in-law for her powers of observation. Another account of the same fête has the princess dipping her handkerchief in the water while she was rowed across a

Gathering roses in East Rumelia (the former name of the southern half of present-day Bulgaria) for attar of roses.

small lake, and then wringing out the scented rosewater into a bottle.

The implication was that this episode launched the Persian trade in attar of roses, but neither account, nor the one in the text of REDOUTÉ's *Les roses*, mentions the essential distillation process by which the true attar is made, and in any case attar was in production centuries earlier. Joannes Actuarios, the Greek physician and governor of Constantinople in the 14th century, described the process, which was probably used much earlier by the Arabs.

The attar of today is made in stills directly from freshly picked rose petals. Water is added to the still until it just covers the petals. This is then brought slowly to the boil and, after being drawn off, is settled in pans and then skimmed. In Europe, Bulgaria was once the primary source of supply and its attar of roses industry still provides the state with much valuable foreign exchange. The main centre of cultivation is in the so-called 'Valley of the Roses' near Kazanlŭk, in the centre of the country. The valley runs east–west and is essentially a corridor between two mountain ranges, one shielding it from the drying winds from the south and the other from icy blasts from the north. There is good drainage, too.

The rose used there is a variety of DAMASK ROSE, and almost all the flower, including even the stamens and calyx, yield some oil. The rose bushes and the mid-pink flowers are both of modest proportions (which may be an aid to the pickers). The picking is begun at dawn as soon as the flowers start to open, and the distillation takes place the same day to reduce loss by evaporation. A 'perfect' day is one when the air is cool and moist.

The Bulgarian attar industry is probably the most widely publicized, but the damask rose has been used in India for the same purpose since the beginning of the 19th century. More recently, the USSR has entered the market as a major exporter of rose oil.

See also SCENT and PERFUMERY, THE ROSE IN.

Australia, the rose in

The problems facing rose growers in Australia are similar to those encountered in the United States – namely, those posed by great distances and extremes of climate. Thus, while the northern margins of the continent are tropical, the highlands and tablelands of Tasmania, the island off the southeast coast and the coldest area of Australia, average a mere 46.6°F (8.1°C) in the coldest month – 12°F (6.6°C) below that of Brisbane's coldest. Western Tasmania has an annual rainfall of up to 140 inches (355 cm), whereas the area stretching from southwest Queensland to the seaboard of Western Australia considers itself lucky if it gets 10 inches (25 cm). Conditions in New South Wales are favourable for roses suited to the warmer areas of the United States.

The rose year differs from one state to another. Thus, rose shows in Brisbane are normally held in August and September (equivalent to February and March in the Northern Hemisphere) and again in May and June (the nor-

thern November and December). But in Perth, where rain seldom falls between November and March, the shows are arranged to avoid the dry season and so take place in October and mid-March – corresponding to the Northern Hemisphere's April and September.

Understandably, given Australia's vast distances, rose societies grew up independently in more than one state. The National Rose Society of Victoria, founded in 1900, was the first, followed by those of New South Wales and Western Australia. The first Australian rose convention was held in Melbourne in 1969, and since 1973, the National Rose Society of Australia (headquarters: 271 Belmore Road, North Balwyn, Victoria 3104) has acted as the parent body of the societies established in individual states. 'Heritage Roses in Australia', with a journal edited by Trevor Nottle, was founded in 1979 to cater for 'old' rose enthusiasts.

During the 1920s and 1930s, Alastair Clark, carried out some crosses with *Rosa gigantea* ('Cooper's Burmese Rose') that proved successful in hot, dry areas (*see* review by Hazel Le Rougetel, *Rose Annual*, 1984). His 'Nancy Hayward' of 1937, a deep-pink, large-flowered CLIMBER, is still obtainable in Victoria nurseries. Fine rose gardens are to be seen in Melbourne, Sydney, Adelaide, Perth, Brisbane, and Canberra.

The popularity of the rose in Australia – and, for that matter, in NEW ZEALAND – owes much to the efforts of Dr A. S. Thomas OBE, VMA, who received international recognition in 1952 when he was awarded the Dean Hole Medal, the highest honour bestowed by Britain's ROYAL NATIONAL ROSE SOCIETY. Dr Thomas's book *Better Roses* (Angus & Robertson), though originally published in 1950 and with only one revision in 1955, is still worth its place on the bookshelf.

Ayrshire roses

These are ramblers, mainly white-flowered and double, that were raised from *Rosa arvensis*, the field rose, by the Earl of Loudon at Loudon Castle, Ayrshire, in the 1820s. Ayrshires are particularly hardy, and sufficiently dense-growing to be used as ground cover. From their extra vigour, they would appear to be hybrids, and may have been crossed with more than one species – for example, with *R. sempervirens*, or with *R. setigera* from seeds that, according to one report, were sent to Loudon from Canada. 'Ayrshire splendens', an attractive mixture of off-white and purplish pink, is, however, confidently billed as a hybrid of *R. arvensis*. Unfortunately, most Ayrshires have little or no scent, and are rarely seen today – though they are still recognized in modern CLASSIFICATION tables. Later hybrids of *R. arvensis* with HYBRID TEAS, *R. gallica* and others have also been classed as Ayrshires.

Right: *A portrait of the alba rose variety 'Greater Maiden's Blush', by Pierre-Joseph Redouté and taken from the first volume of* Les roses *(1817).*

Rosa alba Regalis.

Rosier blanc Royal.

P. J. Redouté pinx.   Imprimerie de Remond.   Bessin sculp.

Above: *Roses cascading over a pergola provides the focus for* In the shade *by the 19th-century artist, G. E. Alluaud.*

Left: La Serre, *by Pierre Auguste Renoir: a mass of roses on a hot summer's day.*

Right: *Edouard Manet's* Fleurs dans un vase de cristal: *although roses are not mentioned in the title, they are clearly recognizable.*

i.ew, qui, hona
of
moon. Query
cinnamon.

flower compared to a sweet smellin
flower, or aromatich flower, sup
-posed to be in the moon. —

月
桂
花

Chinese watercolour of cultivated roses, from the collection
of Bertha and Archie Simons.

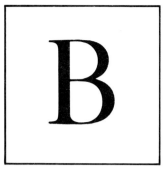

Bagatelle, Château de

The story of the château itself – built by the Comte d'Artois in 1777 in sixty-seven days to win a bet with his sister-in-law, Marie Antoinette, and owned later by Napoleon, the Marquis of Hertford and Richard Wallace, founder of the Wallace Collection in London – need not concern us here. Its famous rose garden is attached to the Orangerie, some distance away from the château and, besides, the garden is a 20th-century creation, first planned in 1905 when the estate was acquired by the City of Paris at the instigation of Jean-Claude Nicolas Forestier, the Conservateur des Parcs et Jardins de la Ville de Paris. He saw that, despite its unrewarding soil, the perfect site for his ideal rose garden lay in the area near the Orangerie that had formerly been used as the royal equitation paddock. Forestier was a friend of Claude Monet and an admirer of the Impressionist school of painting, which perhaps helps to account for the striking juxtapositions and daring use of colour that still characterize the displays of roses at the château.

Today, in 2½ acres (1 hectare) in the Bois de Boulogne, there are 8000 rose plants comprising 889 varieties, some from the last century. Close to the Orangerie that over-looks the grounds are roses famous the world over as past winners of the Bagatelle Gold Prize for new rose varieties. Beyond is an open lawn and below, down a gentle slope, the treasury of roses: ground-cover varieties, bush roses, ramblers on swags, pillar roses on conifers, standard roses with smaller roses planted beneath, weeping standard roses, shrub roses, pergola roses; roses planted individually in lawns bordered with miniature box hedges, arranged formally yet informally to suit the structure of the garden, in cornice beds, in circular beds and in bands – everything that a rose lover could desire.

The Bagatelle Competition for New Roses, instituted in 1907, became the first in the world to require that plants be grown in open ground before they could be considered by the jury. The system of awards and the manner of judging the entries has varied over the years, but because of the prestige which this competition enjoys, and the trouble taken over it, it is worth describing the present procedure in full.

Bush roses, cluster-flowered roses (polyanthas and flori-bundas) and miniatures are all judged in their second season; shrubs, climbers, ramblers and ground-cover roses in their third. Growers send the specified number of plants with the necessary documentation to the Chef de la Circonscription du Bois de Boulogne by the last day of December in the year preceding the start of the competition. The Circonscription forwards the roses to the Bagatelle, unnamed and identified only by an allotted number; they remain anonymous until the final results are announced. The roses are planted at once.

A single first prize, the Gold, is awarded to a rose of any type from any country. A second prize is awarded to the next best – and one or more certificates, if merited, to varieties that have received favourable comments. A separate award is made for the best scented rose, and an additional prize for a rose used in a city landscape is to be awarded from 1986 onwards (*see* AMENITY ROSES).

The full jury for the competition includes the Mayor of Paris and seven officials, nominated foreigners such as directors of public parks, members of rose societies and well-known amateurs, and a number of French personalities including professional producers and growers of roses, directors of rose gardens, members of rose societies, horticultural journalists, artists, perfumery experts and prominent amateur rose-growers. The jury also includes a technical panel of six, nominated and controlled by the Director of Parks, Gardens and Green Spaces of the City of Paris. This panel makes a weekly record of the number of flowers of each variety during the season or seasons previous to the final judging, and notes how many of these flowers were to be seen in September–October.

The permanent commission of the jury, consisting of the French members, examines each rose at the end of June, in the third week of September and at the end of October during the first year, and at the beginning of June in the second year. At the end of the first year, they present a preliminary assessment. In their second season, at the beginning of June, the commission marks each rose separately for vigorous and well-balanced development, resistance to diseases, beauty of bloom or cluster, including quality and constancy of colour and form, scent, duration of flowering and REMONTANT flowering, and profusion of blooms. Non-remontant shrubs are not penalised in cases where hips are exceptionally decorative.

On the basis of these marks, which are treated as indicative rather than definitive, each member of the permanent commission awards a summing-up mark to each variety, ranging from 0 to 10. These marks are then multiplied by a factor that makes them equivalent to 50 per cent of the total mark.

On the day before the conclusion of the competition, a special commission of the jury – known as the Commission of Novelty – examines the roses to consider to what extent they are new varieties. This commission includes breeders and technical experts, both French and foreign, from the jury. They mark the 'new' varieties on a basis of 0 to 10. A large 'E' is placed over the number-plates of those roses that are considered not to be sufficiently novel, the letter indicating that they have been eliminated from the contest. The marks given by the novelty commission are then multiplied by a factor that makes them equivalent to 25 per cent of the total marks.

On the final day of judging, the full jury assembles at about 9.30 am for coffee and orange juice on the terrace of the Orangerie before entering the Orangerie itself for a briefing on the day's programme. Next, the jury tours the garden, re-examining the seventy or so roses still in competition and assessing the scent of each variety – in some cases, no doubt, basing their verdict on the indications previously given by the permanent commission. The final assessment is also made on the basis of awarding points from 0 to 10; these marks count for 25 per cent of the total, so if one particular rose looks especially striking on that day, it is always possible for an upset to occur.

The rose gardens are normally open to the public, and for those without a car, the most economical way of reaching the Bagatelle from central Paris is to take the Métro to Porte Maillot and then a 244 bus.

Balling

Balling occurs when the petals of a rose stick to each other instead of opening out. Dampness after heavy rain is often the reason. Double roses suffer more from this than do single ones.

Barb

See BRITISH ASSOCIATION OF ROSE BREEDERS.

Bermuda, the roses of

Bermuda has proved a happy hunting ground for rose historians, particularly since 1954 when the Bermuda Rose Society was formed with the aim, among others, of 'conserving the old-fashioned roses that have stood the test of time in these islands'. Since then, the islands (there are 140 of them) have turned out to be a living museum of roses. The search for 'old' roses in Bermuda has been all the more enthralling because of the local Bermudian names behind which they lie concealed. Many of these roses are of the China type and seem to thrive in a climate with no dormancy season that is on the same latitude as Shanghai.

A year before the Society was formed, Richard Thomson, at that time chairman of the Old Rose Committee of the American Rose Society, discovered a rose, growing at Belfield, in the Somerset district, that was known in Bermuda as the 'Belfield Rose'. It turned out to be an original 'Slater's Crimson China', known since 1789 or even earlier and, at the time of its rediscovery, thought to be almost extinct (*see* CHINA ROSES). Thomson said he felt like an art collector who had just unearthed a long-missing Rembrandt. Five little plants of this famous rose were carried back to England and re-introduced there at the Chelsea Flower Show.

Another of Bermuda's 'mystery roses', known locally as the 'Spice Rose', was seen and investigated by Peter HARKNESS, member of the well-known rose-breeding family, who decided that, very possibly, it could be 'Hume's Blush Tea-scented China', of which Dr Hurst (in the authoritative work, *Old Shrub Roses*) once wrote: 'Living material of this rose is no longer available.'

Other locally named 'mystery roses' of Bermuda have since been identified. The rose that Bermudians knew for many years as the 'Seven Sisters Rose' has now been correctly identified as the 'Archduke Charles', and the Bermudian 'Emmie Gray' has been placed as the 'Sanguinea', a SPORT of *Rosa chinensis semperflorens*. *R. bracteata*, the Macartney rose, has long been known in Bermuda as the 'Fried Egg', and the 'Duchesse de Brabant' as the 'Shell Rose'.

However, there remain at least five more mystery roses for which no identity has yet been found.

The above information is derived from *Old Garden Roses in Bermuda*, published in 1984 by the Bermuda Rose Society (P.O. Box 162, Paget, Bermuda) and beautifully illustrated with forty-five colour photographs.

Bible, roses in the

There are two mentions of roses in the Old Testament but there are doubts as to how far they can be taken at face value. In the King James version of Isaiah 35:1, there is the prophesy: 'The wilderness and the solitary place shall be glad for them; and the desert shall rejoice and blossom as the Rose'; and Song of Solomon 2:1 reads: 'I am the Rose of Sharon and the lily of the valleys.' Originally, when the Septuagint group – seventy Jewish scholars who were commissioned by Ptolemy Philadelphus (284–247 BC) to translate the original Hebrew text into Greek – came to these verses, they were clearly in doubt as to which plants were intended: in the case of Isaiah, 'rose' was rendered as *krinon*, the Greek word for 'lily'; and in the Song of Solomon, the same word was translated as *anthos*, the Greek for 'flower'. Some improvization seems to have taken place eighteen centuries later during the preparation of the King James Bible, generally known as the Authorised Version, since the 'Rose of Sharon' is no rose but is identified in Britain with *Hypericum calycinum*, a showy member of the St John's wort family, and in the United States, it is the blue-flowered *Hibiscus syriacus*, a member of the mallow family. Neither of these plants grows on the plain of Sharon, which lies between Jaffa and Mount Carmel. A ROCKROSE would have a better claim to the title.

Five references to the rose are to be found in the Apocrypha, but the fact that they were originally written partly in Aramaic, partly in Greek and occasionally in Hebrew cast doubt on their authenticity and led to their exclusion from the sacred canon in England at the time of the Reformation. The verse from the Apocrypha most frequently quoted is Ecclesiasticus 39:13, which reads: 'Harken unto me, ye holy children, and bud forth as a rose growing by a brook of water.' This is assumed by most botanists to indicate a species of iris rather than a rose, though it could be taken in the literal sense to be a plant growing on irrigated land.

Another reference in the Apocrypha to roses is more specific. The Wisdom of Solomon 2:7–8 reads: 'Let us have costly wines and perfumes to our heart's content, and let no flower of spring escape us. Let us crown ourselves with rosebuds before they can wither.' Here, however, we are probably in the company of one of the Alexandrian Greeks of the 1st century BC who were accustomed to wearing coronets of rosebuds at banquets and many other different social occasions. Whether the same flowers were used in King Solomon's time, 900 years earlier, is less certain.

After the Apocrypha came the Targum – consisting of translations, interpretations or paraphrases of portions of the Old Testament and written in Aramaic from about AD 100 onwards for the benefit of Jews in exile. One text clearly translates 'rose' as 'narcissus', of which a species of the tazetta type flourishes in the Holy Land in spring.

No roses are mentioned in the New Testament, and although some SPECIES ROSES, notably *Rosa phoenicia* and *R. canina*, can be found in the Holy Land, they were not, it seems, considered sufficiently important to be included in Holy Writ.

See also ROSE OF JERICHO.

Blackspot

Few complaints are more prevalent – or more disfiguring – to the rose bush than the fungus commonly called 'blackspot'. Botanically known as *Diplocarpon rosae* in its sexual form and as *Actinonema rosae* in the European form for which the exact method of reproduction has not been described, this fungus feeds on the skin cells lying just below the cuticle of the hard waxy surface of the leaflets. The plant's reaction to the fungus gives rise to black spots from which the threads of the fungus can be seen to project like rays. These threads absorb food from the plant and cluster together to produce new spores, which break out from the leaf and are carried by rain, falling dew or garden spray on to other leaves, infecting them in turn. By the time the spots have appeared, it may be too late to save the leaf, which often drops off prematurely, thus weakening and perhaps even killing the plant. In some cases, the stem is also attacked.

The incidence of blackspot varies with the weather and the humidity. If the air is dry, there will be little or no danger because the spores depend on water for life support. Oddly enough, the impurities settling on the leaflets of roses growing in industrial areas are also believed to protect them from infestation.

Blackspot is not confined to cultivated roses but affects wild ones too – in particular, those belonging to the Pimpinellifoliae group (*see* CLASSIFICATION), of which *Rosa foetida* and *R. pimpinellifolia* are members. Roses belonging to the Synstylae group are less prone – among them, *Rosa multiflora*, sometimes known as the 'Japanese Rose' because it was first described in 1784 by the Swedish botanist Carl Peter Thunberg in his *Flora japonica*; *R. wichuraiana* (*see* WILD ROSES); and *R. moschata*, the MUSK ROSE.

No sure method has yet been discovered of producing (intentionally) a worthwhile cultivated rose that is immune to blackspot. 'Allgold', a mid-yellow cluster-flowered variety introduced by LeGrice in 1958, comes very near to being trouble-free, but when its pedigree is examined, it is found that its parents were both hybrid cultivars and its grandparents included one unnamed seedling. Many more expensive trials would be needed before any logical hybridizing programme of this plant would pay its way.

It seems likely, however, that varieties with leaflets covered with tough cuticle are less likely to succumb than roses with tender covering; in addition, those roses with concave leaflets, which curl upwards at the edges and thus hold water, could be more susceptible. Some roses part with their leaves more readily than others, either because of their botanical structure or because they are of a less vigorous constitution.

Blackspot is kept under control by spraying. Since the spores can overwinter in the stems of rose bushes, March is not too soon to start spraying with one of the effective preparations sold for this purpose. (The systemic product Nimrod T, which is absorbed through the leaves, is highly thought of.) However, if the leaves are only just beginning to unfold, the mixture should probably be diluted to half the normal strength. The spray should be applied when the leaflets themselves are dry and early enough in the day for them to dry off again before nightfall. However, it would be unwise to spray if the leaves are afterwards to be exposed to strong sun, as this may lead to leaf scorch. The stems and the undersides of the leaves should also be sprayed as a precaution – a task that is greatly eased if the spray has a nozzle which can be turned upwards. Any fallen leaves should be gathered up and burned.

Books for rosarians: a selection

The *Bibliographa de la rosa* by D. Mariano Vergara (Madrid, 1982) listed more than 1000 books about roses. Of necessity, modern rosarians, conscious of the cost of books and the space needed to accommodate them, have to be content with fewer, and besides, as the discriminating collector realizes, not many of the books currently on sale will remain free from obsolescence.

A group of roses from John Parkinson's classic work Paradisi in sole paradisus terrestris *(London, 1629).*

However, if no work is imperishable, we can at least choose some that were of major importance at the time they were written. One of the more remarkable and percipient surveys to survive from classical times came from Theophrastus (*see* HISTORY OF THE ROSE) who succeeded Aristotle in 322 BC in what would now be called the 'faculty of biology' in Athens. In his *Enquiry into Plants*, Theophrastus by no means wrote entirely of roses, but when he discusses subjects closely related to them – for example, budding, pruning, the mysteries of scent and difficulties of breeding true from seed – the reader cannot but marvel at how often simple powers of observation enabled this self-taught naturalist to anticipate the findings of today by some 2000 years. At least two readable – and re-readable – English translations are worth hunting for: *Theophrastus – De causius plantarum* (3 vols), translated by Benedict Einarson and George K. K. Link, both of the University of Chicago (Heinemann, London and Harvard University Press, 1976); and *Theophrastus – Enquiry into Plants* (2 vols), translated by Sir Arthur Hort (Heinemann, London and G. P. Putnam's Sons, New York, 1916). However, though often quoted, these are hard to find, even on library shelves.

One hesitates about including two other works: *The Herball* by John Gerard (1633 edition) and *Paradisi in sole paradisus terrestris* by John Parkinson, written in 1629. Dover Publications of New York published facsimiles of both them in 1975, and an earlier facsimile edition of Parkinson was brought out by Methuen in 1904. They are weighty tomes, expensive and difficult to accommodate on modern bookshelves, and in each, only one section out of many is devoted to roses. Yet their writings summed up almost all that was of significance to gardeners of the day, and remained unrivalled as a source for nearly 200 years.

The same drawbacks apply to the most famous of all works on the 'queen of flowers', *Les roses*, illustrated by Pierre-Joseph REDOUTÉ, with a text by Claude-Antoine Thory, a French civil servant. In this case, the collector does well to look for the facsimile edition published in three volumes by De Schutter S.A. of Antwerp in 1978, and particularly for the accompanying commentary on the roses of Redouté, which includes a list of synonyms of the varieties mentioned in *Les roses* and a critical analysis by the late Gisèle de la Roche. It also contains some of Redouté's paintings not to be seen in the original folio publication.

Even before Redouté's death in 1834, the growing popularity of the HYBRID PERPETUALS created a market for books that described them. One of the first to appear was *The Rose Amateur's Guide* by Thomas Rivers, a nurseryman of Sawbridgeworth, Hertfordshire. It was published in 1837, and is a practical enough book in its way.

Far more interesting to the modern reader, however, is *The Book of Roses, or the Rose Fancier's Manual*, which appeared the following year. This was the work of Catherine Frances Gore *née* Moody (1799–1861), an indefatigable author who, in addition to her horticultural work, wrote about seventy novels with such titles as *Cecil, or the Adventures of a Coxcomb* and *The Banker's Wife*, which were borrowed with gratification through the newly established lending libraries. In 1832, nine years after her marriage to Captain Charles Arthur Gore, Mrs Gore decided to take up residence in France, and was able through her writing (which also included plays performed at Drury Lane and the Haymarket in London) to support her ten children. Her book on roses was written to encourage English amateur gardeners to pay as much attention to new varieties as French gardeners did, instead of relying solely on such standbys as the cabbage rose, the damask rose and the 'Maiden's Blush'. It is her references to French nurseries and to the customs of France that makes the work such a highly acceptable gift if not a necessary work of reference. A facsimile edition, with a new foreword by Leonie Bell, was published by Earl Coleman in New York and Heyden & Son Ltd, London, in 1978.

In the mainstream of rosarian literature, another facsimile is worth consideration. This is *The Rose Manual* by Robert Buist, published originally in 1844 and republished by Heyden (London) and Coleman (New York) in 1978. Buist, born in 1802, was a Scot who emigrated to the

United States, and established a highly successful nursery business in Philadelphia. He paid frequent visits to England and other European countries to keep abreast of developments, and was able to provide rose lovers in the northeast United States with a wide-ranging, reliable and engaging picture of the world scene.

The Rose Garden by William Paul, published by subscription in 1848, is also highly quotable. The original Paul nursery at Cheshunt in Hertfordshire was founded in 1806 by Adam Paul, who was succeeded by his two sons, William and George. In 1860, however, William moved out and took over the Royal Nursery at Waltham Cross, which thereafter carried the name 'William Paul & Son'. This son, A. W. Paul, was one of the first growers to import roses from the South of France. William Paul's brother George remained at Cheshunt, where the firm continued under the somewhat confusing name of Paul & Son.

The highly readable, and perhaps the best-known and most frequently quoted of all Victorian rose books, *A Book about Roses* by Dean HOLE, is discussed in greater detail elsewhere in this book. Hole's work has been through so many editions that it is still possible to find second-hand copies at reasonable prices.

A small but nevertheless valuable treatise, not easily found, is H. B. Ellwanger's *The Rose*. This book, published by Dodd, Mead & Co., New York, first appeared in 1882, and further editions followed in 1892 and 1914. The second, 1892 edition throws valuable light on the roses available in American, French and English nurseries in the 1890s. Ellwanger, the proprietor of the Mount Hope Nursery at Rochester, New York, made his own assessment of rosarian literature of the time, giving the nod to Thomas Rivers, William Paul and to Shirley Hibberd, the first edition of whose work, *The Amateur's Rose Book*, had appeared in 1864. He also approved of *Cultural Directions for the Rose* by nurseryman John Cranston of Hereford.

In 1902, a joint work by Gertrude Jekyll (the surname rhymes with 'treacle') and Edward Mawley appeared under the title *Roses for English Gardens*; this was republished in 1982 with twenty-four coloured illustrations by Antique Collectors Club Ltd. Edward Mawley concerned himself with the horticultural techniques of rose-growing, while Gertrude Jekyll devoted her attention to the forms of garden design best suited to the roses of her day. Her general philosophy – that nothing was too good for the rose – endears her not only to rosarians but also to students of Edwardian social life.

Some books on roses deserve their place in any bookshelf by virtue of their literary merit. One of these is *Old Garden Roses* by Edward A. Bunyard (Country Life, 1936). Bunyard was a scholar and nurseryman and had the knack of adding life, colour and a trace of good-humoured ridicule to whatever he chose to write about. This work can still sometimes be found in the catalogues of second-hand book dealers, although a facsimile of it has also been produced. In the same year, another treatise of nostalgic appeal appeared, this time by an American author. This was *Old Roses* by Ethelyn Emery Keays (New York: Macmillan), which records the search and research of a devoted rosarian into the whereabouts and well-being of the 'old' roses to be found in private American gardens. This is yet another book that has been reproduced in facsimile by Earl Coleman.

The year 1908 saw the first edition of the Revd Joseph Pemberton's standard work: *Roses: Their History, Development and Cultivation.* Pemberton was Vice-President of the NATIONAL ROSE SOCIETY, as well as a hybridist and rose exhibition prizewinner, and his advice as well as his select list of varieties cultivated in his day may be regarded as authoritative.

It is small wonder that *The History of the Rose* by Roy E. Shepherd (New York: Macmillan, 1954) went out of print so rapidly for, even today, no more thorough, concise and informative exposition of the development of the rose is to be found. In republishing this work in collaboration with Macmillan, Coleman has performed another service to rosarians the world over.

Other works on roses are worth reading at least once, even if they are not to be kept for reference. One of these is *A Rose Odyssey* by Dr J. H. Nicolas (New York: Doubleday Doran, 1937), the account of visits abroad by a distinguished hybridist – and linguist. It is a treasure house of anecdotes about the leading rose breeders of the period, country by country.

A trio of books by Graham Stuart Thomas, hybridist, plantsman and adviser to the National Trust in Britain for many years, carry considerable authority. His *Shrub Roses of Today* (1980), *Old Shrub Roses* (1983) – written with Dr C. C. Hurst, the botanical geneticist – and *Climbing Roses Old and New* (1983), all published by J. M. Dent & Sons, contain penetrating and reflective essays on different aspects of the rose world, as well as comprehensive surveys of the main varieties and species.

Roses, by the late Dr Gerd Krüssmann – available in both English and German – is a fairly expensive encyclopaedic work covering all branches of the development of the rose (Portland, Oregon: Timber Press 1981; London: Batsford, 1982).

The most stylish books on modern roses are probably those by Michael Gibson, President of the Royal National Rose Society. In his latest book, *Growing Roses* (published in 1984 by Timber Press in the US, and Croom Helm in London and Canberra), he sensibly prefers to give generous commentaries on a relatively small number of selected varieties rather than scrappy cameos of a larger number.

Those in search of some of the lesser known Georgian, Regency, Victorian and Edwardian roses will find them beautifully displayed in colour in the relatively inexpensive series of booklets published by Jarrold of Norwich. The elegant and informative commentaries by Peter Beales are worth the cost alone.

In addition, there are a number of ongoing works of reference (apart from the usual periodicals) for which room may profitably be found on the rosarian bookshelf.

One particularly useful publication is the annual *Combined Rose List*, compiled and available from Beverly R. Dobson, 215 Harriman Road, Irvington, New York 10533. This gives all known varieties and species in cultivation, together with the type of rose, the colour, the name of the breeder, the date of introduction and the nurseries where each variety or species is to be found. The same list also includes roses introduced since the latest issue of *Modern Roses*, the standard listing of varieties published by the J. H. McFarland Company of Harrisburg, Pennsylvania. *The Rose Directory*, published by the Royal National Rose Society of Great Britain (and being revised at the time of writing), is an extremely useful booklet and deals with more than 700 varieties and species, with notes on seventeen of the more important qualities (and defects) of each.

Rose lovers in the UK (and elsewhere) planning to add to their libraries will find desirable second-hand copies and facsimile reprints of rose books in the catalogues of specialist dealers, particularly the following:

The Art Book Company Ltd
18 Endell Street, London WC2
(Garden history and facsimile reprints)

Sonia Ewart
3 Kensington Park Gardens
London W11 3HB

Ivelet Books Ltd
18 Fairlawn Drive
Redhill
Surrey RH1 6JP

Watch House Rare Books
43 Belsize Park Gardens
London NW3 4JJ

Wheldon & Wesley Ltd
Lytton Lodge
Codicote
Hitchin, Herts.

Wyseby House Books
Wyseby House
Kirtlebridge
Dumfries & Galloway DG11 3AN

Some rose CATALOGUES are always a pleasure to read, particularly those dealing with 'old' roses, such as those produced by the English growers Peter Beales of Attleborough, Norfolk NR17 1AY, and David Austin of Albrighton, Wolverhampton WV7 3HB. In the United States, an especially praiseworthy catalogue is the one produced by Roses of Yesterday and Today, 802 Brown's Valley Road, Watsonville, California 95076.

Bourbon roses

The arrival of the earliest Bourbon rose (*c.* 1817) in Europe and the United States is described in the section dealing with CHINA ROSES. The original Bourbon was characterized by its vivid rose-coloured flowers with neatly interleaved, rounded, reflexed petals, and broad, tough-looking leaflets on vigorous thorn-protected stems.

When crossed with 'Hume's Blush China', the Bourbons gave rise to the pink TEA ROSES, and when crossed with hybrid Chinas and PORTLANDS, the HYBRID PERPETUALS were the result.

'It is about six years since we predicted that this group of roses in a few years would be the most popular of the "Queen of Flowers",' wrote Robert Buist (*see* BOOKS FOR ROSARIANS) in Philadelphia in 1844. Within sixty years, one nursery alone, that of Jean-Paul Vibert of Chennevières-sur-Marne, had grown 600 different varieties, and Buist's prediction has now been literally fulfilled in the great demand by all admirers and cultivators of the rose for varieties of this family.

True Bourbon-style varieties include:

*'Boule de Neige' (1867): Because of the reflexed petals, this rose was inevitably christened 'Snowball', although its flowers are ivory. Fragrant and autumn-flowering.

*'Coupe d'Hébé' ('Hébé's Cup', 1840) is, as its name implies, a globe-shaped rose, the pink blooms contrasting agreeably with the fresh green foliage. A summer-flowering rose that likes some support.

*'Souvenir de la Malmaison' was introduced as a bush rose in 1843 and was so called, Roy Shepherd tells us, because one of the Grand Dukes of Russia obtained a sample of it from Malmaison for the Imperial Garden in St Petersburg. Now marketed in two forms, bush and climbing. Peter Beales aptly describes the flowers as blush-white with face-powder pink shadings. REMONTANT.

*'Madame Isaac Pereire' (1880), named after the wife of a French banker, scores points mainly for colour (intense purplish-crimson) and a particularly strong fragrance. Untidy flowers with petals quartered and crowded together in a wide open cup; the autumn blooms are said to be superior in shape.

*'Zéphirine Drouhin' (1868) is a favourite because of its thornless stems, and is normally treated as a climber, although it can be disciplined into bush form. Beautifully neat flowers of rather sharp carmine-cerise. Fragrant; remontant.

*'Honorine de Brabant' is of unknown origin but is clearly a very acceptable Bourbon. The flowers are double blush-pink, mottled and striped with violet and mauve. Remontant. Like 'Honorine de Brabant', the roses 'Louise Odier', 'La Reine Victoria' and 'Madame Ernst Calvat' are remontant Bourbons. They improve with support, and are included under RAMBLERS.

*'Gipsy Boy' ('Zigeuner Knabe', 1909), with flowers of deepest purplish-crimson with lemon anthers, is usually classed as a Bourbon, although its general style does not warrant this. It has retained its popularity for more than three-quarters of a century in spite of being only summer-flowering.

Boursault roses

These hybrid climbing roses were first raised by Henri Boursault, a French horticulturalist, from 1817 onwards from crosses between *Rosa chinensis* or *R. banksiae* and (probably) *R. blanda*. The long shoots of Boursault roses are reddish, arching and mostly thornless except at the base; the leaflets are oval and serrated at the tips, but the lower edges are smooth and narrowed into the stalk. The flowers are produced in clusters, and the plants are hardy and early flowering.

One of them – 'Amadis' with dark red blooms, of which Dean HOLE wrote that it 'is very beautiful when the evening sun is low and the soft light rests upon its glowing flowers' – was marketed by the French Laffay nursery in 1829, and is still on sale. 'Madame Sancy de Parabère', a vigorous climber with mauve flowers, launched in 1847 and still going strong, is also usually classed as a Boursault, although Ethelyn Emery Keays, in her classic work *Old Roses* (1935), placed it as a cross between *R. alpina* and a centifolia. Robert Buist, in his *Rose Manual* of 1844 (*see* BOOKS FOR ROSARIANS), wrote of a variety known as 'Purpurea', which was sold 'from the flatboats on the Ohio and Mississippi rivers' under such names as 'Purple Noisette', 'Maheka' and 'Michigan'.

A late Victorian (1889) interpretation of the brier rose by Walter Crane, Principal of the Royal College of Art, associate of William Morris and superb book illustrator.

Brier
The spelling 'brier' is usually preferred to 'briar', but both forms are descended from an Old English word of unknown origin meaning any prickly or thorny bush or shrub, but especially a rose bush. Thus the poet Edmund Spenser wrote 'Sweet is the rose, but grows upon a brere', thus apparently distinguishing the flower from the bush. Shakespeare made the same distinction in Henry VI, Part I (Act ii, Scene 4) when he wrote:

> *Let him that is a true-born gentleman,*
> *And stands upon the honour of his birth,*
> *If he suppose that I have pleaded truth,*
> *From off this brier pluck a white rose with me.*

Today, however, 'brier' is usually taken to mean the whole wild rose bush including the flowers, and sometimes a cultivated variety if it has enough prickles. The experts see no connection between 'brier' and the French *bruyère*, which arose from the Gallic-Roman word for 'heath', and came to mean 'heather'. The root of *Erica arborea* – a white-flowered heather that can grow to nearly 10 feet (3 m) – is used to provide bowls and stems for brier tobacco pipes (thus adding to the philological confusion).

See also AYRSHIRE ROSES, BOURSAULT ROSES, HEDGES, PENZANCE ROSES, RAMBLERS, WILD ROSES.

British Association of Rose Breeders (BARB)
BARB was founded in April 1973 to encourage the introduction and growing of new roses. The active members of the association are professional nurserymen, who are offering, under Plant Breeders' Rights in the UK, either their own varieties or those that other breeders have asked them to introduce. The latter may be varieties from overseas, or from amateurs.

BARB members undertake to sell all new varieties on the same terms to all nurseries and to register them under the provisions of the Plant Variety and Seeds Act of 1964, which requires breeders to declare that they themselves have bred or discovered the variety of the rose in question and that they are free of commercial indebtedness in respect of it. This, of course, protects both breeders and the nurserymen. The rose must be clearly distinguishable from other varieties and be capable of reproducing consistent 'repeats'.

Applicants must furnish particulars of the stem, including its colour, and the number and type of 'THORNS', if any. They must describe the foliage and the neck – whether stiff or pendant – the shape and colour of the bud, the shape, size and structure of the flowers, and the colour of the petals, inside and outside, when opening, half open and fully open. They must also specify the height of the plant two years after its appearance as a MAIDEN, and must present samples of roses grown from it out-of-doors – six in the case of a bush, four in the case of a shrub, and two from climbers.

If applicants are successful, they receive the right to collect a commission from growers who use the buds of their varieties, for a period of twenty years. These commissions are fixed by the breeder in open competition with other breeders. BARB members propagate nearly five million roses every year.

Each spring, BARB circulates the growers with the list of the year's newly protected varieties and receives orders for the numbers of buds required. At the end of September, growers inform BARB of the numbers of buds of both old and new protected varieties they have used, and they are billed in November and the accounts settled in December. BARB acts as a clearing house, forwarding the commissions owed to the breeders. BARB is financed by a levy based on the numbers of roses budded.

See also REGISTRATION OF ROSE VARIETIES.

Budding

Budding is perhaps the most usual way of propagating roses (but *see also* SEEDS, CUTTINGS and LAYERING). Simply put, the buds of the roses that one desires to cultivate are budded on to a vigorous understock that provides them with the nourishment they need for their rapid development

Budding is a knack that is more easily observed than described, but it involves three elements: (1) the UNDERSTOCK to which the buds are to be applied, which can be planted in late autumn or, as a seedling, in early spring; (2) the scion, or shoot from the cultivated variety, which is to supply the buds; and (3) the bud or buds, cut from the wood of the scion. A visit to a rose nursery during the budding season is the best form of instruction, when a team of three can expect to bud between 1000 and 1500 plants or even more in a day.

The following summary does not claim to be more than a condensed account of the procedure:

1. Clean an area of the stem below where the top growth begins on the understock. This can be about 4 inches (10 cm) above the first root in a mature understock (less if a seedling understock is being used). Avoid the sunny side. Of course, in the case of STANDARDS (tree roses), budding is carried out at the top of the understock.

2. Scions that have borne flowers, with buds in the centre of the scions, are the best. The flower on the scion foreshadows those to be expected from the buds. Label the scions and leave in water overnight, or place in a cold store at a temperature of about 37°F (2.8°C) if the budding cannot be carried out at once.

3. Cut off the leaves shielding the buds, leaving ½ inch (1 cm) of stalk; the stalk that remains will make a convenient 'handle' for manipulating the bud.

4. With a sharp pruning knife, cut a thin slice from the scion starting ½ inch (1 cm) above the bud, and finishing 1 inch (2.5 cm) below, leaving a pointed end, so that the slice resembles the shape of a shield.

5. Separate the wood of the slice from the bark, leaving the bud supported by the bark and its green lining. (Where seedlings are being budded, this separation is not practicable.)

6. Make a shallow vertical slit about ¾ inch (2 cm) long in the understock and, at the top of it, a horizontal slit about a third as long – to form a 'T' – so that two flaps of bark, one on each side of the vertical slit, can be separated by inserting the blunt end of the knife. Trim the bark surrounding the bud to suit the size of the slits in the understock.

7. Insert the pointed end of the bud-slice into the vertical slit, press it down and into the slit and fold over the two flaps of bark.

The bud cut from the scion.

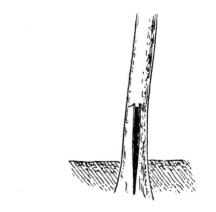

Holding the bud.

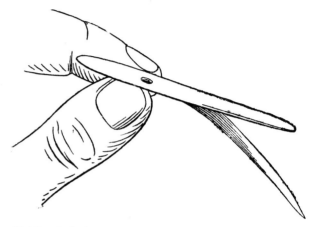

Understock prepared to receive bud.

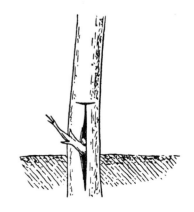

Bud inserted into understock.

8. Growers of the past used to bind the shield on to the stem with bass, a type of flexible binding, but today a self-attaching band, known in the trade as a 'Sleischauer', is preferred. These rot away gradually and do not need to be taken off by hand.

The budding will, in most cases, have been carried out during the summer months; if it is delayed until later, the chances of success are reduced, unless the foliage of the understock is cut back. The bud will usually remain dormant until the following year, but if a shoot materializes in the same year that the plant has been budded, the shoot should be later cut back to one or two buds.

In the following spring, the understock is cut off just above the budding place, and only its lower part and the cultivated bud now remain. Any suckers should also be promptly removed. It is possible to insert two buds in the same understock, and as mentioned above, this needs to be done in the case of standards, to give an even, all-round growth. The rose can be transplanted, if desired, in the ensuing autumn – that is, about fifteen months after budding.

Bush roses

'Bush' and 'shrub' are given much the same meaning in most dictionaries but, in rose parlance, the two are not always synonymous. Bush roses of the kind most often seen in rosebeds are, or should be, smaller than garden SHRUB ROSES, and are not necessarily very bushy. Some of them, however, if cultivated under favourable conditions, can develop into shrub roses.

A rose bush – as distinct from a bush rose – can be of almost any size. MINIATURE ROSES that are less than 18 inches (46 cm) in height are also referred to as 'bushes'.

Button-eye

A button-eye is a deformity of the carpel, the structure that carries and protects the ovules, and is distinguishable as a small green boss or pointel in the centre of the rose bloom. However, the term is often used to refer to the hub of small petals that, in a very full bloom, may be so completely curled over as to show only their reverse sides. Such button-eyes are to be seen in 'old' varieties such as the white damask rose 'Madame Hardy' (1832); 'Königin von Dänemarck' (1826), a rather similar rose with mid-pink blooms; and 'Juno' (1847), a blush Provence rose.

Buttonholes, roses for

Once, when Dean HOLE visited Nottingham for a rose show, he greatly admired a buttonhole worn by the landlord of the General Cathcart Inn. This rose was the HYBRID PERPETUAL 'Senateur Vaisse', which, wrote the Dean, 'glowed amid the gloom like the red light on a midnight train'.

'Senateur Vaisse', a rose from Pierre Guillot *père*, is no longer grown today, and the average rosarian could hardly display such a large bloom without a trace of ostentation. Furthermore, the modern diminutive buttonhole – or 'flowerhole', as it is more properly called – seems more suited to the shape of the button-like *Légion d'honneur* than to a full-sized garden rose.

This marked reduction in the size of the flowerhole by modern designers may account for the virtual disappearance of the tubular water containers that used to hang from the flowerhole behind the lapel, allowing the rose three or four more days of extra life: any tube large enough to be of use would permanently deform the modern flowerhole. However, a magazine in the United States recently advertised, as a suitable present for Mother's Day, a rose tube to be worn in the front of the lapel, made of 14-carat gold with 'a freshwater pearl' at the foot; the price: $495.

President Nehru habitually wore a rose in his lapel, and solved the problem of longevity by wearing a different one every day. Others display a rosebud, since an unopened flower lasts longer than an open one. Another alternative is to choose a double-petalled but small rose, the justification being that a ten-petalled rose lasts longer than a five-petalled one, and a 'full' rose (i.e. thirty to forty petals) longer still. In addition, if the rose is small, it will seldom look dishevelled.

The CLUSTER-FLOWERED deep-red 'Garnette' rose is one such example, and the rose-pink 'Carol Amling', a SPORT of 'Garnette', is another. Both do better under glass than in the open. 'Cécile Brunner' (Ducher, 1881), often classed as a CHINA ROSE, is another possibility. It has decorative buds, too – and some scent. Its yellow counterpart is 'Perle d'Or' (Dubreuil, 1883).

In 1840, Thomas Rivers wrote in *The Rose Amateur's Guide* (2nd edition): 'The "King of Rome" or "Theodore de Corse" (for they are one and the same) is a beautiful and double compact rose so exactly like a double ranunculus that it might almost be mistaken for one.' That, if it had survived, would surely have been greatly admired today.

A wide selection of suitable blooms can be found among the MINIATURES. Those with ornamental sepals, such as 'Jackpot' (Moore, 1985), a fresh yellow, or 'Black Jade' (var. 'Benblack'), a blackish-red introduced by the Savills in 1985, are especially attractive. The fragrant miniature moss rose 'Lemon Delight' (Moore, 1978) would be more familiar in the UK. 'Joan Austin' (Moore, 1981), a pink variety, is also very fragrant, an important asset for the wearer.

The slightly larger PATIO ROSES, such as Poulsen's 'Texas' ('Poultex'), a high-peaked yellow, or one of the Meillandinas from Meilland–Richardier – particularly 'Pink Meillandina' and 'Apricot Meillandina' – would be worth their place on even the most important social occasions.

Buttonhole bouquets, in which the rose is backed with five or so wired leaflets, are, of course, a matter for the florist.

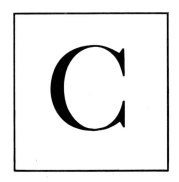

Cabbage roses

See ROSA CENTIFOLIA.

Canada, the rose in

In Canada, roses grow readily in coastal British Columbia (including Vancouver Island), in southwestern Nova Scotia and, to a lesser degree, near Lakes Ontario and Erie in southern Ontario. Elsewhere, Canadian rose growers face much the same problem as the Americans did a century ago: few of the varieties offered to them are suitable for growing in their climate. 'Hardiness,' to quote Professor Patricia Harney, who is in charge of the rose-breeding programme at the University of Guelph, Ontario, 'is undoubtedly the most important character to be incorporated into a new Canadian rose; it is the character most lacking in hybrid tea roses presently on the market.'

Hardiness in roses appears to be controlled not by one gene but by many, and is easily lost if a hardy rose is mated with a tender one. Hence, only a limited number of cultivated varieties are used in the search for the ideal Canadian rose. WILD ROSES are employed as the POLLEN parents, and the seed parents are cultivars that have survived at least one winter at the Cambridge Research Station, some 12 miles (19 km) from Guelph, without any protection except a wood-chip mulch.

As most cultivars have ovules containing fourteen pairs of CHROMOSOMES, the wild roses chosen as the pollen parents must also have the same quantity, and among those that qualify are *Rosa fedtschenkoana, R. pendulina, R. pimpinellifolia, R. arkansana, R. virginiana, R. laxa* and *R. carolina.* However, only hybrids having *R. pimpinellifolia* or *R. fedtschenkoana* as pollen parents have proved truly cold-hardy. Since the bud usually proves to be the plant's weakest link, the practice is to grow the roses on their own ROOTS.

Only summer-flowering wild roses are used. The task of endowing their offspring with REMONTANCY is not, in itself, difficult, but roses that flower a second time do so on new shoots that are often too tender to survive the Canadian winter. What is needed is not merely a rose that flowers a second time but one that is also capable of producing hard wood before the frosts set in. The Agriculture Canada research station in Manitoba is also conducting experiments to find varieties of roses especially suitable to conditions in the Canadian prairie country.

Among the rose gardens of Canada, the best known is probably that of the Royal Botanical Gardens in Hamilton, Ontario, which lies on the northern shore of Lake Ontario about 40 miles (65 km) southwest of Toronto. The latter city was host to the WORLD FEDERATION OF ROSE SOCIETIES at their biennial meeting in 1985.

Cant's of Colchester

The Cant family were growing geraniums in Essex as far back as 1724, and turned to roses in 1765, more than a decade before the American Declaration of Independence. The nursery at that time seems to have been in the care of William Cant (1742–1805), but only came to the fore under his grandson Benjamin Cant (1827–1906). It was under his direction that Cant's entered the first NATIONAL ROSE SHOW held in 1858, and won one of the silver cups awarded by its organizers.

There is evidence that, towards the end of the century, Benjamin was succeeding as a breeder as well as a nurseryman. Thus the great American rosarian H. B. Ellwanger, in his book *The Rose* (1882), gives favourable mention to the Cant rose 'Prince Arthur', introduced seven years earlier. This rose also found favour with Dean HOLE, who described it as a free-flowering form of 'General Jacqueminot'. The great Joseph Pemberton described Cant's 'Blush Rambler', introduced in 1903, as a 'very vigorous pillar rose and one of the best kinds of multiflora'. The HYBRID PERPETUAL 'Ben Cant', a deep crimson rose, was chosen for inclusion in a select list of thirty by the Revd. A. Foster-Melliar in 1905; he described it as being 'tall enough for a middle row', and Pemberton rated it as 'late flowering, vigorous and recommended for exhibition purposes'. Presumably the white 'Dorothy Perkins', introduced in 1908, would have stemmed from Benjamin Cant's efforts.

The Pawsey family, who have contributed greatly to the present success of the firm, are descendants of Diana Cant, Benjamin's granddaughter, who married a Mr Clifford Pawsey. From 1966 onwards, Cant's have maintained an active breeding programme and have scored successes with: 'Just Joey' (1973), a striking coppery-pink-and-buff

LARGE-FLOWERED ROSE that was named for Roger Pawsey's wife Joanna; 'Alpine Sunset' (1974), a large-flowered rose that is creamy yellow and peach; and 'Goldstar' (1984), a large-flowered red or yellow rose, good for cutting and a gold medal winner at the INTERNATIONAL ROSE TRIALS at The Hague.

Catalogues

Catalogues and nurserymen's plant-lists are among the most reliable sources used by rose historians. Catalogues of the 16th, 17th and early 18th centuries were often included in books that otherwise contained no overt sales promotion, a practice which helped to enhance the reputation and prestige of the nurserymen who wrote them. Growers such as Gerard and Parkinson depended for survival on the reputation they enjoyed among a limited and exclusive circle of large estate owners – including members of the Royal family – clients whose interest might have been forfeited if the nurserymen who grew their plants offered them commercially to the public at large.

Few growers' plant-lists were available in printed pamphlet form before 1750. One of these was the catalogue of Robert Furber, a nurseryman 'over-against Hide Park Gate, Kensington', which appeared in 1727. This was three years after Furber's plant-list (which included the first mention of the MOSS ROSE in Britain) had appeared in Phillip Miller's *Gardener's and Florist's Dictionary.*

Trade price-lists in pamphlet form were generally issued free until around 1760, when it became the practice to charge for them. The first catalogues to show prices for forest and fruit trees as well as roses appeared in Britain about the same time as the American Declaration of Independence. The earliest came from John Telford (1744–1830) and his brother George (1749–1834) of Toft Green, York. Their catalogue appeared in 1775 and was followed soon after (1777) by a similar price-list from William and John Perfect of Pontefract. Both offered more than forty varieties of roses.

An early attempt by nurseryman Nathaniel Swinden to attract mail-order business in SEEDS, from which roses were then occasionally grown, is mentioned in Blanche Henrey's work, *British Botanical and Horticultural Literature before 1800* (Oxford University Press, 1975). Swinden's nursery was at Brentford End near the 8th milestone west from Hyde Park Corner, and his catalogue of 1778 suggested that customers who did not wish to make the journey to Brentford could send their orders by letter and have the seeds delivered to St Paul's Coffee House in St Paul's Churchyard, to Messrs Owen & Co., 66 Cornhill, or to any other place in London more convenient.

The arrival of the CHINA ROSES at the end of the 18th century enlarged the amount of space given to roses in general nurserymen's catalogues. For example, Lee & Kennedy's catalogue of 1774 listed fewer than fifty species and varieties, whereas the edition of 1808 contained 220.

Few catalogues devoted entirely to roses pre-date the 19th century, and several of the leading English and American rose growers followed the example of earlier general nurserymen and incorporated their catalogues in books. William Robert Prince of Flushing, New York included in his *Manual of Roses* (1846) 1630 rose varieties, with prices ranging from 18 cents, in the case of some superseded varieties, to $3 for fashionable imports from France. Robert Buist of Philadelphia gave no formal price-list but stated in *The Rose Manual* (1844) that he wanted to help amateurs, particularly ladies, choose their own roses and that he was writing as a nurseryman cultivating the largest collection of roses in the United States. In England, Thomas Rivers of Sawbridgeworth, in *The Rose Amateur's Guide,* described a selection of the outstanding roses from his catalogue, and declared that many of his roses not mentioned in the book were equally good. However, from 1856, rose growers in England were encouraged to give a wider distribution to trade catalogues in pamphlet form when the postage on circulars weighing up to four ounces was reduced to one penny.

The second half of the 19th century saw a flood of colour chromolithographs. Nurseryman William Paul included some in his work *The Rose Garden* (1848), and CANT'S OF COLCHESTER were using colour in their pamphlet price-lists by the turn of the century. A HARKNESS catalogue of 1912 shows a colour picture of a Gertrude Jekyll garden on the front, but the real incentive for breeders to show individual roses in colour was when a system for registering and protecting new varieties came into force in the 1930s. (*See also* PRINTED PORTRAITS OF THE ROSE.)

Some 'old' rose catalogues of permanent value are mentioned in the section dealing with BOOKS FOR ROSARIANS. Some older catalogues of historic interest are to be seen at the Lindley Library of the Royal Horticultural Society and the British Museum, both in London, and at the library of the Botanical Garden in Cambridge.

See also **Selected bibliography**

Centifolias
See ROSA CENTIFOLIA.

Chafers and rose beetles
The rose beetle *(Cetonia aurata)*, with its greenish gold and shiny copper-tinted wing cases, is one of Britain's most beautiful species and one of the most enthusiastic pollinators – or should it be pollen-eaters? – to be found in the rose garden. Unfortunately, in its haste to fulfil its destiny, it attacks and damages petals and anthers.

According to *The Out-door World, or The Young Collector's Handbook* by W. Furneaux, published in 1894 but still widely used by schoolboys of the 1920s, the larva of the rose beetle has a kind of *Midsummer Night's Dream* upbringing: 'Search should be made for this insect on the blossoms of wild roses, strawberries and the privet. Its wood-eating larva often finds both home and food among the chips and tems of an ants' nest, and has consequently been termed the "King of the Ants".' Modern writers are less indulgent, and accuse the larva of finding its home and food in the rose garden, where it feeds on the roots of the plants with alarming results.

Here it is at one with three other less attractive associates: the cockchafer, the summer chafer and the garden chafer. All have white, grub-like larvae, and the prudent rose grower need make no distinction between them. The cockchafer takes about five years to develop, which reduces its life expectancy in the well-tilled garden but leaves the gardener unsure whether the beetles have been completely vanquished.

Regular hoeing will usually detect or even destroy any chafer larvae in the rosebed, but if any are discovered, Bromophos should be added to the soil. The roots of any grass surrounding the rose garden offer a springboard from which chafers can migrate, and drastic measures are advised if an area of grass is to be converted into a rose garden. A season of ridge potatoes is known to discourage chafers, and free-range chickens can help, too.

See also ENEMIES OF THE ROSE.

Children, literature and roses

Gertrude Jekyll's work *Children and Gardens*, published by Country Life in 1908, indissolubly linked her favourite age-group with roses. She lured little ones into the garden with directions on how to get a kettle boiling there in five minutes, and proposed a recipe involving melted Cheddar cheese to which brown sugar was to be added. Her suggestions on suitable roses were, however, less adventurous. She advised children to go for 'the neat little pom-pom rose with pale pink flowers known as "Mignonette", and also to squeeze in a china rose, a damask rose, a cabbage rose and ramblers if the garden had a hedge or fence. The playhouse would be decorated with trellis roses.

More enduring, if more shadow-filled was that fictional rosarium *The Secret Garden*, the inspiration for which came to Frances Hodgson Burnett from the rose garden at Maytham Hall, Kent, her home from 1898. Mary, the orphaned heroine of the story is sent to live at the great house at Mistlethwaite in the Yorkshire wolds that belongs to her uncle. He had married some ten years before the story opens, and in those days, it had been the special pleasure of his young wife to tend the roses in their garden, and to encourage them to grow over an old tree that had a branch bent to form a seat. When she died after being severely injured when the branch broke, her husband was inconsolable, and from that time onwards, the garden was kept locked and the servants forbidden to speak of it. Its existence was kept from Mary, but she discovered it and, with the help of a local boy and Colin, a young cousin who was an invalid, she began to restore the rose garden. In turn, she succeeded in restoring her uncle's faith in humanity as well as Colin's health.

Somewhat further away from real life we have *The Rose and the Ring*, written by William Makepeace Thackeray in 1854 to amuse the children of British expatriots in Rome during the Christmas holidays. Thackeray, who was a gifted artist, also illustrated this fairy tale, which he intended to be read aloud at the fireside. The result was Ruritania with a spice of magic. The ring and the rose, given by the Fairy Blackstick to her two god-daughters, both make their wearers irresistable to all others. The ring and the rose pass by misadventure from one character to another, with satisfyingly predictable results. There are nineteen chapters to this fireside pantomime – each with a kaleidoscopic plot staggering wildly between the plausible and the incredible.

In the next example of a literary encounter between a child and a rose, only one character belongs to the world of reality: Alice. Not long after Alice has dreamed her way through the mirror on the chimney-piece in *Through the Looking Glass and What Alice Found There*, she enters a garden filled with talking flowers.

'There's one other flower in the garden that can move about like you' said the Rose [to Alice] . . . 'But she's more bushy than you are.'

'Is she like me?' Alice asked eagerly, for the thought had crossed her mind: 'There's another little girl in the garden somewhere!'

'Well, she has the same awkward shape as you,' the Rose said, 'but she's redder – and her petals are shorter, I think.'

'They're done up close, like a dahlia,' said the Tiger-Lily; 'not tumbled about like yours.'

'But that's not *your* fault,' the Rose added kindly: 'you're beginning to fade, you know – and then one can't help one's petals getting a little untidy.'

Alice didn't like this idea at all; so to change the subject, she asked, 'Does she ever come out here?'

'I dare say you'll see her soon,' said the Rose. 'She's one of the kind that has nine spikes, you know.'

'Where does she wear them? Alice asked with some curiosity.

'Why, all round her head, of course,' the Rose replied. 'I was wondering why *you* hadn't got some too. I thought it was the regular rule.'

'She's coming!' cried the Larkspur. 'I hear her footstep, thump thump along the gravel-walk!'

Alice looked round eagerly, and found that it was the Red Queen.

Of course, Alice – in *Alice's Adventures in Wonderland* – had already encountered roses: in this, the Queen of Heart's penalty for planting white roses instead of red was . . . death.

Other stories for children that have roses as their centre-pieces are based on folktales. One brilliant adaptation of a myth persistent in many European and some Asian countries appears in Oscar Wilde's *The Happy Prince and Other Tales*, first published in 1888. In 'The Nightingale and the Rose', a student is in love with a girl who demands to be given a red rose if she is to go with him to the ball. But it is winter and only white roses are to be found. A nightingale, taking pity on his plight, tries to comfort the student with a promise that he shall have a red rose. The young man listens as the bird sings on but does not understand what the nightingale is trying to tell him – that the white rose will turn red if the bird keeps singing while pressing his breast against a thorn until the petals of the flower are drenched with his blood. The student gets his red rose and offers it to his love, but the girl throws it into the gutter because the court chamberlain has offered her something better.

Most of the stories in *Grimm's Fairy Tales* are records of folklore. Jacob Ludwig Carl Grimm (1785–1863) was at one time librarian to Jerome Bonaparte, King of West-phalia, and attended the Congress of Vienna in 1815 in the service of the Elector of Hesse to whom he and his brother, Wilhelm Carl Grimm (1786–1859), were librarians from 1814 to 1829. It took the brothers thirteen years to assem-ble their collection of oral tales and songs, many of which were dictated by the wife of a cowherd in the village of Niederzwehrn, near Kassel. The Grimms' objective was to rediscover and preserve the traditional folk legends with exactitude and without embellishment. 'Little Brier Rose' (also known as 'The Sleeping Beauty') is the story of a princess who, in fulfilment of the prediction of a wicked fairy, pricks her finger on a spindle and is condemned, with her family and other members of the court, to sleep for 100 years, while a vast forest of briers grows up to surround the royal palace. A century later, a prince who is passing by hears of the story of the sleeping princess and forces his way through the brier thicket to the palace where he finds the rosebud princess newly awakened. This story, which has been told in many lands in many different forms, was contributed by the old family nurse of Wilhelm Grimm's wife Dorothea.

The Grimms wrote down the tales as they heard them, and not all are sugar and spice – particularly the following, which appears under the title 'The Rose':

There was once a poor woman, who had two children. The youngest had to go every day into the forest to fetch wood. Once when she had gone a long way to seek it, a beautiful little child who was quite strong came and helped her industriously to pick up the wood and carry it home; then before a moment had passed, the stranger disappeared. The child told her mother this, but at first she would not believe it. At length the daughter brought home a rose and told her mother that the beautiful child had given it to her, and had told her that, when it was in full bloom, he would return. The mother put the rose in water. One morning, the mother went to her daughter's bed and found her dead, with a look of happiness on her face. The same morning, the rose was in full bloom.

In Denmark, Hans Christian Andersen, like the Grimm brothers, believed he was writing for all ages and not only for children, and with him too, the rose was in the fore-ground. 'In the centre of a large garden there grew rose trees' begins one of his fairy tales, and, in one of those, the loveliest of all, there dwelt a little Elf . . .' Another rose appears in Andersen's tale of the swineherd:

It happened that where the Prince's father lay buried, there grew a rose tree – a most beautiful rose tree which blossomed only once

in five years, and even then it bore only one flower, but that *was* a rose. It smelt so sweet that all cares and sorrows were forgotten by him who inhaled its fragrance.

The Prince decided to marry and sent the princess of his choice both the rose and a nightingale. Unfortunately, the Princess was disappointed because both of these were natu-ral, not artificial, and she refused even to see the Prince. However, disguising himself as a labourer, he asked for employment at the palace, and the King put him in charge of the royal herd of pigs. The Princess fell in love with the swineherd, but when the King discovered the affair, he was beside himself with rage. The swineherd revealed his true identity but was so disenchanted with the Princess, who preferred a swineherd to a royal lover, and an artificial rose to a real one, that he went home to his own land.

A number of characters beloved by children appear today as names in the catalogues of rose growers. PETER LAMBERT's 'Frau Karl Druschki', an absolutely pure white rose, was rechristened 'Snow Queen' at a time when any-thing of German origin was out of favour in England. The name commemorated Hans Andersen's beautiful Snow Queen who froze her lovers to death. The name is rarely used today, but WILHELM KORDES later neatly avoided dupli-cation by choosing 'Schneewittchen' ('snow witch') for the rose that eventually became 'Iceberg'. Perhaps he was right, but could a witch have been as beautiful as Andersen's Queen?

'Rosenelfe', also by Kordes, is a mid-pink cluster-flow-ered rose. 'Bo-Peep' is a mid-pink MINIATURE by DeVink; 'Cinderella' (white) and 'Tom Thumb' (dark red), both miniatures, came from the same breeder. Another Dutch breeder, DeRuiter, gave the Walt Disney dwarfs a good run, and 'Snow White' – yet another miniature – came from Robinson. 'Rödhätte' (Poulsen) is the Danish form of Red Riding Hood.

China roses

This term is often taken to refer to the species and varieties imported into England from China in the late 18th and early 19th century, which brought with them the combined qualities of delicacy and REMONTANCY that were previously lacking in almost all European varieties. (However, it should be remembered that two of the 'China' roses were fundamentally TEA ROSES.)

For centuries, the movements of foreigners in China had been severely restricted, and it was not until 1842, after Lord Palmerston had sent an expeditionary force there, that the British were permitted to use four designated treaty ports and the island of Hong Kong for trading pur-poses. Consequently, almost all the early China roses imported to Britain were hybrids taken from Chinese gar-dens – particularly the Fa-Tee ('Flowerland') nursery about $2\frac{1}{2}$ miles (4 km) outside Canton in southern China. How-ever, Confucius (551–479 BC) recorded that a large number of roses had been planted in the Imperial Gardens in the capital, Peking, in the north, and it is safe to assume that, although the rose may not have enjoyed the same prestige in China as the peony or the chrysanthemum, it was widely known and cultivated there; certainly it was often portrayed in Chinese works of art. Of equal interest to botanists, as well as to many breeders, was the arrival, sometimes many years after the hybrids, of some original China rose species.

The first arrivals

The first of these roses to arrive was a particularly remontant variety, *Rosa chinensis* var. *semperflorens*, with double flowers and young shoots, both of an intense dark red. This variety has been variously known as the Chinese 'Monthly Rose' and the 'Crimson China Rose', and sometimes as 'Slater's Crimson China' since many cuttings of it were distributed from 1792 onwards by Gilbert Slater, a director of the East India Company, from his garden at Knot's Green, Leytonstone, Essex. It was not found in the wild until nearly a century later. (*See also* BERMUDA, THE ROSES OF.)

The single-flowered wild form – *Rosa chinensis, forma spontanea* – was not known until 1885, when it was discovered in Ichang by Augustine Henry, a doctor from Ireland, then working in the Chinese Imperial Maritime Customs Service.

The next China rose to consider is the one generally known as the 'Parsons' Pink China'. This is a hybrid between two distinct species: *R. chinensis* x *R. gigantea*. The second half of the equation, known as the wild tea rose, is a magnificent climber that sometimes attains a height of more than 50 feet (15 m) and has large lemon- or cream-coloured, scented flowers as much as 5 inches (13 cm) across, and all the more impressive for being single-petalled blooms. It was first discovered in 1888 by General Sir Henry Collett, not in China but in the Shan hills of Burma, though it also grows wild in Yunnan in southwest China, where it was found later by Ernest Wilson. It needs truly mild winters and a southern wall for its well-being and is therefore seldom grown in the UK, but its influence survives in many widely cultivated varieties. It is decidedly remontant, which is more than can be said for the variety sometimes recommended as an alternative – 'Cooper's Burmese rose'.

'Parsons' Pink China' is so called because, according to Henry Andrews, writing in 1805, it had first been seen twelve years earlier flowering in the garden of an amateur rose grower, Mr Parsons, in Rickmansworth. It may therefore have been collected at the same time as *R. bracteata* – the Macartney rose – by Sir George Staunton, who accompanied Lord Macartney's diplomatic mission to China in 1792. The Banks Herbarium (now in the British Museum [Natural History]) contains a specimen of 'Parsons' Pink China', with a note that it flowered at Kew in 1795. William Townsend Aiton, who in 1793 had succeeded his father William Aiton as chief gardener there, reported eighteen years later that he believed that the British naturalist Joseph Banks had secured a plant as early as 1789

After the 'Parsons' Pink China' crossed the Atlantic, John Champney, a prosperous rice plantation owner of Charleston, South Carolina, was the first to cross it with one of the 'old' European species, using pollen from the 'Pink China' to fertilize the white *R. moschata*, the musk rose. He called his rose *R. moschata hybrida* but it soon became known as 'Champney's Pink Cluster' rose. As William Prince stated in his *Manual of Roses* of 1846, his father, William Prince Sr, had already been in correspondence with Champney for some time from his nursery in Flushing, New York, when he was presented with two tubs of 'Champney's Pink Cluster', grown from cuttings. They proved successful as pillar roses and climbers and quantities were exported.

A few years later, Philippe NOISETTE, a nurseryman also located in Charleston, raised the 'Blush Noisette' from seed (as opposed to cuttings) from 'Champney's Pink Cluster'. It was smaller than the original, with more fully petalled blooms and denser panicles. Noisette sent seeds and a seedling to his brother Louis in Paris, and Louis planted these and named the resultant seedlings 'Les Rosiers de Philippe Noisette'. However, they yielded no impressive offspring, and French breeders lost interest until a fresh strain of the original 'Champney's Pink Cluster' arrived from William Prince. When crossed with 'Park's Yellow Tea-scented Rose' (*see below*), it gave rise to the yellowish noisettes that have since been accepted as typical of the class.

'Parsons' Pink China Rose' was also the forebear of the MINIATURE ROSES. The dwarf variety *Rosa chinensis* var. *minima* occurred in Colville's Nursery in Chelsea in 1805, and became known as the 'Fairy Rose' and 'Miss Lawrance's Rose' though it isn't known whether Mary Lawrance, the flower portrait artist, ever painted it (*see* PRINTED PORTAITS OF THE ROSE). The decision to treat it as a variety rather than a species was not taken until 1894.

'Parsons' Pink China Rose' was also the parent of the BOURBON ROSES, so named because they first appeared on the Île de Bourbon (now Réunion), east of Madagascar in the Indian Ocean. The colonists there used both 'Parsons' Pink' and the autumn damask rose, the latter known to them as 'Rose des Quatres Saisons', as hedges. Natural crosses occurred between the two, and a hybrid on the estate of a M. Perichon at St Benoît on the east coast of the island attracted the attention of Émile Bréon, the botanist sent by the French government to establish a botanical garden on Réunion. In 1817, Bréon sent the seeds of this rose to Jacques, the head gardener to the Duke of Orleans at the Château de Neuilly, where REDOUTÉ painted it. One especially remontant seedling of the second generation became known as the 'Rose de l'Île de Bourbon'. In nearby Mauritius, a similar hybrid was already being grown and may have been brought there from the East India Company's garden in Calcutta where it was known as the 'Rose Edward'. The Bourbon rose reached England in 1822 and, six years later, was sent to America by George Hibbert, the Clapham nurseryman.

The original Bourbon rose was of compact, vigorous growth with thick stems and bright green stems and leaves, and reddish-pink flowers with closely packed petals. A proportion of the second generation roses, in response to MENDEL'S LAWS of inheritance, were even more remontant and fragrant than the first. Bourbon roses were also the main source of the HYBRID PERPETUAL roses that eventually supplanted them.

Another cross between *Rosa chinensis* and the wild tea rose, *R. gigantea*, was known as 'Hume's Blush Tea-scented Rose'. It is said to have been sent from India to Sir Abraham Hume in 1809 by his cousin Alexander Hume who was in charge of the East India Company's tea factory in Canton. Because of its unique fragrance, it was known originally as *R. indica odorata*. This scent betrays the strong influence of the wild tea rose, though opinions are divided as to whether it recalls that of fresh tea, the cases in which tea leaves have been packed or the dried leaves themselves; indeed, some experts claim not to have detected any resemblance in the scent of these roses to tea of any form. Special arrangements were made to transport *R. indica odorata* safely to the Empress JOSEPHINE across the Franco-British war zone. Redouté painted a fine portrait of it, captioned *Rosa indica fragrans*, which was just as well as it may no longer be in cultivation, except perhaps in Bermuda. (*See also* ART, THE ROSE IN.) When further hybridized, it provided some fine pink tea roses, including 'Brown's Super Blush' (1815), long extinct but considered by some to be the earliest of all HYBRID TEAS.

The source of many yellow tea roses was 'Parks' Yellow Tea-scented Rose'. The 'scented' was dropped later as more and more varieties appeared without the fragrance claimed for them. Also a hybrid between *R. chinensis* and *R. gigantea*, Parks' rose was brought home from China in 1824 by John Damper Parks for the Royal Horticultural Society and proved to be a large-flowered, strongly scented, double yellow rose, which was named *R. odorata ochroleuca*. When crossed, it led to many intriguing pink-yellow varieties of tea roses and also to HYBRID TEAS, but it proved to be subject to fading, and is no longer to be found in cultivation.

The discoveries continue

The first *Rosa multiflora*, a variety with pink, double-petalled flowers, was sent from Canton by Thomas Evans of the East India Company in 1804. The original wild species came to France from Japan, and was not grown in Britain until 1875. *R. banksiae*, named for Lady Banks, the former Miss Dorothy Huggeson, first arrived in Britain from China in 1807 as a double-flowered white rose. It was named by the eminent botanist Robert Brown, who detected a decidedly violet scent in its cherry-like blossoms: 'Indeed I doubt whether many persons if blindfolded could by the odour distinguish them from violets,' he wrote. The original single-flowered species was first induced to flower in Britain by E. H. Woodall in 1909, who grew the rose

from a cutting taken from a garden at Strathay in Scotland, from a rose said to have been planted there in 1796 by Robert Drummond after he returned from a voyage with his brother Admiral Drummond, in the China Sea. It was said that the rigours of the Scottish climate had prevented the rose from flowering earlier. Roy Shepherd has pointed out that it cannot definitely be proven that the plant at Strathay is the one originally planted in 1796 and that it might be the offspring of a later importation, but he concedes that the appearance and size of the crown 'denote that it is quite aged'. Of this rose, Robert Buist in Philadelphia wrote regretfully:

It is in the states south of this [Pennsylvania] where it must be seen to be pronounced the most graceful, luxuriant and beautiful of roses; there it is a perfect evergreen covering the ends, fronts, and in some instances the entire dwellings of many of the inhabitants, who name it the 'Evergreen Multiflora'. To us, the beauty of the plant is nearly lost, being too tender for the garden, and when grown in the greenhouse, its beauty and luxuriance almost disappear.

The double yellow form, *R. banksiae lutea*, with recurved petals was brought back by Parks at the same time as the 'Parks' Yellow Tea-scented China' in 1824. He had seen it growing on walls in Nanking where it is almost evergreen. The single yellow form *R. banksiae lutescens* was not introduced until 1870.

Three new hybrid China roses were discovered by Robert Fortune between 1844 and 1850, but the individual species from which they sprang are not beyond dispute. The first of these, *R. anemoneflora*, has been described as a hybrid of *R. setigera*, of *R. moschata* or of *R. laevigata* and *R. multiflora*. The second variety, 'Fortune's Double Yellow Rose', which he found in the garden of a mandarin in Ningpo in 1845, has been given the botanical name *R. odorata pseudindica*. Some see it as having affinity with *R. moschata*, others with the noisettes or with *R. banksiae*. Fortune's third rose, *R. fortuneana*, though found in a Shanghai garden, is thought to have been a natural hybrid between *R. banksiae* and perhaps *R. laevigata*,

Towards the end of the 19th century, when there were fewer restrictions on travel, more of the original China species began to arrive. Paul Guillaume Farges, Jean André Soulié and Jean-Marie Delavay, all French missionaries, sent seed to Maurice de Vilmorin, enabling him to raise *R. moyesii*, *R. setipoda*, *R. sertata*, *R. soulieana* and the four-petalled *R. sericea* var. *pteracantha*. Another missionary, Giuseppe Giraldi from Italy, sent home that interesting species *R. caudata* in 1897. It has bright red flowers in clusters and orange-red pear-shaped hips nearly 1 inch (2.5 cm) long.

R. hugonis, advertised, justifiably, as the 'Golden Rose of China', was sent to Kew Gardens by the Revd Hugh ('Pater Hugo') Scallan in 1899 and officially named after him six years later. It was marketed by the Veitch nurseries in England in 1905 and sent to the Arnold Arboretum in the US three years later.

More species from China arrived during the first decade of the 20th century, largely through the efforts of E. H. ('Chinese') Wilson. They included: *R. omeiensis*, the four-petalled close relative of *R. sericea*; *R. sweginzowii*, with bright red stalks and showy hips; *R. willmottiae*, a dense-foliaged bush with fragrant leaflets and rose-purple flowers; *R. helenae*, a fragrant white-flowered relative of *R. moschata*, which Wilson named in honour of his wife; *R. rubus*, closely related to *R. helenae*; *R. corymbulosa*, with small white-centred red flowers, and an almost complete absence of prickles; *R. davidii* with a profusion of pink blossom protected in bud by unusually long sepals; *R. filipes*, an extremely hardy, semi-climbing shrub that yearns for a pillar from which to show off its fragrant white flowers; and *R. multibracteata*, rather similar to *R. willmottiae* but with pink flowers. Like all the other early 20th-century China roses, this last is in cultivation but is probably the least hardy of Wilson's later discoveries.

Another Chinese treasure, the double-flowered form of *R. xanthina*, was sent to the US from China by Frank N. Meyer in 1906, and the single form, *R. xanthina spontanea*, soon after. The hybrid known as 'Canary Bird' was formerly thought to have sprung from *R. xanthina spontanea*, but may in fact have been a hybrid of *R. xanthina* with *R. hugonis* or possibly with *R. pimpinellifolia*. The circumstances in which this particular alliance took place have not been recorded.

Descendants of China roses

Some direct descendants of the original China roses are still cultivated. The first of these is the rose known as 'Old Blush' which is considered to be almost identical to 'Parsons' Pink China Rose'. Redouté's portrait, labelled *Rosa indica vulgaris*, shows a truly 'feminine' rose with buds of deep rosé and semi-double blooms of softer pink, disposed in clusters, set off by delicately pointed leaves. 'Old Blush' is grown today on both sides of the Atlantic, and is able to prosper in many different types of soil. 'Hermosa', a variety first noted in 1840, is a similar plant, but smaller and with lilac-pink flowers; two or three bushes together look effective.

There seems to be no record of who introduced 'Sophie's Perpetual' or when, but this vigorous eight-footer with silvery-pink flowers has been known to flower continuously for thirteen months. 'Cramoisi Supérieur' (1832) is thought to be a modern lookalike of the original 'Slater's Crimson China Rose' and is available from nurseries in both the US and the UK. A climber under this name (one of the few to retain its deep crimson colouring) appeared in 1885, at the time when the original form of 'Slater's Crimson China' was discovered growing wild in China.

'Sanguinea', a 3 feet × 3 feet (1 m × 1 m) China rose with dark red, almost single flowers and unknown origin, is cultivated mainly in the United States. 'Archduke Charles', of which the flowers develop in traditional China-rose fashion from pale pink to deep rose, is also grown in the United States by heritage-rose lovers. The 'Comtesse du Cayla', a fine orange-red China rose of normal bedding size, has both British and American supporters.

'Grüss an Teplitz', grown in Australia and Japan as well as in the US and the UK, is sometimes classed as a China rose because the colour of its dark crimson blooms intensifies as they develop; it is, however, often listed as a Bourbon. It can be used as a large shrub, or, with support, for pergolas and the like.

Another interesting variety is *R. chinensis* var. *mutabilis*. This SPORT of *R. chinensis* illustrates an attractive feature possessed by many Chinese varieties: their petals deepen in colour during the flowering period. The flowers of this variety are single, and the petals, on opening, are coloured saffron within and orange on the reverse, but within a day, they turn to coppery salmon and later change again to dark crimson.

Another Chinese curiosity, *R. chinensis* var. *viridiflora*, looks like a throwback to prehistoric times, when flower petals were still modified leaves. The blooms of this rose are double, the petals green, sometimes with a bronze margin; they stand out in a whorl reminiscent of a flue-brush ready for use in some miniature chimney. The petals, being thick, are long-lasting, and stand up particularly well to rain. One plant of this variety is said to have originated in 1833 as a mutation of *R. chinensis* at a nursery in Charleston, South Carolina, and was transported to Thomas Rivers' nurseries at Sawbridgeworth in England four years later, but it does not seem to have been widely distributed until after 1856, when it was put on sale by Bembridge and Harrison. Although a normal diploid (*see* CHROMOSOMES), this rose appears to be sterile. However, its curiosity value is such that it is still cultivated on both sides of the Atlantic, and can be seen in the gardens of the ROYAL NATIONAL ROSE SOCIETY near St Albans, Hertfordshire.

R. chinensis var. *longifolia* has, as its name implies, outsize leaflets up to 2 inches (5 cm) long, but this attraction has not proved sufficient to keep it in general cultivation.

See also HISTORY OF THE ROSE (19th century), CLASSIFICATION OF THE ROSE and WILD ROSES (Himalayas and eastern Asia).

Christmas rose

The Christmas rose *(Helleborus niger)* is not actually a rose at all, but is a member of the family to which buttercups and peonies belong. The adjective *niger*, meaning black, refers to its black roots and equally black seeds. The flower does indeed resemble a beautiful white single rose with five petals, though these are not petals but sepals.

For centuries, it has been known as the Christmas 'rose' or 'flower', which could be expected to appear for that feast if the weather were mild and warm. It was given its Yuletide name before 1752, the year when England adopted the Gregorian calendar already observed in other parts of Europe for the previous 170 years. The effect of this change was to advance the date by eleven days so that the 'new' Christmas Day was celebrated on the 'old' 14 December, and has remained so ever since.

Chromosomes

Chromosomes are a crucial factor in the inheritance passed on from one generation of roses (and other living things) to the next. Each cell nucleus contains a substance called *chromatin*. This chromatin is normally dispersed, but at certain stages, when the cells are about to divide (MEIOSIS and MITOSIS), it concentrates into bodies that can be stained and examined under the microscope (hence the name *chromosome*, meaning 'colour body').

Each chromosome carries with it hundreds of chemically active and self-reproducing bodies – the *genes* – which, working separately or together, affect the hereditary features transmitted from one plant generation to the next – for example, flower coloration, leaf shape, hairiness, etc. The genes are each a unit of *deoxyribonucleic acid*, or DNA for short. The arrangement of the DNA molecules is the key that determines the form of the plant (e.g. whether it is to become a rose or a lily). The control over the development of the plant is exercised by a twin compound – *ribonucleic acid* (RNA) – which modifies metabolism and cell formation in accordance with the pattern set by the DNA.

Each plant cell normally contains two sets of chromosomes: one set that we can think of as *A*, *B*, *C* and so on, inherited from its male parent; and a matching set (*a*, *b*, *c*) inherited from the female side. At times of cell division, the chromosomes are arranged in pairs in the same sequence so that *A* matches with *a*, *B* with *b* and so on; there is no cross-pairing between chromosomes of different letter-groups.

The number of chromosomes in each cell nucleus of a rose can be counted by examining a section taken from the growing tip of a shoot, or from a root, under a high-powered microscope. There are normally seven pairs, so the basic, or *haploid*, number of chromosomes in the rose is said to be seven. A rose nucleus with twice that number of chromosome pairs – that is, fourteen – is therefore said to be a *diploid*. Other roses are *triploids* (having three times the basic number), *tetraploid* ($\times$ 4) and so on up to *octoploid* ($\times$ 8).

These variations from the basic seven may well be the consequence of natural and unrecorded hybridization, which often results in irregularities during meiosis. By examining the chromosome structure, it is often possible to trace the family history of a rose, the ancestry of which would otherwise remain a mystery.

CIOPORA

The aim of this organization – Communauté Internationale des Obtenteurs de Plantes Ornementales de Reproduction Asexuée (International Community of Breeders of Asexually Produced Ornamentals) – with its worldwide membership and headquarters at 4 Place Neuve, Geneva, Switzerland, is to extend plant breeders' rights to all countries, and to represent breeders at government level where possible. It covers all ornamentals, including roses.

See also REGISTRATION OF ROSE VARIETIES.

Classification of the rose

Botanical

The botanist distinguishes one rose from another according to its structure rather than by its behaviour in the garden, which is the aspect of most interest to the horticulturalist (*see below*).

All roses belong, botanically, to the family Rosaceae, which also includes plums, pears and strawberries among many others. Roses are a sub-genus of this family, and within this sub-genus, various sections have been defined, each with different characteristics. However, there is no recognized world authority that can determine, once and for all, how many sections of roses there should be, or which roses should belong to them, and during the past two centuries, the solutions offered have differed according to whether the taxonomist (specialist in the classification of plants, etc.) concerned was a *synthesist* (someone who believes in grouping together as many varieties as possible) or a *segregationist* (one who favours maximum differentiation). Thus the Herbarium of the British Museum (Natural History) in London still uses the system devised by the Swiss botanist Augustin Pyramus de Candolle in 1825 which divides the sub-genus into four main sections, but the Revd Joseph Pemberton, in his authoritative work *Roses: Their History, Development and Cultivation*, first published in 1908, gave the accepted number as sixteen. Since then, four CURIOSITY species differing greatly from the normal rose have been transferred to three separate sub-genera. The system put forward in 1949 by the American botanist Alfred Rehder is generally regarded as an acceptable compromise: this is an amalgam of earlier systems, and recognizes ten sectors:

Section 1 Pimpinellifoliae. Among these are the burnet roses, the stems of which are densely clothed with bristles and scattered straight prickles. The name 'burnet rose' was bestowed on these roses because their leaflets, being small and almost oval, resemble those of the wild salad burnet.

This sector has provided the gardener with the bright yellow *Rosa hugonis* (named after the Revd Hugh Scallan), and the golden *R. xanthina* that, when crossed with *R. hugonis*, yielded the modern variety known as 'Canary Bird'. Other species in this sector have been hybridized to give the Frühling series of early-flowering garden varieties. *R. foetida*, from which most modern yellow and orange garden roses have been directly or indirectly derived, also belongs to this section, though it previously enjoyed a section of its own. The double-yellow 'Sulphur Rose', *R. hemisphaerica*, is also in this group.

Section 2 Gallicanae. The wild *Rosa gallica* is thought to be the ancestor not only of the ROSE OF PROVINS but of DAMASK ROSES, ALBA ROSES and, probably, ROSA CENTIFOLIA, all of which are members of this section. Thus we have rather a mixed company here. One characteristic they have in common is that their sepals droop after anthesis (flowering) and sometimes drop off, too; the outer ones are slashed on both sides. The prickles are hooked and, in the

Section 5   Cinnamomeae. Members of the group are to be found in Asia and North America as well as in Europe. The stems are upright and slender, the flowers red (seldom white) and the sepals remain upright long after the petals have been shed. The prickles are in pairs at the base of the leaves.

There are two particularly valuable species in this group. One is *R. moyesii*, so named in honour of the Revd J. Moyes of the China Inland Mission by Ernest ('Chinese') Wilson in gratitude for the help the latter had received. Gardeners have tried without much success to improve on its fine ruby-red flowers and flask-shaped hips. The other species is *R. rugosa*, almost as hardy as its fellow section member *R. acicularis*, which can flourish even within the Arctic Circle.

R. cinnamomea, the rose most typical of this sector, is now called *R. majalis* because of its ability to flower in May. Its solitary crimson flowers make a fine contrast to the dull green leaves.

Historical development of bush roses and climbers

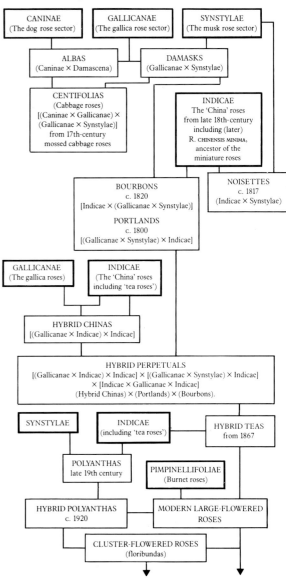

Rosa pimpinellifolia (R. spinosissima), *parent of many garden and hybrid roses, from H. C. Andrews'* A Monograph of the Genus Rosa *(1805).*

cases of *R. gallica* and *R. x centifolia*, scattered and unequal. The stems are erect and scent glands are often to be seen on them.

Section 3   Caninae. These are the dog roses, so called, it is thought, because their prickles resemble dog's teeth. The two star performers in this sector are the sweet brier, which Linnaeus called *Rosa eglanteria* (whereas others prefer *R. rubiginosa*), and *R. glauca*, (formerly *R. rubrifolia*), of which the young shoots are almost dove-grey and prized for flower decorations. Roses of this group are distinguished from the Pimpinellifoliae by their arching stems and curved prickles, and from the Gallicanae by their seven or more leaflets (the Gallicanae have five or fewer).

Section 4   Carolinae. This group consists exclusively of North American species and includes *Rosa palustris* and *R. virginiana* (with leaflets unpointed and almost elliptic), as well as *R. carolina*. They are small upright shrubs, with seven to nine leaflets to each leaf stalk, and small, curved down-turned prickles arranged in pairs. Most yield only a few flowers.

Rosa multiflora

Section 6 Synstylae. Botanically, this is the easiest group to distinguish, since the styles are fused into a single column and the flowers are usually arranged in corymbs (inflorescences in which the flower stalks at the top are shorter than those below, giving a flat-topped effect).

This sector contains some very valuable species – in particular *Rosa multiflora*, believed to be the progenitor of that bamboo-leaved little 'Rosa watsoniana' featured by ELLEN WILLMOTT in her great work. *R. setigera*, the prairie rose, has impressively long leaflets, and has given rise to many good climbing hybrid roses. *R. moschata* is a strongly scented rose and, under favourable conditions, an autumn-flowerer. *R. longicuspis* is a vigorous evergreen climber, and *R. wichuraiana* is an excellent ground-cover plant. The humble field rose, *R. arvensis*, belongs to this sector, as does that influential rose from the Middle East, *R. phoenicia*.

Section 7 Chinenses. This group – the CHINA ROSES – contains both species and some stabilized hybrids that have long been cultivated in China but have never yet been found in the wild. Most are thinly armed with translucent 'thorns', with delicate pointed leaves and loosely formed silky-petalled flowers, on long flower stems.

The most striking species is the large-flowered, dedicated climber, *Rosa gigantea*. The dark-flowered *R. chinensis*, though less ambitious in structure, has led to numerous garden hybrids.

Section 8 Banksianae. *Rosa banksiae* and its near relative *R. cymosa* are evergreen climbers with many small, clustered flowers – white or cream in the case of *R. banksiae*, white in that *R. cymosa*. Both species are natives of China.

Section 9 Laevigatae. The best-known species in this section is the glossy-leaved *Rosa laevigata*, the Cherokee rose, its flower stems and hips armed with a formidable profusion of prickles. Common enough on rocky ground in China and other parts of the Far East, it is also well established in the southeast United States.

Roy Shepherd notes in his valuable *History of the Rose* that the name *Rosa laevigata* was first applied to this species by Michaux in 1803. There were, of course, two people named Michaux in the annals of botany. The better known of the pair, André Michaux, the French botanist-explorer, undertook several expeditions in the south and east of the United States; his son, François André Michaux, accompanied him on the first of these. In 1796, Michaux senior left America for the last time, returning to France to establish a garden of exotics. He sailed away again in 1800 to accompany Baudin's expedition to Australia; he parted from it *en route* and died of fever in Madagascar in 1803. His son, however, saw to the publication of his father's work *Flora borealis americana*, which appeared the same year.

Section 10 Bracteatae. *Rosa bracteata* is known as the Macartney rose, after Lord Macartney who introduced it into Britain in 1793. Like its near relative *R. clinophylla*, it is another evergreen rose. The leaflets of *R. bracteata* are rounded, and the plant is also notable for the number of its stamens – 300–400 to a single flower. The stems, stalks and sepals of both these species are densely covered with soft hair, as are the hips; the stipules are deeply slashed.

R. bracteata has become naturalized in the United States from Virginia to Florida and as far west as Texas. *R. clinophylla* is native to India and Burma, and is one of the few roses that will flourish in swamps and on riverbanks.

Horticultural

Attempts have been made for at least two centuries (some would say for at least 2000 years) to classify garden roses into groups that could be easily recognized and compared with one another. Until recently, these attempts proved unsuccessful, mainly because of the inconstancy of the rose itself. The lineage of some of the best varieties of roses is indeterminate and sometimes intentionally unrecorded. Furthermore (as breeders are only too willing to confirm), garden roses have few heritable attributes that can be predicted with confidence.

At the close of the 18th century (*see* HISTORY OF THE ROSE), there were a dozen easily distinguishable roses – either species or 'historic hybrids' such as ROSA CENTIFOLIA, ALBA ROSES and DAMASK ROSES– which had become seemingly stabilized through the survival of the fittest and had established their identity in the garden. These are called, by some, the 'ancient roses'. However, these botanical navigation marks gradually disappeared beneath the rising flood of new hybridizations.

Nehemiah Grew showed hybridizers the way forward in his *Anatomy of Plants*, the earliest volume of which was published in 1682. He was the first to suggest that the stamens of flowers were the 'male' organs and that the 'farina' – his name for pollen – was the fertilizing agent. However, it was not until 1717 that Thomas Fairchild, the Hoxton nurseryman, made the first intentional hybrid by applying the pollen of a carnation to the stigma of a sweet william: the resulting plant had the general habit of a sweet william but the flowers were larger, double-petalled and red. Nevertheless, his rivals noted with complacency that 'Fairchild's mule' was infertile, and interest in hybridization quickly lapsed among his compatriots. In France, however, the botanical writings of Sebastien Vaillant, which led Linnaeus to base his classification on the sexual organs of plants, concentrated the attention of horticulturalists on the potentialities of using the organs for cross-breeding, and André Dupont at the Jardin du Luxembourg became one of the pioneers of rose hybridization.

His interest coincided with the arrival of the CHINA ROSES: their tenderness made it essential for them to be crossed with hardier species if their fragrance, their translucent flowers and their REMONTANCY were to be preserved out of doors and enjoyed in the colder winters of western Europe. But some of these roses were already hybrids, notably 'Parsons' Pink China', which combined elements from *R. chinensis* and *R. gigantea*. When crossed with *R. moschata*, it gave rise to 'Champney's Pink Cluster Rose' and, in a second generation, to the NOISETTES. These in turn were crossed with another China rose, 'Parks' Yellow Tea-scented', to produce yellow climbing tea roses.

'Parsons' Pink China Rose' was also the parent, with another historic hybrid *R. damascena bifera*, of the BOURBON ROSES, which, in an improved form, constituted one element in that miscellaneous aggregation of roses known as the HYBRID PERPETUALS. Already the family tree of the rose was becoming more complex, less discernible.

Another China rose, 'Slater's Crimson China', when crossed with *R. damascena bifera* gave rise to the PORTLAND ROSES, which in turn provided some hardy and vigorous hybrid perpetuals. Thus the hybrid perpetuals were indeed hybrids, though not always perpetually flowering in the first generation, since the gene of remontancy is recessive. Their existence was not officially recognized in England until 1843.

In parallel with these groups was another, namely the tea roses. Pink tea roses were derived from a cross between 'Hume's Blush China Rose', itself a modified hybrid, and the Bourbon rose. The yellow tea roses came, as indicated above, from the noisettes and 'Parks' Yellow Tea-Scented

China'. The tea roses thus became as hybrid as the hybrid perpetuals, although in general, this class could be distinguished as floriferous, fragrant, finely shaped and remontant. In each case, these special qualities can be traced back through these various hybridations to the influence of *R. gigantea*, the wild tea rose.

The final marriages of convenience within the rose family took place unofficially from as early as 1815, and officially from 1867 onwards, and amounted to an alliance between the delicate, finely scented tea roses and the hardier but less well-shaped hybrid perpetuals – to form the HYBRID TEAS, embodying the virtues of both parties. The hybrid tea class was not officially recognized in England until 1893.

Earlier in the century, the naming of varieties was left, as it is today, to breeders who, if they were sufficiently methodical, also kept records of the seed parent of the new varieties they grew. New varieties were then placed in the same group as the female parent. Records of the pollen parent, even if known, were considered to be of lesser importance, if not immaterial. If the new variety differed too greatly in appearance from that of the seed parent, the word *hybrid* was placed in front of its name. The results were unfortunate.

William Robinson stated the case for reform in his usual robust fashion when he wrote in *The English Flower Garden* (14th edition, 1926):

The attempted classification of roses into teas, hybrid perpetuals, etc., is confusing and not sound as all these roses are hybrids. What is wanted in the trade and other catalogues is alphabetical lists of the best varieties without following the absurd attempt at classification. It would be difficult to imagine anything more confusing than the writings on the rose and our catalogues of the present day!

Almost useless groups like the BOURSAULT [a little cultivated China rose hybrid of *Rosa blanda*] are dignified as classes, while the more important groups like the noble teas often receive no due notice.

And, if they did, you took your chance on whether they were climbers or not. The terms 'Bourbon', 'noisette' and 'hybrid tea' were equally indefinite in as much as the roses might or might not be climbers.

Robinson might well have added another vexatious example. A complete range of hybrids declared to be 'hybrid musks' were actually crosses between hybrid teas and noisettes, the earliest and most successful of which was with a German rose named 'Trier' derived from a variety known as 'Rêve d'Or'. The relationship of the hybrid musks with *R. moschata*, the MUSK ROSE, was a remote one that only depended on the element of *R. moschata* present in the original noisettes.

Before Robinson's death in 1935, the hybrid tea community had been further diluted by the arrival of the PERNETIANAS, which came from crosses between various forms of *R. foetida* and the hybrid teas. In addition, the year 1930 witnessed the arrival of yet another class of roses

– the FLORIBUNDAS. Their lineage sprang originally from a cross between the 'Dwarf Pink China' and the species *R. multiflora,* and their offspring became known as the POLYANTHA ROSE. The polyanthas were then crossed with various hybrid teas to give hybrid polyanthas, and these were crossed in turn with pernetianas and hybrid teas to give the large-flowered polyanthas on which, partly for commercial reasons, the new designation 'floribunda' was bestowed.

By now, it had become clear that any attempts to classify garden roses according to their antecedents was doomed to failure since most were not merely simple hybrids, but hybrids of hybrids. Furthermore, analysis of the CHROMOSOMES of a number of roses showed that their parentage was, in any case, materially different from the ones that had been traditionally assigned to them. And even those who judged by outside appearance only were prepared to admit that it was illogical to have yellow damasks and pink albas.

It was therefore a major triumph when the members of the WORLD FEDERATION OF ROSE SOCIETIES agreed among themselves to consider an entirely new system that classified roses, not according to the variety or species from which they might originally have been derived in the distant past, but on the way in which they could be expected to behave in the garden today. This is the pragmatic functional classification that allows the nurseryman to arrange his catalogue in a logical manner for buyers to order their plants.

The new classification was based largely on a draft prepared for the World Federation by the ROYAL NATIONAL ROSE SOCIETY of Great Britain in 1971. Some modifications were adopted at the World Federation meeting at Oxford in 1976, and these were ratified at Pretoria three years later.

The resulting system (*see chart*) recognized three main divisions:

(1) *Modern garden roses* – that is, those varieties bred after 1867, the year generally recognized as that in which the first hybrid tea appeared, and including SHRUBS and MINIATURES.

(2) *Old garden roses:* the traditional classes established before the advent of the hybrid tea. These, it was thought, were unlikely to be developed further, though exceptions do occur. One of the latter is that popular *gallica* derivative 'Constance Spry', which first appeared in 1961.

(3) *Wild roses:* both species and varieties, or hybrids, single- or double-flowered, that bear a strong resemblance to species.

Modern garden roses are subdivided into two categories: (a) *non-climbing roses,* i.e. roses with self-supporting stems; and (b) *climbing roses.* The non-climbing roses can in turn can be either (i) recurrent, i.e. REMONTANT or repeat-flowering roses, or (ii) non-recurrent roses in which case the rose flowers in spring or summer with, at best, only a few blooms in the autumn. The recurrent flowering roses are further subdivided into shrub roses (a term used on this occasion to mean plants that are too large for the normal bed), ground cover roses, bush roses and miniatures. All modern bush roses and non-climbing miniatures are assumed to be recurrent. The bush roses are subdivided into (i) LARGE-FLOWERED varieties (previously called HYBRID TEAS), (ii) cluster-flowered roses, and (iii) POLYANTHA roses – the latter with smaller flowers often in large, short-stemmed clusters or bouquets. Non-recurrent modern garden roses are subdivided into shrubs and ground cover.

International rose classification chart

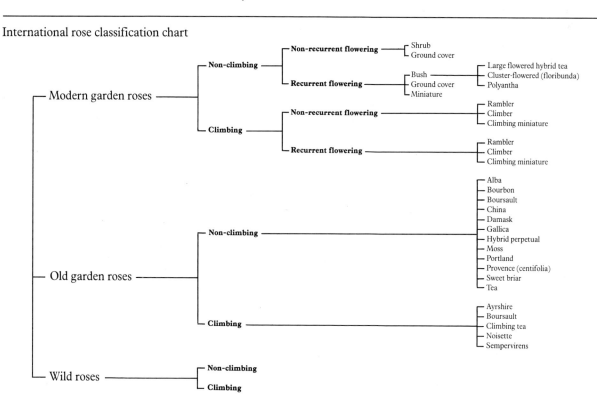

All classifications are subject to revision, and as far back as the mid-1920s, there were signs that the dividing line between large-flowered roses and cluster-flowered and polyanthas roses might not be permanent. From 1925 onwards, breeders in the United States engaged in an extensive programme of crosses between polyanthas and hybrid teas (as the latter then were), which resulted in roses with larger flowers than the normal polyantha hybrids. Dr J. H. Nicolas, then Director of Research at the famous JACKSON & PERKINS rose nursery, marketed them under the name 'FLORIBUNDA', a commercially astute decision. Not too much attention was paid to the critics who pointed out that the title was botanically unsound as it had been used at one time for *Rosa micrantha* as well as for *R. helenae*, a close relative of *R. moschata*. Matters were carried still further in 1946 when the American breeder W. S. Lammerts crossed the hybrid tea 'Charlotte Armstrong' with a floribunda known as 'Floradora'. The result was a rose with flowers midway in size between those of a floribunda and those of a hybrid tea. The ALL-AMERICA ROSE SELECTION body considered that this rose, which received many international awards, should be placed in a class of its own – named 'GRANDIFLORA'. However, this name, too, had already been applied in former days to other roses – varieties of *R. gallica* and *R. pimpinellifolia*. Of course '*Rosa grandiflora*' is only grand in comparison with the ordinary floribunda, but on seeing a tall hedge of 'Queen Elizabeths', the observer might wonder how much larger the flowers of such roses can grow, and by how much the numbers in each cluster can be reduced without their becoming almost indistinguishable from the present large-flowered roses.

The modern climbing roses are, like the modern shrub roses, divided into two groups – those that are remontant and those that have but one flowering season. Each of these groups is subdivided into three sections: (i) RAMBLERS (with pliable stems), (ii) CLIMBERS (with relatively stiff stems) and (iii) climbing miniatures.

The second category – *old garden roses* – is similarly divided into two groups, the climbers and the non-climbers. The non-climbers include eleven of the 'old' classes (in alphabetical order): ALBA, BOURBON, CHINA, DAMASK, GALLICA, HYBRID PERPETUAL, MOSS, PROVENCE (centifolia), PORTLAND, sweet brier and TEA.

The climbers include AYRSHIRE, BOURSAULT, climbing tea, NOISETTE, and sempervirens. The term *sempervirens* is used here to include roses showing the evergreen influence of *R. sempervirens*. 'Ayrshire' includes those showing the influence of *R. arvensis*.

The third main group – *the wild roses* – is also divided into climbers and non-climbers, and includes (*see above*) species and varieties that bear a strong resemblance to the wild species. This still leaves rugosa rose hybrids 'doing the splits': some of them closely resemble the original species *R. rugosa* and should therefore be counted as wild roses, whereas others such as 'Max Graf' and *Rosa x paulii* do not. In addition, rugosa hybrids, particularly 'Roseraie de l'Hay', and 'Frau Dagmar Hastrup (Hartopp)', were pro-

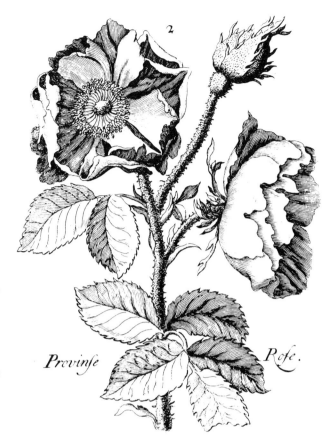

Rosa centifolia, *the 'cabbage' rose, from* A Compleate History of Drugs *by P. Pomet, 1725.*

duced during the 20th century and are large enough to qualify as modern shrubs. But 'Blanc Double de Coubert', an equally desirable and large-structured rugosa hybrid, was bred by Cochet-Cochet in 1892 and thus would not qualify.

Attention has been focused on the family tree of the rugosa hybrids simply because they are, like the modern *R. pimpinellifolia* shrub hybrids, a recent development fresh in our minds and as yet comparatively uncomplicated. In time, we may be content to consider the rugosas like other derivatives of species – according to their behaviour in the gardens of the future – and not mind if they are not all to be found in a single tidy compartment. With roses, nothing, not even the latest classification chart, is final.

Climbing roses

All roses that need support for their upward growth can be regarded as climbers – even if they have no climbing apparatus of their own save their 'thorns'. In addition, 'Climbers' are not differentiated from 'ramblers' in the CLASSIFICATION adopted by the WORLD FEDERATION OF ROSE SOCIETIES. It is, however, convenient to draw a distinction between roses of fairly rigid growth that can be depended on to clothe the front of, say, a three-storey Queen Anne house, and 'RAMBLERS' that are not at ease against vertical walls but which, nevertheless, have long springy canes that can be relied on to arch over pergolas and arbours. Most ramblers are closely linked with species that are not REMONTANT, whereas many climbers have in them a Chinese strain that endows them with REMONTANCY. Accordingly, ramblers are dealt with in a separate section.

We should also differentiate between 'old' climbers, which are related to groups established before the watershed year of 1867, from the new discoveries raised later (except in those cases where the new arrival is unmistakeably linked with one of the 'old' groups).

Some of the modern climbers are climbing SPORTS of modern bush roses; they have been isolated and developed by budding, cutting, etc. In such cases, the word 'climbing' is usually placed before the name to make it unmistakeably clear that there is also a bush form. Thus climbing 'Cécile Brunner' is easily distinguishable from the original 'Cécile Brunner'.

In general, the development of the 'old' climbers followed a parallel course with that of other garden roses, with successive attempts to balance the climbing ability and remontancy of the Chinese strain with the hardiness of the 'European'. Thus the BOURBON ROSES gave rise (eventually) to climbing 'Souvenir de la Malmaison' and 'Zéphirine Drouhin', both remontant. The NOISETTES, also derived from the CHINA ROSES, gave us the white-flowered 'Aimée Vibert' (1828), the first really vigorous remontant climber rising to 12 feet (3.65 m). (The original 'Blush Noisette' averages 8 feet [2.4 m] and is therefore often treated as a shrub.)

The tea noisettes offer a wider choice of climbers. '(Mademoiselle) Claire Jacquier' is among the most energetic, rising to as much as 30 feet (9 m) and yielding well-shaped and finely scented double blooms of a colour described as 'eggy'. 'Madame Alfred Carrière' is almost as vigorous and is a favourite at the ROSERAIE DE L'HAY gardens in Paris, where it is trained to grow in swags. The flowers are large, globular and sometimes quartered, but this rose is generally accepted as a noisette; it is hardy, remontant and sweetly scented, with a colour that is described as white with a faint discernable blush.

The grand old classic climber 'Maréchal Niel', which needs a sunny position if it is to show its summer-butter flowers at their best, is more widely offered by nurseries in England than by those even in the southern states of the US. It is known to be tender, and Roy Shepherd recalls that when Pradel introduced it in 1864, he insisted on each purchaser ordering at least a dozen plants. According to Dr J. H. Nicolas, Maréchal Niel, Secretary of War to Napoleon III, was entertained at a banquet in Avignon during a tour of inspection. The hall was decorated with sprays of a beautiful yellow rose and, on asking what the rose was called, Niel was told that it had been grown by Pradel, a local nurseryman, but it had not yet been named. Pradel gallantly offered to name the rose for the Maréchal's wife, but the soldier was a confirmed bachelor, and so the flower received a somewhat incongruous name. Niel

later fought in the Crimean war in the siege of Sebastopol, which fell soon after the capture by the French of the Tour de Malakoff – the name of another rose, a violet-magenta centifolia introduced in 1856.

'Gloire de Dijon' (1853) was preferred among all other climbing roses by Dean HOLE and, judging by the frequency with which it appears in catalogues, is still very popular. It was the result of a cross between a tea rose and the Bourbon 'Souvenir de la Malmaison', but its flowers – buff yellow with tinges of pink and apricot – justify those who have classified it as a climbing tea rose, even though it has the hardiness of the noisettes.

'Rêve d'Or' with yellowish-buff blooms with a hint of pink is sometimes listed as a climbing noisette though the colouring is tea-ish. 'Desprez à Fleur Jaune' (sometimes 'À Fleurs Jaunes' or, even more simply, 'Jaune Desprez') is another borderline case. This arose from a cross between 'Champney's Pink Cluster' (or its immediate descendant) and 'Park's Yellow Tea-scented Rose'. The result was a rose described variously as creamy yellow, or apricot, pinkish and coppery, the typical colour tints of a tea rose, yet it is sometimes grouped with the noisettes. It is vigorous, heavily scented and near-perpetual.

Of the unequivocally climbing tea roses, the best known are:

Climbing 'Devoniensis': The bush version of this, sometimes known as the magnolia rose, was first introduced in 1841 by a Devonshire nurseryman; the climbing version came eighteen years later. Recurrent and richly scented. Raised in both Britain and the United States.

A rose bower of pillar roses, from a French agricultural encyclopaedia and reproduced in Popular Gardening (c. 1895).

'Fortune's Double Yellow' discovered in 1845 by the explorer Robert Fortune in a Chinese mandarin's garden at Ningpo (*see* CHINA ROSES). Rather neglected both in Britain and the United States, perhaps because it needs a friendly climate if it is to prosper or because it flowers on wood of the previous year, which is all too often pruned away prematurely by the over-zealous.

'Marie van Houtte' (1872), a low-profile climber, has followers in the US as well as in Europe. The blooms are creamy suffused with carmine pink and golden at the base.

Climbing 'Sombreuil' (1850), a tea, like the previous rose, with flat quartered flowers of white, tinged with pink in the centre, is also grown by both British and American fanciers.

Modern introductions

We now come to those modern climbers that have been introduced since 1867 and are not attributable to any of the classes existing prior to that date. It would be nice if they could be divided neatly into two classes – namely, those that are LARGE-FLOWERED and those that are cluster-flowered – and at one time it seemed as though this might be possible. However, recently more and more new varieties have appeared that show large flowers growing in clusters, and some plants produce some flowers in clusters and others singly. The WORLD FEDERATION OF ROSE SOCIETIES recognizes two distinct types of modern climbing roses – those that are remontant and those that are not – but even here, the dividing line is often somewhat smudged.

Some of the finest modern shrub roses have given rise to climbing SPORTS. Among the pinks and reds are: Climbing 'La France' (1893), Climbing 'Madame Abel Chatenay' (1917), Climbing 'Madame Caroline Testout' (1901); Climbing 'Ophelia' (1920), Climbing 'Madam Butterfly' (1926), Climbing 'Lady Sylvia' (1933) and Climbing 'Queen Elizabeth' (1957). Smokey-pink Climbing 'American Beauty' (1909), Climbing 'Crimson Glory' (1916) and coral-flowered Climbing 'Fragrant Cloud' (1973, one of the most strongly fragrant of all roses) can be added to the list. Still more recently, JACKSON & PERKINS have produced a climbing version of their highly rated pink rose named 'First Prize': Climbing 'Shot Silk' adds gold to the pink of its blooms. In addition, there are two admirable pink roses that are natural climbers and not sports. These are 'Cupid' (1915) and 'Madame Grégoire Staechelin' (1927) – the latter also known as 'Spanish Beauty'. 'Parade' (1953) is a deep pink, well-scented, remontant climber that has lasted the course well.

Large-flowered modern climbers with copper- or flame-coloured flowers include: Climbing 'President Herbert Hoover' (1937), reliably remontant; Climbing 'Flaming Sunset' (1954), fairly remontant; and Climbing 'Sam McGredy' (1938), fully remontant. 'Madame Édouard Herriot' in bush form was the *Daily Mail* 'Rose of 1913'; the climbing sport arrived in 1921. 'Joseph's Coat' (1964), from Armstrong & Swim, with golden flowers flamed with orange and cerise, can be grown as a shrub; it is remon-

tant. The climbing sport of 'Soraya' – with flame-coloured cerise and coppery flowers – appeared in 1960 but appears not to be in great demand in the US. Nor is the orange-blended Climbing 'Bettina', which is also from the otherwise successful Meilland nursery.

There is a large choice of yellow-flowered climbers, including sports of 'Lady Forteviot' (1935); 'Ellinor LeGrice' (1950), which is particularly remontant; and 'Golden Dawn' (1947). Climbing 'Peace' (1950), tinged pink, is hardly a 'yellow' but fits in here as well as anywhere else. 'Elegance' (1937) has fully double but well-shaped flowers of summer-butter yellow fading to lemon; some blooms can be expected in late summer.

For those who like lavish and long-lasting displays on their walls, there are three large-flowered climbers that are especially remontant: 'Étoile d'Hollande' (1931) and 'Crimson Glory' (1946), both sports; and 'Souvenir de Claudius Denoyel' (1920), a variety in its own right. Climbing 'Ena Harkness' (1954) is another medium red that, for some reason, is well liked in Britain, but has not caught on in the US. Climbing 'Josephine Bruce' is among the darker reds, together with the still darker Climbing 'Château de Clos Vougeot' and its near relative 'Guinée', which is both fragrant and remontant. 'New Dawn' (1930), pale pink, is a steep climber although it was a sport of a rambler 'Dr W. van Fleet'. Well scented and large flowered, with clusters that are long stalked, it was the first rose to be patented in the US – a remarkable rose. 'Aloha', a descendant of 'New Dawn', is a large-flowered remontant climber that can be grown as a shrub too. The flowers are scented, warm pink and long-stemmed; good for cutting.

Of the above roses, 'Crimson Glory', 'Madame Édouard Herriot', 'Shot Silk', 'Ena Harkness' and 'Souvenir de Claudius Denoyel' all have nodding blooms that may commend them to all who have to admire their climbers from below.

Next, there are what might be called the ultra-modern climbers, based mainly on the cluster-flowered roses. Once again the yellows offer a wide choice. 'Leverkusen' is a favourite from Kordes (1955), with long arching sprays and a profusion of neat, fragrant, lemon-coloured, rosette flowers and some remontancy; it is sometimes listed as a shrub. Unlike Leverkusen, 'Golden Showers' (1956) does not grow thickly enough for it to become an effective shrub but it needs very little support on a wall. Its semi-double flowers are a warm primrose and, in Sussex at least, it lasts well into the New Year. 'Royal Gold', a repeat-flowering, upright and vigorous plant with deep golden-yellow, fragrant blooms seems to have come to the fore since it was introduced in 1957, despite the fact that it needs the protection of a south-facing wall.

'Lawrence Johnston' was raised from *Rosa foetida persiana*, the double form of the Persian brier, and, when cultivated and exhibited by Mr G. S. Thomas in 1948, it won the Royal Horticultural Society's Award of Merit. It is a very vigorous climber with medium-sized, scented, yellow flowers, and will bloom through the summer. Of this rose, a satisfied customer of the Roses of Yesterday and Today nursery wrote from Michigan to say: 'Please stress the hardiness and toughness of "Lawrence Johnston". [Its] old canes are in a class with oak flooring. I've had a plant for years and it is an opulent 6-foot [1.8 m] shrub despite the fact that it is planted beside the road where it is completely exposed to winter winds and sun and subject to regular battering from snow plows.'

Climbing 'Grüss an Aachen' shows an off-white bloom with flesh-pink tints and is remontant. The fully double cluster flowers of 'Dream Girl' are of a blended pink and open late in summer; they are quite large enough for this 10-foot (3 m) climber. 'Ritter von Barmsted' (1959) is a rather similar rose and perhaps better known. 'Bantry Bay' has well-scented flowers of a deeper pink and is much the same size as the last two roses. It has good stems for cutting as also has Climbing 'Cécile Brunner', usually billed as a China rose. McGredy's 'Handel' (1965) has proved a great success on both sides of the Atlantic. The flowers are cream edged with carmine, and they contrast well with the dark green, bronze-tinted foliage. It flowers well into the autumn.

The remontant 'Pink Perpétué', introduced in 1965, has double flowers of bright rose pink set off by glossy foliage; it has a wide following. 'Nymphenburg' (Kordes, 1934) is rated in the US as a hybrid musk and sometimes is placed elsewhere in the shrub sector, but it can reach 18 feet (5.5 m) with support. The flowers – salmon pink with shades of orange and yellow – are very double.

'Meg', an almost single rose, is nearer to apricot than pink, with petals that show off the dark amber stamens; it is fragrant but not particularly remontant. 'Schoolgirl' (1964) has proved very successful, but deserves the name becauseof its leggy appearance; blooms of orange-apricot against glossy dark green foliage; remontant.

'Compassion' ('Belle de Londres') (Harkness, 1974) is widely praised for its ornamental scrolled apricot buds opening to pale salmon pink; well scented and repeat flowering. It is sometimes classed as a large-flowered climber. 'Albertine' (1921), with its large coppery pink flowers, has retained its popularity for generations. It can be grown as a climber or a shrub and gives a fine display in midsummer. There is some fragrance.

Among the scarlet climbers, 'Danse du Feu', alias 'Spectacular', is outstandingly floriferous and immensely popular in the UK but is less fully appreciated in the US. On the other hand, 'Blaze', reputed to be the most popular climber launched by Jackson & Perkins during the 113 years of their existence, is scarcely seen east of Maine, though its near relative, 'Paul's Scarlet Climber', is offered by many British nurseries. Blaze's scarlet clusters appear from June to September. Its successor, 'Tempo', has somewhat darker blooms and is confusing to the pedants because its $3\frac{1}{2}$–4-inch (9–10 cm) cluster flowers are high-centred like the large-flowered roses. 'Altissimo' (1967), of unknown parentage, is especially interesting for its single-petalled blooms of intense scarlet, centred with golden anthers; remontant.

Three other cluster-flowered climbers at the red end of the spectrum deserve special mention: 'Dortmund', 'Parkdirektor Riggers' and 'Hamburger Phoenix'. All three are derived from a hybrid of 1919 between *R. rugosa* and *R. wichuraiana* known as 'Max Graf', and sometimes used as ground cover. Some twenty years later, some seeds of 'Max Graf' sown at the Kordes nursery were found to have a complement of twenty-eight CHROMOSOMES, twice the expected number, and this mutation resulted in a rose that is healthy, vigorous and fertile and behaves just as if it were an entirely new species, although it is correctly shown as *R.* x *kordesii*. 'Leverkusen', already mentioned, is another member of the Kordesii clan.

One unusual climber that would look well against a wall of reddish brick is another Kordes rose (but not one of the Kordesii), 'Ash Wednesday' ('Aschermittwoch'). It shows violet buds opening to soft grey blooms.

Finally there are a number of SPECIES ROSES that are either natural climbers or 'scramblers', including:

Rosa banksiae	*R. laevigata*
R. moschata	*R. setigera*
R. brunonii	*R. wichuraiana*
R. filipes	*R. bracteata*
R. longicuspis	*R. sempervirens*
R. helenae	*R. sinowilsonii*
R. multiflora	

Some climbers particularly associated with individual species are mentioned separately with the species concerned.

Cluster-flowered roses
See CLASSIFICATION (Horticultural), POLYANTHAS, FLORIBUNDA ROSES, GRANDIFLORA ROSES, PATIO ROSES.

Cocker, James & Sons of Aberdeen
This family's nursery was founded in Aberdeen in 1841 by James Cocker, who left his job as head gardener on the Castle Fraser estate, west of Aberdeen, because of his unwillingness to break the Sabbath by picking fruit on a Sunday. He was soon offering a general list of plants – including seedling conifers and strawberries – sold in quantity, and opened a seeds office in the centre of Aberdeen. On his death in 1880, his son James succeeded to the nursery, and he and his three sons – William, James and Alexander – began to specialize in garden plants and, later, roses. James Cocker Jr died in 1897, a year before the firm's first big success. This was 'Mrs Cocker', a light-pink rose that won a gold medal at the National Rose Show. 'Mrs Andrew Carnegie', though white and somewhat frail, was awarded the same honour in 1912.

James Cocker Jr's youngest son, Alexander, eventually succeeded to the business, but when he died in 1920 at the age of sixty, his son Alexander Morison Cocker was only thirteen years old. Much to Alec's disappointment, the family trustees closed down the nursery, and when Alec reached adulthood, he had to start up all over again from scratch, helped by his wife Anne. They eventually decided to specialize in growing roses and succeeded in winning the NATIONAL ROSE SOCIETY's Autumn Challenge Trophy for five consecutive years. It was not until 1963, however, that Alexander Cocker decided to move from growing and showing roses into breeding them.

He had an early success with 'Alec's Red', a name given to it not by Alec himself but by various nurserymen to whom he had sent it as an unnamed rose for trials. 'Alec's Red' is a LARGE-FLOWERED ROSE with impressive blooms of luminous crimson. It won the highest award of the (now) Royal National Rose Society – the President's International Trophy and Gold Medal – as well as the Edland Medal for Fragrance – all in the year of its introduction, 1970.

In 1975 James Cocker & Sons received the Royal Warrant as Supplier of Roses to Her Majesty Queen Elizabeth II. 'Glenfiddich', an amber-yellow cluster-flowered rose, followed in 1976. This was SPONSORED by the whisky distillers and happened also to be a drink that Alec admired.

The next year, Alec achieved lasting fame with 'Silver Jubilee', which, like 'Alec's Red' seven years earlier, won the RNRS President's International Trophy and Gold Medal. As recently as 1985, in a poll of growers conducted by the *Sunday Times Colour Magazine* (London), every breeder, except the becomingly modest Anne Cocker, voted it the best of all the large-flowered roses. In the same year, it was awarded the James Mason medal, presented in memory of the actor by his rose-loving wife Clarissa for roses that have given particular pleasure.

Alec Cocker died in 1977, the year of his final triumph, but his son Alexander James Cocker, with the help of Anne Cocker, has kept up the rose business, and new roses – such as 'Sweetheart' (1980), a warm, rose-pink, fragrant large-flowered rose; 'Remember Me' (1984), a coppery seedling of 'Silver Jubilee'; and 'Abbeyfield Rose', a warm-pink large-flowered variety bred from 'Silver Jubilee' crossed with 'National Trust' – have continued to delight rose enthusiasts.

Colour in roses

The colours of roses do not lend themselves easily to spectral analysis – particularly not by judges at conventional rose shows, or even in laboratories – for the benefit of those who seek to patent a certain variety. One of several difficulties arises from the fact that blooms on the same plant are not necessarily identical nor are the individual blooms uniformly coloured all over. Most roses show more colour at the centre of the flower than at the edges of the petals, and, on examination, the petals themselves, which might, for example, appear to be shell pink, turn out to carry red veining against a cream background, or are composed of two different layers of pigment, pink and yellow, at varying distances from the surface of the petal. In addition, no single colour gives rise to the much prized velvet look to be found in some dark red roses, which is probably generated by reflections from the raised, cone-like papillae on the upper side of the petals. Rose growers make no pretence of dodging this problem, describing 'Souvenir d'Alphonse

Lavallée' as showing 'many shades of crimson to purple maroon', or 'Souvenir de Pierre Vibert' as 'dark red, shaded carmen and violet'.

The fact that the colour of a rose will vary from one shade to another during the development of the flower adds to the difficulty of describing its colouring satisfactorily. The extreme case is that of *Rosa chinensis mutabilis*, of which the flowers are cream-coloured at one stage and copper at another. In the case of REMONTANT roses, blooms at the first flowering may differ in colour from those of the second. Other non-China roses, such as *R. alba maxima* and *R. foetida bicolor*, have attractive coloration at the bud stage that is not present when the flower is at its best.

Some roses – in many cases, but not always, the 'older' varieties – fade with age or vary with the temperature during the day. Some of the reds show bluish tints – a development regarded with aversion by the *cognoscenti* – while other old-fashioned roses acquire mauve or purplish hues that are declared to be perfectly acceptable. Thus, to take one example, the variety 'Tour de Malakoff' is described as 'magenta flowers flushed purple and fading to a soft lilac grey' (*see also* CLIMBING ROSES). Descriptions based on the colour of the rose when exhibited at rose shows may tell only half the story. Each colour really needs to be qualified in two ways: according to its degree of saturation (its intensity), and according to its luminosity (the total amount of light in and reflected by the colour).

The 'white' of some white roses is due to the reflection or refraction of light in the spaces between the transparent cell walls. The colour in the remainder comes from pigments either in spherical bodies known as *plastids*, which line the inner walls of the cells, or from pigments dissolved in the cell sap that fills the cell.

The pigments in the cell sap are collectively known as *anthocyanins*, and consist of basic compounds named *anthocyanidins* combined with, in the case of the rose, one or more molecules of glucose. Those anthocyanidins to which two molecules of glucose are attached are more strongly coloured than those with only one molecule.

Anthocyanidins provide the reds and purples of the rose garden. One of them, pelargonidin, accounts for the brilliant orange-based scarlets to be seen in 'Paul Crampel', and in American varieties such as 'Independence' and 'Gloria Mundi'. Pelargonidin was first detected in roses in 1930 but is unknown in WILD ROSES – a unique colour mutation. Cyanidin, another of the anthocyanidins, yields the deep reds and magentas of roses such as GALLICA ROSE varieties and 'Wendy Cussons'. It is reinforced by peonidin, particularly in the Cinnamomeae, Carolinae and Minutifoliae groups. Two other water-soluble pigments, which provide mid-yellow, pale yellow and near-white tints, belong to a group known as the *flavonols*. They can absorb ultra-violet light, and are sometimes able to combine chemically with anthocyanidins to produce bluish tints.

In addition, however, there are, in roses and other plants, the insoluble pigments contained in the plastids lining the inner walls of the cells. These include chlorophyll (green), carotene (deep yellow) as in *R. foetida* and xanthophyll (yellow) pigments.

Attempts have been made – unnatural though it might seem – to produce a true-blue rose. Botanical physicists have pointed out that the cyanidins that generate red coloration in roses are similar to those that produce the blue in cornflowers – possibly because of minute mineral traces taken up by the latter plant. This suggests that it might be possible to 'blue' roses in the same way as hydrangeas are 'blued' by watering the soil with a solution of sulphate of aluminium; individual blooms can also be 'blued' by dipping their stems in a mixture of household ammonia and detergent. It has also been pointed out that some pink varieties of hydrangea turn purple or blue on acid soils. However, no satisfactory method of applying this knowledge to roses has yet been discovered.

Attention has also been focused on *Pulmonaria officinalis*, that favourite plant of cottage gardens that is known as 'Soldiers and Sailors' because the pink buds turn, without artificial stimulants, into blue flowers. However, no way of reproducing the same process in the rose has yet been found. Attempts to isolate the blue pigments that appear when certain red or purple roses, such as 'The Bishop', start to fade have been no more successful. An obvious line of approach to rose growers is that of breeding selectively from the existing purplish roses such as 'Reine des Violettes', but while some of the genes controlling pigment production (for instance, of cyanin and peonidin) have been shown to have some dominance, others such as pelargonidin are partly recessive, and these differentials add to the costs of lengthy and uncertain experiments.

Breeders have also to consider whether the hunt for a blue rose should take precedence over the search for other new varieties of rose that are hardy, remontant, well-structured and foliaged, with freshly coloured, non-fading fragrant blooms that do not wilt in the rain or fail to shed their petals when flowering is over. Most surveys by breeders and florists have rated red, scarlet and vermillion as the most popular colours for roses, with pink, yellow, white and lavender following in that order. A place could certainly be found for blue but just where remains uncertain.

There is a widely believed story according to which Alexander DICKSON III succeeded in raising a true-blue seedling and showed it at Southport in 1925, but when his father, Alexander II, got to hear of it, he had the rose destroyed to prevent it from debasing rosarian standards. A similar story has been told in which the protagonists are Sam MCGREDY II and III.

One other possibility is that, just as pelargonidin, the pigment that gives red to the geranium, appeared unexpectedly and for the first time in roses in 1930, so perhaps delphinidin, the pigment that gives blue to the delphinium, might just as unexpectedly occur in some breeder's rose. Biotechnicians, too, might succeed in inducing normal *Rosa* genes to yield delphinidin (which, chemically, is not far removed from pelargonidin) or its equivalent, but progress towards success has been slow.

Nurserymen, because the limited space available in their catalogues, have to dispense with glimpses of the obvious, and are obliged to take it for granted that buyers already have some idea of the colour of the varieties they are considering, and tend therefore to emphasize the features that are outside the normal. This helps to explain why, in addition to the basic rosarian palette range – ivory, cream, lemon, straw, canary, sulphur, saffron, apricot, buff, salmon, copper, bronze, blush, crimson, scarlet, pink, coral, lilac, plum, magenta, maroon, etc. – we find references to 'grape purple', 'cerise with silvery highlights' and even 'transparent blush pink'.

The AMERICAN ROSE SOCIETY has simplified matters for us all (but made them more prosaic) by officially adopting sixteen colours (and no more) as descriptions for rose varieties.

White or near white	Medium pink
Medium yellow	Deep pink
Deep yellow	Pink blend
Yellow blend (i.e. with some pink or red)	Medium red
Apricot blend	Dark red
Orange, and orange blend	Red blend
Orange-red	Mauve
Light pink	Russet

Compass rose
A term used as far back as 1527 to describe the printed card of a mariner's compass. Also known as a 'wind rose', since it allowed the direction of the wind to be determined.

Compatible plants for the rose garden
Opinions are divided on which plants – if any – are suitable for setting alongside roses. At one end of the spectrum, the Revd A. Foster-Melliar in *The Book of the Rose* unreservedly argued that roses should be grown in isolation. He wrote:

It should be understood that in this I am speaking of the best Roses, HP's and Teas . . . For me, beds must be made for the Rose and the Rose alone. No! no mignonette or other annuals 'to hide the bare ground'! . . . Let 'the small man', if he be a true Rose-lover and has a mind to grow them really well, harden his heart against all rival flowers, and go in, practically, for Roses alone. In every department of life a man must be a specialist now if he wants to succeed, and the Rose will amply repay devoted care.

In contrast, William Robinson, describing his new rose garden at Gravetye in Sussex, wrote:

Instead of mulching the beds in the usual way, and always vexing the surface with attentions I thought were needless, we covered them with Pansies, Violas, Stonecrops, Rockfoils, Thymes and any little rock plants to spare. Carpeting these Rose-beds with life and beauty was half the battle. We do not mulch with these living plants, many of which are so fragile in their roots that they cannot have much effect in a bed of 3 feet of moist, good soil. So that instead of the bare earth on hot days, the flower shadows are thrown on to soft carpets of fragile rock or mountain plants.

When Vita Sackville-West ventured to ask Robinson how, under these circumstances, he manured his roses, the Master replied, with some acerbity: 'They don't need it.'

Since Robinson's day, the problem of how to grow rock plants on soil that has been or is about to be newly enriched with horse-manure or other dung has been solved for most gardeners by the difficulty of getting any. Substitutes such as formula fertilizers can be easily restricted to the ground beneath the rose itself and worked or watered in, and when the soil has warmed up and is not too dry, a covering of chips or other MULCH can be applied – again around the rose bush itself.

Assuming that the whole bed is not to be mulched, the next question is to decide what other plants can add to the attraction of the rosebed at times – admittedly shorter than in the past – when no rose blooms are to be seen. If the rose bushes are in flower almost continuously, there may be no need for any other adornment of the bed, but at other times, rose bushes, irrespective of whether the earth around them is bare, are inclined to look somewhat skeletal, and the bed needs some fleshing out.

The choice of plants must in the first instance depend on the size of the rose bushes and the manner in which they have been pruned. If the immigrants to the rosebed are bushy undershrubs such as lavender, sage or rue, designed to cover up the bare stems of the roses, they may not need to be more than a foot or so in height. If, on the other hand, the incoming plants are to provide a foil to the rose or a colour contrast to the blooms, they will need to be plants that can almost reach to the same height as the rose bush itself. Or there could be a sprinkling of each kind – some stubby undershrubs and some tall spires such as are provided, for example, by the taller phloxes. The mignonette and other annuals so strongly deplored by Foster-Melliar would fit in nearer to the border of the rosebed.

The time at which the 'bed-friends' of the rose are expected to flower is important. If it is accepted that the rose looks at its most haggard in the early months of the year, then spring flowers are what are wanted – perhaps small narcissi, sky-blue chionodoxas, starry-blue ipheion or even the ever-present grape hyacinth or the humble snowdrop.

Plants with silver foliage – for example, *Anaphalis margaritacea* (the pearly everlasting), *Stachys lanata* (lamb's tongue), 'snow in summer' or a small variety of *Santolina* – provide a more or less continuous contrast to the darker foliage of the rose.

Colour is the factor that determines whether an incoming plant is compatible with roses or not. Modern roses tend to have sharper colours than formerly, and in this case, plain white sometimes provides the necessary relief. The soft true-blue of the delphinium or of love-in-a-mist (but not the violet-blue of some campanulas) is often acceptable.

The background to the rosebed is equally important. A hedge of dark-green yew, fronted by a strip of grass, is almost ideal, if you can wait long enough for the hedge to grow. If the rosebed is near the border of the property, it could be seen against a background of mauve buddleias – or an extra rose hedge. The much abused privet is another possibility, provided that it takes no nourishment from the rosebed itself; it also requires careful trimming if it is not to become ragged. If there is a herbaceous border within sight of the rosebed, it can usefully contain a blue streak of larger plants such as blue geraniums, globe thistles and delphiniums. Climbers and ramblers go well with the blue and mauve varieties of clematis, and with some sweet peas. They contrast well against separate dark-leaved shrubs such as *Laurus nobilis* (the bay).

For the miniature rose or the standard rose in a small bed, the minute, pale-green leaves of *Hebe pageana* make the perfect ground cover.

Crystallized rose petals and rose-petal jam

Individual rose petals can be candied by dipping them first in thin gum arabic or beaten egg-white. They are then laid out on a sheet of greaseproof or waxed paper that has been covered with caster sugar. More sugar is sprinkled on top so that both sides of the petals are covered. When dry, the petals are stored in an air-tight container, between layers of greaseproof paper. Alternatively, the petals can be pounded with pestle and mortar to form a conserve.

A classic recipe for rose-petal jam, recommended by Edward Bunyard in his splendid work *Old Garden Roses*, calls for 1 lb (0.45 kg) of sugar to be added to $\frac{1}{2}$ pint (285 ml) of water and brought to the boil. When the resulting syrup is clear, 1 lb (0.45 kg) of well-washed and dried petals is added for each pint (0.57 l) of syrup, and the mixture is boiled to a jam-like consistency.

The Greeks, it appears, make their rose jam using rosewater instead of tap water. For this purpose, rose petals, well pressed down, are placed in a saucepan with just enough water to cover them, and this is then brought to the boil. The mixture is simmered for a few minutes and then strained.

In any case, the tough flange joining the petals to the flower stalk should first be removed.

Cultivar

A variety stemming from cultivation.
See also NAMING OF ROSES.

Curiosity roses

Most roses were once curiosity roses until gardeners got used to them. But for some, however, eccentricity is their chief merit. Among them are:

**Rosa sericea:* the 'Himalayan Rose' with only four petals.
**R. multiflora* var. *watsoniana:* the 'Bamboo-leaved Rose'.
**R. viridiflora:* the 'Green-flowered Rose'.
**R. centifolia cristata:* 'Napoleon's Hat' rose.
**Hulthemia persica:* a member of the rose family placed in a separate sub-genus. Flowers resemble those of a rockrose with central dark blotches. Leaves greyish in alternate, not opposite, positions.

R. roxburghii: the 'Chestnut-bur Rose' (a near-rose belonging to the sub-genus Platyrhodon).

R. stellata: wedge-shaped leaves, dark purple single flowers (a near-rose belonging to the sub-genus Hesporhodos).

Cut roses

Commercial cultivation

The methods used for selecting and growing roses under glass for florists' shops, hotels, offices, etc. differ sharply from those of field nurseries selling plants to the public – and even more so from the practices of the amateur rose grower.

The dozen or so varieties grown on an all-year-round basis by a modern establishment in the UK – such as Southdown Flowers at the Pollards Nursery near Barnham, West Sussex – can be expected to average twenty-five blooms a year each on stems of 24 to 28 inches (60–70 cm). At this rate, the rose trees have a life expectancy of five to six years, after which they are discarded. They are planted at a density of 30,000–35,000 trees per acre of glass.

Soil is prepared for planting by adding base fertilizer and some peat. Before each new planting, the soil is sterilized by fumigating with methyl bromide gas – a method that is less expensive than using steam. The work, which takes a week, is carried out by contractors who lay perforated pipes on the soil and blanket the area with polythene sheets in order to maintain the necessary concentration of gas.

Some of the roses for new planting, having been grown in the favourable climate of Spain, will arrive at the cut-rose nursery as one-year-old rose trees, in which case they are likely to have been BUDDED on UNDERSTOCKS of *Rosa indica major* or on *R.* x *noisettiana* 'Manetti', which has particularly shallow roots and is therefore easily mechanically undercut and lifted out of the ground without damage to the root fibres. The majority, however, will arrive from Holland in November and December as six-month-old bushes that have been budded the previous summer on to understocks, probably of the 'thornless' *R. canina inermis.* If the budding took place early in the summer, the bud will probably have been encouraged to form a shoot by cutting back the understock. These roses will be lifted in October or November to avoid the risk of their becoming frozen into the ground.

When they arrive in the UK, the usual practice is to heel in the plants in the open and leave them in the ground for five to six weeks before planting in the greenhouse in January. If, however, the budding was made later, the understock will have been allowed to grow on, and in this case, the bud will still be dormant when it arrives at the nursery. The plants with dormant 'eyes' will then be placed in a polythene 'tent' that is heated and constantly misted to encourage the dormant eyes to sprout before planting. The planted roses will then be 'built up' in such a way as to encourage two shoots to break from the base of the plant. The shoots from these base-breaks provide the first long-stemmed roses, and these can be cut in early June.

Each different type of planting material – the one-year-old trees, the six-month-old bushes, those with dormant eyes – are treated slightly differently, but in essence the original growth is pinched when the bud appears in order to stimulate base-breaks, and blooms are taken only after these base-breaks have been trimmed back. The aim is to discourage the growth of short-stemmed roses – which is especially important when launching a new variety.

After the first year – or even earlier – the new plants will need additional undercutting to prevent them from becoming unmanageably tall. This operation takes place during the growing season, and not, as in ordinary garden practice, when the plant is dormant. Up until January, whenever blooms of all-year-blooming roses are cut, two or more stalks of five leaflets are left on the branch on which the flower has grown. As a result, the rose tree gradually increases in height and, by December, will have reached its maximum height for the year, which, in the case of large-flowered roses, can be as much as 10 feet (3 m). In late January, however, the flowering stems are cut at full length, taking all the leaflets on the branch with them. In addition, a length of the stem from which the flowering shoot has grown is also removed, so that a general reduction in the height of the plant takes place. This operation is known to growers as *undercutting,* and it ensures that the growth of the rose tree occurs within a band of about 2 to 3 feet (0.60–0.90 m). This method is used only for roses that are grown to flower throughout the year (including the winter), and not to varieties such as 'Gabriella', which, as explained later, are pruned section by section.

Every bed has a piped water supply close to ground level, and one circuit might feed 3000 plants. The water carries nutrients in solution and is passed through pinwheel jets that dispense it as fine droplets. Each circuit can be pre-timed separately to run for the required number of minutes. The moisture content of the soil can be tested satisfactorily by hand with an auger.

Temperature can be a decisive factor in growing cut roses. With heating costs averaging more than £1 per plant per annum in a nursery of 100,000 roses, a variety such as de Ruiter's orange-red 'Madelon' (1981), which can prosper at a night temperature of 59°F (15°C), has a telling advantage over a rose such as 'Ilona' that needs 63°F (17°C). Georges Delbard, the French breeder, has recently specialized in roses that will flourish at even lower temperatures. 'Lancôme' is a deep-pink large-flowered rose that requires a mere 50°F (10°C) until the buds are formed, and only 46°F (8°C) up to the time of cutting. 'Madame Georges Delbard', a velvety red rose, is one of those few which does well both as a cut rose and in the garden. 'Malicorne', an orange-red large-flowered rose – to which the Delbard catalogue does scant justice – needs still less heat: 46°F (8°C) until the buds are formed and 43 to 46°F (6–8°C) up to the time of cutting.

'Malicorne' is one of the roses that can be cut while the buds are still closed, whereas in many cases it is recommended that the stems should not be cut until the first petal of each bud is almost fully unrolled. If, as sometimes happens, the grower chooses to disregard this advice in the hope that a tight bud will last longer after cutting than a partly opened one, the result may well be disappointing. The rose either fails to open fully or does so, but with an unsound neck.

In a relatively favourable climate such as in the south of England, a nursery is able, by heating with gas or coal rather than with oil, to cut roses every day of the year. In order to conserve heat at night, thermal screens of porous woven nylon are drawn across underneath the glass roof under the automatic control of a time-switch. In the English climate, it is not necessary to spray the glass with a heat-protecting substance in summer as happens in the US, but during really hot spells, the thermal screens may be occasionally half-closed.

This measure is resorted to with reluctance, as English nurseries need all the light they can get. Roses, like other plants, need carbon dioxide (CO_2). When enough light is available, plants remove CO_2 from the surrounding air and use it to convert inorganic chemicals into living cells. This process is known as *photosynthesis*, and can take place only during the hours of daylight or under very strong artificial light. Within limits, the higher the light intensity and the temperature, the faster the available CO_2 is used up. Normally 'fresh air' contains 300 parts per million of CO_2 but if, in a greenhouse, the vents cannot be opened without an unacceptable drop in temperature, the percentage of CO_2 drops, because the amount used up by the roses during daylight is not replaced. In such conditions, the development of the rose trees is slowed up or, in extreme cases, may cease altogether.

Consequently extra carbon dioxide has to be provided from October to April – until the temperature outside allows the vents to be opened and fresh air to enter freely. (The extra CO_2 is not, of course, needed during the hours of darkness because the plants are inactive then.) It can be obtained by burning either propane gas supplied in liquified form or paraffin. The latter is the cheaper method: low-sulphur paraffin is used and precautions taken to keep atmospheric impurities due to incomplete combustion out of the greenhouse. The CO_2 gas is piped in large diameter ducts to reach every part of the greenhouse, and growth accelerates so rapidly under its influence that it has proved economic to raise the CO_2 level as high as 1000 parts per million.

To maximize the amount of light reaching the plants, the glass of the greenhouse is regularly cleaned outside with diluted acid spray and inside with pressure-hosed water. Dust seems to accumulate on glass, even in areas remote from large cities.

When cut, the roses are placed in a canvas 'sling', a hammock-like device with a loop at each end that is stretched half-open between a pair of hooks. The hooks are fixed at opposite ends of a kind of travelling workbench that is suspended from a gantry on a monorail. The gantry travels along the main alleyway as the picker moves from one row to the next. The cut roses are laid in the sling with their stems level and, when there are enough of them, one loop of the sling is taken off its hook, and is doubled across to the other hook, thus closing the sling. The sling is then lifted and its cargo of roses is deposited at once in a bucket of water.

The roses are collected from this every twenty minutes, and are taken to the cold store, where they are placed in water cooled to a temperature between 36 and 41°F (2–5°C). There they remain for a cooling-off period of some twelve hours. The water in which they stand contains a preservative – often the one marketed under the name 'Chrysal'.

The stems are then passed to a grader who places them on a belt marked with graduations in such a position that superfluous parts of the stem are automatically cut off. The machine also sorts the roses electronically into groups with stems of the same length. These are bunched into 10s or 20s, and each bundle is then automatically wrapped in a fine-polythene cylinder open at each end, before being returned to the cold store.

In many cases, cut roses are ordered by wholesalers 'on sight', but a large nursery in the UK will also dispatch flowers unseen to every major city. In this case, the roses are packed in tough carton boxes and held in position by 'pin-strips' – strips of springy metal fitted at each end with a sharp arrowhead that pierces the sides of the box and is folded back flat against the outside. In the US, where the demand can fluctuate considerably, rose blooms are sometimes stored in sealed containers at temperatures just above freezing for up to two weeks. Some roses there are dispatched in insulated cartons as a protection against excessive heat or cold.

Popular varieties

Florists' roses are selected on a strictly commercial basis, according to public preference which, in the UK, places red roses first, followed (in order of popularity) by pink (both salmon and what is known in the trade as 'blue pink', typified by the strawberry-ice rose 'Bridal Pink'), yellow, white and apricot-orange, though the last named has recently been coming to the fore. In the US, the order is much the same, but there is a steady demand for novelties such as bicolour roses, and for the long-stemmed cluster-flowered varieties.

Competition among breeders is intense. In the UK in the early part of the 19th century, TEA ROSES such as 'Catherine Mermet' (pink), 'Perles des Jardins' (yellow) and 'Niphetos' (white) were especially in favour. They were superseded by the HYBRID PERPETUALS, which offered stronger stalks. Much later, MEILLAND's 'Baccara', once regarded as the ultimate rose because of its long stems and splendid lasting qualities, was largely superseded among red roses by the more floriferous 'Ilona', a Gijsbert Verbeek rose from AALSMEER in Holland, which in turn has since been threatened in the mid-1980s both by 'Madelon' (de Ruiter), an orange-red large-flowered rose, and by 'Gabriella' (sometimes 'Gabrielle'). The latter is an unusual rose, discovered as a SPORT of the Kordes cluster-flowered rose 'Mercedes' by Lars Berggren at his nursery in Sweden. It is marketed by Kordes.

It is all too rare for a sport to turn out as well as the original, but 'Mercedes' has given rise to two winners: 'Gabriella' and 'Jaguar', another cluster-flowered rose popular in the cut-rose trade. 'Gabriella' is, however, light-demanding, and in the twilight of an English winter, it has proved economical to 'go cold' with this variety of cut rose from November to March, and to fill orders for it by importing from Israel. Meanwhile, the sections of 'Gabriella' are pruned one at a time, so that from March they will come into flower successively and not all simultaneously.

'Sonia' – otherwise known as 'Sonia Meilland' and 'Sweet Promise' with pink-coral-salmon blooms, and listed in the US as a GRANDIFLORA – has proved to be the backbone of the European cut-rose industry since the early 1970s, just as another French rose, the pink 'Madame Abel Chatenay Pernet Ducher' was eighty years earlier. In 1983, 'Sonia' headed the list of the top ten large-flowered cut roses sold at the vast international auctions held in the Netherlands, with a total of 209 million stems sold there as compared with 71 million stems of 'Ilona', the runner-up.

'Golden Times' (Kordes), classed in the US as a cluster-flowered rose, is in the front row of the mid-yellows, as is 'Mercedes' among the orange-reds. 'Jack Frost', a lightly scented, globose, creamy-white American rose with dark foliage, is favoured for weddings, but in general, the demand for scented cut-flower roses in the UK is not sufficient to warrant the extra expense of growing them.

The cut-flower industry is, of course, subject to peaks at Christmas, Valentine's Day and Mother's Day (celebrated in the US on the second Sunday in May and in the UK – 'Mothering Sunday' – on the fourth Sunday in Lent; *see* GOLDEN ROSE, THE), but experience has shown that, where possible, it is more economical to arrange production in a steady flow rather than in 'flushes'.

The cut-rose industry
United Kingdom and the Continent. The current (1985) wholesale value of cut roses sold in the UK, including imports, amounts to about £12 million per annum, and the retail value to probably more than double that, at £25 million. However, Britain spends less on flowers than consumers in other EEC countries. The UK figure of £4.64 per head per annum is about one-seventh of that in the Netherlands, the largest consumer within the EEC, and is about one-third of the level of France, the second lowest consumer.

West Sussex, the Lea Valley in Essex and Lincolnshire account for about half the national rose acreage, which has shrunk since 1973 to less than half of the 109 acres under cultivation in that year. The rising cost of heating oil, which more than doubled during the 1970s, was partly responsible for this shrinking acreage and, although some firms were able to continue all-year production by investing in energy-saving devices and by switching from oil to coal or gas (which is 30–40 per cent cheaper than oil), other nurseries have been compelled to go over to growing with little or no heat. Labour costs also doubled during the same period, while the selling price of cut roses scarcely changed.

Foreign competition, too, increased in the third quarter of the century, and today more cut roses are imported into Britain than are grown there. More than half of the imports come from the Netherlands where natural gas fuel is subsidized: in 1984, 22.7 million stems were imported into Britain, and at least one Dutch nursery sends lorries across the Channel twice a week to canvas casual trade from florists' shops near the coast. Israel, with 17.5 million stems, is the other prominent supplier during a season that ran originally from November to April but now extends from October to May.

Lesser quantities come to Britain from (in order of importance) the Canary Islands, Zimbabwe, Greece, Colombia (a threat more to the United States than to Europe), Spain, Portugal, Italy, Brazil, West Germany, Peru, Morocco and Bermuda. Exports from Spain and Portugal are likely to grow as these countries become full members of the European Community. The climate in Almeria, the province immediately to the east of Granada, is similar to that of parts of California, and could be attractive to American investors once Spain has duty-free access to the European market.

In Europe, the largest auctions for cut flowers are held in the Netherlands, with AALSMEER as the main centre. The rose was still the leading flower there in 1984, with cut roses to the value of £121 million sold that year. Recent trends, however, have favoured chrysanthemum sales, which in 1984 were valued at £95.2 million.

United States. The cut-rose industry in the United States is proportionately larger than that of the UK, and it has been estimated that more than 300 million blooms of large-flowered roses and 120 million blooms of long-stalked cluster-flowered roses are sold there annually, with the wholesale value of the crop between six and seven times that of the UK. As in Britain, the leading roses change almost from year to year as breeders launch varieties with improved staying powers, yield and vigour.

Some 50 per cent of the cut roses in the United States are grown in California but there are also centres in Colorado, Illinois, Indiana, Pennsylvania and in other states where climatic conditions are favourable. Most are dispatched by air-freight.

See also GARDEN ROSES FOR CUTTING.

Cuttings

There are divided views about the wisdom of amateurs growing roses from cuttings, although large-scale nurseries thrive on the practice. Theophrastus (*see* BOOKS FOR ROSARIANS), who knew about budding (on trees) and about the layering of roses (*De Causius Plantarum*), tells us (*Historia Plantarum*): 'The Rose also grows from the seed . . . nevertheless, since it matures slowly, they cut up the stem and propagate it this way.' He also wrote that 'it is reasonable that plants propagated from slips should sprout and be grown faster than those propagated from seed, especially if the slips are taken with some roots attached, for in slips many parts are already present, needing only to be fed, whereas in a plant produced from seed, all these parts must first be generated and only then can grow.' He might have added that roses grown from a cutting can be depended on to produce the characteristics of the parent, whereas SEEDS can seldom be relied on to do so.

Roses grown from cuttings may take longer to flower than those budded on brier rootstocks, but they are said to live longer, and of course there will be no suckers. One disadvantage, however, is that, if truly successful, the cutting may take up more room in the rosebed than the brier rootstock might have done, and the proportion of blooms to foliage may be less. Equally, the cutting may prove less resilient and tough than the brier would have been.

Not all roses respond readily when propagated as cuttings. RAMBLERS and the rugosas do best, and there have been successes with CLIMBERS such as 'Zéphirine Drouhin' and some large-flowered roses such as 'La France'.

Cuttings from roses growing in the open can be taken as early as August. Young shoots with ripened wood and which have borne a flower are best, and lateral shoots are preferable to leaders. Those growing low down on the plant, on the shady side, are favoured, and those with the leaf joints close together will prove the most vigorous.

The rose cutting can be taken from the parent plant either by making a clean cut immediately below one of the leaf joints, or by pulling the desired shoot downwards at the join with the main stem, to give a 'heel' of bark and wood. Ideally the finished cutting should be a sprig of

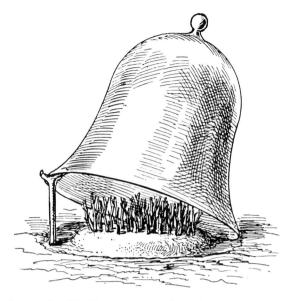

Rose cuttings à la *France (not to scale) under a bell cloche, from* Agricole: Encyclopédie Illustrée *(Larousse, Paris, 1921).*

about 9 inches (23 cm) with two leaf joints in the top 3 inches (8 cm). The tip of the cutting that has borne the flower, and the leaf immediately below it, should be cut off obliquely.

Leaves (but not the buds) on the lower two-thirds of the cutting are removed as this section will be planted in the ground. The soil should consist of a mixture of loam and silver sand mixed to a depth of about 9 inches (23 cm) in a pot or V-shaped trench.

Before planting, first make a hole in the paper and soil with a cane to allow the cutting to enter freely; then moisten the lower end of the cutting with damp cotton wool and dip it into root hormone powder. Insert the cutting and press the soil down firmly around it. Cover with leaves or sacking over the winter if protection is needed against frost. The cutting should have formed a root by the ensuing summer and can be transplanted in the autumn. Full size is normally reached in four to five years.

A cold frame full of rose cuttings planted directly into the ground, from Popular Gardening *(c. 1895).*

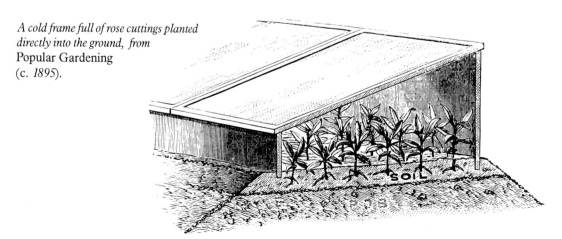

Rosa gigantea: *a botanical portrait by* *John Nugent Fitch, nephew of the great* *Walter Fitch* (SEE PRINTED PORTRAITS OF THE ROSE).

A Christmas rose (Helleborus niger), *from* Curtis's Botanical Magazine *(1793). The black roots help to account for the adjective* niger.

Above: A Cottar's Garden, *by Edward Kington Brice (1860 – 1948):*
almost a 'wild' garden but with campanulas, lilies and ox-eye daisies
as suitable companions for the rose.

Right: Rosa canina, *the dog rose, by Jacques le Moyne de Morgues,*
c. 1560.

The royal virgin rose without thorns, *by Georg Dionysius Ehret. This is a more finely finished portrait than Redouté's of the same species,* Rosa pendulina, *then known as* R. alpina pendulina. *However, neither artist showed the drooping hips in sufficient quantity.*

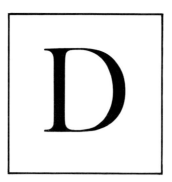

Damask roses

Damask roses are regarded today as historic hybrids derived originally from *Rosa gallica* (*see* GALLICA ROSES), and they may never have grown in the wild. There are, however, two distinct strains: the summer-flowering damasks, *R. gallica* x *R. phoenicia* denoted as *R.* x *damascena* or (more often) *R. damascena;* and the autumn-flowering damask, *R. gallica* x *R. moschata*, usually written as *R. damascena bifera*.

In so far as they differ from the gallicas, the damasks can be said to have arching stems (often green), plenty of stout, hooked prickles, and leaflets that are deeply nerved, light green, downy and rounded, tending to droop. The flowers are frilly and dishevelled with large golden eyes, in colours ranging from blush to pale rose and translucent near-white. They also have their own unmistakeable fragrance. The hips are narrowly elliptic or tapering and thus easily distinguishable from the rounded receptacles of the gallicas. In the autumn damasks, the distance between the leaf stalks diminishes towards the top of each branch so that the flowers at the end appear to be surrounded by a 'ruff' of green foliage.

R. damascena trigintipetala, the 'thirty-petalled' pink-flowered rose traditionally used in Bulgaria for the distillation of ATTAR OF ROSES, is REMONTANT and is close to the cultivated variety Kazanlik. The rose known as the 'Quatre Saisons' is apparently the type of rose most typical of the autumn damasks. (*See also* PORTLAND ROSES.) The 'Quatre Saisons Blanc Mousseux' – the perpetual white MOSS – is a SPORT of the last-named rose, which suggests that mossing, both in centifolias and damasks, may have been derived from their common ancestor *R. moschata*, the MUSK ROSE.

The damasks, including the autumn-flowering variety, seem to have been lost to sight in the centuries following the fall of the Roman empire and, as far as we know, were not rediscovered until the 16th century, when Pierandrea Matthiolus (1501–77), the eminent Italian botanist, declared in 1544 that they had only recently appeared in Italy. Michel de Montaigne (1533–92) the French philosopher and moralist, was astonished, on visiting a monastery in Ferrara, Italy in 1580, to see roses blooming there in November, and obtained a plant for his garden in France. Thus, even if the damask rose did come originally from

Damascus as its name suggests, it seems unlikely that the Crusaders were responsible for its spread through Europe. It seems more likely, as Graham Thomas has suggested, that the damask rose's connection with Damascus came from the comparison between its petals and the rich fabrics

Rosa damascena versicolor – *the 'York and Lancaster' rose – from* Les roses *by Pierre-Joseph Redouté.*

woven there. It seems to have first appeared in Britain as the 'Monthly Rose', described as a damask in Sir Thomas Hanmer's *Garden Book* of 1659 (*see* HISTORY OF THE ROSE).

'Leda', the rose otherwise known as the 'Painted Damask', is also remontant. It is a compact plant with blush flowers margined with crimson – an interesting combination. Little is known about its origins or about the first date of its appearance, but it is generally assigned to the early 19th century. The most widely known variety of the summer damasks is the blotched pink-and-white 'York and Lancaster rose', which is dealt with in the section on the rose as a SYMBOL.

Other well-known varieties among the summer-flowering, non-remontant damasks include 'Madame Hardy', a lavishly petalled, white variety that has led some experts to link it with *R. alba* or possibly *R. centifolia*. 'Celsiana' is another summer-flowering variety with attractive greyish foliage and pale pink flowers that fade to a darker blush colour. REDOUTÉ's portrait labelled *Rosier damascena Celsiana prolifera* somewhat exaggerates this colour change and hardly does justice to the leaves. The 'Isfahan' rose (which appears in most rosarian literature as 'Ispahan'), though not a remontant variety, has a long summer-flowering season, and its bright pink flowers hold their colour well. The 'OMAR KHAYYAM' rose, also summer-flowering, is described in detail in the section of that name.

The damask 'Marie Louise' was grown at La Malmaison but received its present name in 1813, three years after Napoleon married the Archduchess Marie Louise, JOSEPHINE's supplanter. It has very large double, reflexed mauvish-pink flowers, the weight of which tax the branches of the plant to their utmost. Offered mainly by nurseries specializing in the 'old' roses, it is summer-flowering.

Design of the rose garden

For the true rose lover, gardens should be designed to meet the needs of roses and not the other way round. One might even go further and say that the very site of the house should be the first element to be taken into consideration when planning a rose garden.

The over-riding priority must be for a *well-drained site*, for no roses, except for a few American species such as *Rosa palustris*, will flourish in ground that becomes waterlogged after heavy rain. Nevertheless the soil reserved for roses must also include sufficient humus so that such moisture as the soil contains will be held there long enough for the rose to profit from it. Soil of a light sandy nature does not fulfil this requirement, nor will it hold the roots of the rose firmly enough for the plant to withstand the force of winter gales.

Two further essentials for the rosarian homestead are *fresh air*, without over-exposure to high winds, and *sun*. These last two requirements are admirably discussed in Victorian style by Dean HOLE in his chapter on position in *A Book about Roses*. 'Some, having heard that a free circulation of air and abundance of sunshine are essential elements of success, select a spot which would be excellent for

Design for a rose garden. The rose arbour played a prominent role in this illustrated history of gardening written in 1577, the author of which showed a commendable desire to forsake the open-plan garden for one revealed with reticence.

a windmill, observatory, beacon, or Martello tower,' he wrote,

and there the poor Rose-trees stand or, more accurately speaking, wobble, with their leaves, like King Lear's silver locks, rudely blown and drenched by the 'to-and-fro contending wind and rain'. I have seen a garden of Roses – I mean a collection of Roseless trees – in front of a 'noble mansion proudly placed on a commanding eminence' where if you called on a gusty day, the wind blew the powder from the footman's hair as soon as he had opened the front door, and other doors within volleyed and thundered a *feu de joie* in honour of the coming guest.

Others, who have been told that the Rose loves shelter, peace and repose, have found 'such a dear snug little spot', not only surrounded by dense evergreen shrubs, but overshadowed by giant trees. Repose is there, assuredly – rest for the Rose when its harassed life is past, when it has nothing more for disease to prey upon, no buds for the caterpillar, no foliage for the aphis – the rest a mausoleum! You might as well expect a canary to sing in a hat-box as a Rose to bloom in this dreary dell.

Within the available space, the design of the rose garden should be such that the rose can show itself to best advantage. For Dean Hole, this raised no problems. 'There should be beds of Roses,' he wrote, 'banks of Roses, bowers of Roses, hedges of Roses, edgings of Roses, pillars of Roses, arches of Roses, fountains of Roses, baskets of Roses, vistas and alleys of the Rose.' However, in any garden, each of these features must be assigned its correct place. BUSH ROSES, for example, are better shown on a slope or in terraces than on the flat, a slope being preferred even though the beds on it might be more difficult to work. (The only risk incurred by planting on a slope comes from the possibility of frost pockets forming in the winter at the foot.)

Elsewhere the placing of the roses within the garden will be influenced by the classes of roses that are to be grown in it. Stiff CLIMBERS are best seen against the walls of an old house, and SHRUB ROSES where they can be admired or the flowers picked without the trouble of a long walk. BRIER species, on the other hand, look better in a more remote position away from the formal garden – perhaps in the orchard or rambling along a boundary hedge.

STANDARD and PILLAR ROSES introduce an element of formality that may be at variance with the style of the rest of the garden, and a site of ample proportions is needed to justify the expense of constructing and maintaining a rose pergola because, to be fully appreciated, the roses growing on it need to be viewed from outside, from above, and from a distance as well as from within the structure.

In the case of 'OLD' ROSES that flower only once during the summer, the original practice was to plant them in a separate 'rosarium' set apart from the rest of the garden and forgotten except when the roses were actually in bloom. However, before the end of the 19th century, the concept of a separate rose garden was strongly assailed by William Robinson who wrote in *The English Flower Garden*:

The idea of the Rose garden itself, as laid down in all the books, i.e. a place apart where one can only see flowers at a certain season, was harmful, as it led to the absence of the Rose from the flower garden. Instead of seeing the Rose in many different attitudes in a country place, we see a wretched mob of standards and half-standards rising out of the ground, generally in a miserable formal arrangement called the 'Rosery'. The Rose exhibitor's Rose garden is even uglier than the so-called Rosery in the large country seat, and thus the beautiful human and artistic side of the Rose garden has been forgotten.

The exhibitor's garden to which Robinson so scathingly referred consisted of long beds of a prescribed width in which roses of each variety were placed together in tasteless clumps so that they could be found, examined and treated at the same time with the least possible delay. Any other arrangement, as the exhibitors confessed, would involve a waste of precious space that might be used for growing one more rose. To the exhibitors, plants were not natural objects of beauty, becoming so only when the blooms arrived on the trestle tables of a rose show. At least one showman of the time suggested that the rosebed should enjoy the sun only in the morning and early after-

noon; it should, he thought, be in shade from 4.30 onwards, so that the flowers would be in the right condition for cutting for the following day's show.

One way of retaining a separate rose garden but maintaining its attractions when the summer-only roses have finished flowering was to mix in other more accommodating plants (*see* COMPATIBLE PLANTS). Another solution was to plant some early-flowering roses and some late bloomers, to give a display, albeit a limited one, over a longer period.

For the non-exhibitor, the difficulties of designing a modern rose garden have since been immensely lightened by the arrival of newer varieties capable of flowering for longer periods. In general, the modern trend is towards the less inflexible style of the rose garden, say, of the Parc de la Tête d'Or in Lyon in place of the geometrical magnificence of LA ROSERAIE DE L'HAY-LES-ROSES, near Sceaux.

However, if the rose garden is to be formal, and space and contours allow, then the style adopted in the Parc de la Grange on the south bank of the lake at Geneva has much to recommend it. The roses there are arranged in an octagon with beds set on three levels, so that visitors can stand, if they wish, on the stage, so to speak, of an amphitheatre and look at the stalls and, above them, the dress circle and the upper circle with its beds of large-flowered roses; or, if they prefer, they can climb up and look down from above on the weeping standards and ramblers around the fountains beneath. In addition, there are pillar roses and Italian pergolas to be admired along the boundary.

In the end, however, the style of every rose garden must be a matter for each individual. A collective decision on the perfect design has never been taken and probably never will be.

See also ROSE GARDENS, A SELECTION OF INTERNATIONALLY FAMOUS.

Dickson nurseries

The mayoral chain of the Borough of Newtownards, Northern Ireland, presented to it in 1937, was made from the gold medals won by the Dickson family of rose growers during the firm's first century. This nursery was founded in 1836, the year preceding the dawn of Queen Victoria's golden reign, by Alexander Dickson, and originally cut flowers and general nursery stock were grown there. It was more than forty years before Alexander Dickson II, the founder's grandson, began to specialize in roses. Dickson roses were exhibited at the NATIONAL ROSE SOCIETY for the first time in 1887. A gold medal followed in 1892 for 'Mrs W. J. Grant', a pink rose and the first of the newly named HYBRID TEA class to be so honoured. By 1908, twenty-five out of sixty-six prize-winning rose varieties listed by the *Journal of Horticulture* were Dickson introductions; the remaining forty-one were divided between twenty-three other raisers.

'George Dickson', a scented rose of rich velvet crimson, came in 1912 and stayed at the top of the NRS's list of exhibition roses for the next twenty years. 'Mrs Wemyss

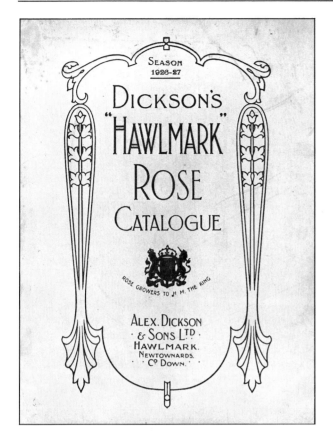

Alex Dickson & Sons Ltd, by then rose growers to King George V, used a contemporary art-deco design for the cover of their 1926–7 catalogue.

Quin', a chrome-yellow PERNETIANA introduced in 1914, and the first really hardy rose of its type, missed the National Rose Society's Gold Medal but won a similar award at the BAGATELLE rose trials in Paris.

'Betty Uprichard' won a gold medal at the NRS show in 1921 and was introduced the following year. It was named for a woman from Northern Ireland who was fond of hunting and was thrown from her horse and killed not many years afterwards. 'Shot Silk', a large-flowered rose described sometimes as cerise, sometimes as bright orange-pink with carmine, won the NRS's Gold Medal in 1923 and it too was introduced the following year.

In 1926, yet another Alexander Dickson was born, known by his second name, Patrick. Alexander Dickson II retired in 1930, leaving the business to his sons, George and Alexander III (born 1893 and father of Patrick). Within nine years, World War II put an end to rose-growing for a further six, but a small stock of the best varieties was kept for the future. In 1957, Patrick Dickson, now just thirty, took over the work of hybridizing, representing the fifth generation to work in the family firm.

The next year the NRS President's International Trophy was awarded to 'Dickson's Flame' – a dazzling red cluster-flowered rose – the first British rose to win this award. 'Silver Lining', a pink large-flowered rose, appeared the same year, and 125 bushes of it were planted in the grounds of Buckingham Palace to celebrate the birth of Prince Andrew. This rose later won a gold medal at the PORTLAND ROSE FESTIVAL in Oregon. Also in 1958, 'Shepherd's Delight', an orange-red and yellow cluster-flowered rose, won an NRS Gold Medal. 'Dearest', a rosy-salmon cluster-flowered rose, raised by Alexander Dickson and named for his wife, Maud Dickson, won gold medals both from the NRS and the Hamburg shows in 1960. The Royal Horticultural Society also gave it a first-class certificate (seldom awarded to a rose).

In 1964, 'Happy Event' became the first rose to be awarded a gold medal at the international trials in Tokyo – though it seems since to have fallen into disuse. The following year, Dickson's again won a gold medal in JAPAN from the Japanese Rose Society with 'Shiralee', a large-flowered, yellow-blend rose. In that year, 1965, Patrick Dickson won his first President's International Trophy and Gold Medal from the Royal National Rose Society with 'Grandpa Dickson' ('Irish Gold'), a large-flowered lemon-yellow rose, flushed pink, which is believed to have earned the firm as much as £600,000. In 1969 Patrick Dickson won his second President's International Trophy with 'Red Planet', a large-flowered bright crimson rose.

Alex Dickson III died in 1975 and, two years later, it was decided to separate the retail side of Dickson's from the breeding sector, which was considerably less profitable. Patrick took control of the breeding nursery as Dickson's Nurseries Ltd, and his brothers the retail garden centre. Patrick Dickson's new discoveries are now introduced by HARKNESS.

For the next few years, 'Memento' – a cherry-pink and salmon, cluster-flowered rose – provided the main encouragement, winning a silver medal in Geneva in 1977, and one in Baden-Baden the following year, followed by top awards in Belfast and The Hague, but in 1983, things began to happen. 'Beautiful Britain', an orange-red cluster-flowered rose, was voted 'ROSE OF THE YEAR', and 'Ards Beauty', a mid-yellow cluster-flowered rose, won the RNRS President's International Trophy and Gold Medal.

The following year was equally successful. 'Ainsley Dickson', named for Patrick Dickson's wife, won the President's International Trophy and Gold Medal, and 'Dickerry', a cluster-flowered hand-painted pink, was also awarded a gold medal.

Another Dickson rose, a PATIO ROSE unnamed at the time of writing, has been voted 'Rose of the Year' for 1986, and others are in the pipeline. Patrick's son, Colin, is already working in the hybridizing sector, becoming the sixth generation of dedicated Dicksons.

Dwarf roses

A term used, particularly in 19th-century books about the rose, to distinguish ordinary bedding roses from the larger STANDARD ('TREE') ROSES, and sometimes today to distinguish low-growing cluster-flowered roses (e.g. PATIO ROSES) from larger cluster-flowered bushes.

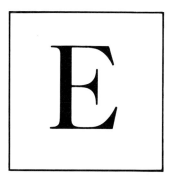

E

Ehret, Georg Dionysius

Georg Dionysius (sometimes Dyonysos) Ehret (1708–70), has been acknowledged as the leading painter of flower portraits (including many of roses) throughout the middle years of the 18th century, He was born, according to his own memoir, the son of a Heidelberg market gardener. Though apprenticed to the seed bed, the drawings he did in his spare time attracted the attention of the Margrave of Baden, and later that of a Regensburg banker named Lesenkohl, by whom he was employed for several years of unrewarding copy-work. Then, fortunately, some of his sketches of common local plants, painted on small scraps of writing paper, were seen by Dr Christof Jacob Trew, a wealthy naturalist and collector of Nuremberg. Trew at once recognized the talent of the twenty-one-year-old artist and offered him, sight unseen, an open-ended contract for large-scale paintings of the new exotic plants that were then flooding into Europe from across the world. Trew, who was to become Ehret's lifelong friend and patron, was especially interested in the morphology (i.e. structure) of plants and in the botanical importance of their reproductive organs, and it was largely on Trew's advice that Ehret made the serious study of botany that endowed his portraits with a special worth.

In the years that followed, Ehret searched for unusual plants in many of the leading botanical gardens of Europe in Basle, Zurich, Bern, Geneva, Strasburg, Montpellier and in Paris where he arrived with an introduction from his old employer, the Margrave of Baden, to Bernard de Jussieu, then lecturer in botany and director of cultivation at the Jardin du Roi. When he left, on de Jussieu's advice, to visit Britain, Ehret took with him not only a passport signed by Louis XV, but also letters of introduction from de Jussieu who had himself recently returned from London.

Ehret's first stay in England was only to be short as he had intended first to visit the famous botanic garden at Leyden in the Netherlands, before travelling on to London. In Leyden, he heard that the great LINNAEUS was staying with his patron George Cliffort, the banker and director of the Dutch East India Company, at Haarlem, and he tramped there on foot to meet them. Linnaeus, who was preparing a work on Cliffort's famous garden, had already formulated his system for classifying plants according to their sexual characteristics, and found in Ehret the ideal botanical illustrator for his new theories. *Hortus Cliffortianus*, written by Linnaeus and illustrated by Ehret, was thus the first published work to make use of Linnaeus's new system of classification.

In 1736, with an unassailable reputation, Ehret returned to England where he was to spend the rest of his life. He settled in Chelsea near to the residence of Sir Hans Sloane and the Physick Garden that the great man had established. Soon he had almost more work than he could handle, and prints hand-coloured and, in a number of cases, etched by the artist himself, are to be found in many important works on exotic plants of the time. Ehret married the sister-in-law of Philip Miller, who presided over the Chelsea Physick Garden for forty-eight years and wrote there his *Gardeners' Dictionary*, the sixth edition of 1752 being recognized as the initial reference point for the names of all garden CULTIVARS. In 1757, Ehret was elected to the 'English List' (as opposed to the 'Foreign List') of the Royal Society, a signal honour for a foreigner.

Some of Ehret's finest paintings of roses are to be seen in the print room of the Victoria & Albert Museum. In these, the precision and botanical accuracy achieved, often with the help of a microscope, together with his sureness of touch and sense of design, more than compensate for the somewhat formal style of presentation.

See also PRINTED PORTRAITS OF THE ROSE.

Ellacombe, Canon Henry Nicholson

A close and persistent connection seems to have existed during the late 18th and 19th centuries between the Church of England and gardening. In the literary field, there were the Revd Gilbert White (1720–93) at Selborne, and the Revd Charles Kingsley (1819–75) in his garden at Eversley in Hampshire. (Kingsley's daughter Rose wrote *Roses and Rose Growing*, published in 1908; in Susan Chitty's biography of Kingsley *père*, she mentions an article in *The Rose* journal of spring 1969, according to which Rose's book, which dealt with the rose scene from 1860, was surprisingly modern and independent.) The Revd John Henslow was the botanist who recommended his pupil Charles Darwin as naturalist to the *Beagle*, and the Revd William Wilks was Rector of Shirley, Surrey, the village from which his Shirley poppies took their name.

In the more strictly rosarian sense, there was the Revd s. REYNOLDS HOLE, Dean of Rochester, and the Revd Joseph Pemberton who, as a schoolboy, used to take a bud of 'Souvenir de la Malmaison' back to school in a barley-sugar box, and who afterwards became Vice-President of the NATIONAL ROSE SOCIETY and a professional rose grower. The Revd A. Foster-Melliar of Sproughton Rectory near Ipswich wrote *The Book of the Rose*, which was first published in 1894 and became a bestseller in its field, and the Revd Henry Honywood D'Ombrain, Vicar of Westwell, near Ashford, Kent, helped to found the National Rose Society.

However, in none of these is the connection between roses and the country parsonage as intimate as in the case of Canon Henry Nicholson Ellacombe (1822–1916), who succeeded his father as Vicar of Bitton, Gloucestershire in 1850 and remained in the same post until his death sixty-six years later at the age of ninety-four. His garden filled a mere one-and-a-half acres, and lay on the chalk, yet his skill was such that he regularly exchanged plants with Kew, and succeeded in cultivating that strange variety *Rosa watsoniana* about which ELLEN WILLMOTT so aptly wrote, as well as the original MUSK ROSE that had almost vanished from cultivation.

He was a gardener of the modern persuasion and his philosophy was to 'let Nature in at the gate' so that wild flowers could grow alongside his roses. In fact he went even further: 'I would rather see a flower border with a mixture of flowers and weeds than one with a few plants and large continents of bare soil.' Weeds, he believed, were sometimes useful if they saved the soil from losing too much of its moisture.

Ellacombe eventually fathered ten children (three sons and seven daughters), and was a man of wide interests with enthusiasm for madrigals, old glass, old silver and the correct hanging of church bells. When travelling to London after one of his canonical visits to an outlying parish, he would, as the train passed through Bitton, throw his vestments out through the train window for the stationmaster to collect and keep in safe custody, and he used to write to his more scholarly friends in Latin elegiacs.

Today, however, the articles that he wrote for the *Guardian* newspaper are his finest memorial. They were collected and first published in 1895 by Edward Arnold under the title *In a Gloucestershire Garden*, and in 1982 it were reissued in paperback by Century Publishing. The reader's sympathy immediately goes out to the Canon on learning that he was prepared to sacrifice good Brazil nuts in order to keep the mice away from the roots of his apple trees, and that he learned the hard way that 'sowbread' (a popular name for the cyclamen) was not food for pigs, a hungry porcine family having invaded his garden and rooted up most of the plants in a bed but left the cyclamen roots untouched. He was fond, it is said, of yuccas, but it was the

rose that above all other plants claimed his attentions, and his tribute to the rose can hardly be bettered:

In May and June come roses of all kinds, except the musk, which comes later, says Bacon; and though I so far follow his lead as to place the rose among the chief glories of the garden in June, and though it is in June that they are seen in the fullest abundance and beauty, yet it is one of the great charms of the rose that they brighten our gardens for so many months of the year. We may almost say that, weather permitting, a good garden is never entirely without roses in flower. I have picked good flowers from the monthly China roses in January, and in 1881 I picked a good bunch of fairy roses on Christmas Eve. I know of no other flower that comes near the rose in this respect; the daisy possibly comes the nearest. This may perhaps be gathered during nine months of the year, but very seldom in November, December and January.

And this must be one of the reasons (independently of the beauty and scent) why the rose is so dear to us, and is so closely interwoven with English country life. It is not only that it is the national emblem, and has been so from very early times, for other nations have national floral emblems, which do not enter into their home-life as the rose does with us; nor is it because it is surrounded with so many historical associations – the red rose of Lancaster, the white rose of York, the Tudor Rose, the musk roses, the Eglantine of Shakespeare and Milton – but it is, I think, that from its easy cultivation especially in our climate, it is found in every garden, and can be grown in full beauty in the great gardens of the rich, but in equal beauty in the small garden of the poorest cottager. It is the favourite everywhere; in the child's garden, and in the garden of the florist, who watches and nurses it for exhibition – pruned or unpruned, highly cultivated or neglected, it is always beautiful and always prized.

Enemies of the rose

Animal kingdom

Enemies from the animal kingdom include such insects as bees, moths, beetles, APHIDS, weevils – all with six legs and antennae – and mites, which are arachnids with eight legs when fully grown, and no antennae. In some cases, as with beetles, the fully developed insect is responsible for damaging the rose by chewing leaves or petals. In other cases, the caterpillar is the culprit, and the adult insect (the moth) is guilty only to the extent of laying the eggs that give rise to the caterpillars.

Pests that eat leaves or blossoms can be attacked with sprays that coat their food with poison. Some pests, including froghoppers, leafhoppers, aphids and mites, are not equipped with mandibles (jaws) for chewing. Instead, they are able to pierce the stems or shoots of the rose, and draw out sap. The food supplies of sap-suckers cannot be reached with surface sprays and so other methods have to be used. In the case of insects, it is possible to spray a liquid that either dries and blocks the spiracles on the insect through which it 'breathes', or paralyses its nervous system. Mites have different breathing apparatus and other methods of control are employed.

Systemics – that is, deterrents that are absorbed through the leaves as well as the roots and are thus passed through

The yellow-tail moth. This male specimen has a more modest 'tail' than the female. The caterpillar, with a vermilion stripe down its back, attacks leaves in the autumn.

the entire system of a plant – now play an increasing part in the war against pests. Both insecticides and fungicides can be introduced into the sap of the plant to deal with sap-suckers and fungi that could not easily be combated in any other way. The trend today is towards single all-purpose products designed to deal with every animal or vegetable ailment of the rose, but inevitably if one particular complaint is predominant in the rose garden, there may be an advantage in using the remedy specifically prepared to deal with it. Equally, a specific remedy recommended for one complaint may be effective for others too, as the instructions for use will no doubt make clear.

Regulations regarding sprays and powders that can be used in gardens vary from country to country, as do the brand names under which the products are sold. In some cases, the impressively lengthy chemical formula of the active ingredient is disclosed (though it would be unwise for the amateur to endeavour to duplicate it); in others, the important constituent goes under a more easily pronounced but legally protected name, but this is unlikely to be the same worldwide. Rose lovers will come to no harm provided that they buy the products of reputable firms and follow the instructions. Continuing research leads to new products, and those mentioned here are examples only and are by no means an exhaustive list of effective remedies.

Many products are sold as powder in sachets for dissolving in water, a practice that sometimes involves mixing larger quantities than are needed. The surplus will lose its value when stored, and those with small rose gardens do better to buy products in concentrated liquid form. Hand-sprays holding as little as a pint of liquid may prove adequate and, in any case, are easily refilled.

Leaves. Several species of sizeable caterpillars habitually feed on the leaflets of roses; others normally found on hawthorn, pear and other relatives of the rose occasionally enter the rose garden. The one most commonly found there is the caterpillar of the vapourer moth, coloured smokey blue, red and white, with toothbrush tufts of yellow hair. The rose-slug caterpillar (*Eucloa indetermina*) – orange with tufted spines – is a similar pest in the US. The lackey moth, whose caterpillars construct silken greyish tents several inches long between shoots, is another frequent visitor as is the buff-tip moth, whose caterpillars travel in battalions. There are also caterpillars that walk with a looping motion, including the green and yellow larva of the shoulder-stripe moth, which stands up rigidly like a twig when at rest. The winter moth caterpillar, also a loop-walker, prefers to conceal itself by drawing two leaves together.

The caterpillars of the micro-sized tortix moth (*Lozotoenia rosae*) also cause trouble by sewing together the edges of rose leaflets to make shelters for themselves and sometimes sallying forth to eat into rosebuds. There are half-a-dozen different kinds of these micro-moths, the caterpillars of which are generally described as rose maggots. Some, when disturbed, pretend not to be at home by suspending themselves below leaflets on silken threads.

Hexyl-Plus – a combination of derris and benzene hexachloride – is a convenient preparation for dealing with caterpillars, rose maggots as well as hoppers. It is not systemic.

The female of the leaf-rolling sawfly species, *Blennocampa pusilla*, causes rose leaflets to curl up dramatically by injecting toxin into them as she lays her eggs. The pale green or whitish larva can be distinguished from that of any moth since it has more than five pairs of claspers in addition to the normal three pairs of thoracic front legs. Remedies containing trichlorphon are usually effective, but since the leaflet will have already been spoiled by the time the caterpillar appears, it may be best to remove and destroy the leaflet.

Leaves are also attacked by the larvae of the rose slug-worm sawfly (*Endelomyia aethiops*) and its near relative, which reduce the leaflets to mere skeletons, as does the bristly rose-slug (*Cladius pectinicornis*). Again, Hexyl-Plus is an effective remedy, provided that special attention is paid to the underside of the leaves on which the larva often stations itself.

The larva of the rose-leaf miner (*Stigmella anomalella*) disfigures the leaf with brown serpentine tracks eaten between the leaf surfaces. In this case, either a remedy containing trichlorphon, or fenitrothion (sometimes called Fentro), is prescribed. The leaf-cutter bee, which bites out circular portions of rose leaflets for its nest, can best be combated by discovering and destroying its nest.

Less obvious forms of damage are caused by the rose leafhopper (*Tyflocyba rosae*), which takes up residence on the undersides of leaflets. There, the almost colourless nymphs of the post-larval stage feed on the sap, imparting a mottled brown appearance to the leaf. Here a systemic, such as Benlate, is recommended, with fenitrothion as a second string.

The so-called red spider (*Tetranychus telarius*) – which is neither a spider nor red, but a mite – also lives on the underside of leaflets under the protection of a silky web. Along with mealy bugs (*Pseudococcidae*) and whiteflies (*Aleyrodidae*), it is a pest in glasshouses as well as in the garden. Chlorobenzilate or Benlate have been found effective.

Shoots and stems. Here the most frequent attacks come from aphids, the subject of a separate section. But the attentions of the froghopper (*Philaenus leucophthalmus*) are equally unwelcome. The frothy, so-called cuckoo-spit, usually found at the junction of a shoot, shelters a nymph or partly grown froghopper that is feeding off the sap. Hexyl can be sprayed, but the none-too-squeamish can use their fingers with economy.

Weevils, distinguishable from other beetles by their long snouts, come, from the gardener's point of view, in two varieties: those that sleep by day and those that sleep at night. Both types feed on all parts of the rose including the stem. The day-feeding weevils often congregate at the tips of the shoots and, when seen, can be knocked off into an inverted umbrella. When not active, they shelter at the foot of the plant and can be caught there in boxes filled with waste paper or dead leaves.

The common green capsid plant bug (*Lygus pabulinus*) attacks rosebuds and shoots with the result that they look withered and mis-shapen. This is a sap-sucking insect and is best tackled with systemic insecticide.

Two species of sawfly – *Ardis brunniventris* and *A. sulcata* – lay their eggs in the main shoots of roses, and on hatching, the larvae bore their way down into the stem, hollowing it out. They tend to feed on the edges of leaves and can sometimes be detected before too much harm is done; wilting shoots sometimes also give a clue to their presence. Systemic spraying is the best deterrent.

Other insects attack the lower parts of stems. These are scale insects, or coccids, which grow scaly structures on shoots and stems while feeding on the sap of the plant. The active coccids are best attacked with sprays of ICI's Sybol 2 containing pirimiphos methyl, in the early autumn before they have had time to grow scales. The eggs can be killed off in the winter with Mortegg, of which tar-oil is a constituent. This should be sprayed on to the ground as well as on the rose plant.

For rose galls, *see* ROBIN'S PINCUSHION; for crown galls, *see below.*

Buds and blooms. Thrips (*Thripus fuscipennis*) and other similar species are delicate-looking insects about one-tenth of an inch (2 mm) long, and appear in swarms, particularly during heat waves. They attack not only leaves and shoots, but also the buds and petals of the flowers, scraping away the surface of plant tissues in order to suck the juices beneath, and depositing eggs inside the petals of the flower causing unsightly deformities in the bloom. They are a

menace in the greenhouse as well as in the garden. Spray once every fourteen days with derris.

CHAFERS can cause large-scale damage to rose blooms, and growers in the United States have to wage un unending campaign against the Japanese beetle, which was imported there in the days before strict controls were introduced.

The immature nymph capsid bugs, already mentioned unfavourably for their attacks on the shoots of rose plants, also damage rose blooms throughout the summer.

Roots. The grubs of chafers and weevils damage the roots of rose plants, and rose root aphids (*Cinara rosae*) cluster on the lower parts of stems and the upper root system in the same way as its relatives further up the plant. The eggs, which are black and shiny, are laid in the autumn and should be rubbed off and destroyed, together with any visible insects. Some species of nematodes, otherwise known as eelworms – small, thread-like, transparent and therefore not easily detected – attack the roots of roses and are a serious problem in the United States.

Professional nurserymen take the precaution of sterilizing their soil to free it from nematodes, using either steam or methyl bromide gas – methods that are impractical for average gardeners. In times gone by, they were instructed to discourage nematodes by planting tagetes (African marigolds) in the rosebed – a not-very-appealing suggestion – but it is now possible to buy an effective deterrent marketed as Bromophos. This will kill not only nematodes but also chafer grubs and sawflies in the chrysalis stage.

Vegetable kingdom (including viruses and bacteria)
Fungi, including moulds, cankers, MILDEW, BLACKSPOT and rust, are among the most persistent enemies of the rose. They reproduce themselves as airborne spores, which grow into thread-like hyphae that penetrate the host and are able to absorb food from it. New spores are formed incredibly rapidly in various ways, differing according to the class of fungus. There may be 'winter' and 'summer' forms of spore.

Rust is so called because of the colour of the particular strain that was first noticed on wheat. In the UK, the rust that attacks the rose – *Phragmidium mucronatum* – appears, however, in the form of orange spots that can be seen in spring on the undersides of the leaves. Risk of infection is increased when drops of water remain on leaf surfaces for prolonged periods. The disease later spreads over the upper surfaces of the leaves and over the stem, leading to open cracks that favour the entry of other infections. A really severe attack can kill a rose bush in a single season. The leaves can be sprayed with Plantvax, which includes the active ingredient oxycarboxin, or with Calirus, which contains benodanil. This treatment should be repeated once every two weeks and should be followed up in the autumn with a spray of tar-oil emulsion, such as Mortegg, to deal with the successive life forms of this pest. Remember to spray the ground as well as the plant itself.

At least six different kinds of rust have been identified in rose gardens in the United States, some adapted to a particular species of rose, others to the climate of a particular region. Local advice should be sought.

Anthracnose (*Sphaceloma rosarum*) is another highly infectious complaint, giving rise to circular spots on leaves, pale at first but darkening later. They are often dark-rimmed at the edges, and this, and the fact that they eventually rupture, help to distinguish them from the more frequently encountered blackspot. Similar spots, which later join together, may appear later on the stem. The affected parts should be removed and burned; the rest of the plant should be thoroughly sprayed with a wash such as copper sulphate, for which a glass, plastic or copper receptacle should be used – not one of iron or tin. The term *anthracnose* is often used in the US to include diseases caused by other organisms such as *Gloeosporium*, *Colletotrichum* or *Elsinoe rosarum*.

Leaf-scorch (*Septoria rosae*) is another leaf complaint due to attacks by a fungus; it should not be confused with the kind sometimes produced by spraying plants when the sun is hot. It shows on the leaves as yellowish-green patches that later become brown and, later still, when spores are present, appear as whitish spots. Spraying with colloidal cuprous oxide or ICI's Roseclear should be begun in the spring.

Silver-leaf (*Stereum purpureum*) is characterized by the metallic appearance of the leaves, but this is hardly detectable until just before the leaf dies and falls. The dead leaves later show brownish or purplish marks. At the time of writing, there is no effective remedy, and roses seldom survive an attack by this fungus. The plants should be dug up and burned.

Botrytis cinerea is known in the UK as 'grey mould' and in the US as one of a large group of blights that also include cane blight (*Physalospora obtusa*), southern blight (*Sclerotium rolfsii*) and thread blight (*Pellicularia koleroga*). Botrytis favours decaying vegetation, and will settle on any damaged tissue including wood, buds, shoots and flower stalks. Attacks can be controlled with Benlate.

Black mould (*Chalaropsis thielavioides*) is a fungus that interferes with rose-grafts, causing them to fail. It is frequently met with and deservedly feared in the United States. No effective remedy is known.

Various species of *Cladosporium*, which attack the leaves and buds of roses, and can be dealt with normal fungicides, are known in the US as *leaf moulds*.

Fungi are also responsible for various forms of *canker*: e.g. stem canker (*Coniothyrium fuckelii*), brown canker (*Cryptosporella umbrina*), brand canker (*Coniothyrium wernsdorffiae*) – so called because the stems of the rose appear to have been branded – crown canker (*Cylindrocladium scoparum*), which attacks the area around the point where the UNDERSTOCK has been budded, and *Griphosphaeria corticola*, not seen sufficiently often in gardens for it to have been given a common name. The rate of success in combating any of these fungi is not encouraging, and often the only course is to cut out and burn the diseased stem.

Spraying roses with a solution of water, soft soap and a dash of turpentine to kill aphids (Cassell's Family Magazine, *1891*).

Crown gall – as distinct from crown canker – is not a fungoid disease but results from the attacks of *Bacterium tumifaciens*; the swellings disfigure, even if they do not mortally damage, the rose. The galls should be cut off and the scar treated with a bactericide to prevent reinfection. One more bacterium, *Agrobacterium rhizogenes*, afflicts roses in the US with *hairy root* but is not a problem in the UK.

'*Die-back*' in garden roses is not a disease in itself, but may follow severe frost or drought, especially if injudicious pruning has left a SNAG on the plant. Any part of a rose tree that has died will automatically attract one or more of the diseases to which the rose is liable.

Armilleria mellea, known in the UK as *honey-tuft* and in the US as *root-rot*, attacks both the stem and the root of the rose. In the final stages, a display of honey-coloured toadstools is seen, in which case it will be too late to take counter measures, and the plant should be dug up and burned.

The unaffected roses should then be given a precautionary spray with Armillotox.

Virus diseases that lead to strange patterns appearing on the leaves of roses are as yet the province of specialists. Nurserymen rid their own understocks of viruses by cultivating them for a period under heat (100°F, 38°C) and then sterilizing their soil with steam or methyl bromide. To this extent, the gardener who buys from a reliable nursery is safe. MICROPROPAGATION of roses from virus-free stock is an alternative form of insurance.

'Buy My Fine Myrtles and Roses!' from a print published by the Catnach Press, Seven Dials, London.

Evolution and the rose

Many serious botanical works list the plants they are describing in an order corresponding to the position that each family is thought to have occupied in the sequence of evolution – thus, the 'primitives' appear at the beginning of the work, and the more 'advanced' plants at the end. For instance, in the prestigious *Flora of the British Isles* by A. R. Clapham, T. G. Tutin and E. F. Warburg, the Rosaceae family is placed as number 52 out of a total of 146 families and comes immediately after the peas and vetches and just before the plane trees. But what are the features that make

a flowering plant such as the rose 'primitive' or 'advanced', and where does the rose stand in the mainstream of botanical evolution?

Not even the experts are entirely of one mind on these matters, for while the fossilized remains of earlier primitive plants (gymnosperms, such as conifers, which develop from naked seeds) date back 350 million years, it is difficult to establish an orderly connection between them and the later and very much more successful angiosperms – including the rose – in which the seeds develop in a protected ovary following dual, and more or less simultaneous, fertilization of the ovule and the endosperm that is to nourish it. This is because the earliest fossilized angiosperms date back only some 100 million years – by which time they were already widely spread across the globe and had branched out into some fifty distinct families. We know nothing of the earlier history of the angiosperms, which ones were the most primitive and where, when and from what older plants they developed.

Since direct evidence is lacking, botanists have had to fall back on their powers of deduction. In these circumstances, the question of where the first of the 'modern' flowering plants first appeared is perhaps the least difficult. It is assumed that they would have developed in the region containing the widest variety and greatest profusion of primitive plants – which, from the numbers of species still surviving, would seem to be in an area lying between Assam in northeast India and the islands of the western Pacific.

Unfortunately, none of the existing naked seed plants can be directly associated with the rose and other angiosperms, since over the years the primitives, too, have all progressed beyond the point where they could be related hypothetically with the first angiosperms. Thus the specific ancestor of the rose is probably untraceable.

The birth-date of the first angiosperm is also a matter for conjecture, but since they were pollinated by insects, we might justifiably assume that their arrival would not be earlier than that of the earliest pollinators, the beetles, which took place in the early part of the Permian period – that is, about 280 million years ago. It is widely accepted that the first angiosperms might have arrived in the first half of the Jurassic era between 195 and 135 million years ago. This period then would have witnessed the original planting of the rose's family tree.

The rose was well equipped to flourish in the new world of beetles. These insects and their like would have been attracted to the flowers by scent, and they would also have come to eat pollen. Butterflies, moths, bees, wasps, mosquitoes and other insects equipped to suck up nectar did not play an influential role in plant development until much later. From this it follows that flowers offering liberal supplies of nectar are 'advanced', while those (including the rose) mainly supplying pollen for pollination by beetles are 'primitive'.

It has also been observed that, if two plants have the same characteristics, one of which is known to be primitive, other features common to both often turn out to be primitive, too. Thus plants pollinated by beetles tend to have cup-shaped flowers that, it is suggested, serve to provide a resting place for the pollinators and easy access for them to the pollen. This would hold true of many of the SPECIES ROSES and the older garden varieties. In the more advanced plants, the nectaries are often concealed from the view of casual passers-by, and are accessible only to those insects of the right size and weight and then only if they are equipped with the right length of proboscis – an arrangement that helps to ensure that pollen taken from one plant is carried to another plant of the same species and so is not wasted.

Flowers that develop at the end of a flower shoot, as with the rose, are another sign of primitiveness. This is because the early flower petals developed from modified bracts at the end of the vegetal shoots. For the same reason, the 'early' petals would be separated from one another and not joined together to form a funnel or hood.

It is also assumed that, since the early angiosperms would have developed from woody tropical plants, the more primitive species would also be woody trees and shrubs rather than herbs, many of which die down after seeding.

In other respects, the rose shows 'primitive' characteristics. The leaves of primitive angiosperms, as can be seen from the structure of the nodes (the points on the stem from which the leaves, as distinct from leaflets, arise), are arranged in spirals as in the rose, a formation loosely described as 'alternate', and not placed in pairs opposite to one another or in whorls. The stipules – leafy growths associated with the leaves – are also prominent in primitives.

The seeds of some primitives are uncomfortably large and would have been distributed via the stomachs of animals – originally by reptiles and later, as in the case of the rose, by birds. In modern plants, however, the trend has been consistently towards lighter seeds distributed in other ways.

In all these respects, therefore, in the shape, character and, to some extent, the positioning of its flowers, from its stems, its stipules, its seeds and the arrangements of its leaves, the rose may be regarded as being among the primitives. Some botanists rate roses as not being far removed from the magnolia, which is widely held to be the most primitive of all angiosperms.

However, in the course of time the rose has modernized itself somewhat. The geological pressures that raised the world's great mountain ranges during the Cretaceous era (135 to 65 million years ago) set the conditions for rapid developments in the plant world. The differences of altitude to be found on mountain chains offered new challenges to those species capable of adapting to extremes of heat and cold. Away from the tropics, the climate was seasonal, and in summer, some plants had to contend with hot drying winds from the south. In consequence, it is widely believed that heat rather than sharp winters may have led to the appearance of the first deciduous plants, which shed their leaves in order to reduce loss of water through evaporation. Certainly the rose has joined the company of deciduous plants, even though its leaves are now shed in winter when conditions are unfavourable for growth.

Another advance by the rose lies in its ability to impart dormancy to its seeds. These, though they may be formed during one season, are required not to germinate until after the following winter. This is widely regarded as an 'advanced' feature shown only in plants that have learned to survive in a seasonal climate. In addition, roses that have acquired higher CHROMOSOME counts either through hybridization with other species in the wild or by a failure by the nucleus to divide during MITOSIS are considered to be more advanced than the 'older' species with lower chromosome counts.

The rose has also learned how to travel, with the help of horses, birds or possibly humans themselves. In the days when the climate of the north was far less severe than at present, the rose had no difficulty in spreading right across the Northern Hemisphere. One route to the Americas – and probably the most important link – lay north-eastwards through Asia and along the Aleutian island chain and the Bering Strait, but an alternative route led across the North Atlantic landbridge over Iceland and Greenland, which at that time were joined to the North American continent.

Angiosperms that developed in the Southern Hemisphere did so in a different fashion and spread along different routes – across Antarctica to Chile, across Australia to New Zealand and across the vast land mass that, early in the Tertiary era (about 65 million years ago), had split up to form Africa and South America. However, the wild rose remained exclusively on the north side of the tropical heat barrier, and none grew wild south of the equator, though many, of course, are now cultivated in Australia, New Zealand, Africa and in South America.

We may conclude, therefore, that the rose is, in many respects, a primitive plant and of indeterminate origin, even though its future may be secure.

F

'Floribunda' roses

'Floribunda' roses – the cluster-flowered roses, as they are now officially called – evolved in the present century from the smaller and less significant cluster-flowered, almost scentless POLYANTHA hybrids that failed to fulfil the hopes of rosarians, particularly in respect of fragrance and freedom from MILDEW.

A Levavasseur rose of 1903, 'Madame Norbert Levavasseur' ('Crimson Rambler' x 'Gloire des Polyanthas'), was the ancestor of many of the modern floribundas. One of her progeny, from an unknown pollen parent, led to the vivid crimson, white-centred 'Orleans Rose' – an influential rose – the descendants of which, each of them important in the history of the floribundas, occur in two main groups.

One branch of the Orleans Rose's descendants turned up in Denmark where Svend POULSEN of the Planteskole nursery at Kvistgaard had decided to raise roses that could withstand Denmark's hard winters, and yet also produce a really good show of flowers within the short Scandinavian flowering season. His first move was to cross 'Madame Norbert Levavasseur' (alias 'Red Baby Rambler') with the mid-red LARGE-FLOWERED rose, 'Richmond'. This produced 'Rödhätte' ('Red Riding Hood'), in which the HYBRID TEA influence was clearly shown in the flower structure. This rose is no longer in cultivation, but Poulsen was sufficiently encouraged by its performance to make fresh crosses, using the 'Orleans Rose'. From this, he was able to raise two winners: the mid-pink 'Else Poulsen' and the mid-red 'Kirsten Poulsen', both of which were introduced in 1924. Their success drew worldwide attention to the possibilities of developing cluster-flowered roses with larger blooms.

The other main branch in the family tree led from the 'Orleans Rose' to a variety no longer with us, 'Edith Cavell', and to 'Iceberg' (1947), probably the first of the cluster-flowered roses to bear scented blooms of a modern high-peaked scrolled structure. Finally came 'Evelyn Fison' (alias 'Irish Wonder'), an outstanding garden floribunda with bright red flowers, which was awarded the UK NATIONAL ROSE SOCIETY's Gold Medal in 1963.

'Baby Château', mated with *R. multibracteata*, produced the magnificent 'Floradora' (Tantau, 1944), the parent of 'Queen Elizabeth' named in the US as the first GRANDI-FLORA. Crossed with the large-flowered 'Golden Rapture', 'Eva' produced (1940) the famous 'Pinocchio', a rose that was unusual in having a cluster-flower structure although it had sprung from two large-flowered roses.

A 'Pinocchio' cross with 'First Love' produced 'Pink Parfait', a grandiflora, and a 'Pinocchio' seedling crossed with 'Goldilocks' (which had a strain of copper in it that came from the Austrian brier) resulted in 'Masquerade', the flowers of which range, while blooming, between pink, orange and crimson.

'Masquerade', crossed with Meilland's large-flowered rose 'Sultane', produced the orange-red floribunda 'First Choice'. So developments in this sector have been very active.

The term *floribunda* did not come into use until 1930 when Dr J. H. Nicolas, hybridizer and manager of the rose division of the US firm, JACKSON & PERKINS, suggested it as a promotional (if unbotanical) description for the new roses. It was some years before the term received official approbation among botanically minded communities elsewhere.

Having now surveyed the mainstream of developments of the earlier floribundas, we may, perhaps, stop to look at some of the more outstanding varieties that have come to the fore in recent years.

Many have overcome the defect of comparative scentlessness that had held back the polyanthas. In 1963 MCGREDY & Son's floribunda, 'Elizabeth of Glamis', won the Clay Challenge Cup awarded by the National Rose Society to the raiser of the best new scented rose in one year. Other well-scented cluster-flowered roses are: 'Arthur Bell' (McGredy, 1965), mid-yellow; 'Fragrant Delight' (Wisbech, 1978), apricot; 'Lilac Charm' (LeGrice, 1962), mauve; 'Scented Air' (Dickson, 1965), pink; and 'Yvonne Rabier', an exceptional white polyantha by Turbat (1910), which was one of several so-called polyanthas derived in fact from *R. wichuraiana*.

When choosing a floribunda, rosarians do well to pay a visit to the nursery from which they plan to order it. This is because the combined effects of genealogy, variations in habit, in the structure of the clusters and in the flowers carried on them cannot easily be conveyed in cold print. There is, however, less difficulty in describing the colour of the bloom, and in grouping the varieties together accordingly, which is the system used here.

*'Allgold' (LeGrice, 1956) is one of the best of the yellows, bushy, compact and non-fading; it attains a height of about 2 feet (0.60 m). The scent is slight but the flowering period prolonged. This rose was awarded the Gold Medal of the Royal National Rose Society in 1965.

*'Korresia' (sometimes known as 'Friesia' or 'Sunsprite'), a Kordes introduction of 1973, has bright yellow flowers that are larger than those of 'Allgold'; well-scented, too.

*'Chinatown' (Poulsen, 1963) and 'Mountbatten' (Harkness, 1982) are fine yellow, cluster-flowered roses, large enough to be classed as shrubs. 'Chinatown' has large double, clear yellow flowers. The flowers of 'Mountbatten' have been compared to the paler tones of mimosa.

*'Amber Queen' (Harkness, 1984), 'Anne Harkness' (Harkness, 1980) and 'Apricot Nectar' (Boerner, 1965) are in the apricot range. 'Amber Queen' and 'Apricot Nectar' grow up to 3 feet (0.90 m), but 'Anne Harkness' reaches 4 feet (1.2 m) and is vigorous enough to make a low internal hedge.

*'Southampton' (Harkness, 1972), with apricot flowers, is another hedging possibility, though it looks excellent in the ordinary rosebed.

*'Arthur Bell' and 'Glenfiddich' are also appropriately, since they commemorate famous brands of Scotch whisky, in the apricot-amber range, with 'Arthur Bell' the brighter of the two. (See SPONSORED ROSES.)

*In the pink sector, 'English Miss' (Cant, 1978) has light-pink and rose flowers and good scent; 'Dainty Maid' (LeGrice, 1938) shows rose-pink petals deeper on the reverse; 'Daily Sketch' (McGredy, 1960) delivers high-peaked blooms of deep pink with silvery reverse (this rose was awarded the UK National Rose Society's Gold Medal in 1960); 'Regensberg', a McGredy rose of 1979, has pink and white flowers; McGredy's 'Paddy McGredy', another gold medal winner in 1961, has carmine blooms, and it is somewhat susceptible to BLACKSPOT.

*'Sweet Repose', a National Rose Society Gold Medal winner of 1955, has cream and pink flowers, and 'Old Master' (McGredy, 1974) is 'painted' deep carmine with a white eye.

*Those who prefer salmon to rose can choose from 'City of Leeds' (McGredy, 1966), a National Rose Society Gold Medal winner in 1965; 'Memento' (Dickson, 1978), which mixes cherry and salmon tints; and 'Elizabeth of Glamis' (McGredy, 1964), which blends salmon with light orange.

*Two of the best cluster-flowered pinks are imposing enough to be classed as grandifloras. They are the already-mentioned 'Queen Elizabeth' (Lammerts, 1955), and 'Pink Parfait' (Swim, 1960), a gold medal winner in the UK. 'Queen Elizabeth' is tall enough to make a hedge; 'Pink Parfait' is an ideal bedding plant.

*Among the more modern bright reds, 'Evelyn Fison' (McGredy, 1962), National Rose Society Gold Medal, 1963, is one of the best to be found in European gardens.

Meilland's scarlet 'Sarabande' of 1957 still has admirers, and the Dickson nursery produced a 'Scarlet Queen Elizabeth' in 1963. The stately 'Rob Roy', with perfectly formed, sharp crimson flowers, was introduced by COCKER OF ABERDEEN in 1970. 'Stephen Langdon' (Sanday, 1969) follows the modern trend of larger flowers, but fewer to a cluster; it has attractive frilly petals.

*Included among the more unusual colour-mixes, we find 'Bonfire' (sometimes 'Bonfire Night', McGredy, 1971), orange-scarlet; 'Escapade' (Harkness, 1967), mauve and white; 'Angel Face' (Weeks, 1968), lavender-mauve; 'News' (LeGrice, 1968), Royal National Rose Society Gold Medal (1970), sharp reddish-purple. 'Intrigue' (Warriner, 1984) is a cluster-flowered rose with the same plummy-to-beetroot colouring as 'News', and with long cuttable stems and some scent; as yet, it is still an exclusively American rose.

*In the United States, 'Marina' (Kordes, 1974), orange-red; 'Matador' (Kordes, 1972), red with orange reverse; and 'Interama' (de Ruiter, 1970), crimson, are all in the forefront, together with 'Angel Face' and 'Sunsprite', mentioned above.

Recently, new roses described as 'bouquet-branching hybrids' have come on offer as decorative shrubs with six-to-twelve branch clusters of flowers on stems 10–15 inches (25–38 cm) long so that they can be used for bouquets. 'Intrigue' (Warriner, 1984), red-purple; and 'Showbiz' (Tantau, 1981), scarlet, are other cluster-flowered roses marketed in the 1980s by JACKSON & PERKINS. The name 'flora-tea' has been coined – and patented – by the same company to describe these large-flowered cluster-flowered roses.

Umbrella training-stand for weeping roses from Popular Gardening *(c. 1895).*

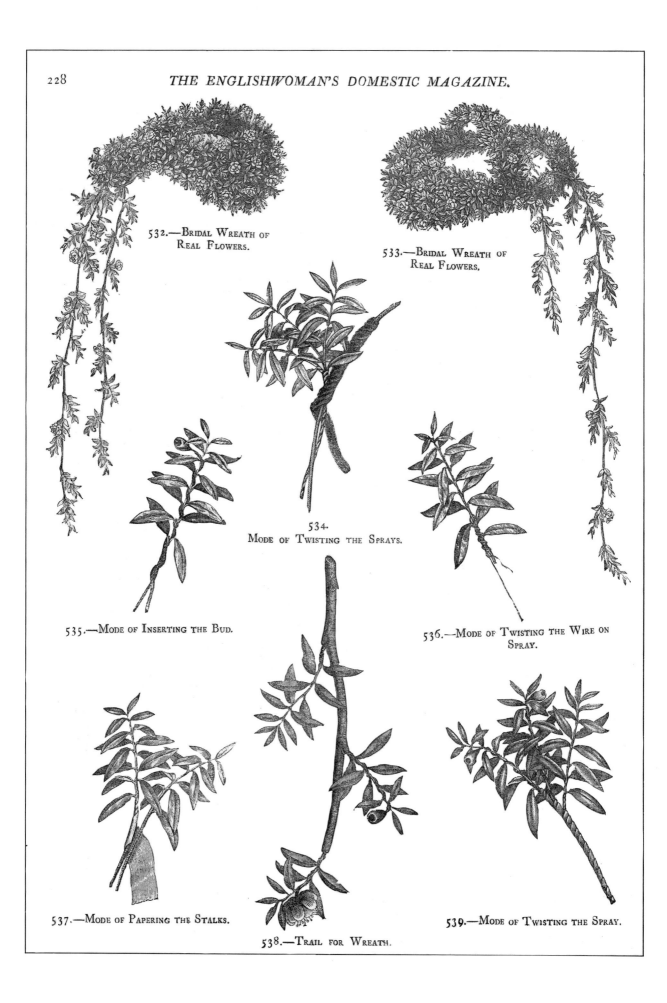

532.—Bridal Wreath of Real Flowers.

533.—Bridal Wreath of Real Flowers.

534.
Mode of Twisting the Sprays.

535.—Mode of Inserting the Bud.

536.—Mode of Twisting the Wire on Spray.

537.—Mode of Papering the Stalks.

538.—Trail for Wreath.

539.—Mode of Twisting the Spray.

Florists and the rose

Florists admit that roses are the most popular of all flowers – and yet they find them the most difficult to handle. CUT ROSES delivered to florists' shops are often claimed to have a vase-life of ten to fifteen days, but the florists' best efforts are needed if this target is to be reached.

Much depends on the condition of the blooms when they are delivered to the shop. Some varieties can be picked when the bud is still fairly tight, but others have to have at least one petal already unfurled before the stem is cut – otherwise, the flower may fail to open properly or may droop with a weak neck. Some red roses do not tolerate sudden changes of temperature, and develop a faint black edging round the tips of the petals. An investigation by the Society of American Florists has established that roses last longer and can take up more water if temperatures are in the range of 65–75°F (18–24°C) during the three weeks preceding harvesting; results have proved less satisfactory with roses harvested after a spell of temperatures in the 54–59°F (12–15°C) range. The life expectancy of the rose is also less if it has been deprived of sunlight. These matters are not, of course, the direct responsibility of florists, who will, however, rely on their suppliers to replace any deliveries that fall short of the required standards. Local suppliers obviously have the advantage over more remote growers who may have to contend with unfavourable conditions on aircraft or at loading or unloading docks.

The main responsibility of florists is to prevent airlocks subsequently occurring in the rose stems. After their arrival at the shop, the stems will be re-cut under water to avoid the risk of air rather than water rushing into the stems. To avoid damage to the tissues of the stem, the cut is made with a sharp knife rather than with scissors or secateurs. In exceptional cases, roses that appear dried out can sometimes be brought back to normal by first placing them in warm water (100°F, 38°C) and then keeping them at a temperature of 33–35°F (just above 0°–1.6°C) for six-to-twelve hours. In any case, roses not required for display will be kept in a cool dark cellar or a specially cooled cold store. Removing 'thorns' from the part of the stem that is to be in water is also said to prolong the life of roses.

Most florists add some form of preservative to the water in which roses are stored (and wish their customers would do the same). A commercially marketed preparation, Chrysal VB, is especially intended for roses, but a solution containing up to 2 per cent of glucose or sucrose can be made up that has proved effective especially if dissolved in carbonated water. The mixture should, however, also include an additive to ward off infection by bacteria, fungi and insects.

Great importance is attached to this last precaution because attacks by insects or fungi can lead not only to stem blockage but also to the development of ethylene

(C_2H_4), a gas that can drastically shorten the life of a rose. Ethylene in strong concentrations can be detected as an odour that is both sweet and acrid. It is generated by any form of vegetal decay or damage, not necessarily connected with the rose itself. Absolute cleanliness has to be maintained in storerooms and shops, and care must be taken to isolate roses from fruit and vegetables that can generate ethylene even when apparently in good condition. All containers are regularly rinsed out and disinfected.

The reception and storage of roses are, of course, only part of the florist's accomplishments. Roses also have to be displayed effectively in the shop and sold, possibly with a gift wrapping and card – or perhaps even with a suitable vase.

Roses are one of the more difficult plants handled by florists and are not easily re-arranged. There are advantages, therefore, in keeping all the roses of one variety together and not displaying them 'tutti-frutti' fashion, mixed in the same vase with other varieties or even other flowers. The use of the rose as a decorative flower – as part of a bouquet or a floral arrangement for a hotel, office, bank, exhibition hall or church – forms part of the practical training of florists and is supplemented by studies at local technical colleges. In the UK, examinations in theoretical and practical floristry are held by the City and Guilds London Institute in close cooperation with the Society of Floristry, which also supervises examinations at the more advanced level, for the Diploma of the Society of Floristry.

The Constance Spry Handbook of Floristry by Harold Piercy (Croom Helm, 1984) is worth consulting.

Flower arrangements, the rose in

Those considering flower arrangements devoted to the rose alone would do well to study Julia Clements' *The Book of Rose Arrangements* (Batsford, 1984), which also explains many of the fundamental principles of flower arranging.

The part played by the rose in more general floral arrangements is referred to briefly in the sections on SHOWING ROSES and FLORISTS AND THE ROSES. Whereas florists entering examinations or competitions will be asked to design an arrangement with a commercial application (e.g. a wedding bouquet for a 'pop star'), the theme set in an amateur flower arrangement contest is often based on a non-commercial concept such as 'East and West' or 'Persian Carpet' (both of which, as it happens, offer wide scope to the rosarian arranger).

The National Association of Flower Arrangement Societies (21a Denbigh Street, London SW1V 2HF) coordinates the activities of the 1400 flower arrangement clubs and societies in the UK affiliated to it, and is, in turn, affiliated to the Royal Horticultural Society and the National Council of State Garden Clubs of America (4401 Magnolia Avenue, St Louis, Missouri 63110). It is responsible for the flower arrangements in Westminster Abbey for the seven main festivals during the year, and members travel from many different areas of Britain to arrange the flowers there. A magazine, *The Flower Arranger*, with articles relat-

Floristry in the 19th century, from The Englishwoman's Domestic Magazine *of 1872.*

ing to flower arrangements and activities of interest, is published quarterly. Members are encouraged to take City and Guilds examinations in flower arranging, horticulture, botany and design.

Foliar feeding

Plants, including roses, can absorb added chemicals through the cuticle of their leaves as well as through their roots. Tests with electrically charged trace elements have shown that absorption into the leaves can take place in as little as fifteen seconds. Younger leaves absorb and retain more feed than elderly ones, and the undersides, where the cuticle is thinner, are more receptive than the upper surfaces of leaves.

Foliar feed can be misted on to the leaflets and will include compounds of nitrogen, phosphorus and potassium as well as trace elements such as magnesium, iron, manganese, boron, molybdenum in addition to niacinamide.

Foliar feeding is particularly effective in the case of pot-roses, which are otherwise often dependent on slow-release fertilizers. Systemic remedies against MILDEW, BLACKSPOT, APHIDS, etc. can also be absorbed by rose plants through their leaves.

Fragrance

See SCENT.

Future of the rose

Two main factors will affect the future development of the rose: labour costs and customer demand.

The work of BUDDING, on which, in the past, rose production has largely depended, is an operation requiring great skill, and it can be performed only during a short season. Consequently, there is a scarcity of budders. Large nurseries can sometimes overcome the difficulty by drafting in staff from other sectors of the business, but smaller nurseries are compelled to rely on casual part-time workers – students, housewives, etc. – at a time when farmers and fruit-growers can offer them better wages. In addition, even if the grower is successful in assembling a workforce, the weather or some other unforeseen obstacle can disrupt the budding operation, and therefore the whole of next year's breeding programme.

This situation is unlikely to change in the future and, therefore, growers have turned to methods of production that need no large workforce and can be carried out indoors, without the need to occupy expensive agricultural land or pay for the costs of planting UNDERSTOCKS, budding them and digging them out later. They are tending to grow roses under glass either from GRAFTS or CUTTINGS, and to bring them on rapidly by forcing them with warmth and artificial mist.

The use of light fibrous rockwool, glued to paper sheets, in place of soil makes it possible to move roses more easily from one part of a glasshouse to another and to pick out individual seedlings far more easily than would be possible

if the plants were growing in compost (*see* POTS AND OTHER CONTAINERS, GROWING ROSES IN). Fluid nutrient containing the requisite mix of chemicals can be trickled through the rockwool and even re-cycled, with a considerable savings in costs. It follows that, irrespective of the possibilities of MICROPROPAGATION, the day of the green-fingered plantsman may be vanishing, to be replaced by that of the bio-chemist.

Fortunately for the growers, the limitations of space in the glasshouse that make it more profitable for them to concentrate on smaller roses have coincided with some radical changes in the demands of consumers – the second determining factor of the future of the rose.

Customers, like the growers, have encountered labour problems. Few can afford a garden larger than they can manage by themselves. Smaller plots are demanded, particularly by richer clients with weekend 'cottages' in the country and with money to spend on roses, but who do not wish the flowerbed to pre-empt the leisure time they could devote to alternative hobbies such as golf, tennis or sailing. The smaller garden calls for smaller roses, and this preference is reinforced by the tempo of life today. A sense of urgency now leads amateurs to reject the idea of buying a bare-root rose and waiting six months for it to flower. They would rather obtain a rose in a container at a garden centre at any time of the year and plant it at once.

This trend, like the move towards smaller gardens, makes for smaller roses that garden centres have space to store. Given modern slow-release fertilizers and hydrogel moisturizers, roses can be stored in containers for as long as six weeks and even restored, if unsold, to give a second flowering season. Thus both the grower and the customer are turning towards smaller roses for equally good reasons. These need not be MINIATURES, which, to some people, are too small to possess the differentiation of character to be seen in larger roses. But they would be smaller than the ordinary BUSH ROSE, and thus suitable for flat-dwellers who may have no more than a terrace or even a balcony as their garden. In these circumstances, few breeders are likely to search for new varieties of CLIMBERS that require so much glasshouse and housewall space.

Predicting fashions in roses is a gambler's throw, but with leisure time becoming more and more precious, it can be assumed that the most popular varieties will be those that need the least attention, that will be healthy but not too exuberant. There is also room for a really efficient ground-cover rose, provided it is floriferous and knows its place.

Roses with a prolonged flowering season are essential for those who have time only at weekends to admire them, and for this reason the present enthusiasm for 'old' roses, which need plenty of space and are by no means all REMONTANT, may not last indefinitely. Out-of-doors, there is a growing market for AMENITY ROSES, which the French call 'landscape roses', for planting *en masse* by city councils. As for flat-dwellers, the rose of the future is the one that flowers well indoors without the need for artificial lighting.

1	Perennial dwarf Sun flower.	8 Pansies, or Hearts-ease.	17 Fraxinella.	26 White Jasmine.
	Ultamarine & Prusian blew	9 Maidens blush Rose.	18 Moss province Rose.	27 Scarlet Geranium.
	Iris Major.	10 Yellow Jasmine.	19 Double Verginian Silk-grass.	28 Yellow Martagon.
3	Blew Nigella,	11 Blew Corn flower.	20 White Rose.	29 Red Martagon.
	or Fennel flower.	12 Blush Belgick Rose.	21 Dutch Hundred Leav'd Rose.	30 Teucrium or Germander.
4	Moon Trefoile.	13 The Francford Rose.	22 White Batchelors Button.	31 Mountain dwarf Pink.
5	Upright Sweet William.	14 Double Martagon.	23 Rosa Mundi.	32 Yellow Corn Mary-gold.
6	Saxifrage.	15 Orchis or Bee flower.	24 Mountain Lychnis.	33 Purple Sweet Pea.
7	Cinque foile.	16 Scarlet Colutea.	25 Dwarf Iris Strip'd.	34 Greek Valerian.

JUNE

Flower-arranging in the 18th century: 'June' from Robert Furber's
Twelve Months of Flowers *(1730) illustrated with engravings by H. Fletcher*
from paintings by Pieter Casteels (1684–1749).

Left: Rosa gallica officinalis, *from Mary Lawrance's* A Collection of Roses from Nature, *the first illustrated monograph to be devoted entirely to roses.*

Below: *'Rose and Coronet' wallpaper designed for the Houses of Parliament in the 19th century by Augustus Pugin.*

Gallica roses

LINNAEUS named this red rose 'gallica' because, having found the first reference to it in Roman (and not in Greek) sources, he assumed that it had originated in Roman Gaul. But *Rosa gallica*, the 'French rose', is to be found wild in Italy, Switzerland and Austria, as well as in France, and was stated by the 19th-century nurseryman Thomas Rivers to be the only WILD ROSE to be found in the Papal States. *R. gallica* was also known to the Greeks, and before them to the Median fire-worshippers of Persia in the 12th century BC.

It is a true species, and the ultimate parent of some of our most beautiful hybrids, both wild and cultivated. The wild *R. gallica* has stiff, upright flowering shoots, few prickles, upstanding green leaflets and rosé-wine-coloured single flowers, held aloft and carried alone rather than in clusters. 'Pink' as an adjective was not in use until the 18th century, which accounts for the gallica rose usually being described as red; today we know it as a mid-pink.

Its legendary medicinal properties and its pleasing scent when dried commended it to the Roman military doctors who took it with them on campaigns and planted or sowed it whenever possible in their fortified camps. Its fertility, copious seed production, ability to spread by underground SUCKERS and tolerance of extremes of heat and cold and of different types of habitat and soil enabled it to survive in the military outposts as well as in the thousands of monasteries in which the relicts of former civilizations were preserved through the early Middle Ages.

CHROMOSOME analysis has led to the conclusion that *R. gallica* influence can be traced in both summer- and autumn-flowering DAMASKS, and in ROSA CENTIFOLIA and thus, indirectly, in the PORTLANDS, the BOURBONS, the HYBRID PERPETUALS and thence to the HYBRID TEAS, the LARGE-FLOWERED ROSES as they are now called. One of the earliest crosses led to the 'Frankfurt Rose', sometimes known as *R. turbinata* because of its top-shaped hips. It is probably *R. gallica* x *R. cinnamomea*.

In the Middle Ages, a highly scented semi-double variety of the species was adopted by apothecaries as their favoured rose and thus acquired the title of *R. gallica officinalis*. It has been cultivated for some seven centuries at PROVINS near Paris. 'Rosa mundi' (*R. gallica versicolor*) is a bizarrely red-and-white striped SPORT of *R. gallica officinalis*, and is different in almost every respect from the pallid 'York and Lancaster' damask rose. It was described as far back as 1583 by Clusius (Charles de l'Ecluse), and was drawn by the French artist Nicolas Robert in 1640.

Some other specially fine garden varieties are classed as gallicas. Many of them, though introduced in the first half of the 19th century and before the arrival of the hybrid teas, are still on sale. 'Assemblage des Beautés' produces flowers of a sharp crimson, with reflexed petals exposing a green BUTTON-EYE in the centre. The fragrant blooms of 'Belle de Crécy' are pink as they open, turning violet and then a soft grey. 'Camaieux' (1830) is equally fragrant and colourful, the pink flowers striped with light crimson in the opening stage and fading to violet grey on white. The semi-double petals are loosely arranged, the canes are arched as in the damasks, and the leaflets are an attractive greyish-green.

No prelate's robe could surpass the rich velvety purple of the blooms of 'Cardinal de Richelieu' (1840), one of the most celebrated of the gallicas. The variety 'Tuscany' is the modern equivalent of the old dark red velvet gallica rose. 'Charles de Mills' (early 1800s) and 'Cramoisi Picoté' (1834; the name means 'crimson speckled') are both very full gallicas, with forty or more petals to the bloom, and both are deep crimson marked with purple.

'La Belle Sultane', sometimes called 'Violacea', 'Gallica Maheca' or even 'Cumberland', is a spectacular, almost single-flowered gallica with flowers of almost black violet-crimson with a white halo around the golden stamens; it was known earlier than 1824. The 'Duc de Guiche' also has blooms of rich violet crimson, but they are double; the date of its introduction is unknown.

Another of the gallicas, the 'Duchesse d'Angoulême' (pre-1827), has been called the 'wax rose' by virtue of its delicate pink flowers with translucent petals; they are produced early in summer. The 'Gloire de France' (1819) has been much praised for its tightly packed, mauvish-pink blooms that hold their colour in the centre while fading to paler shades at the edges. The rose 'Président de Sèze', which first attracted notice in 1836, shows even sharper contrasts than 'Gloire de France'. Its flowers are very full and quartered, opening crimson purple in the centres and shading to the palest lilac at the edges.

No firm date is given for the first appearance of 'Jenny Duval', though the *Combined Rose List* (1985; *see* BOOKS FOR ROSARIANS) suggests the year 1821 with a cautionary question mark. The colour of this rose is equally uncertain – varying with the weather. On cool days, it can open a plain grey, on hot days a sharp magenta. In full flower, it can show a spectrum ranging from cerise to violet, mauve and grey.

The gallicas are by no means all pre-1867 varieties. 'Marcel Bourgouin', with loosely disposed petals of darkest velvet crimson sometimes mottled with purple, first appeared in 1899. The 'Rose des Maures' was surely an 'old' rose, but remained in obscurity until 1947 when it was discovered (or rediscovered. and possibly renamed too) at Sissinghurst in Kent. It is deep crimson, semi-double and slightly scented.

Finally, there is the case of 'Scharlachglut' ('Scarlet Fire', 1952), a direct hybrid cross by WILHELM KORDES between *R. gallica* and the large-flowered variety 'Poinsettia', a medium-red rose introduced in the US in 1938. It is a fine example of the unexpected that can happen in rose breeding. The result is an imposing shrub some 5 feet (1.5 m) tall, spreading to 7 feet (2.1 m), and fully deserving of a solus position in the rose garden. The flowers are single but large – up to 5 inches (13 cm) – with petals that blaze with intense, vivid scarlet-crimson colour, and also have a tinge of the magic gallica velvet; these are followed in late summer by decorative hips. The flowers are carried all along the arching, rambler-type canes.

The late appearance of this rose – less than fifty years ago – would not of itself be a sufficient reason for treating it as a modern rose if its appearance had not warranted this. But its 'wild' look and its rambling habit set it apart, however direct its lineal relationship may be with *R. gallica*, and accordingly it is now properly regarded as one of the modern shrub roses – though unfortunately not a REMONTANT one.

The useful thick-set shrub *R. macrantha* with heavy pink flowers is believed to be a natural hybrid of *R. gallica*.

Other gallica varieties still obtainable include:

* *'Agatha'* (pre-1815), deep pink.
* *'Alain Blanchard'* (1839), red.
* *'Anaïs Ségalas'* (1837), crimson.
* *'Antonia d'Ormois'* (no date), light pink.
* *'D'Aguesseau'* (1837), deep pink.
* *'Duchesse de Buccleugh'* (no date), deep pink.
* *'Duchesse de Montebello'* (no date), pale pink.
* *'Georges Vibert'* (1853), striped pink and crimson.
* *'Henri Foucquier'* (no date), pink.
* *'La Plus Belle des Ponctuées'* (no date), spotted pink.
* *'Nanette'* (no date), crimson purple.
* *'La Rubanée'* ('Perle des Panachées') (1845), white, pink markings.

* *'Petite Orléannaise'* (no date), pink.
* *'Pompon Panachée'* (no date), ivory striped pink.

Garden roses for cutting

These, of course, are distinct from the CUT ROSES grown intensively under glass for the florist trade.

Among the garden types are two tall, back-of-the-bed star performers: 'Alexander' (Harkness, 1972) with large blooms of luminous vermilion, and the cluster-flowered GRANDIFLORA 'Queen Elizabeth' (Lammerts, 1955), which has blooms of the pink colour often to be seen on painted china. Other pinks include: 'Congratulations' (Kordes, 1978), almost thornless; 'Blessings' (Gregory, 1968); 'Paul Shirville' (Harkness, 1983); and 'Dearest' (Dickson, 1960).

In the yellow-apricot-orange-copper range are: 'Anne Harkness' (Harkness, 1980); 'Grandpa Dickson' (Dickson, 1966); 'Remember Me' (Cocker, 1984); 'Doris Tysterman' (Wisbech, 1975); 'Just Joey' (Cant, 1973); and 'Whisky Mac' (Tantau, 1967).

The whites and near-whites include: 'Pascali' (Lens, 1963), usually thornless; 'Polar Star' (Tantau, 1982), ROSE OF THE YEAR 1985; 'Margaret Merill' (Harkness, 1978); and 'Peaudouce' (Dickson, 1985).

For 'reds', 'National Trust' (McGredy, 1970) is recommended as a durable though almost scentless rose, which is also the drawback to two otherwise commendable McGredy roses: 'Evelyn Fison' (1962) and 'City of Belfast' (1968).

In the US, JACKSON & PERKINS have registered the tradename 'flora-tea' for roses that can be used for cutting as well as landscaping, and have launched new and exciting, if more conventional, varieties in most seasons. One of the most unusual is 'Intrigue' with blooms of a plum colour akin to that of 'News', and which has fewer stems of 12–18 inches (0.30–0.45 m). The fragrance is described as 'lemony, old rose'. This is a 1984 ALL-AMERICA ROSE SELECTIONS winner, which means that it has come through the AARS trials with special credit.

Gesellschaft Schweizerischer Rosenfreunde

The Gesellschaft Schweizerischer Rosenfreunde – the Swiss Society of Friends of Roses – was founded in Zurich on 23 May 1959, largely through the efforts of Dietrich Woessner, instructor at the School of Agriculture of the Canton of Schaffhausen. It now has a membership of more than 3000. In celebration of its 25th birthday, it published, in 1985, *Rosen in der Schweiz* (Roses in Switzerland), an elegant and lavishly illustrated survey appropriate to its title. Although the text is mainly German, with the rest in Italian, the illustrations speak for themselves, and the coloured reproductions of the coats of arms, designed for more than a hundred Swiss villages to honour the rose, are memorable.

In particular, one article by Dietrich Woessner himself, on the results of twelve-year trials of roses grown at high altitudes of between 3975 and 6240 feet (1210–1900 m) above sea-level, deserves international attention. These trials, which have been carried out continuously at the village of Braunwald in the Glarner Alps, southeast of Zurich and northeast of the St Gothard pass, have led to some unorthodox – perhaps disturbing – conclusions.

One of these is that many of the new varieties that are supposed to be tough and more resistant than the older ones are not. Another surprise is that roses that fail in the trials are successfully replaced in the same soil by other roses. The absence of rose sickness in the soil is ascribed to the large amounts of sediment deposited by the melting snow and to the rinsing action of the water itself. In practice, a pH value of 7 to 7.5 has been found to give the best results.

Experiments have shown that the following precautions are the most effective: Before the onset of winter – at the end of September or the beginning of October – all bush roses are cut down, irrespective of the number of eyes, to 6 inches (15 cm) above ground level. Remontant shrub roses are shortened to 24 inches (60 cm); summer-flowering shrub roses are untrimmed.

A list of the roses that can be successfully grown at altitudes of up to 5250 feet (1600 m) is also given. Above this level, the short flowering season – three weeks – is thought not to justify the outlay.

Rosen in der Schweiz is distributed by Rapperswiler Buechlade, Verkehrsbüro, 8640 Rapperswil, Switzerland.

Gibberellic acid

Gibberellic acid (GA3) – so called because it was first isolated from the fungus *Gibberella fujikuroi* – is known to plant breeders for its effectiveness in overcoming dormancy in buds and in increasing the stem length of plants. It has been used with success by E. F. Allen, Honorary Scientific Adviser to the ROYAL NATIONAL ROSE SOCIETY, to increase the numbers of HIPS formed, and the SEEDS yielded per hip. The flowers were treated ten days after pollination with a solution of gibberellic acid in alcohol, and it is believed that this served to prolong the life of the flowers and enabled more pollen tubes to reach the ovules before the styles were shed. The operation needs careful timing, however, since premature application will cause hips to be formed before fertilization can take place.

See also SEEDS, PROPAGATION OF ROSES BY.

Golden Rose, the

The papal Golden Rose is an ornament wrought in pure gold awarded by successive popes to persons, churches or cities deserving of special commendation.

The Golden Rose is traditionally blessed by the Pope on Laetare Sunday, the 4th Sunday in Lent, also known as the 'Sunday of the Rose' *('Dies Dominica in Rosa')* and, in Britain, as 'Mothering Sunday' (from the ancient custom of paying a visit on that day to the oldest or 'mother' church in the area).

Though many types of Golden Rose have been presented, the design we see today, chosen by Pope Sixtus IV

(1471–84), consists of a stem with thorns and leaves, and flowers with jewelled petals. The tip of the stem bears an open rose with a small phial into which balsam and musk can be poured.

As early as AD 1049, a Golden Rose was present *to* Pope Leo IX by the nuns of the convent of Tulle in gratitude for their exemption from certain obligations, but the first recorded presentation *by* a pope was that made by Pope Urban II to the Count of Anjou in 1096 at a time when the Pontiff was encouraging Christian leaders to take part in the First Crusade.

Several kings of France – including Charles VII ('the Victorious') – have been so honoured, as were Henry VI and Henry VIII of England – the latter twice (in 1518 and 1524) before his quarrel with the Church. Many women have also been awarded the Golden Rose and, since 1759 when Francisco Loredan, the Doge of Venice, was honoured, the award (when made to individuals) has been reserved for women only – mainly female Catholic sovereigns. Among these have been Queen Isabella of Spain (1490), Catherine de' Medici (1548), Mary Tudor (1555) and Empress Eugénie of France (1856) whose Golden Rose was kept at Farnborough Abbey, Hampshire until it was stolen in 1974. Princess Charlotte of Nassau, the Grand Duchess of Luxembourg, received a Golden Rose in 1956.

A fuller and more detailed account of the Golden Rose and its recipients is to be found in *Orders of Knighthood, Awards and the Holy See* by Archbishop Cardinale (Van Duren Publications).

See also SYMBOL, THE ROSE AS A.

Rosa eglanteria (R. rubiginosa).

Grafting

Stem-grafting, as distinct from bud-grafting, is the method used by professional growers who wish to produce flowers of a new or rare variety in the shortest possible time. Grafts made in January can yield flowers in the following June. However, the process is one for the expert and calls for culture in heat and under rigorous controls.

Grandiflora roses

The term *grandiflora* was coined in the United States in 1954 to describe a particular type of FLORIBUNDA ROSE with modern high-peaked flowers, its exceptional vigour distinguishing it from earlier floribundas with peaked flowers.

The rose for which the AMERICAN ROSE SOCIETY created this category was 'Queen Elizabeth', the result of a cross between Lammert's LARGE-FLOWERED ROSE, 'Charlotte Armstrong', and the floribunda rose, 'Floridora'. This splendid pink-flowered variety is tall enough to make a boundary screen, though it can be leggy in the lower reaches.

At the time of writing, 'Pink Parfait' (Swim, 1960) and 'Love' (Warriner, 1980) are two other examples of grandiflora roses, though such matters are constantly under review.

Gregory's Roses

C. Gregory & Son Ltd of Stapleford, near Beeston, Nottinghamshire, is a four-generation family rose growing and breeding firm due to celebrate its 50th anniversary in 1986. It has an eight-acre exhibition rose garden placed conveniently close to the M1 motorway (open daily to visitors from July to mid-October – including Saturday and Sunday evenings).

Charles Gregory, the firm's founder, had to leave home in 1886 at the age of nine following the premature death of his father, and took a job as a gardener's boy. By the time he was married, he had set himself up as an independent nurseryman and, with the help of his son, Charles Walter, specialized in roses. Today, although more than $1\frac{1}{2}$ million roses are grown each year on the firm's 200-acre rose farm, the company avoids accepting contracts from breeders on the grounds that this might prejudice their freedom of choice.

More than 60,000 MINIATURE ROSES are produced annually from bench graftings. The firm has had notable successes with its own hybrids, as, for instance, with the pink large-flowered climber 'Pink Perpétué' which looks like an old-fashioned rose, but was launched in 1965. 'Apricot Silk', a large-flowered bush rose was introduced in the same year. The almost legendary 'Wendy Cussons' appeared in 1963.

Other members of the family include Tony (Charles Anthony); Gregory, the son of the late Charles Walter, who is responsible for the impressive catalogue and works on the sales side of the business; and his son Charles Michael, born 1960, who represents the 4th generation of Gregorys to devote itself to the rose.

Ground-cover roses

The reluctance of gardeners to undertake weeding, as well as the limits of space in the modern garden, have encouraged the demand for small ground-cover roses. Since 1983, the WORLD FEDERATION OF ROSE SOCIETIES has distinguished them as a separate branch in its CLASSIFICATION table.

Here we are not considering AMENITY ROSES, which if planted closely enough will smother weeds; nor are we thinking of roses that will serve to ornament a bank, or even RAMBLERS, the canes of which may eventually return to the ground of their own accord and, if pinned down, may be persuaded to stay there. What is looked for are roses that cling to the ground with such persistence and produce foliage of such density that there is no place there for any other form of vegetation – in short, almost a mat, or cushion, of foliage.

'Snow Carpet' is mat-forming and a 'buy' for those who are attracted to white flowers. The three POULSEN roses – 'Pink Bells', 'Red Bells' and 'White Bells' – are close-growing with clusters of unusual bell-shaped flowers. 'Grouse', a gold medal rose with pinkish creamy-white, single flowers, is also among the favourites.

Many of the roses appearing in rose catalogues under the heading 'Ground-cover roses' do not provide the kind of ground cover offered by, say, the smaller geraniums, phlox, subulata or the polygonums, so careful buyers go to rose nurseries to see for themselves what is on offer.

Guelder rose

This is a shrub of the hedgerows, woods and damp bushy places, but it is not a rose. In fact, *Viburnum opulus* belongs to the same family as the honeysuckle and the elder bush, which has led at least one botanist to surmise that it should really have been called the 'elder rose' instead of the guelder rose, a name that links it, without any special reason, to the Dutch province of Gelderland that lies to the southeast of what was once the Zuider Zee.

Guelder rose flowers are white, single and small, and are arranged in lax heads. The flowers in the centre of each head measure about $\frac{1}{4}$ inch (6 mm) across and are fertile; those on the fringe of the heads are twice or three times as large and are sterile.

A cultivated form known as the 'Snowball Tree' is often seen in gardens.

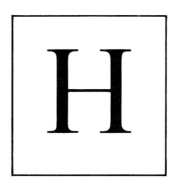

Haggard, H. Rider

Sir H(enry) Rider Haggard – best known for his romantic
novels *King Solomon's Mines* (1885), *She* (1887) and *Ayesha*
(1905) – also wrote *A Gardener's Year* (Longmans, Green &
Co., 1905), and confessed in it his love for roses:

Among these aristocrats, and dozens of others on the garden
border, are one or two of the common little Pink Roses, which I
grow here because they remind me of the hedges of them that
rambled round my garden in Pretoria five-and-twenty years ago,
and, indeed, all about that pretty Dutch town and many another
city in South Africa. Also there is an ungrafted bush of Manetti,
the common stock. How that came here I know not, but we must
work something on to it when we find time.

My way to the Stable bed is along the old wall upon which
other Roses hang, and past the Mushroom house, where years
ago, I planted a climbing 'Nephitos', now covered with its pure
white blooms. It runs over the roof also, but this spring the cold
winds and frost have caught it here and made its top unsightly.
The Stable border is, if anything, even more beautiful than that
of the Flower-garden, although it has never been re-made like the
latter. Perhaps its effect is due to the planting of standards and
half-standards at intervals among the bush Roses, thus breaking
the line; also it owes something to the large clumps of Pinks, now
a mass of flowers, that grow between them.

Among my best sorts here are 'Caroline Testout', a hybrid, tea-
scented, a very large, deep pink, single, and showing the eye,
sweet-scented also, like a wild Rose (by the way, these are lovely
on the hedges now); 'Monsieur Victor Verdier', a rather small,
bright crimson; 'Paul Neyron', hybrid perpetual with huge
crimson flowers. This rose I have found hardy and an excellent
grower. 'Annie Laxton', hybrid perpetual, a bright red, that varies
to crimson. This is a tremendous bearer, and we arch down
sprays of it, which carry a wonderful show of blooms. 'Cheshunt
Hybrid', a hybrid tea of a carmine hue, a glorious Rose, most
fruitful of flowers, but I like it best as a climber. 'Madame Van
Hout', a sweet, cream-coloured tea, and others 'too numerous to
mention'.

On the wall at the end of this bed is one of the old-fashioned
white Moss-roses which, when in bud, can hardly be surpassed
for beauty. It is now a fine specimen, but I find it a slow grower.
Also there is a copper-coloured Briar, that is lovely, but soon
passes out of bloom.

I have instanced the foregoing sorts among my Roses because I
think that anyone who has only room for a few of these delightful
flowers cannot do better than plant them. One question – why are
the Hybrid Perpetuals so named? The description 'Perpetual'
surely applies better to the Teas, which bloom for a much longer
period.

Haggard's 'Nephitos' should have been 'Niphetos', still
obtainable in the UK from Peter Beales' nursery at Attleborough, Norfolk. However, as Haggard himself wrote a
few lines earlier: 'The great curse of gardening is names,
that are as the sand of the seashore for number, and seem
to add to their multitude year by year.'

Harkness: a family of rose growers

More than a century ago, John and Robert Harkness, then
schoolboys, sold their first plants – wallflowers grown from
a fourpenny packet of seed. Their father, a tailor living in
Allendale, Northumberland, expected his sons to follow his
trade, but instead, he was persuaded in 1879 to set them up
in a nursery business in a slightly more clement area near
Bedale in what is now North Yorkshire. The young Hark-
nesses soon became renowned for their dahlias, which
brought them international honours in 1881 and 1882. In
all, they won over 700 prizes during their first five years in
business.

Five years later they were competing in London for the
Championship event of the NATIONAL ROSE SOCIETY, which
required entrants to present 72 perfect blooms in 72 distinct varieties. To everyone's astonishment, the young
Harkness boys from Yorkshire swept the board. A hand-
shake, some congratulations and a shrewd comment came
from the famous Dean HOLE, the founder of the Society:
'Well, boys, you've done it, but you'll never do it again. The
season has been all in your favour for once, and against the
rest of us.'

The Dean, of course, was right. Only once in a great
while would roses grown in North Yorkshire be in a good
enough condition to compete against south country plants
in the National Rose Shows in London. And so in 1892, we
find Messrs Harkness paying rent for a rose field at Charlton in an area southwest of Hitchin, Hertfordshire. Two

years later, their employee, William Gooch, who was waiting to take their roses to the National Rose Show at Crystal Palace on the 2 am train, was 'taken in a fit' (to use the words of the *Hertfordshire News*) and died shortly after.

It thus became clear to the Harkness brothers that they would have to give up the idea of running their rose garden at Hitchin by remote control from Yorkshire. One of them would have to go and live in the south.

Neither of the brothers was anxious to move to a strange part of the country, so they tossed a coin to decide who should go. Robert lost, and took the road south, together with his half of the nursery's dormant stock. For nearly twenty years, Robert continued in business, eventually moving his headquarters to Oakfield Farm, near Hitchin. Unfortunately, a series of devastating May frosts, and the effects of World War I, were disastrous for the nursery, as William Harkness, Robert's son, learned when he came back from the war. In addition, while William had been away, his sister Lena had married a Mr G. H. McGready (no relation to the MCGREDY family) who had bought the goodwill of the nursery and set himself up as a managing partner; when his tenancy at Oakfield Farm expired, he left, and the firm was defunct. However, William Harkness now decided, even before he had been demobilized, to resurrect his family nursery. With his savings he bought the goodwill and a list of former customers from Mr McGready. With the help of sparetime army clerks, he wrote to these clients, found a rose crop that someone else

had grown and could not sell – and was in business.

Once the war was over, he had enough capital to make a modest start but not enough to keep a wife and family while the rose plants were growing into money, so he took on the tenancy of the Raven Inn at nearby Hexton. His wife – daughter of the landlord of the Angel Vaults – saw to the premises by day, and William saw to the roses until opening time in the evening. The Raven had a large garden and William extended it by renting extra land. Within two years he was acquiring extra ground near Hitchin for his dream rose nursery, and in 1925, he was able to leave The Raven for good. In 1932, after an absence of twenty-five years, the Harkness name was once more engraved on the National Rose Championship Trophy.

That was the turning point. More land was acquired along the A505 road between Hitchin and Letchworth, and the Harkness Nursery showed its mettle by winning twenty-two National Championships, a record that has

---

Above right: *Horse-hoeing at the Harkness nursery: the leggings stop the roses scratching the horse; the string muzzle stops the horse eating the roses.*

Below right: *A Farmall tractor does the work of three horses, c. 1950.*

Below: *Cultivation of roses at the Harkness nursery: hand-hoeing the maiden roses (1928).*

remained unassailable, as the Championship is no longer held in its original form.

Even in the late 1920s, however, the Harkness rose garden was still cultivated by plough, drawn by a horse provided with a string muzzle to prevent it from eating the roses, and with cyclist's leggings to save it from scratches. During World War II, roses had to be put aside, and Bill Harkness grew potatoes, carrots, onions and Brussels sprouts. Soon after VE Day, however, the Harkness nursery took off again when Albert Norman, an amateur, brought some rose seedlings to Bill Harkness 'to see if they were any good'. Norman wanted to call the best one 'W. E. Harkness', but Bill preferred it to be named for his wife instead, and so the rose world learned to love 'Ena Harkness', the large-flowered crimson-scarlet rose that for many years was the red most frequently grown in Britain. Ten women of the Harkness family have had roses named after them, the latest (1985) being Rosemary Harkness, great-granddaughter of John Harkness and daughter of the firm's joint managing director, Peter Harkness, who annually writes one of the most interesting and informative of rose catalogues. 'Rosemary Harkness' is a large-flowered rose with blooms of a blended orange-yellow and orange-salmon.

Ena Harkness is now a director of the firm. Jack and Peter Harkness, her co-directors, are grandsons of John Harkness. Robert, joint managing director, and Philip Harkness, another director, are both sons of Jack Harkness, the author of *The Makers of Heavenly Roses* (1985) who was for many years the firm's chief hybridizer.

Successes in recent years have included: 'Margaret Merill' (1977), a cluster-flowered white rose, pinker and more upright than 'Iceberg'; 'Compassion' (1972), large-flowered apricot-pink climber; 'Amber Queen', ROSE OF THE YEAR 1984, a cluster-flowered rose with orange-apricot, wavy petals; 'Alexander' (1972), almost a shrub, deep vermilion; 'Anna Ford' (1980), RNRS Gold Medal, an orange-red cluster-flowered rose suitable for patios; and 'Mountbatten', Rose of the Year 1982, a shrub rose with double light-yellow flowers.

l'Hay-les-Roses, La Roseraie de

In 1892, when Jules Gravereaux, partner of the main founder of the Grands Magasins du Bon Marché, the French department store, bought an estate south of Paris, overlooking the River Bièvre, he found that the garden contained about a hundred different roses. From that moment he became passionately interested in roses. He sought the advice of Charles Cochet, whose firm had just launched the pale pink and lemon 'Maman Cochet', one of the most beautiful of all TEA ROSES. By 1900, when the first list of Gravereaux's collection appeared, it contained thirty times as many varieties as it had originally. To accommodate them, he had the garden redesigned by Édouard André. The fame of his collection became such that, from 1914, the inhabitants of l'Hay (formerly Lay), were permitted to rename their village l'Hay-les-Roses.

In the early years of the century, Gravereaux provided many of the roses planted at the CHÂTEAU DE BAGATELLE, and during 1909 and 1910, he re-established at La Malmaison a collection of the 197 varieties of roses known in the lifetime of the Empress JOSEPHINE. The work at the Château was carried out with the cooperation of Jean Ajalbert (at that time, the Conservateur of the Château), with assistance from M. Vigier, then Minister of Agriculture and from Madame Philippe de Vilmorin, and with financial aid from the American banker, Edward Tuck, whose benefactions to the city were such that he was created a *citoyen de Paris* in 1932 and awarded the *Grand Croix de la Légion d'honneur*. The roses, of which few, if any, now remain, were grouped around the Château in accordance with plans prepared by Theuriet, the garden designer, and at the same time, Gravereaux planted a duplicate collection in his own rose garden.

Following his death in 1916, his family continued to maintain his collection to some extent, but in 1937 the Départment de la Seine took matters in hand and acquired the estate. The Département du Val de Marne to which the estate devolved in 1968 has continued the good work, and the garden, now in splendid condition, is in the care of the Direction des Parcs, Jardins et Éspaces Vertes de la Ville de Paris.

Today, within an area of about 5 acres (2 hectares), the visitor will find La Roseraie de Madame, a sector for CUT-ROSE varieties, beds illustrating the HISTORY of the garden rose, a collection of notable hybrids, and one of GALLICA ROSES, the roses of La Malmaison, roses of the Middle and Far East, a decorative rose garden surrounding a 'mirror pool', new hybrids from French breeders, and a similar collection from foreign hybridizers, a collection of WILD ROSES, and one of TEA ROSES, another of *R. rugosa* and *R. pimpinellifolia* varieties, and a 'theatre of the rose' – the setting for fêtes, concerts, song recitals and ballets staged in honour of the rose.

The rose museum, which contained samples of almost everything connected with the rose – for example, some of REDOUTÉ's engravings, costumes, fabrics, enamels, lace and paintings by the French artist Diaz de la Peñã (1807–76) and the more recent specialist flower painter Madeleine Lemaire (1845–1928) – is unfortunately no longer to be seen. It was broken into some years ago and the contents removed.

Some guidebooks have rightly placed this garden as being close to Sceaux, but the simplest way of reaching it from central Paris, for those without a car, is to take the fast Metro (RER) to Bourg-la-Reine, a journey of perhaps half an hour, followed by a five-minute ride in Autobus 172 or 192 to the gates of the Roseraie.

Hedges

Here a distinction has to be drawn between the impressive rose hedge that forms the external boundary of a property – an effective security measure – and those internal rose hedges that are purely ornamental and serve to divide one part of a garden from another, for the latter can take almost as many different forms as there are gardens. For token hedges, the hand-painted pink and white 'Regensberg', the red-to-orange 'Anna Ford' or the mauve-crimson 'Manou Meilland' might serve.

The boundary hedge may rise to 6 feet (1.8 m) – or more if it is unchecked – and may stretch as far in depth. Though informality is one of its charms, ramblers of the kind that decorate the hedgerows of the countryside are not wanted here, because they need the support of posts, with all the trouble and expense that this involves.

For those needing protection rather than decoration, the best hedge of all is that of *Rosa multiflora*, sometimes used in the United States as a crash barrier on motorways. With plants set 1 foot (0.30 m) apart, it is said to be 'horse high, bull strong and goat tight'. Other keep-your-distance roses are 'Cantabrigensis' (a Hugonis hybrid), *R. sericea pteracantha* and that fine modern but not REMONTANT, purple-flowered rose 'Zigeuner Knabe' (Gipsy Boy). If there are no horses, bulls or goats around, the discerning gardener turns to the HYBRID MUSKS and the rugosa hybrids. Among the former, those particularly recommended include 'Buff Beauty' with fragrant apricot-coloured blooms, and 'Penelope' with creamy pink blossoms. The hybrid rugosas can offer 'Schneelicht' with large single white flowers, which grows to a height of 6 feet (1.8 m) and, if planted at 3 feet (0.90 m) intervals, is said to be impenetrable to cats and rabbits after two or three years. The same applies to 'Blanc Double de Coubert' – another white rugosa. There are also 'Roseraie de l'Hay' (purple-flowered) and the purple variety 'Scabrosa', both of which have good hips. 'Sarah van Fleet' – another rugosa derivation – offers light pink flowers and, although this variety grows to six feet, it takes up less ground space than some of the larger rose hedge plants. All the above are 'repeaters', as are the fragrant Bourbon-derived rose 'Boule de Neige', the cream-coloured 'Nevada', and the 'Reine des Violettes' – one of the old HYBRID PERPETUALS.

Those who prefer the species briers for their less formal habit, and (in some cases) spectacular hips, must reconcile themselves to a show of flowers during the summer only. Here the sweet brier and its close relations are outstanding for fragrance.

See also AMENITY ROSES.

Heraldry, the rose in

The rose, so easy to draw and so clearly recognizable from afar, has been found especially suitable for emblazoning heraldic coats of arms. In England, it was first used by the Royal family in the reign of Edward I (1272–1307), who chose a heraldic golden rose.

Henry IV (1399–1413) used a red rose, and Edward IV (1461–83) a *rose en soleil* (a white rose framed in a circle of sunrays), a device adopted as the Yorkist rose after the victory of Mortimer's Cross, which won Edward the crown. It still forms part of the arms of the York Herald. Henry VII and Henry VIII chose what came to be known as the Tudor

rose (a white rose placed in the centre of a red rose surmounted by a crown), and Edward VI a Tudor rose impaling a pomegranate. Queen Elizabeth I favoured a Tudor rose accompanied by the motto *'Rosa sine spina'* (the rose without a thorn).

The Stuarts, on the other hand, divided the rose into two halves and added the thistle with its thorns (the latter symbolizing Scotland, of which the Stuarts were also monarchs). Queen Anne (1702–14) outraged the botanists still more by adopting as her personal badge, (the last monarch to have one) a rose and a thistle growing from the same stalk.

Since then, the form of the rose has been decreed by Royal Warrant. In heraldic terminology, the rose is 'slipped' when it is shown with a stalk, 'slipped and leaved' when there is one leaflet and 'stalked and leaved' when there are several leaflets. It is a 'barbed' when the sepals are shown projecting from behind and between the petals, and it is 'seeded' when anthers are visible.

The rose in heraldry has no 'proper' colour, and must therefore be specifically described – for example, as 'gules' (red), 'argent' (silver), 'or' (gold), 'vert' (green), etc. A bloom of *Rosa gallica* might, for instance, be described as a 'rose gules, seeded or and barbed vert'. Alternatively, since green is recognized as the proper colour for sepals, and gold for the anthers, it could equally well be described as a 'rose gules, seeded and barbed proper'.

Outside the Royal family, the rose, when added to a coat of arms, as a cadency mark (showing the status of a younger branch of a family), indicates that the wearer is 7th in line of succession to the individual whose coat of arms he is bearing. The 7th son of a 7th son is entitled to wear two roses.

Hips

These are assumed by the unwary to be the fruit of the rose, but mistakenly so, since the true fruits, known as *achenes*, each containing a single SEED, lie concealed within the hip's showy covering. 'Hep' is accepted by the *Shorter Oxford English Dictionary* as an alternative to 'hip', but the latter is clearly preferred.

Hips can be reddish-brown as in *Rosa brunonii*, red (*R. multiflora*), orange-scarlet (*R.ecae*), blackish-purple (*R. pimpinellifolia*), globose (*R. gallica*), urn-shaped (*R. canina*), ovoid (*R. chinensis*), flask-shaped (*R. moyesii*), and even hairy (*R. pomifera*).

The flesh of the hip contains substances that inhibit the seeds from developing during the winter, and germination often takes place after the flesh of the hip has been eaten and digested by some obliging animal; this releases the seeds undamaged, which are then free to sprout in a new location. Humans, too, may have helped to propagate the rose by eating rose-hip tarts and pies.

Hips from the sweet brier were used in medieval times to flavour the fermented honey-and-water concoction known as mead, and rose-hip syrup had the official seal of approval in Britain as an alternative source of vitamin C at a

(1.) THE FLOWER-BUDS AND LEAVES.
(2.) VERTICAL SECTION OF FLOWER. (3.) CARPEL. (4.) FRUIT. (5.) SEED.

The wild rose, or dog rose.

stage in World War II when the German submarine blockade cut off normal supplies of oranges and lemons.

The accepted method for preparing rose-hip syrup is to gather the hips as soon as they are ripe, wash them and weigh them. If a blender is available, they can be thrown into it and broken up there. Otherwise they must be topped and tailed, and cut in two by hand. They are then placed in a saucepan with just enough water to cover them, and brought to the boil and simmered until reduced to a pulp. The pulp is squeezed through a muslin bag, sieve or strainer to get rid of the achenes and other undesirables, and the simmering and squeezing process repeated. Sugar equivalent to half the weight of the original hips is then added, and the mixture is brought to the boil and held there for a few minutes. The syrup can be bottled and sealed when hot – just like jam.

Rose-hip jelly can be made by adding $\frac{1}{2}$ pint (285 ml) of water to each 1 lb (455 g) of hips. Boil until tender; then sieve. Add 1 lb of preserving sugar for each 1 lb of pulp, and boil until a small sample, removed and cooled, proves sufficiently firm.

Those more interested in the shape rather than flavour of rose-hips will plant *R. rugosa* and their hybrids for round or oval ones, and *R. moyesii* and hybrids for pear- or flagon-shaped hips. Hybrids of *R. canina* and *R. macrantha* have generously large hips, and those of *R. pendulina* and *R. sweginzowii* are, among many others, especially decorative.

History of the rose

Ancient times to the Renaissance

The story of the rose begins some 5000 years ago when the Sumerians settled in the fertile area lying between the River Tigris and the former bed of the Euphrates, in what is now Iraq. They were among the first to use the wheel, and the first to divide the circle into sixty parts – a concept still used today on analog clock-faces and compass dials. In their strange cuneiform writing, their wedge-shaped characters (produced by dipping the end of a reed-stalk obliquely into soft clay) give us what is thought to be the first written mention of the rose. It appears on tablets found by the British archaeologist, Sir Leonard Woolley, during the excavation of the royal tombs at Ur of the Chaldees, and is thought to refer to rosewater if not to the flower itself. Also, in a fine example of the jeweller's art, an ancient Sumerian modelled a golden ram caught in a thorn bush, on the fringe of which (and very much as an accessory) there blooms a golden rose.

The Sumerian civilization had passed its peak around the year 2000 BC, and for the next significant appearance of the rose, we turn to the island of Crete, which lay across the trade routes to Europe from the Nile delta and the Levant. The Minoan kings built many fine palaces, the most magnificent, completed *c.* 1700 BC, being at Knossos on the north coast of Crete. It is in the remains of a fresco at this palace, generally known as the Blue Bird Fresco, that the rose reappears. Those who first saw it believed that the artist had included a fictitious rose, because the flower had been gilded and was endowed with six petals instead of five. However, later excavations revealed that the palace had been severely damaged by the earthquake that struck Crete in about 1450 BC and, later still, had been partly burned down. By a miracle, another portion of the original fresco had survived, and on it was a rose with five petals coloured pink. It was a restorer and not the original artist who had gilded the other rose and painted in an extra unwanted petal.

From the Cretans, the cult of the rose spread northwards to the Greeks, originally more famous for their warlike qualities than for their culture. In keeping with this, we learn from Homer's *Iliad* that, when Hector was slain by Achilles during the siege of Troy in *c.* 1206 BC, the victor's shield was decorated with roses. Homer also reported that Aphrodite came by night to annoint Hector's body with rose-oil before it was embalmed. However, it was not until the days of Herodotus (*c.* 485–425 BC) that the rose as a flower received particular attention. During a journey he took towards the end of his life, Herodotus visited the fabled gardens of Midas, King of the Phrygians, who was reputed to have lost his throne and had been exiled to Macedonia in north Greece. With him, the ex-king had brought roses with sixty petals to grow in his garden. They are thought to have been either the double form of *Rosa gallica* or of the autumn damask rose.

Meanwhile, the island of Rhodes was featuring the rose on its coinage. The early coins that came into circulation around 400 BC show the sun god Helios on one side and a rose, with heavily bearded sepals, on the other, the latter being the emblem of Rode, the nymph beloved of Helios. A later coin circulating in Rhodes and worth 3½ drachmas bore the same sun god on one side and a rose with buds on the other. In each case, the rose is shown in profile – an indication that these were no mere conventional devices but executed as works of art.

Both the rose and its cultivation were examined in detail by Theophrastus (*c.* 372–286 BC), the Greek philosopher who inherited Aristotle's library and succeeded him as chief lecturer in the complex of halls and classrooms known collectively (because of their proximity to the Athenian temple of Apollo Lyceius) as the Lyceum. In the sphere of natural science, Aristotle had made a special study of the biology of the animal kingdom, and Theophrastus now turned to the world of plants and speculated on the miraculous way in which the torch of life passes from one plant to another through the medium of a small cutting.

Thus in his *Historia plantarum*, Theophrastus notes: 'The rose and the lily are also generated when the stems are cut up, and so also the dog's tooth grass . . . The rose also grows from seed . . . nevertheless since it matures slowly, they cut up the stem and propagate it this way.' In his *De causis plantarum*, full instructions are given for budding and for plastering the scion bud with a bandage of lime bark and mud mixed with clay to hold it in place, though to be precise Theophrastus is talking about trees and not roses. On roses, Theophrastus related how the citizens of Philippi, the city founded by Philip II of Macedon, father of Alexander the Great, used to collect wild roses from the Pangaeus mountains to grow in their gardens, some of them, he had heard, having as many as 100 petals. He also distinguished the single wild dog roses that he called *kynosbaton* (literally 'dog brambles') from the double flowers of the Rhodon roses.

The Romans copied the Greeks in their love for the rose. In Rome, as at Troy, victors were awarded roses as battle honours, and civilians were forbidden in wartime to deck themselves out with garlands of roses as they normally did at banquets and other celebrations in order to mask the odour of wine in their hair. Gerd Krüssmann, author of *Rosen, Rosen, Rosen* (English translation published as *Roses*), recalls the case of a money-lender, Lucius Flavius, who, during the 2nd Punic War (218–201 BC), incautiously looked out of his window in broad daylight while wearing a chaplet of roses; the Senate awarded him a prison sentence.

In the long run, however, though wars continued, the rose could not remain the monopoly of the warrior class. The Emperor Nero, who reigned from AD 54 to 68, chose rose petals as the ideal carpet for a banqueting hall, and is said to have spent enormous amounts of money to purchase the rose petals he considered necessary for a single entertainment. He was the first, but not the last, Roman to arrange for rose petals to be showered on to his guests from the ceiling of a dining hall, and he even demanded that part of the seashore near Naples be strewn with rose petals in preparation for his visit there.

Naturally there was an evergrowing demand for roses in Italy, and more and more time was spent on their cultivation. Horace, the poet and satirist (65–8 BC), complained that too many roses were being grown in Italy and not enough corn, and Martial (AD 41–100), the poet and epigramatist, said as much when a consignment of roses arrived in Rome from Egypt instead of the infinitely more useful grain.

However, other writers praised the rose and particularly those grown in the Bay of Salerno at Paestum, the site of the famous temple built by the Greeks in honour of Poseidon. For example, Virgil (70–19 BC) made a glancing reference to Paestum in the *Georgics* (IV:116), which later led to much confusion among rosarians:

> Now, did I not so near my labours end,
> Strike sail, and hastening to the harbour tend,
> My song of flower gardens might extend
> To teach the vegetable arts, to sing
> The Paestan roses, and their double spring.

(Translation by John Dryden, 1693)

The last line was at first taken to mean that the Romans already grew a REMONTANT rose that flowered twice during a season. However, no reference to such a rose can be found elsewhere among works by Virgil's contemporaries, and the modern view is that it was Paestum and not the roses that produced twice as many flowers. Possibly the growers of Paestum had found a way of getting an early crop of bloom from some of their rose plants by forcing, followed later by a second crop from roses such as *Rosa x bifera*, the autumn DAMASK ROSE that normally flowers later, or by late pruning that sacrifices summer flowers in return for autumn ones. Already in Virgil's day, because of a change in the course of the river Silarus that left the surrounding marshland undrained, Paestum was acquiring a reputation for '*mal aria*' (bad air), and in time the rose growers moved elsewhere.

The division of the Roman Empire into two halves in AD 364, one based on Rome, the other on Byzantium, signalled the end of the *Pax romana*, and imperilled all branches of learning and culture in Europe. The Roman army withdrew from Britain in AD 407 and Rome itself was nearly destroyed by Attila the Hun in 453. For various reasons, however, the cult of the rose survived the turmoil, and much of the scholarship of classical days was preserved in the Eastern Empire of Byzantium whose rulers were also in close touch with the rose culture of Persia (now IRAN).

When, in AD 711, the Moors (Arab Berbers from north Africa) drove the Visigoths from Spain, the foundations were laid for the splendours of the Muslim caliphate of Córdoba under Abd ar-Rahman III, and for the gardens filled with roses and other flowers that still delight the visitor to southern Spain. However, the rose was not forgotten under the cloudier skies of the north. King Hildebrand (reigned AD 511–58) is said by the poet Venatius Fortunatus to have laid out a rose garden for his queen Ulthrogoto in what is now the St Germain-des-Prés area of Paris, and in Aachen, in a decree issued in the closing years of the 8th century, the Emperor Charlemagne called on the cities of his dominions to plant lilies and roses (among other plants) in the civic gardens. It has been suggested that the 30-foot (9 m) 'Rose of Hildesheim', which may have lived for more than 1000 years, was planted under his orders (*see* VETERAN ROSES).

At the same time, the principles and practices followed by the Greeks and Romans in the cultivation of roses were preserved in many monasteries. The Venerable Bede, the monk of Jarrow (673–735), was among those possessing a copy of Pliny the Elder's 160-volume *Historia naturalis*, which first appeared in AD 77 and in which a full chapter is devoted to roses. In Switzerland, plans for the monastery at St Gall, built between 816 and 836, provided for rose beds to be included in the infirmary garden. In England, the foster brother of Richard Coeur de Lion, Alexander Neckham (1157–1217) who was elected abbot of the Augustine monastery of Cirencester in 1213, described roses as 'clad becomingly in ruby purple, blossoming as the glory of the garden'.

In Spain, Christian, Muslim and Jewish scholars worked together in the School of Translators founded in Toledo by Archbishop Raimondo (*fl.* 1125–49) to provide Latin versions of Arabic texts of ancient Greek works – especially Aristotle – for distribution to the universities of Europe. Theodora Gaza's translation of Theophrastus followed in 1451, though it was not published until 1483.

Apart from this, the First Crusade (1095–99), and those that followed during the next two centuries, familiarized the leaders of the West with the status of the rose in Asia and with the varieties cultivated there. The future Edward I of England, after his return in 1272 from his expedition to relieve Acre, ordered rose trees for his garden in the Tower of London, and chose a golden rose as his personal emblem (*see* HERALDRY). As Teresa McLean has noted in her work *Mediaeval Gardens*, Edward I specifically referred to the rose that we know as *Rosa gallica* in his 1306 Bill of Medicines.

During the 14th and 15th centuries, the rose received increasing attention in the fields of ART, POETRY, HERALDRY and as a SYMBOL – just one small sign among many that the otherworldly asceticism of the Middle Ages was soon to be replaced by the realization that beauty was desirable for its own sake.

The Renaissance to John Gerard's *Herball*

The circumstances of the Renaissance favoured the development of the rose in the gardens of western Europe.

The capture of Constantinople (formerly Byzantium) by the Turks in 1453 led to an exodus of scholars, bringing with them Greek and Latin texts. When studied, these disclosed that the writers of classical times, in particular Theophrastus, knew more about horticulture and rose growing than some of their successors more than 1000 years later. At the same time, contacts between the West and the newly established Ottoman empire revealed the former had much to learn from the style and methods of horticulture pursued so successfully in the gardens of Asia Minor and Persia. Many unfamiliar plants grew there, too: chief among these was, of course, the tulip, but two yellow roses (*described below*), which were unknown in England before the 17th century, came from Asia Minor by way of the Danube.

The invention of the printing press, which occurred only thirteen years before the fall of Constantinople, allowed these new plant discoveries to be publicized and, in some cases, made it possible to distinguish between varieties of roses shown in illustrations. Early printing centres were established by Johann Gutenberg at Mainz (1450), by William Caxton (on the Continent in 1474 and at Westminster in London in 1477), by Aldus Manutius in Venice (1494) and later by Christophe Plantin at Antwerp (1555) – the last named being a particularly important source of botanical illustrations of the 16th century.

Matthias de Lobel, in his *Icones* published in 1581, described ten different roses, mainly species, though some of the illustrations are hard to match with the text. For the rosarian in England, however, the most useful and readable treatise was the *Herball* of John Gerard, first published sixteen years later and then edited and republished in an enlarged and improved form by Thomas Johnson in 1633. This latter edition contains more than 1600 pages of text, describing about 2850 plants with woodcut illustrations – most of them from the collection accumulated by Christophe Plantin.

Gerard's great work is divided into three parts: the first dealing with grasses, grains, reeds, irises and bulbs; the second covering food, medicinal plants and some aromatic herbs; and the third includes shrubs, trees, heathers and mosses, and other plants that, as Gerard said in a foreword, would have appeared earlier but for 'slackeness of the Cutters or Grauers of those'.

The rose appears in the third part, or 'Booke' as Gerard called it, where there are descriptions of eighteen, most with illustrations. The esteem in which he held the rose is not in doubt:

The Plant of Roses, though it be a shrub full of prickles, yet it has been more fit and convenient to haue placed it with the most

The title page of the 3rd (1636) edition of the Herball *of John Gerard.*

Ceres

Pomona

Ecce dedi vobis omnes herbas sementantes semen, quæ sunt Gen. 1. 29.

Excideret ne tibi diuini muneris Author,
Presentem monstrat quælibet herba Deum.

THE
HERBALL
OR GENERALL
Historie of
Plantes.

Gathered by Iohn Gerarde
of London Master in
CHIRVRGERIE

Very much
Enlarged and Amended by
Thomas Iohnson
Citizen and Apothecarye
of
LONDON

THEOPHRASTVS

DIOSCORIDES

London Printed by
Adam Islip Ioice Norton
and Richard Whitakers
Anno 1636.

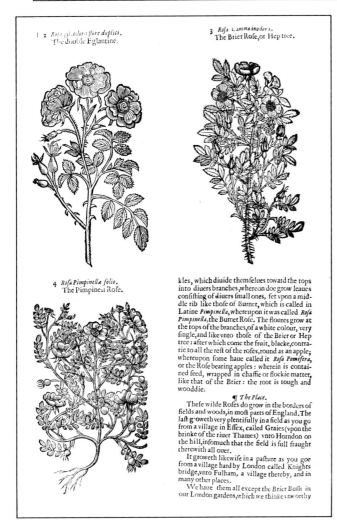

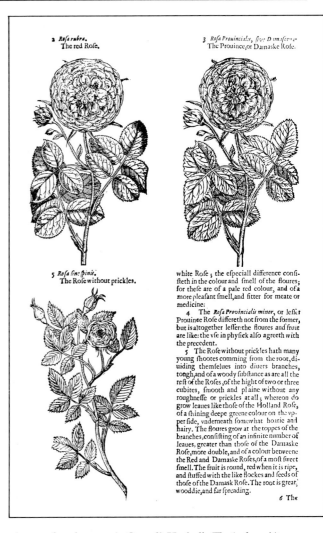

A page from Gerard's Herball *(1636), showing wild roses including* Rosa canina *(the dog rose),* R. pimpinellifolia *(the burnet rose) and a double form of* R. eglanteria *(the sweet brier), which was not shown in the original 1597 edition.*

A page of garden roses in Gerard's Herball. *The 'red rose' (top left) was the name often given to* Rosa gallica, *but there is little to distinguish its portrait from that of its next-door neighbour.*

glorious floures of the world, than to insert the same here among base and thornie shrubs; for the Rose doth deserue the chiefest and most principall place among all floures whatsoeuer, beeing not onely esteemed for his beautie, vertues, and his fragrant and odorisroue smell.

Gerard apologized for treating his roses in detail:

If the curious could so be content, one general description might serue to distinquish the whole stocke or kindred of the Roses, beeing things so well knowne: notwithstanding I thinke it not amisse to say something of them seuerally, in hope to satisfie all.

Gerard began with the ALBA ROSE, the white rose, and remarked on the fragrance of the white flowers, on 'the ouerworne green colour' (or, as we would say, the pale dull glaucous green) of the leaflets, and on the 'yellow threds or chiues' as the stamens were then called. The accompanying illustration correctly shows the prickles: large, hooked and distant from one another.

He next described *Rosa rubra,* the red rose – a double-flowered form of the rose since renamed *Rosa gallica* (*see* PROVINS, THE ROSE OF) and the illustration duly shows a rose without large prickles. Gerard remarked on the brown colour of the wood, but of the leaves, he wrote that they were of 'a worse dustie colour [than those of *R.* x *alba*]'. Was there, perhaps, a touch of mildew in Gerard's garden?

For his third rose, Gerard chose 'Rosa Provincialis sive Damascena, The Prouince, or Damaske Rose'. This, he said, resembles the white rose in size and in its prickly branches, but its flowers are of a pale red, and have a better scent (than the gallica's) 'fitter for meate or medicine'. The illustration shown could be a damask rose, though it is without the prickles that should have been there; the illustration also shows no hips. Gerard is imprecise as to the flowering time, and lumps his garden species into one short paragraph: 'These floure from the end of May to the end of August, and diuers times after, by reason the tops and

superfluous branches are cut away in the end of their flour-
ing: and then do they sometimes floure euen vntill
October, and after.' It seems likely that he may have grown
both forms of the damask rose – namely, the summer-flowering damask and the autumn-flowering damask, which
is recurrent to a limited extent.

Next, Gerard described 'Rosa sine spinis, the Rose without prickles'. With this caption, one might have expected to
see *R. pendulina* (synonym *R. alpina*) – a SPECIES ROSE that
grows wild in central and southern Europe, and is often
completely without prickles. However, we are shown what
is clearly a garden rose with flowers 'consisting of an infinite number of leaves, greater than those of the Damaske
Rose, more double, and of a colour between the Red and
Damaske Roses, of a soft sweet smell'. A double variety of
R. pendulina has since been cultivated, but its flowers are
pink or purple rather than red. The leaves of the spineless
rose are said by Gerard to be shiny and deep green above
and somewhat hoary and hairy beneath, which matches
the unarmed form of *R. canina*, but the flowers of this are
normally single and white or pink. John Parkinson, when
describing a thornless rose in his *Paradisi in sole paradisus
terrestris* (1629), said that its flowers were of a pale rose-red
colour with pale veins throughout the petals, adding that
he had heard of, but had not himself seen, a white rose of
the same kind. *R. glauca* (synonym *R. rubrifolia*) is also
almost thornless, but the leaves are unlike those described
by Gerard or Parkinson.

Gerard said that this rose came from Clusius's garden in
Vienna but the description that most nearly fits Gerard's
rose without a thorn is that of the so-called Frankfurt rose,
said by Parkinson to be almost thornless with a pale purplish bark. This rose, as Graham Thomas has pointed out,
was painted by REDOUTÉ as *R. turbinata*, and is probably a
cross between *R. cinnamomea* and *R. gallica*. Gerard's illustration shows the strongly veined leaves and the sepals
that, as Parkinson remarked, had no 'jagge' at all. Parkinson noted the great 'bud or button' under the bloom that
caused it to disintegrate frequently before it had properly
flowered. This hip is properly described as 'turbinate' or
top-shaped, though Gerard termed it 'round'. The latter
concluded by saying that the rose without prickles was
then a stranger in England – and it does not appear to have
become well known since.

He mentions one more truly garden rose – 'Rosa Hollandica, sive Bataua, the Great Holland Rose, commonly
called the great Prouince Rose'. This is today more commonly called the cabbage rose, or ROSA CENTIFOLIA.

Gerard went on to name other roses, which, though
reckoned by most writers of the day to be wild plants,
deserved, he said, to be in a separate chapter placed
between the garden roses and the brier roses, since they
have been planted in gardens with good reason. Among
these he included the single and double MUSK ROSES, which,
he noted, flowered 'in Autumne, or the fall of the leafe'.
There was also 'the great Muske Rose', said to bear single-
petalled flowers of white dashed over with a light wash of

carnation, which Gerard said flowered at the same time as
the damask, i.e. in the summer. The colouring was that of
the York and Lancaster rose (*R. damascena versicolor*), but
the flowers of this last rose are double or semi-double. The
hips in the illustration are still in the process of formation
but appear more like the oval ones of damascena than the
rounded hips of *R. gallica*.

Gerard's next plant, 'Rosa holosericea, the Velvet Rose',
was so called because of its dark red, almost black colour,
suggesting red crimson velvet. Both the colouring and the
hip shown in the illustration stongly suggest that this was a
variety of *R. gallica*.

The 1633 edition of Gerard's herbal included the two
yellow roses already mentioned: the single variety that he
called *R. lutea*, and the double rose which he named *R.
lutea multiplex*. He found *R. lutea* to have an excellent sweet
smell – more pleasant than the leaves of the sweet brier –
but later gardeners disagreed and renamed it *R. foetida*.
The double-yellow rose, which we now call *R. hemisphaerica*, did not appear in the 1597 edition of the *Herball* but
was added by Johnson, who admitted (as did many others
after him) that this rose was something of a disappointment, seldom flowering and rapidly deteriorating.
Redouté's painting called *The sulphur rose* shows it in a
much better light. (The double version of *R. foetida*, known
as *R. foetida persiana* was not introduced to Britain until
1837.)

Finally among the species roses grown in gardens, Gerard mentioned the single (only in the 1633 edition) and
double cinnamon roses. These were originally known as,
respectively, *R. cinnamomea flore simplici* and *R. cinnamomea
flore pleno*, but these names had to be dropped as they
resembled a synonym for *R. pendulina*. Now the cinnamon
roses are called *R. majalis*. Here is another rose that is
almost thornless except for the two prickles protecting each
pair of stipules. The leaves, dull green above and hairy
below, are exactly as Gerard described those on the spineless rose, but if *R. majalis* had been the rose without a
thorn, he would hardly have gone to the trouble of listing
the two roses separately.

The 17th and 18th centuries

By the start of the 17th century, only eight garden roses
were considered important. *R. alba* (the white rose); *R. gallica* (the red rose); *R. damascena* (the summer-flowering
damask); *R. damascena bifera* (the autumn-flowering
damask); *R. moschata* (the musk rose); *R. lutea* (first called
the yellow rose and, later, the Austrian brier); *R. centifolia*
(the cabbage rose); and *R. hemisphaerica* (the double yellow). There was, of course, no intentional hybridizing in
those days, and any varieties from these roses were SPORTS,
or casual hybrids, of an unpredictable character.

The four 'wild' roses that Gerard did not think belonged
in the garden were *R. eglanteria* (the sweet brier), in single
and double forms (the latter not shown in the first edition
of his book); *R. canina* ('the Brier Rose or Hep Tree'); and
'*Rosa pimpinellae folia*, the Pimpernell Rose'.

Sir Thomas Hanmer, *by Sir Godfrey Kneller. The great plantsman, whose* Garden Book *of 1659 lay undiscovered until its publication in 1933.*

A sidelight on the cultivation of the rose on the Continent in the early 17th century is cast by Emanuel Sweerts' *Florilegium*, which appeared in 1612 – that is, in the period between the 1st and 2nd editions of Gerard. It was first printed in Frankfurt and reprinted there in 1614, with five more reprints in Amsterdam between 1620 and 1655. Although Sweerts' production was, in essence, a catalogue of his own wares, the illustrations were executed in copperplate, allowing roses and other plants to be shown in much finer detail than could have been obtained with woodcuts. Sweerts showed the double cinnamon rose, the double musk rose, *R. centifolia* and *R. hemisphaerica*, and also included *R. alba*, the striped *R. gallica versicolor* and a double pink *R. damascena*.

John Parkinson's *Paradisi*, mentioned above, listed twenty-four roses – ten more than Gerard. New varieties included: the York and Lancaster rose, which Parkinson rightly associated with the damask family; *R. pomifera*, 'the Great Apple Rose'; and *R. sempervirens*, the evergreen rose, from which several fine hybrid ramblers (e.g. 'Aimée Vibert' and 'Félicité et Perpétué') have been derived. The remainder seem to be the same as those described by Gerard or else varieties closely related to them.

One garden that a member of the well-to-do of Britain was able to set up and maintain in the 17th century despite the Civil War was that of Sir Thomas Hanmer at Bettisfield, Clwyd, in north Wales. He was an expert plantsman and had travelled widely. In his *Garden Book*, dated 1659 but first published in 1933, he described twenty-one different roses. Among them was the spectacular *R. foetida bicolor*, the Austrian brier, with scarlet petals that were yellow on the reverse. Hanmer, like Gerard and Parkinson, grew several varieties of *R. gallica* – including the velvet rose, and the striped *R. gallica versicolor*. He included *R. alba maxima* (the white rose of the Jacobites), the damask rose and the York and Lancaster rose as well as *damascena bifera* (the autumn-flowering damask), *R. majalis* (*cinnamomea*) and *R. hemisphaerica*, which he found no easier to grow than others had before him.

Two landmarks in the botanical history of the following century enable us to verify the types of rose that were cultivate in England under the Hanoverians. The first of these was the appearance in 1753 of LINNAEUS's *Species plantarum*, in which he set out the first-ever classification of wild plants, using binomial names. In it, he set out twelve species of roses:

Rosa cinnamomea
Rosa eglanteria
Rosa villosa (now *R. pomifera*)
Rosa canina
Rosa spinosissima (now *R. pimpinellifolia*)
Rosa centifolia
Rosa alba
Rosa gallica
Rosa indica
Rosa sempervirens
Rosa pendulina
Rosa carolina

R. indica, one of the 'new' species on Linnaeus's list, is really the first of the CHINA ROSES, but acquired its Indian name because most of the plants coming from China passed through the East India Company's garden at Calcutta on their way to England. Indeed, this and other similar roses were popularly known as Bengal roses. But Linnaeus, whose information in this case came from the English naturalist James Petiver, noted that *R. indica* was a native of Chu San, an island southeast of Shanghai.

Linnaeus's *R. pendulina*, the pink alpine rose, is still offered by nurserymen on both sides of the Atlantic, and is treasured by gardeners for its drooping flask-shaped hips. His *R. carolina* is also still grown in the United States, the UK and Denmark. It is, however, not limited to the Carolinas, as Linnaeus implied, but ranges from New Brunswick to Florida and from west Texas to Wisconsin; it is also the state flower of Iowa.

Colefax & Fowler's chintz 'Bailey Rose',
based on a mid-19th-century English fabric that was originally made
as a block print in reds and greens.

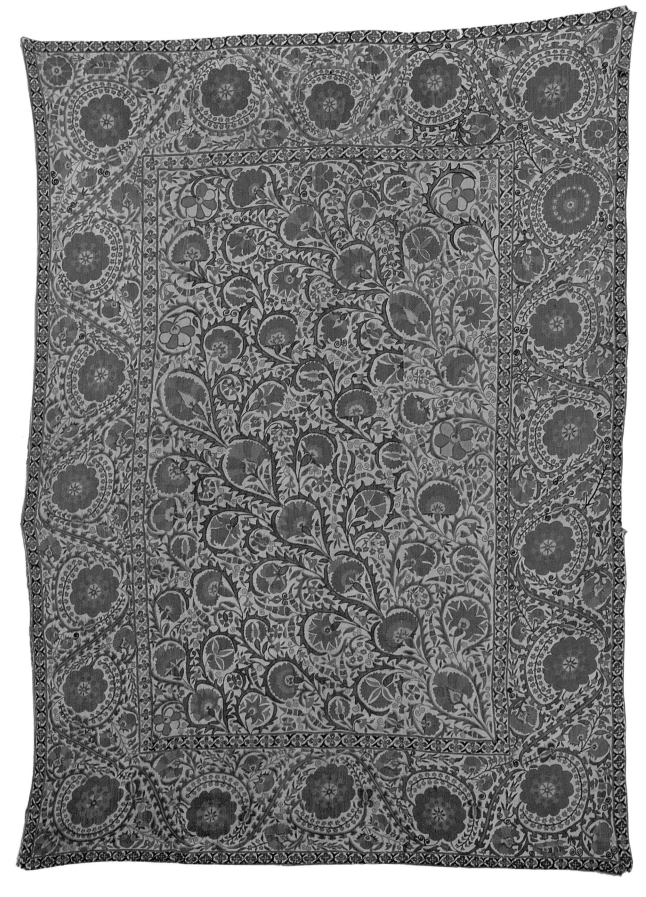

*This Russian Bokhara Suzani carpet of the 19th century
suggests a garden of roses, even though the flowers themselves
are an indefinable species* (courtesy Sotheby & Co.).

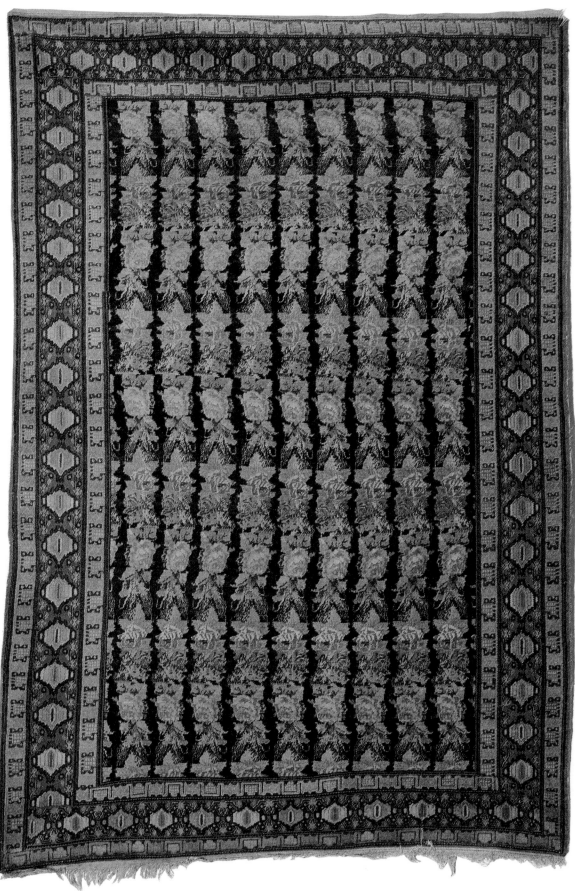

This Persian carpet with its softly blended colours
offers row after row of rose blossoms of such quality that they deserve
permanent display on a wall (courtesy Sotheby & Co.).

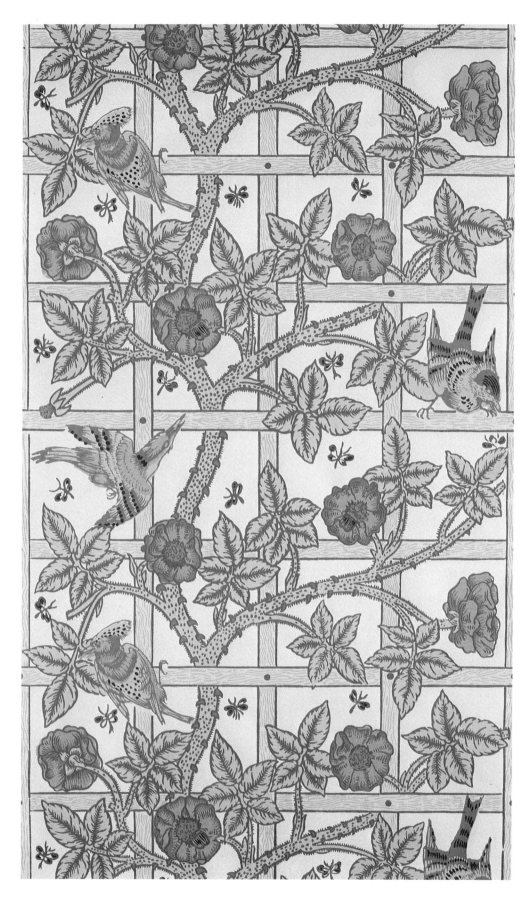

'Trellis', a block-printed wallpaper produced in 1864 by William Morris.
This was the first wallpaper designed by Morris, and is said to have been inspired
by the garden trellis at the Red House, his home in Bexley Heath.

The second botanical landmark in the story of the rose during the 18th century occurred in 1752 when the 6th edition of Philip Miller's *Gardener's Dictionary* appeared. This is the horticultural equivalent of Linnaeus's *Species plantarum* – the earliest valid list of the names of garden varieties – and in it, Miller named twenty-six roses compared with Linnaeus's original twelve.

Miller adopted the Linnaean system for his edition of 1768 and examination of it shows that he included nine of Linnaeus's species: *Rosa canina, R. spinosissima, R. villosa, R. eglanteria, R. sempervirens, R. centifolia, R. alba, R. gallica, R. cinnamomea.* In addition, he incorporated, as garden varieties, *R. muscosa* – the MOSS ROSE, reported in the UK by Robert Furber in 1724 and three years later by Miller himself – and *R. damascena* and its relatives, the 'Monthly Rose' and the 'Striped Monthly Rose' (the York and Lancaster rose). He lists *R. lutea bicolor* under its pseudonym *R. punicea,* and also *R. scandens,* which was probably a variety of *R. sempervirens.* Miller's *R. hispanica* is thought to have been a relative of *R. canina* or possibly *R. micrantha.* Apart from these, there is little advance on those described by Gerard 170 years earlier.

Lee & Kennedy's catalogue of 1744 listed forty-four varieties. One notable rose grown by them at this time was *R. centifolia pomponia,* the pompon or miniature cabbage rose, which was the forerunner of the De Meaux varieties known as 'Miniature Provence'. (These were, of course, distinct from the true miniatures that were grown from *R. chinensis minima,* imported to Britain from Mauritius around 1810.) Many of their other listings at this time were, however, modifications of varieties that were already well known.

There was at this time a feeling in some quarters that rose breeders had led themselves into a cul-de-sac. There is a touch of despair in the descriptions of roses written by Thomas Mawe, gardener to His Grace the Duke of Leeds, and John Abercrombie in their *Universal Gardener and Botanist* of 1778 which is said to describe 'every Tree, Shrub and Herbaceous Plant that merits culture either for use or ornament or curiosity in every department of gardens'. In it they took rather the same line with garden roses that Linnaeus had followed with the wild varieties:

The sorts of Roses are very numerous, and botanists find it very difficult to determine with accuracy which are species and which are varieties, as well as which are varieties of the respective species, on which account Linnaeus, and some other eminent authors, are inclined to think that there is only one real species of Rose, which is *Rosa canina* or Dog Rose of the Hedges, and that all the other sorts are accidental varieties of it; however, according to the present Linnaean arrangement, they stand divided into fourteen supposed species, each described to have some particular mark of distinction, though in several sorts this is not very conspicuous and agreeable to the specific description . . .

Within a few years, however, much of this fatalism was to be dispelled by the arrival of new and more scrutable species from the Orient.

The 19th century

The story of the garden rose during the period linking the Empress JOSEPHINE with that other imperialist, Queen Victoria, proves to be one of continuous specialization.

The infusion of the new blood of the CHINA ROSES led, in the first quarter of the century, to the NOISETTE hybrids between 'Parsons' Pink China' and *Rosa moschata;* to the BOURBON ROSES derived from a cross between 'Parsons' Pink China, and *R. damascena bifera;* and to the PORTLAND ROSES, which were derived from a cross between a China rose, probably 'Slater's Crimson China', and *R. damascena bifera,* the autumn damask.

These, however were surpassed in the second quarter of the century by the HYBRID PERPETUALS, in which the elements of all the main earlier groups – hybrid Chinas, noisettes, Portlands and Bourbons – were represented. The hybrid perpetuals held the field until around 1880, when gardeners began to realize that development of this class had become almost static, and that a new distinct type of rose – more delicate with better high-peaked, scrolled, helical blooms, and more reliable remontancy – had in the meanwhile grown up almost unnoticed, made up of hybrids containing a larger proportion of TEA ROSE in their constitution. These were the HYBRID TEAS, which finally became the class of the future in the closing years of the century.

At about the same time, a number of new and interesting WILD ROSES – such as *R. hugonis,* a SHRUB ROSE with a great profusion of cup-shaped flowers of cream yellow, and *R. wichuraiana,* the begetter of so many valuable hybrids – first made their appearance.

The efforts of hybridizers to introduce true yellows into hybrid tea roses did not bear fruit until 1900, when the first of the PERNETIANA ROSES appeared, but they deserve mention here because they led to the LARGE-FLOWERED varieties of the future with orange, apricot, flame and copper-coloured petals.

An extremely useful survey of the international scene in the world of roses was prepared by H. B. Ellwanger, the American author and horticulturist, in his work *The Rose* (1882). At that time, Ellwanger reckoned that, of the nurserymen who had raised the best roses then (1880) obtainable, 41 were French, 11 English and 6 American.

Ellwanger placed Lacharme first in order of merit, giving special praise to him for having raised 'Victor Verdier', 'Alfred Colomb', 'Coquette des Alpes' and 'Charles Lefebvre', commenting: 'He has sent out few poor or indifferent sorts than any other large grower. He raises few Teas.'

Of Guillot *fils,* he said: 'In "La France" and "Catherine Mermet", he has given us new types of wondrous beauty. "Horace Vernet", "Eugénie Verdier" and "Marie Guillot" are scarcely less fine. He furnishes about equal numbers of Teas and Hybrid Remontants.' Eugène Verdier he placed third because he had raised 'Maréchal Niel' (launched by Pradel) and some lovely dark roses: 'Prince Camille', 'Madame Victor Verdier', and 'Fisher Holmes' (all three still obtainable in 1985). Antoine Levet is placed fourth with a note that he was profuse in his production of climbing teas of the Dijon type. Joseph Ducher was placed fifth with the comment: 'Strong in Teas'. Seven of the French working nurseries mentioned by Ellwanger were centred in or around Lyon. No doubt the favourable climate, allowing a longer growing season for seedlings, may have helped to bring about the French superiority.

In the United States, James Pentland and Anthony Cook (Koch) were each in business in a small way in Baltimore, and the Revd James Sprunt was active in Kenansville, North Carolina. Feast of Baltimore was out of commission.

The first English nursery to be mentioned by Ellwanger was Paul & Son (George Paul) whose plants, he said, were not always at home abroad:

He has given us some dark kinds of wondrous beauty, but they do not thrive in our extreme climate. Perhaps some of his newer ones will be better adapted to our requirements. We miss very much in not being able to grow well 'S. Reynolds Hole', etc.

Henry Bennett, who in conjunction with the French growers of Lyon had launched the term 'hybrid tea' as a commercial venture, figured in Ellwanger's survey and his ten hybrid teas were listed, sixteen years before they were recognized as a show class. Charles Turner of Slough was praised as 'a raiser with an active conscience. Would there were more!' Other English working nurseries were scarcely touched on, but their turn came when a revolution of a different kind occurred, not so much in the type of roses grown as in the people who grew them.

In the opening days of the 19th century, the impetus for rose cultivation had come from those on high – from royalty or from wealthy landowners or inspired amateurs such as Sir Joseph Banks – and the new varieties of that time bore titles such as 'Rose du Roi', 'Souvenir de la Princesse de Lamballe' or 'Adelaide d'Orléans' (sister of King Louise-Philippe). However, as the demand for new hybrids increased, the importance and influence of the breeders mounted and new varieties were given self-advertising names such as 'Gloire de Ducher', 'Madame Laffay' and 'Mademoiselle Thérèse Levet'. Raisers also became aware of the commercial advantages to be won by bestowing on a rose a name such as 'Pâquerette' (daisy) and 'Soleil d'Or' (golden sun), which would convey its special character more vividly to the potential buyer. There was even a hint or two of sponsorship.

A new market was waiting for rose growers. It consisted of the ever-increasing population that no longer lived in the inner cities but had spread out into the suburbs and into houses with some kind of garden. At first, their attention was drawn to roses by rose shows. However, this had the disadvantage of encouraging a type of rose that looked good at the right moment in exhibitions but might not retain its good looks in the garden for days on end, or stand up to the rain or be self-cleansing when flowering was over. The link between the nurserymen and the millions of small amateur gardeners was forged by a band of talented and far-seeing writers who grasped how the rose could be popularized and transformed from a showman's treasure into something that everyone could grow. Among the most influential of these authors and their books were Thomas Rivers' *The Rose Amateur's Guide* (1837), John Cranston's *Cultural Directions for the Rose* (1857), William Paul's *The Rose Garden* (1848), the Very Revd Dean Samuel Reynolds HOLE's *A Book about Roses* (1869) and the Revd Henry D'Ombrain's *Roses for Amateurs* (1887). Shirley Hibberd's *The Rose Book* appeared in 1863 and a 2nd edition, under the title *The Amateur's Rose Book*, appeared in 1894.

A similar service for rosarians was performed in the United States, first by Robert Buist, whose *Rose Manual* appeared in 1844 followed by *Culture of the Rose* in 1854, and later by H. B. Ellwanger, whose invaluable work, *The Rose*, ran to a 2nd edition in 1892 and a 3rd in 1914. The benefits of their work have been enjoyed throughout the 20th century.

See also BOOKS FOR ROSARIANS.

Hole, The Revd S. Reynolds

There can have been few more enthusiastic rosarians than S. Reynolds Hole (1819–1904), Dean of the cathedral city of Rochester, Kent, and President of Britain's NATIONAL ROSE SOCIETY for the first twenty-eight years of its existence.

Hole was the son of a prosperous cotton merchant and, as a young man, rode to hounds and took part in archery contests – at one of which he met his future wife. He enjoyed cricket and bowls, too – roses came later.

Hole, like his friend William Thackeray, hated snobs, and poured scorn on those who considered it demeaning to work alongside their gardeners in the rosebed. His philosophy was well set out when he was asked to judge a show of roses (which had been grown under glass) staged by working men at the General Cathcart Inn in Nottingham one April. His fears that a journey to a rose show in April might prove to be an April Fool's outing were dispelled when 'the landlord met me, with a smile on his face and with a "Senator Vaisse" [a strongly scented hybrid perpetual] in his coat, which glowed amid the gloom like the red light on a midnight train.' He and the contestants got along splendidly.

Hole's work, *A Book about Roses*, first published in 1869, became a bestseller. The above quotation is taken from the 15th edition that appeared nearly thirty years later in 1896. He further popularized the rose in articles written for William Robinson's magazine *The Garden*.

Nor was he merely a rosarian on paper. In 1869, for example, he won fourteen first prizes from the sixteen collections he had shown, including the first prize awarded to an amateur at the Grand National Show of the Royal Horticultural Society. When first appointed Dean of Rochester in 1887, he visited the deanery garden and was horrified to find that there were no roses to be seen. By 1903 there were more than 130, including varieties such as 'General Jacqueminot', 'Grüss an Teplitz' and 'Caroline Testout', still grown today.

Rudyard Kipling asked Dean Hole for advice on roses and, in 1895, wrote him a specially warm latter of thanks from Vermont after a New Jersey nurseryman had presented the thirty-year-old author, then resident in the United States, with a gift of forty-five rose trees out of regard for Dean Hole.

Dean Hole's pre-eminence as a rosarian is commemorated today in the 'Dean Hole Cup', awarded each year by the Royal National Rose Society to the amateur exhibitor who becomes national champion by gaining the highest aggregate points in designated classes and shows held during the season. In addition, the 'Dean Hole Medal', the highest honour bestowed by the RNRS, is awarded for specially commendable services to the rose.

Those wishing to learn more about this remarkable rosarian can consult his own reminiscences: *Memories* (1892), *More Memories* ((1894) and *Then and Now* (1901). His letters, edited, with a memoir, by G. A. S. Dewar, were published in 1907. A more modern perspective is provided by Betty Massingham's biography *Turn on the Fountains*. The apt title was inspired by an occasion recalled by the actress, Dame Sybil Thorndike: The Dean had turned up – invited but unannounced – to look round the Duke of Rutland's gardens at Belvoir Castle. After some minutes of conversation, the gardener ventured to ask to whom he was talking. When he learned that his visitor was the Dean of Rochester, he was so deeply impressed that he cupped his hands and hollered to the under-gardener: 'Turn on the fountains, turn on the fountains!'

Hugo, Victor

Victor Hugo, an incurable romantic, often used to say that he would like to die when roses were in bloom. His death at the age of eighty-three occurred on 22 May 1885, so his hopes were realized only to a limited extent. However, he may have been consoled by the fact that several roses were named after him.

William Paul, whose work *The Rose Garden* appeared in 1848, recommended a 'Victor Hugo' as a hybrid Bourbon 'for those who cultivate for exhibition or who admire a large full flower', adding that the flowers were 'rosy lilac, shaded, very large and full; form globular. Habit, erect; growth, vigorous. A fine pillar rose, and a first-class show rose.'

However, Joseph Schwartz, one of the leading rose growers in Lyon in the 19th century, appears in the *Combined Rose List* (*see* BOOKS FOR ROSARIANS) as having introduced, thirty-six years after Paul's recommendation, a dark red HYBRID PERPETUAL also named 'Victor Hugo'. The uncharitable might be excused (but not for long) in wondering whether the last two digits of 1848 had not been transposed into 1884, the year before Hugo died. But, no, the Revd Joseph Pemberton credits Schwartz with a 'Victor Hugo' rose in that year.

Two roses were named 'Souvenir de Victor Hugo', and one further 'Victor Hugo' variety is mentioned in Jäger's *Rosenlexicon*.

A symbolic treatment of the rose by Walter Crane.

Hybrid musk roses

The roses known as 'hybrid musks', the originals of which were bred by PETER LAMBERT around 1904 from a white rose known as 'Trier', owe little to the musk rose, and show a strong resemblance to NOISETTES. Many are now classed by the Royal National Rose Society as REMONTANT SHRUB ROSES. *Rosa multiflora* was the main influence on one side of the pedigree of 'Trier', and 'Rêve d'Or', a noisette of 1869 from Ducher, on the other. The first noisettes were influenced by *R. damascena bifera*, which in turn owed its parentage in part to *R. moschata* – the musk rose – so that the latter might have had only one-sixteenth direct share in the hybrids from 'Trier', although the discerning can detect a musk scent in the best varieties.

Lambert's roses came from crosses of 'Trier' with TEA ROSES, HYBRID TEAS, CHINA ROSES or HYBRID PERPETUALS, but the results were only moderately successful, and his originals are difficult to find today. However, the Revd Joseph Pemberton, at Havering-atte-Bower (so called because Elizabeth I owned an enclosed herb garden at Pyrgo Place nearby) in Essex, took to breeding hybrid musks that were then marketed for him by J. A. Bentall (who advertised them as hybrid teas), and these are still widely grown.

Following Pemberton's death in 1926, his sister and lifelong companion, Florence, continued to run the nursery until her own death three years later. Bentall subsequently raised a number of varieties on his own account, the best of which are: 'Autumn Delight' (1933), pale buff-yellow; and 'Ballerina' (1937), pink, white centres.

American breeders have had several successes in this field, including 'Bishop Darlington', raised by Captain G. C. Thomas in 1926. Several blush-white varieties have also come from Francis B. Lester at Watsonville, California.

WILHELM KORDES added a sequel to the story of the hybrid musks, with 'Wilhelm' (1934), marketed as 'Skyrocket' in the US. This has soft crimson, slightly scented flowers, and merges well in the garden with 'older' roses. The same cannot be said of 'Will Scarlet', a brilliant SPORT from 'Wilhelm', raised by Graham Thomas in 1948. It is, however, popular on both sides of the Atlantic.

Hybrid perpetuals

The hybrid perpetual roses, which dominated Victorian rosaria from about 1840 until almost to the end of the century, represented the hectic efforts of rose breeders, particularly in France, to extend the flowering period of roses beyond the conventional few weeks of June and July.

Many experiments were tried, and some rose growers feared that the older varieties that they had grown to love would disappear for good. Shirley Hibberd, in his work *The Rose Book* (1864), wrote: 'This [hybrid perpetual] class is like Moses' serpent, it swallows up all the rest; or rather it would do so, were there not always a few resolute rosarians blessed with large and ecclectic tastes to save the others from the total eclipse that constantly threatens them. Of their pedigree, who shall tell?'

No convincing reply has been given to this last question since few records of crosses were kept in those days, but the general intention was to infuse more of the CHINA strain into BOURBONS and to some extent into the PORTLANDS, both of which already had an element of it. The two principal China hybrids chosen for this purpose were the 'Gloire des Rosomanes', a glowing scarlet Bourbon x China cross introduced by Vibert in 1825, and sometimes known as 'Ragged Robin'; and 'Malton' (alias 'Fulgens'), another bright scarlet rose. 'Athalin', a crimson Bourbon, was crossed with them and with the autumn damasks and the Portland 'Rose du Roi', and from a meld of all these elements, the hybrid perpetual group began to take shape.

The French rose breeder Jules Laffay took the lead in the development of the hybrid perpetuals, and though some of his earliest introductions such as 'Princess Hélène', 'Prince Albert' (both 1837) and 'Madame Laffay' (1839) are no longer in circulation, the 'Duchess of Sutherland' (1839) with light pink blooms is still to be found. In 1842, he launched 'La Reine', a mid-pink that is still obtainable, and the success in the same year of the amateur breeder Romain Desprez's 'Baronne Prévost' made it clear that a new type of rose had arrived.

From then on, progress was meteoric, and many varieties that had been formerly listed under other categories were reclassified as hybrid perpetuals. By the following year (1843), Adam Paul of Cheshunt, Buckinghamshire, founder of what was later to become the two firms William Paul & Son, and Paul & Son, had forty-three hybrid perpetuals on his books. Ten years later the figure had risen to 150. The numbers doubled in the following decade, and by 1884, according to Roy Shepherd, they had passed the 800 mark.

Robert Buist who had emigrated from Scotland to become a leading rose specialist in Philadelphia was equally enthusiastic. Writing about hybrid perpetuals in his book *The Rose Manual*, published in Philadelphia in 1844, he declared:

This is a new tribe, that has originated within a few years, between the Perpetual and Bourbon roses, possessing the beauty and fragrance of the former with the growth and foliage of the latter; they produce an abundance of flowers from June to November; they open a field of pleasure to the northern grower and amateur, which had hitherto been reserved only to the fanciers of more favoured climes . . . The varieties are yet limited, compared with many of the families we have described, but a few years will multiply them to a greater extent.

Buist then described nearly thirty varieties, noting, however, that the group was still deficient 'in flowers of a pale or white colour', a defect that he believed would soon be remedied.

Dean HOLE wrote equally enthusiastically of

that section, the most perfect and extensive of all . . . so far as its garden roses are concerned, viz. the hybrid perpetual, a family so numerous and so beautiful withal, that two of our most fastidious rosarians, Mr George Paul [grandson of Adam], and Mr [Thomas] Rivers [another famous rose nurseryman], ejecting from a select list every flower which has not some special excellence, gives us the names of 120 varieties as being *sans reproche*.

In addition, Jules Gravereaux is believed to have assembled 1700 varieties in his garden at L'HAY-LES-ROSES.

Such a class is not easily described, but in general, they were large plants (almost too large for the average bed) with large blooms, almost always of a single colour, ranging from white (so the defect Buist pointed out had been remedied) through clear pink and bright crimson to dark maroon. It has been conjectured that the whites have some connection with *Rosa alba*, the pinks with *R. damascena bifera*, and the dark red, at least indirectly, with the GALLICAS. Attempts to introduce a worthwhile yellow came to nothing.

Taking some of the characters of the hybrid perpetual story more or less in the order of their appearance, we have, first, 'Général Jacqueminot', a splendid, intense, dark red rose, strongly scented, a begetter of many other fine varieties. (The General owed his promotion to Napoleon and his popularity to the Munich lager that he brewed in Paris after his return from the wars: he fought at Austerlitz and Wagram, endured the retreat from Moscow and was present at Quatre Bras.) The rose was raised in 1853 by Auguste Roussel, an amateur rose grower. 'Reine des Violettes', with large double flowers with cerise tints fading quickly to violet-purple, is one of the most popular but not by any means the most typical of the hybrid perpetuals; it is, however, only moderately REMONTANT. This variety was introduced by Millet-Malet in 1860.

The following year saw the launching of 'Prince Camille de Rohan', a dark-red rose from the Verdier nursery, and 'Charles Lefebvre', another dark-red variety from the Lacharme nursery. 'Beauty of Waltham' from William Paul & Son at Waltham Cross followed in 1862; this is a medium-red still obtainable on both sides of the Atlantic. Three other roses of the 1860s are less easily come by but can still be found: 'Alfred Colomb' (Lacharme, 1865), deep pink; 'Horace Vernet' (Guillot *fils*, 1866), dark-red; and another dark-red, the 'Duke of Edinburgh', from Paul & Son, Cheshunt, 1868. The dark red 'Souvenir du Docteur Jamain' (Lacharme, 1865) and 'Baronne Adolphe de Rothschild' ('Baroness Rothschild'), a light pink rose from Pernet *père*, are far more popular today.

Although the hybrid Chinas used by the growers were self-pollinated to increase the element of remontancy before being crossed with the Bourbons and Portlands, by no means all of the resulting crosses were reliably remontant, still less perpetual, even in the first generation. One reason suggested for this was that the factor of remontancy was often linked to a gene that, according to MENDEL'S LAWS, was recessive and would therefore disappear in the first generation and reappear only in a proportion of the second.

A new infusion from the TEA ROSES, in which the strain of remontancy was differently linked, was therefore needed, and although the tea roses were known to be even more tender than the hybrid Chinas, it was found, in practice, that the hybrid perpetuals were strong enough to be crossed with the tea roses without wilting. Thus a rose could be developed that was both hardy and long-flowering – an experiment that had probably been tried, intentionally or otherwise, even before Lacharme's rose, 'Victor Verdier' (1859). However, the potential of this new approach was not fully appreciated until a quarter of a century after the acknowledged prototype of the new rose, 'La France', had been launched.

In the meantime, rosarians continued to produce new hybrid perpetuals in the same old way up to the end of the 19th century and even beyond, and many are still in cultivation:

'Paul Neyron' (Levet, 1869), which out-cabbages the centifolias with its tightly packed, rose-pink petals in blooms up to 6 inches (15 cm) across.

'Mrs John Laing' (Bennett, 1887) was declared by Dean Hole to be 'not only in vigour, constancy and abundance, but in form and feature, Beauty's Queen'. It has mid-pink, fragrant flowers.

'Baron Girod de l'Ain' (Reverchon, 1897) is an exceptional hybrid perpetual in having crimson wavy petals edged with white. Like many other hybrid perpetuals, it is large enough to make a good shrub.

'Georg Arends' (Hinner, 1910), a true pink, has scrolled buds nearer to the modern image and, from its parentage – 'Frau Karl Druschki' x 'La France' – could well be regarded as modern, though it appears as a hybrid perpetual in catalogues.

'Ruhm von Steinfurth' (Weigand, 1920), which many prefer to call by the more compendious name of 'Red Druschki', is the offspring of a cross between 'Frau Karl Druschki' and a vigorous red-flowered climbing hybrid tea, 'General MacArthur', and should therefore look 'modern'. However, it wears the traditional features of the hybrid perpetual and is also included in that sector.

'Ferdinand Pichard' (Tanne, 1921) is at one with 'Baron Girod de l'Ain' in having unusual colouring: double crimson flowers with paler pink or white striping. It is understandably popular on both sides of the Atlantic. It is a spreading shrub with attractive lettuce-coloured leaves, but has sometimes been treated as a rambler.

In Britain, a fine assembly of hybrid perpetual roses, including the rare variety 'Le Havre' intermingled with other classic varieties, is to be seen in Humphrey Brooke's Lime Kiln Rosarium, at Claydon, 3 miles (4.8 km) north of Ipswich. Others are on view at the Hon. Robin and Mrs Walpole's Heritage Rose Garden at Mannington Hall, near Norwich, which is conveniently near to Peter Beales' specialist 'old' rose nursery at Attleborough, Norfolk; and at Mottisfont Abbey, near Romsey in Hampshire. In the United States, 'old' roses are to be seen at Colonial Williamsburg, in Virginia, and at other public displays. They are also found in specialist nurseries such as the Heritage Rose Gardens run by two sisters, Virginia Hopper and Joyce Demits, at Fort Bragg and Branscomb, both in California, and at Patricia Stemler Wiley's Roses of Yesterday and Today nursery, at Brown's Valley, Watsonville, California.

An especially comprehensive historical survey of the hybrid perpetual class is to be found in an article by L. Arthur Wyatt in the 1981 edition of the *Rose Annual*, published by the Royal National Rose Society.

Hybrid tea roses

The use of the term 'hybrid tea' is now officially frowned on and, instead, these roses are today described as 'LARGE-FLOWERED ROSES'. However, since we are dealing here with the history of these flowers beginning in the 19th century, we may, perhaps, be excused for keeping to the style of former times.

Fundamentally, the hybrid tea rose was the outcome of efforts by the breeders to satisfy the public's thirst for novelty. This demand for new roses could not be met merely by re-hybridizing the HYBRID PERPETUALS that already existed. Almost every alternative was tried in an effort to break new ground, but because so little was known about controlled hybridization and the application of MENDEL'S LAWS, it was no easy matter to map out a logical breakaway programme. The manner in which varieties were named added to the disorder, for in those days it was customary to call each new variety after the seed parent. Thus a Portland x tea rose cross would, if it differed from the Portland, be regarded as a hybrid Portland, whereas the same cross with the seed and pollen parents reversed would be seen as a hybrid tea.

Furthermore, whereas up until 1873, the majority of breeders crossing hybrid perpetuals and teas had used teas as the seed parents, the success of the tea rose 'Safrano' as a pollen parent of 'Captain Christy' led them to prefer the tea rose as the pollen parent.

Nevertheless, despite all the confusion, rosarians had begun to realize, by the mid-1880s, that there had come into existence a certain type of rose with a special style and virtues, that the new roses were more REMONTANT than the average hybrid perpetual, and that their new blooms with their high-peaked structure were built to last and retain their scent longer.

However, it was hard to draw the line between the old and the new, and success came slowly. The description 'hybrid tea' was officially recognized in 1884 (sixteen years after Henry Bennett launched the term), and that year Dicksons of Newtownards, Co. Down, Northern Ireland, published the first catalogue listing the class as such. But when George Paul, Jr – author, breeder, nurseryman and nephew of William Paul – addressed the National Rose Conference held in London in 1889 by the Royal Horticultural Society, he reported that 'the class of hybrid teas does not seem to have made real advance.' There were several reasons for this. Apart from the difficulty of distinguishing between hybrid perpetuals and hybrid teas, there was a feeling among the more conservative nurserymen, and thus among their clients, that any new rose known as a hybrid tea would be associated with tea roses as such, and tea roses were known to require extra care in cultivation and had suffered disastrously during the exceptionally hard winter of 1860/61. Consequently it was no great hardship for growers for those of their new roses that were not clearly pure teas to remain known as hybrid perpetuals.

The famous rose, 'La France' (silver-pink and scented), which had been launched by Jean-Baptiste Guillot in 1867, was a case in point. It failed to win the top prize at the Paris World Fair in that year because the judging took place two days after the appointed date and the flower was, by then, not at its best. However, in his classic work *The Book of the Rose*, the Revd A. Foster-Melliar, one of that immortal band of Victorian ecclesiastical rosarians, wrote:

Mons. Guillot must have been inspired when he gave the name dearest to Frenchmen to the best rose 'La France' had produced . . . It is emphatically everybody's rose, the one indispensible variety for exhibitors, gardeners, cottagers and all, on all soils and stocks, standard or bush. In America it is as popular as it is here, as good an autumnal after the fierce heat of summer, and as hardy in winter against the severe frost. The same report comes from Australia, and I believe it to be equally popular wherever

roses are grown. In Cairo I am told that it 'grows like a weed', and the local rose society had thoughts of barring it in their classes for roses of one variety, as they could get nothing else shown.

Yet, although the 1st edition of this book appeared in 1894, 'La France' is described as a hybrid perpetual, and this classification remained unchanged in the 3rd edition of 1905.

Meanwhile the shock value of 'Madame Caroline Testout' had encouraged hybridizers to redouble their efforts. This was a rose that had bright pink blooms with darker centres. The raiser, Pernet-Ducher, thought little of the seedling, but Madame Testout, a Parisian dress designer, chose it to be her rose. It was introduced in her showroom in 1890 and was an instant success.

In 1893, the Selection Committee of the NATIONAL ROSE SOCIETY issued a list of ten approved varieties of hybrid tea, of which five – 'Augustine Guinoiseau' (a white version of 'La France'), 'Captain Christy', 'Kaiserin Augusta Victoria', 'La France' and 'Viscountess Folkestone' – are still in cultivation. The Committee implied that 'La France', the oldest of those mentioned in their list, was the first and original hybrid tea rose. Since then, however, there have been half-a-dozen roses, going back to 1815, for which priority or preference has been claimed. One of these is 'Smith's Yellow' (1833), wrongly regarded and named as a NOISETTE because the seed parent was a noisette. It has also been argued that 'La France' has more non-tea than tea in her and that Jean-Baptiste Guillot once said that he could not be certain of her parentage because she was a chance seedling. 'Victor Verdier' (1859), 'Cheshunt Hybrid' (1872) and 'Captain Christy' (1873) are other roses on behalf of which claims have been made. It seems doubtful, however, whether anything other than an open verdict will be returned.

It was only after 1895, when breeders began crossing hybrid teas among each other and back-crossing them with hybrid perpetuals, that hybrid teas really began to take off with greatly improved varieties. 'Grüss an Teplitz', from Rudolf Geschwind who was born in that (now) Czechoslovakian city, was one of these, although its mixed ancestry, containing elements of the BOURBONS, NOISETTES, CHINAS and tea roses, make it something of a mishmash. The blooms are dark scarlet, plentiful and fragrant.

In 1898, the National Rose Society agreed that hybrid teas could be exhibited at their shows as a separate class, and from 1900 on, the hybrid teas received a fresh impetus with the arrival of the PERNETIANA ROSES. However, all this success brought nearer the day when hybrid teas became less easily recognizable as such and could be more appropriately described as just 'large-flowered roses'.

Hybridizing roses

Hybridization is the story of the rose itself and it is hardly surprising that most rosarians at one time or another have felt like adding a chapter to the book. While it is dangerous to be dogmatic on such matters, the first intentional rose hybridization appears to have been 'Pearl of Weissenstein' – made by Herr Schwarzkopf, head gardener to Landgraf Frederick II of Hesse at Schloss Weissenstein near Kassel (now West Germany) from 1769. The practice has since shown no signs of abatement.

As well as optimism and a willingness to spend money, patience and resignation are required. For example, Dr Wilhelm KORDES, perhaps this century's most successful rose hybridizer, has reckoned that he needed to make 20,000 crosses a year for his firm to retain its leading position in the world of roses.

Ideally, breeders look for a rose with hardiness, resistance to disease and a prolonged flowering season. They hope for plentiful durable, non-fading, well-structured flowers impervious to rain, and carried on long, strong stalks. The foliage needs to be vigorous and attractive, and the scent memorable. Breeders who produce new roses possessing, say, five of these qualities in any marked degree will consider themselves in luck.

The obstacles are formidable, since, when hybridizing roses, we are not dealing with fixed elements. Almost any rose that is not a wild one has, in its makeup, the traces of so many crossings and *mésalliances* of the past that it is difficult to predict with any certainty how a new marriage will turn out. To cite one example: the LARGE-FLOWERED white rose 'Elizabeth Harkness' was derived from a cross between the cluster-flowered 'Red Dandy' and the large-flowered, scarlet and gold 'Piccadilly'.

Every crossing is fraught with insecurity. Thus, although in theory it makes no difference whether, when you cross two roses, you apply the pollen of one to the stigma of the other, or the other way round, it is unsafe to assume that in reality this is so. When Pernet-Ducher was endeavouring to introduce notes of orange and flame into the modern rose with the help of *Rosa foetida persiana*, he found that the yellow rose was infertile as a seed parent, but he was able to fertilize 'Antoine Ducher', the other parent, with pollen from *R. foetida*. No doubt prolonged hybridization of earlier days had caused the pollen of 'Antoine Ducher' to degenerate.

Hybridizers have also to allow for the laws of inheritance as originally investigated by Gregor MENDEL, and have to bear in mind which of the qualities that they wish to see in the new variety are to be linked to dominant and which to recessive genes. Thus mossing in roses (i.e. the thick covering of hairs tipped with scent glands) is thought to be a dominant characteristic, whereas REMONTANCY is recessive and will appear only in the second generation of a hybridized variety. In COLOUR, cyanidin is believed to have a dominant tendency in some varieties of rose, whereas pelargonidin is recessively linked.

There is also the difficulty of gene linkage. Some characteristics, such as a climbing habit or resistance to MILDEW, appear to be inherited primarily through a single dominant gene. On the other hand, attributes such as SCENT, the shape of the flowerbud, the presence or absence of THORNS,

the length of the stem and the strength of the neck are controlled by a number of genes working in combination, and are inherited only if all the necessary genes are present.

In addition to these uncertainties, hybridizers are faced with the possibility of mechanical breakdown of the arrangements that they have made. For instance, it is known that the genes that will control the characteristics of the future variety are arranged on the CHROMOSOMES in a definite sequence. If during MEIOSIS this sequence is disturbed either by chromosomes becoming transposed, reversed, disrupted or separated, or if crossing-over during meiosis is incomplete, then hybridizers will not achieve their objectives.

Having regard to all the accidents that can happen, and all the uncertainties involved, it might seem presumptuous for hybridizers to exercise any choice over what is to be hybridized. Yet the decisions have to be taken. If they are nurserymen, they must estimate what is likely to be the demand for the type of rose they are hoping to introduce. They must have in their mind's eye the picture of their intended variety; and they must choose as the parents two roses that are noted for their vigour and fecundity. For example, single roses are likely to be more fruitful than double ones as less of the plant's vigour has been expended on petals. If there is a choice between two parents, the one with fewer chromosomes should be selected as offering better chances of consistency. If either parent shows signs of a MUTATION of any kind, the chances of finding a really new variety are improved. In addition, it is usual to make the cross in both directions as a safety precaution.

Hybridizing techniques
Henry Bennett, the farmer-turned-rose-breeder who almost single handedly established the HYBRID TEA ROSES as a distinct class, carried out all his most important hybridizing operations under glass. However, this may be difficult for most amateur gardeners and so the following assumes that they will be working out-of-doors.

The hybridizer's equipment is of the simplest:

*a small pair of scissors for removing the stamens, tweezers for collecting the pollen, and small container in which it can be stored.
*a camel-hair brush or disposable blotting paper for applying the pollen to the stigma of the seed-parent.
*a small medicine glass containing alcohol to be used for sterilizing the brush before and after use.
*some hoods (paper or plastic bags that can be closed) of two different sizes to protect the blooms of the seed parent.

The timetable of operations has to be arranged with care, and the pollen prepared in advance of the time when the bloom of the seed parent will be ready to receive it. The pollen to be used for the crossing is contained in the pollen sacks carried in the anthers on the end of the stamens (*see* ANATOMY OF THE ROSE), and when the pollen ripens, the sacks burst open, scattering the pollen grains hither and thither.

It is therefore important to remove the stamens before this happens, thus allowing the pollen to ripen safely in a container.

The bud that is to provide the pollen can be cut from the rose bush just before it is about to open. The stamens are removed, and the anthers are allowed to ripen in a dry, warm (68°F, 20°C) place in the shade: in a day or two, the pollen sacks will burst and the pollen is then ready for use. The pollen grains can be expected to retain their potency for a week to ten days, if protected from the sun. If, however, pollen from an early-flowering rose is to be used later in the season, it should be wrapped carefully in foil and stored in a refrigerator until needed.

The preparation of the bloom of the seed parent also needs to be carefully timed. Although there is no objection to beginning operations early in the season, the most successful attempts are those made at the peak of the flowering period.

The best plan is to make a search before sun-up for those blooms that are about to open on that day, for if the sun's rays reach the stamens, this may ripen the seed parent's pollen, which will then fall on the stigmas, thus aborting the project. If a cluster-flowered variety is being used as a partner, ignore the buds in the centre of the cluster since experience has shown that they are rarely effective. Having selected the likely blooms, all the petals except the outer ring of five are removed. The stamens are also cut off, taking great care to avoid damaging the styles and stigmas of the bloom. It is important to make sure that all the stamens are removed since, if any are left, the rose could be fertilized with its own pollen instead of by the pollen from the intended variety. As soon as this has been done, hoods of the larger size should be placed over each of the selected blooms. About one day later, it will be seen that the stigmas have exuded a sticky secretion, thus creating conditions favourable to the reception of the 'foreign' pollen.

The pollen can then be applied – choosing a dry, and preferably windless, day. If a brush is used for pollination, it must be cleaned with spirit after each application to free the hairs from excess pollen and from any secretion from the stigma. All the alcohol must then be removed from the brush, for if any is left the next batch of pollen will be sterilized. For this reason, some hybridizers prefer to use disposable blotting paper as the applicator instead of a brush, especially if they consider it desirable to make several applications of pollen to ensure a good 'take'.

After the pollen has been satisfactorily applied, the remaining petals can be removed and a hood of the smaller of the two sizes placed over each flower. Fertilization will be promoted if the hood is made of water-proof material, and it should be large enough to allow air to circulate freely around the styles. The hoods may be removed after about five days.

Changes in the colour and appearance of the receptacle will soon show whether fertilization has taken place and a hip is to be formed.

Hybrid success rates

Many successful hybrids – notably 'General Jacqueminot' (1853) and, more recently, 'Frensham' and 'Ena Harkness' (both 1946) – have come from amateurs. Nevertheless the odds against a winning coup by the average rose grower are formidable.

MEILLAND, for example, has reckoned that of 80,000 seedlings grown in his nursery every year, all but 2000 will have been discarded by the end of the first three-year trial period. These 2000 will be budded in the open, and are given a further two-year trial, after which 150 to 200 will be retained and sent for trials both in France and abroad. This reduces the number of hybrids to perhaps 30, and these select few are then submitted to yet another trial, lasting for three years, by Meilland agents in some twenty-two countries.

Statistics for hybridization in the United States seem to be similar. JACKSON & PERKINS, the highly successful hybridizers of Medford, Oregon, reckon that often as many as 100,000 seedlings are grown, examined and discarded before one is found that is worthy of introduction to the public. The firm estimates that, on average, it takes eight years and costs about $100,000 to develop each new variety from the initial selection of a seedling.

Their practice is to wait until their rose seedlings have bloomed in the research greenhouse, approximately eight weeks after germination, before making a preliminary selection when 'very many' are eliminated. Many more are taken out on the second cycle, and only about 1 per cent go forward to budding in the field. During their first year outdoors, they are examined for habit, foliage, abundance of blooms and resistance to disease. At this point, workers are to be seen in the fields carrying canes 6 feet (2 m) long, which they stick into the ground to mark the position of roses showing particular promise. Those that qualify (perhaps no more than 100) are budded on a larger scale for a second year in the fields.

Those that survive this second year of trials are planted for testing in a variety of other locations. This third year continues the process of selection with still fewer varieties being budded in increasing quantities.

By the fourth year of testing, the number of seedlings will have been reduced to 'a small number', and some of the more promising will be entered for the ALL-AMERICA ROSE SELECTION trials. Four plants of each variety are sent to each of the AARS test gardens where they are judged for two years. If one of the varieties is selected for an award, plants are budded and grown to saleable size, a process that takes another two years – adding up to a total development period of at least seven years that does not include the time spent selecting and preparing the hybridization. In addition, as part of their programme, hybridizers may also be involved in rose shows, INTERNATIONAL ROSE TRIALS, advertising, the preparation of catalogues, the management of stocks and the registration of any new varieties they may wish to protect.

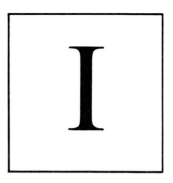

International rose trials and awards

The great European rose shows, with their coveted gold medals, are held in a sequence that best suits the rose. The big show in Rome usually takes place at the end of the 3rd week of May; that of Monza, near Milan, a week later. Madrid is to be expected at the end of the 1st week of June, the CHÂTEAU DE BAGATELLE trials in Paris are held during the 3rd week in June; Geneva follows at the end of June, and Baden-Baden in the 1st week of July. There are also prestige contests at Baden near Vienna, Courtrai in western Flanders, Roeulx near Mons, Copenhagen, Lyon, Orleans, The Hague and Belfast.

Sometimes two prizes are offered, one for a rose grown in the home country and another for the visitors. A rose that has earned a gold medal in, say, Rome will not, however, necessarily suit gardens in Geneva or Copenhagen, nor are the same qualities relevant in every city. Each country has its own system of rose trials, and its own method of assessment

Here, there is space for only some of the many important trials to be discussed.

Britain

The ROYAL NATIONAL ROSE SOCIETY's Festival of Roses, with accompanying National Rose Show, is normally held at Bone Hill, near St Albans, in the first week of July, but the trials leading up to the gold medals last for three years. Applicants are required to submit six specimens in the case of large-flowered and cluster-flowered roses, and two in the case of climbers. These are planted in the Society's trial beds and identified by numbers only. They are inspected by a panel of expert rose breeders and growers – some amateur and some professional – once every week from June to October. The judges mark their books separately – awarding points for vigour, habit, resistance to disease, colour and form of blooms, duration of flowering, general effect, novelty and scent – but meet in a body to decide the final awards. A gold medal implies that the variety is outstanding in its class. Certificates of merit are awarded at the end of three years to roses that fall just short of the 'gold' standard, and trial ground certificates are given to roses considered to be good reliable varieties. The Henry Edland Memorial Medal is awarded to the best scented rose. The President's International Prize for the Best Rose of the Year is the most important British award. Winning roses are planted not only in the Society's garden at Bone Hill, but also in display gardens in Cardiff, Colwyn Bay, Edinburgh, Glasgow, Harrogate, Norwich, Nottingham, Southport, Taunton and Redcar.

United States

The ALL-AMERICA ROSE SELECTIONS are run by professional rose growers with a keen eye to sales potential, and are held at selected nurseries on a two-year basis. Roses are assessed for points twelve times in a season, with a spring report and a fall report in the first year, and a spring report and a final report in the second year. A dozen or more different merits are considered, with various weightings according to the character of the rose. Thus lack of fragrance is penalized more in a large-flowered rose than in, say, a grandiflora, in which other characteristics are considered more important.

France

The Château de Bagatelle International New Roses Contest is described under that heading.

West Germany

The rose trials at Baden-Baden are supervised by three separate juries. There is first the local jury, which examines all the trial roses once or twice a month from May to September and records any noteworthy details. Secondly, there is the permanent jury of international rose experts, each member of which makes an independent one-day inspection of the roses. Thirdly, there is the international prize jury, on which international experts, representatives of the leading European trials gardens and officials from the VEREIN DEUTSCHER ROSENFREUNDE (the Assocation of German Friends of Roses) are represented; this meets in the first week of July. Points are derived from the findings of all three juries: 100 points is the maximum count, but few roses top 85 points. The main criteria are: novelty, 25 points; scent, 15 points; health, 10 points; general impression, 15 points; and colour of bloom, 10 points. The highest distinction for the finest scented large-flowered rose is the Gold Medal presented by the Casino of the City of Baden-Baden. Next comes the prize for the rose with the finest perfume, and then the Prize of Honour of the VDR.

Additional assessment trials are held by the Association of German Nurserymen (headquarters at Pinneberg, near Hamburg); these are for German and foreign roses alike. Applicants must submit examples of each rose – ten in the case of bush roses, and three for climbers and shrub roses – to each of nine trials gardens in different parts of the Federal Republic. The trials last for two seasons in the case of bush roses, and three for climbers and shrubs. Roses meriting 80 points out of 100 are granted the status of All-German Roses (ADR).

Northern Ireland
Since 1965, the City of Belfast has held international rose trials at the Sir Thomas and Lady Dixon Park, Upper Malone; and Belfast Rose Week, with competitions judged by an international panel, was inaugurated in 1975. The Rose Society of Northern Ireland provides a panel of judges to assess the roses' performance during their first season and the early part of their second season in the trials garden. A gold medal and City of Belfast Award are given for the best large-flowered rose; the Golden Thorn is awarded by the North of Ireland Ministry of Agriculture for the best cluster-flowered rose; and the Uhlad Award for Fragrance is given by the Belfast Chamber of Commerce.

Republic of Ireland
St Anne's Park, northeast of Dublin and about half an hour's bus ride from the city centre, is the setting for the City of Dublin International Rose Trials. A century ago the estate belonged to the newly wedded Arthur Guinness and his young wife Olive. It became a public park in 1949, and in addition to its thirty-four football pitches and eighteen tennis courts, it has a rose-garden, set up through the joint efforts of the Clontarf Horticultural Society and the Dublin Corporation Parks Department. The garden, fortunately shielded from the easterly sea breezes by a plantation of evergreen oaks, has more than 100 beds and about the same number of modern rose varieties, contributed by, among others, DICKSON, HARKNESS, Mattock, MCGREDY, GREGORY, KORDES and Belfast City Council. The trials have been held since 1980 and prizes are awarded for unnamed seedlings of three types: large-flowered roses, cluster-flowered roses, and miniatures, shrubs or climbers.

The Netherlands
Westbroekpark in The Hague is the setting for the highly rated annual international competition, at which the best rose of the year is named 'The Golden Rose of The Hague'. Gold medals are also awarded to winners of three other, separate contests.

One, judged by professional growers only on the basis of reports by the Royal (Netherlands) Horticultural Society, is for varieties not yet marketed. A second contest judged by a mixed jury of amateurs and professionals, also with assessments from the Royal (Netherlands) Horticultural Society, is for varieties that have already been launched; and a third contest is for roses suitable (but not exclusively so) for growing in parks. The prize for fragrance – the Crystal Award for Scent – applicable to sections one and two, is assessed by a panel of women judges.

Efforts are being made by the WORLD FEDERATION OF ROSE SOCIETIES to standardize the organization of rose trials, the criteria for judging and the methods of recruiting juries.

See also ROSE GARDENS (Switzerland).

Iran, the rose in
The native roses of Iran (formerly Persia) are described under WILD ROSES. The following is a vivid account of the role played in Persia by the garden rose. It comes from a distinguished English artist and traveller of the 19th century who held the unusual appointment of 'Historical Painter' to the Tsar of Russia. An ancestor of Sir Robert Ker Porter had fought at Agincourt, and he himself had campaigned in the Peninsular War with Sir John Moore before Coruña. At the Court of the Tsar, he met, and later married, a Russian princess, and when he visited Persia, it was with introductions to the highest in the land. His very readable account of his wanderings was published in 1821 under the title *Travels in Georgia, Persia, Armenia, etc. 1817–1820.*

One of the most delicious spots on which I paid the most frequent visits was the garden of Negauristan, another palace of the King's . . . On my first entering this bower of fairyland (indeed I may call it the very garden of Beauty and the Beast!) I was struck with the appearance of two rose-trees, full fourteen feet high, laden with thousands of flowers, in every degree of expansion, and of a bloom and delicacy of scent, that imbued the whole atmosphere with the most exquisite perfume. Indeed, I believe that in no country of the world does the rose grow in such perfection as in Persia: in no country is it so cultivated, and prized by the natives. Their gardens and courts are crowded with its plants, their rooms ornamented with vases, filled with its gathered bunches, and every bath strewed with the full-blown flowers, plucked from the ever-replenished stems. Even the humblest individual, who pays a piece of copper money for a few whiffs of a kalion, feels a double enjoyment when he finds it stuck with a bud from his dear native tree! But in this delicious garden of Negauristan, the eye and the smell were not the only senses regaled by the presence of roses. The ear was enchanted by the wild and beautiful notes of multitudes of nightingales, whose warblings seem to increase in melody and softness, with the unfolding of their favourite flowers; verifying the song of their poet, who says: 'When the roses fade, when the charms of the bower are passed away, the fond tale of the nightingale no longer animates the scene.'

Israel, the rose in
Although roses had long been grown in the Holy Land to provide the Arabs with rosewater, the first serious cultivation of roses was begun in the 1850s by German Templars at Sarona near the southern end of the Sea of Galilee, who used *Rosa canina* as the UNDERSTOCK. Their efforts were

overtaken, however, by some of the Jewish pioneers in the settlements at Petach Tikva, Ekron and elsewhere, founded through the efforts of Baron Edmond de Rothschild. He imported DAMASK ROSES on their own roots from Cannes in 1890 and set up a rose-oil distillery at Yesud Hama'ala. The roses, though planted for shelter between olive trees, suffered badly from the effects of the prolonged Sirocco winds, and irrigation in those days was of the primitive open-channel variety. The factory was closed in 1905.

Rose growing continued sporadically until soon after the establishment of the State of Israel in 1948. A Ministry of Agriculture survey published in 1949 showed that the total area devoted at that time to rose cultivation was a mere 12 acres. By 1959, however, this had risen to 49 acres, and more than twice as many plants were produced per acre; some stems were also exported – initially to Switzerland. The rose export industry was reorganized in 1964, and as a result, the number of rose plants increased from 700,000 in that year to a total of about 4 million in 1980; the number of blooms was, of course, much higher.

In 1964, about 120,000 CUT-ROSE blooms were exported to Europe as compared with 215 million in 1980. Two Boeing 747 jets now take off every evening from Israel, their loads of roses coordinated in advance by telex to respond to the latest demands of the market.

The greenhouse production of cut flowers for export is confined to a 30-week period in winter, during which roses are cut twice a day and transported to the packing station in refrigerated trucks, with a forecast of the next day's crop sent to a central office in Frankfurt. No flowers are cut during the summer. Medium-height pruning is carried out during early summer with continuous removal of laterals from the new shoots in order to promote the formation of renewal canes from the bases of the plants.

The Israeli Rose Society was established in 1956 and the Wohl Rose Park of Jerusalem was set up in 1981 opposite the Knesset (Parliament) building through the generosity of Maurice and Vivienne Wohl of Geneva. Its opening coincided with 'Rose Pilgrimage '81' – the fifth conference of the WORLD FEDERATION OF ROSE SOCIETIES, which was held in Jerusalem in that year.

The History of the Rose in the Holy Land throughout the Ages by Asaph Goor (Massada/Am Hassefer, 1981), on which part of the above is based, contains many other items of interest to the historically minded rosarian.

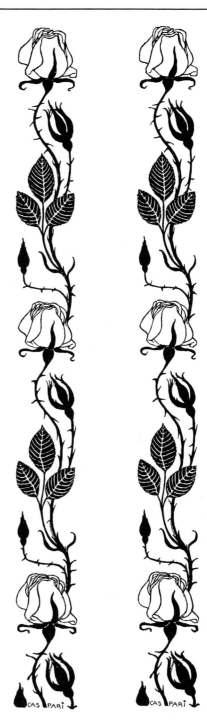

Early 20th-century decorative rosebuds from Jugend *(1904).*

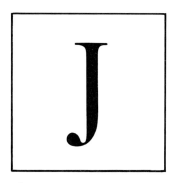

Jackson & Perkins Company

The Jackson & Perkins Company, renowned as the world's largest rose grower, raises more than 16 million rose plants each year in the San Joaquin Valley northwest of Los Angeles. The company records can be traced back to 1873, when Charles H. Perkins formed a partnership with his father-in-law Albert E. Jackson to grow strawberries, raspberries and blackberries in a market garden at Newark, New York (near the shore of Lake Ontario and not to be confused with Newark, New Jersey). To Perkins, who had other interests, the market garden was initially something of a sideline, but then, along with many other horticulturalists, he read H. B. Ellwanger's classic work, *The Rose*, and became fired with the ambition to grow roses. In 1884, he expanded the nursery, and hired Alvin Miller, who had studied propagation in Germany and had worked for the Ellwanger & Barry nursery at nearby Rochester. In 1892, Charles' son, George C. Perkins, who had just graduated from college, joined the business, and it was with his encouragement that, in 1901, Alvin Miller introduced the famous 'Dorothy Perkins' (named for George's daughter; *see* RAMBLERS) from a cross between *Rosa wichuraiana* and 'Madame Gabriel Luizet'.

In the 1900s, Jackson & Perkins established a nursery near Bakersfield in southern California though this was for production rather than for breeding. The firm had, however, never been completely monopolized by roses, and even in the 1920s – after the famous rose hybridist, Dr Jean Nicolas, had produced some exceptional roses for Jackson & Perkins, as well as the original idea of selling roses with roots packed in compressed moss – there was also an annual output of 300,000 evergreens, 125,000 hardy hydrangeas, 80,000 weigelas, 50,000 philadelphus, 40,000 loniceras, 175,000 clematis and 300,000 phlox, so that, with the necessary plantings, the total population of the nursery exceeded 4 million plants. In addition, a large herd of cattle was kept and wintered in barns attached to the various nurseries in order to get a winter crop of manure. In the meantime, three nephews of the founder – Charles Perkins, and his brothers Clarence G. Perkins and Ralph E. Perkins – had joined the company, still very much a family business and exclusively wholesale.

In 1927, Eugene (Gene) Boerner, who had come to J & P in 1920, succeeded Dr Nicolas as director of the breeding programme and continued to produce worthwhile if not spectacular varieties, mainly FLORIBUNDAS. One of these, 'Ma Perkins' (1952), was named after a radio soap opera heroine (no relation to Dorothy).

The firm set up a small stand at the 1939 New York World's Fair to take orders for rose plants, one of which was a deep-red cluster-flowered rose that Kordes had launched as 'Minna Kordes'. With some acumen, J & P renamed it 'World's Fair', still with an eye to the wholesale trade, but there were many more retail customers than wholesalers, and they liked getting their plants by mail. Repeat orders followed, so Jackson & Perkins found themselves in the mail-order business, with requests for roses streaming in from all over the country.

In the 1960s, however, as more and more garden centres were established, the company began to rely less heavily on mail order and developed their interests in the cut-flower trade, which requires very large quantities of a limited number of varieties – a demand especially suited to Jackson & Perkins' massive structure. Nevertheless, under Bill Warriner who succeeded Gene Boerner in 1966, sensational new roses continued to come for the average gardener.

In 1966, with the three brothers no longer young men, Jackson & Perkins was acquired by another family business – the Bear Creek Orchard Company of Medford, Oregon, run by Harry and David Holmes who had made their reputations in the none-too-easy business of selling gift boxes of their Royal Riviera pears by mail. The Holmes brothers afterwards became leading shippers of fine food and fruit gifts, and the founders of the 'Fruit of the Month Club'. Bear Creek is now part of an even more extensive conglomerate, R. J. Reynolds, with interests in, among other things, fine foods, tobacco, Ritz crackers, Shredded Wheat, wine and even oil prospecting.

Jackson & Perkins is now run from Medford, where newly harvested roses are prepared for shipment. This is also the site of the Jackson & Perkins test and display garden, one of the twenty-one accredited by ALL-AMERICA ROSE SELECTIONS. The roses are actually grown some 300 miles south in the San Joaquin Valley near Bakersfield where the growing season lasts for 262 days – that is, nearly nine months – and the company's research facility is at Tustin, southeast of Los Angeles. To those who wonder whether a rose grown in California can stand up to the less friendly climates of states such as Maine and Minnesota, the Jackson & Perkins' reply is that a rose's hardiness is inherent in its genetic background and is unaffected by where it has grown. Nevertheless, roses raised in California have a head start because of the long build-up they get before facing their first winter.

Japan, the rose in

Though the cherry and the chrysanthemum are the traditional favourites of Japanese gardeners, the number of Japanese rose breeders and nurseries operating in the international field has recently shown a sharp increase.

Tokyo is the headquarters of the Keisei Rose Nurseries and of the Komoba Nursery. The Keihan Hirakata Nursery is based in Osaka nearly 300 miles to the southwest, and the Itami Rose Nursery is situated in a residential suburb of Osaka.

The climate of Japan is clearly suited to rose growing, and many ancestors of the finest garden roses grow wild there, among them *Rosa rugosa, R. acicularis, R. banksiae, R. laevigata, R. multiflora* and *R. wichuraiana*. However, gardeners in Japan showed little interest in modern garden roses until the 1930s, and the Rose Society of Japan – *Nippon-Bara-Kai* – was formed only in 1949 after an amalgamation of local groups in Tokyo and Osaka. Emperor Hirohito, already the author of a work on the wild flowers of the island of Nassu, is a member of the Society, as is the former Prime Minister, Mr S. Yoshida, who possessed a very fine garden of his own.

Since those early days, a number of successful hybrids have been bred locally, in particular 'Olympic Torch' (Suzuki, 1966), a large-flowered, red and yellow rose that seems to have taken hold in Australia; and 'Eiko' (Suzuki, 1978), another large-flowered rose of a blended yellow that is marketed in India. In 1968, Toru F. Odonera, a professional scientist but an amateur rose breeder, secured a truly international breakthrough with 'Nozomi', which has caught on in Canada and the US as well as in some of the best nurseries in Britain. It offers pearly-pink single flowers in profusion in summer, and is versatile enough to be ranked as a climbing miniature, a small cluster-flowered rose, a standard rose, a patio rose or a ground-cover rose – a conundrum here for classifiers. A large-flowered but modest-sized Japanese rose – lemon-yellow and fragrant, and the first to be sold commercially in the UK – is marketed under the name of 'Ama Tsu Otome', by Gandy Roses Ltd.

Josephine and her roses at La Malmaison

It is generally thought that Pierre-Paul Prud'hon's portrait of Josephine in her garden at La Malmaison most nearly recaptures the elegance and seductive charm that so deeply impressed her contemporaries. However, rosarians may

The Empress Josephine: a watercolour by Jean-Baptiste Isabey (1767–1855), painted in 1809, the year of the annulment of her marriage with Napoleon.

prefer to admire the miniature by Jean-Baptiste Isabey, which offers a more coquettish Josephine wearing a gauzy décolleté dress, tear-drop earrings and a coiffure of curls and coils adorned with half-a-dozen miniature roses. The latter was a particularly appropriate touch for a woman who had been christened Marie-Joseph-Rose and had, until her marriage to Napoleon when she was thirty-three, generally been called Rose by her family and friends.

The estate of La Malmaison, some 9 miles (15 km) west of Paris, where Josephine was to create her famous rose garden, had remained in the possession of a single family for nearly 400 years. In the second half of the 18th century, it was bought by the financier Jacques-Jean le Couteulx du Molay, who improved and 'modernized' the building and grounds. He was, however, ruined by the Revolution and was obliged to put it up for sale. Josephine took Napoleon to see the property, but he considered the price too high for a house of fairly modest proportions. Josephine, however, was determined to have her way, and while Napoleon was away on his expedition to Egypt in 1798, she prevailed on Mayor Chanorier, of nearby Croissy, to negotiate the purchase on her behalf, borrowing 37,000 francs to pay for the furniture and the costs of the sale. Napoleon eventually found the balance of 300,000 francs and the property was registered in his name. Laughable as it might now seem, he hoped to run it profitably as a stud farm.

The house itself was in poor shape and needed extensive

restoration and redecoration, and Pierre-Joseph REDOUTÉ's first commission there was to execute some floral portraits on vellum for Josephine's bedroom, while his elder brother Antoine-Ferdinand, a theatrical designer, decorated the walls.

In the grounds, Josephine favoured the unexpected – sweeping lawns interspersed with glades and waterfalls. She approved of the informality of the *jardin anglais*, and liked a disordered profusion of different species and varieties of plants that would grow naturally together, as they did in her native Martinique.

Her particular interest in roses seems to date from 1804 (the year Napoleon became Emperor and she Empress of France), probably because of the new varieties of CHINA ROSES reaching England through the efforts of Sir Joseph Banks and others. The Hammersmith (London) nursery of Lee & Kennedy had long been noted for its success in cultivating roses, as well as the seeds that Banks had brought back from his expedition with Captain Cook to Australia, and Francis Masson from his travels in South Africa. Redouté's patron, M. Héritier de Brutelle, had, as a letter in the Hammersmith Borough Library shows, been ordering plants from Lee & Kennedy as far back as 1783. *The Gentleman's Magazine* of 14 November 1811 reported that: 'Curious plants to the amount of £700 have lately been shipped at Portsmouth for the *ci-devant* Empress Josephine. They are the produce of the Nursery garden at Hammersmith from which she also got a supply in 1803 to the amount of £2,600.'

Although the fighting barely ceased between the two countries during the years that Josephine occupied La Malmaison, John Kennedy was, at the request of French scientists and largely through the efforts of Sir Joseph Banks, provided with a *laissez-passer* allowing him to travel freely between England and France, partly so that he could put his knowledge and his roses at her disposal. (*See also* PORTLAND ROSES for an alternative explanation of how he was able to travel freely to France.)

A letter from him dated 24 October 1808, and preserved in the library of the Royal Botanical Gardens at Kew, suggested a list of roses to be supplied to La Malmaison but declined to disclose their names because they were 'unbotanical'. This list might have included the unbotanically named 'Great Maiden's Blush', which was already known before the 15th century, but there are many other possibilities. 'Hume's Blush Tea-scented Rose' is dated as first appearing in 1809 but perhaps Kennedy had already budded a specimen; the 'Royal Virgin' rose, painted earlier by EHRET, weas another variety that he might have felt would cause embarrassment at La Malmaison.

Josephine also did much to encourage rose growing in France. André Dupont, who had established the rose garden in the palace grounds of the Luxembourg and was also an enthusiastic hybridizer, was commissioned to assemble an even more magnificent rose collection at La Malmaison. Fine specimens came from Jacques-Martin Cels, who was officially recognized as a Cultivateur de l'Institut National de France. His nursery on the plateau of Montrouge, $3\frac{1}{2}$ miles (6 km) south of Paris, provided among other plants that freakish near-rose *Hulthemia persica*, which Redouté was to include among the first portraits in *Les roses*. Other celebrated French rose nurseries of the time included those of Boursault at Yerres, about $12\frac{1}{2}$ miles (20 km) south of Paris; De Brisset in the Rue St Maur; Fion in the same neighbourhood, on the Rue Trois couronnes; and Descemet, whose seedlings at St Denis were later to be rescued by his fellow nurseryman, Jean-Paul Vibert, from the path of advancing British forces. However, as Ventenat, Josephine's botanist, admitted, 'Most of our roses came from England.'

The main entrance to La Malmaison is now up a straight drive flanked by orange trees. On the right of the drive is an enclosed rose garden with modern varieties of BUSH ROSES; a collection of WILD ROSES, including some of the varieties painted by Redouté, is now to be seen in geometrically disposed triangular beds on steep ground behind the row of lime trees to the left of the drive. Formerly, as can be seen from paintings now in the Malmaison Museum, visitors approached the '*château*' by a curving drive that took them through the park.

During the ten years from 1804 to her death in 1814, Josephine amassed a collection of more than 250 different varieties of rose. Roy E. Shepherd, in his classic work, *The History of the Rose* (1954), stated that her roses included, in addition to the aforementioned *Hulthemia persica*, 167 different varieties of *Rosa gallica*, 22 China roses, 9 damasks, 3 mosses, 27 centifolias, 1 musk rose and some transatlantic species possibly brought home earlier by André Michaux.

Josephine, so insouciant in many other respects, took a serious interest in botany and in the welfare of her plants. One of her ladies-in-waiting, Georgette du Crest, bore candid witness to this in her memoirs of the Empress Josephine, published anonymously in 1828:

When the weather was fine, the greenhouses were inspected; the same walk was taken every day. On the way to that spot, the same subjects were talked over. The conversation generally turned on botany, upon Her Majesty's taste for that *interesting* science, her wonderful memory, which enabled her to name every plant – in short, the same phrases were generally repeated over and over again, and at the same time, circumstances well calculated to render the promenades exceedingly tedious and fatiguing. I no sooner stepped on to that delightful walk, which I had so admired when I first saw it, than I was seized with an immoderate fit of yawning.

Further confirmation of Josephine's personal and abiding interest in botany can also be found in the memoirs of Mlle d'Avrillon, edited by M. Dervelle (Mercure de France, 1969). If anything, Josephine's interest in her garden increased after her marriage to Napoleon was annulled in 1810, and it may have been with satisfaction rather than self-pity that she was able to say in 1813: 'My garden is now more popular than my salon.'

Her expenditure continued uncurbed. As part of the annulment settlement, the Emperor had made over to her both La Malmaison and the Château de Navarre near Evreux, and paid off debts amounting to 3.6 million francs. Two years later, she confronted him with liabilities amounting to 1.2 million francs, and the Emperor settled these as well. Yet when she died, there was a further 3 million francs to be found. However, not all of this was spent on the gardens: at her death, Josephine's wardrobe contained 220 gowns, more than 300 blouses and 158 pairs of stockings.

Following the defeat of Napoleon at Leipzig in 1813 and the occupation of France by his enemies, Josephine felt called on to entertain the conquerors. Indeed it was a boat-ride taken on a summer's evening with Alexander I of Russia that proved fatal to her. Characteristically she had worn a thin off-the-shoulder dress, and returning home, she at once took to her bed with a chill and died three days later.

With Josephine's death, the glories of La Malmaison faded. After his final defeat at Waterloo in 1815, Napoleon paid a last visit to La Malmaison with the thought that he might retire there as a private citizen, but he found that the house was empty and had not been lived in since her death. The poet Chateaubriand, who visited La Malmaison in that year, found weeds and grass growing in the paths. The exotic trees were dying and the black swans that Baudlin had sent from Australia had vanished from the waters. Presumably the roses had been no better cared for – unless they had already been dug up.

Since those days, La Malmaison has been privately owned, repurchased by the state, disposed of once more. It finally came into the possession of a Monsieur Osiris who, after restoring it, presented it to the French nation in 1904. Two years later, a museum was opened there. The original furniture had long since disappeared – the indefatigable Miss Mary Berry, who had visited La Malmaison in 1816, had noted that, even then, the chair covers and the paintings had already vanished – but some authentic furniture has since been assembled from elsewhere, including some from the Rue de la Chantereine (now the Rue de la Victoire near to the Gare St Lazare) where Napoleon and Josephine had first set up house after their marriage in 1796.

During 1909 and 1910, Jules Gravereaux, the founder of the Bon Marché department store, enthusiastic rosarian and creator of the ROSERAIE DE L'HAY-LES-ROSES near Sceaux, collected 197 of the varieties of roses grown by Josephine at La Malmaison and these were again assembled in a garden there. (The bush and climbing roses known as 'Souvenir de la Malmaison' date from 1843 and 1893, respectively, and thus were not contemporary with Josephine.)

The fact remains that the achievement of Josephine lay not so much in the varieties that she herself grew as in the impetus that she gave to French rose breeders to produce so many fine new varieties in the years that followed.

To reach La Malmaison from Paris by public transport, take the fast Metro (RER) to La Defence, and then a No. 158A autobus.

Judging roses

Judges can make or mar a rose show. If they are known to be painstaking, observant, knowledgeable and impartial, their decisions will probably be accepted without demur. However, if they are unfamiliar with or have never grown the particular roses that they have undertaken to assess, and then award honours to an undeserving exhibit, they are deluding not only the competitors and the public but also the organizers of the rose show.

For this reason, national rose societies are becoming increasingly careful about whom they invite to be judges at their shows. In Britain, the ROYAL NATIONAL ROSE SOCIETY holds periodic examinations for would-be judges and, in 1985, announced that only judges who had passed either the RNRS judges' examination or attended an RNRS judges' seminar within the previous three years would be included in their future lists.

In the United States, the AMERICAN ROSE SOCIETY is equally strict. Applicants for an 'apprentice rose judge' certificate must, among other qualifications, 'know intimately the characteristics and the range of variability of at least 100 varieties, largely in the grandiflora, hybrid tea, floribunda, miniature, climber and "old" garden rose classes and be able to verify labelling', and 'must have successfully exhibited by winning more than five blue ribbons for at least three years in at least five shows'. They must also have worked as clerk with other apprentices and accredited judges in a minimum of three rose shows, and must, in their application, declare for how many years they have grown roses and what varieties, and how many plants they have cultivated and are cultivating. The qualifications required of an 'accredited judge' are, of course, even more demanding.

The Royal National Rose Society's official publication *Judging Roses* gives much useful practical advice on how to go about judging, and suggests the commonsense system of weeding out entries that are obviously inferior before starting to arrange the others in order of merit.

Both the American Rose Society's *Guidelines for Judging Roses* and the Royal National Rose Society's booklet take the view that judging skill will, in most cases, lead to the correct decision, without the need to evaluate each flower according to a points system, which would make a job that could and should be done in minutes take hours. The points system should be used mainly as a general guide that allows members of the judging panel to assess characteristics on a common basis – for example, occasionally points may decide the issue between two varieties of almost equal merit. However, even in the system used in judging the international competition for new roses at the CHÂTEAU DE BAGATELLE, points are treated as indicative rather than binding.

See also ALL-AMERICA ROSE SELECTIONS.

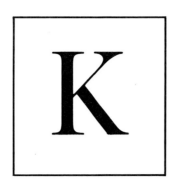

K

Kordes, Wilhelm and family

Wilhelm Kordes senior was twenty-two years old in 1887 when he founded the firm that bears his name. The original site of the nursery was at Elmshorn between Hamburg and Kiel, and before the outbreak of World War I, Kordes had also established a nursery in England, at Witley near Guildford, in partnership with Max Krause. Unfortunately Kordes was visiting it when war broke out and both he and his partner were interned on the Isle of Man for the duration of the war and expelled afterwards as undesirable aliens.

On his return to Germany at the age of fifty-four, he transferred his nursery to Sparrieshoop, a nearby village, and made over his business to his two sons, Hermann Kordes and Wilhelm Kordes II (1891–1976). The latter, a hospitable and popular character with his square-cut white beard and (frequently) Hamburger sea-captain's cap, took over the HYBRIDIZATION programme in 1920, and was responsible for many of the best known of the Kordes varieties. 'Geheimrat Duisberg' ('Golden Rapture') had an immediate success as a unique yellow cut-flower rose, and 'Crimson Glory' (1935), a dark-red LARGE-FLOWERED ROSE, brought him international renown. The very next year he had a success with 'Rosenelfe', a mid-pink cluster-flowered rose that had the peculiarity of bearing high-peaked blooms typical of modern large-flowered roses.

In 1930, Wilhelm Kordes II decided to cross varieties of *Rosa pimpinellifolia* (which, being summer-flowering only, had been somewhat neglected) with the vigorous large-flowered mid-yellow rose 'Joanna Hill' ('J. H. Hill'), which had been introduced only two years before. From these, he obtained the successful Frühlings series, which, although not REMONTANT, more than compensate for this by the profusion with which they flower and by their exceptional hardiness. He had the same kind of success with *R. eglanteria* var. *magnifica*, also crossed with 'Joanna Hill' to produce 'Fritz Nobis' (1940), a vigorous shrub with clove-scented, semi-double pink blooms. Other successes with *R. eglanteria* var. *magnifica* include 'Sparrieshoop' (1952); 'Flammentanz' (1955), a mid-red large-flowered climber;

and 'Aschermittwoch' (1955), a pearl-grey-to-white climber.

Another series of triumphs came when the much-neglected varieties raised by PETER LAMBERT and other HYBRID MUSKS were crossed with large-flowered roses to produce remontant SHRUB ROSES, dealt with in detail in that section.

We owe to the Kordes family the new breed of perpetual-flowering climbing and shrub roses derived from *R. kordesii* (a rose equivalent to 'Max Graf' but with double the number of chromosomes). This range includes: 'Dortmund' (1955), single flowers, red with white eye; 'Hamburger Phoenix' (1954), dark crimson; 'Leverkusen' (1954), lemon yellow; and 'Parkdirecktor Riggers' (1957), crimson.

Reimer Kordes, son of Wilhelm Kordes II, began serious hybridization around 1955 and became managing director of the firm in 1964. His first success came with the famous and much-loved white cluster-flowered rose 'Iceberg' ('Fée des Neiges', 'Schneewittchen', 1958), which was a cross between the mid-red hybrid musk 'Robin Hood' (Pemberton, 1927) and the white large-flowered rose 'Virgo' (Mallerin, 1947).

'Congratulations' (1978), an impressively fine, dark-red, large-flowered rose, worthy of a solus position or as a hedge, was another Reimer Kordes winner. He is helped in the business by his son Wilhelm III and his two cousins, Hermann and Werner.

Right: A fine portrait of Rosa damascena versicolor *by Georg Dionyisus Ehret. The somewhat pretentious title was first given to this rose in 1629 when John Parkinson referred to it as* 'Rosa versicolor – *the party coloured rose, of some Yorke and Lancaster', nearly 150 years after the Wars of the Roses had ended on the field of Bosworth.*

ROSA rugosa.

Rosa rugosa, *Japan's 'ramasa rose'. Hand-coloured lithograph from* Flora japonica, *by P. F. von Siebold and J. G. Zuccarini (1835).*

Right: *Four stages in the blooming of a large-flowered rose ('Silver Jubilee') from the transparencies of F. C. H. Witchell.*

1. *The 'bud stage' showing full colour with one or two petals beginning to unfurl above the opening calyx.*

2. *The rose half-open.*

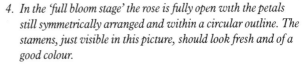

3. Left: *The rose three-quarters open. The 'perfect stage' for which exhibitors and judges hope is when the rose is half to three-quarters open, with the petals symmetrically arranged in a circular outline and, in the case of a large-flowered rose, evenly surrounding an upright, well-formed centre.*

4. *In the 'full bloom stage' the rose is fully open with the petals still symmetrically arranged and within a circular outline. The stamens, just visible in this picture, should look fresh and of a good colour.*

Lambert, Peter

By the time he was twenty-four, Peter Lambert (1859–1939) was able to write authoritative articles on rose culture and to describe himself as 'garden artist and rose breeder'. He had been born in the town of Trier, in what is now West Germany, near the border with Luxembourg. He was the son of Jean Nikolaus Lambert, founder of the fruit tree and rose production firm of Lambert & Reiter, which as early as 1879 had been exporting roses to Britain, Belgium, Norway, Sweden, Russia and the US.

Peter Lambert's first success came in 1891 with the launching of a rose named in honour of Queen Victoria's eldest daughter who was married to the German emperor, Wilhelm II. 'Kaiserin Auguste Victoria' was a magnificent 100-petalled rose treasured for many years for bridal bouquets, and as Roy Shepherd pointed out, it was still to be found in some rose catalogues as late as the mid-1950s. The Empress rewarded Lambert with a portrait of herself in oils. In the same year, Lambert took over the business management of the VEREIN DEUTSCHER ROSENFREUNDE (VDR, the Association of German Friends of Roses), and set up his own nursery at Trier–Sankt Marie.

Shortly before the turn of the century, he married Leonie Lamesch, whose family lived across the frontier in Luxembourg. His honeymoon was spent in St Petersburg (now Leningrad), where he and his young bride were invited by the Tsar to attend a court ball at The Hermitage at which Lambert roses formed part of the decorations. On this occasion, he was presented with a golden brandy glass as a mark of the Tsar's favour.

In 1895, Lambert made a cross between two roses – 'Merveille de Lyon', a light-pink HYBRID PERPETUAL, and the darker-pink 'Madame Caroline Testout'. One of the resulting seedlings developed as an absolutely pure white rose, untinged with cream, pink or green. Those who came to see it in Lambert's garden christened it the 'Snow Queen',

but Lambert found this name unappealing, and preferred to keep the rose unnamed in order to compete for the prize offered by a gardening journal for the best unnamed rose of German origin exhibited at the Frankfurt Fair of 1900 – the winning rose was to be named 'Count Otto von Bismarck'. As it turned out, Lambert did not carry off the prize – the judges may well have considered a pure white rose to be an inappropriate tribute to that artful practitioner of *realpolitik* – and in 1901 the rose was named 'Frau Karl Druschki' in honour of the wife of the President of the VDR.

The aforementioned roses, 'Kaiserin Auguste Victoria' and 'Frau Karl Druschki', together with the pure white polyantha 'Katherina Zeimet', make a unique trio of outstanding white roses from one breeder.

Lambert's rose 'Trier', also white and a rambler, appeared in 1904 and proved to be a truly historic variety, being the ultimate progenitor of the *Kordesii* hybrids such as 'Heidelburg' (1959). A 'family tree' in the magnificent rosarium at Baden, near Vienna, traces the connection between 'Trier' and its descendants. The contribution made by Lambert's roses to the development of the HYBRID MUSK ROSES bred by the Revd Joseph Pemberton is dealt with under that heading. More recently, 'Trier' was named as the co-parent of *Hulthemosa* 'Tigris' (Harkness, 1985) – the first hardy variety to be bred in 150 years from the rock-rose-like *Hulthemia persica*.

Lambert's nursery disappeared in the tumult of World War II, but his rose 'Trier' has lived on.

Large-flowered roses

Although the high-peaked, large-flowered, scented, remontant roses known as HYBRID TEAS have officially been traced back to 1867 and beyond, they were not established as an influential class until almost the end of the 19th century – by which time they carried so many non-tea strains that they scarcely justified their original name. Therefore, since 1971, by agreement among the members of the WORLD FEDERATION OF ROSE SOCIETIES, they have been officially designated as 'large-flowered roses'.

With their delicately scrolled buds, their alluringly hesitant mode of self-revelation and their classical simplicity of

---

Left: *Gardening under the Mogul emperors. The channels of running water and the division of the garden into four quarters were typical features of the period. From the Baburnama Manuscript.*

form, they come nearest to the ideal rose, the florist's perfect bloom, the rose of love and of gardeners' dreams. Yet their future is uncertain. As long ago as the 1950s, Roy Shepherd was surmising: 'Perhaps this class, like others that preceded it, is destined eventually to be replaced by a new class in which the good qualities of hybrid tea will be combined with the greater hardiness and disease resistance of others.'

One handicap to their future progress as a rose-type is commercial. In order to stay in business, nurseries are obliged to offer a continual string of new large-flowered roses, but only some of these are better than the varieties already on offer. In 1906, when Léon Simon and Pierre Cochet published their *Nomenclature de tous les roses connus*, they listed 10,953 entries. Yet today, even including the varieties since introduced, fewer than half that number are now grown at all and fewer still commercially. There is market competition, too, not only from the cluster-flowered varieties and the MINIATURES, but also from the 'old-fashioned' hybrid perpetual roses, with their soft colours that mix so well together in the same bed; their nostalgic appeal seems likely to remain at least for a while.

Even the casual observer cannot fail to notice how few of the large-flowered roses popular today are survivors from the first quarter of this century. 'Grüss an Aachen' (Geduldig, 1908, light pink), 'Ophelia' (Paul, 1912, salmon colour), 'Madame Édouard Herriot' (Pernet-Ducher, 1913, multicolour) and 'Souvenir de Claudius Pernet' (Pernet-Ducher, 1920, corn-cob yellow) are the ones that come readily to mind. One wonders why, in the past forty years, no rose has caused the same thrill of delight as 'Peace' (*see below*). This said, it is certainly a cause for satisfaction that at least forty really good large-flowered roses, which have appeared at the rate of one a year since the 1940s, are still in wide demand. Space allows only a few out of many to be mentioned here.

'Peace' ('Madame A. Meilland', 'Gloria Dei', 'Gioia'), produced by MEILLAND in 1945, comes first in the pageant. Few colour photographs capture the fascination of its large luminous pale yellow flowers, lightly suffused with cerise, and decorated with a coronet of golden anthers. Meilland-Richardier's later lists consider it unnecessary to enter any description except for that given to the climbing version, which is designated as 'canary yellow, bordered with carmine'. The lightly coloured blooms of 'Peace' are matched by its vigorous growth, and are backed by rich glossy green foliage. However, even given such vigour, it has been a phenomenal achievement to have produced the millions of 'Peace' roses sold the world over from a single plant.

'Josephine Bruce' (Bees, 1949) is another rose of the 1940s that is still in favour. The blooms are dark scarlet with shadows of blackish maroon, and the plant, at $2\frac{1}{2}$ feet (75 cm) is small enough for any bed. We are warned, though, to take the normal precautions against MILDEW.

'Sutters Gold' (Swim, 1950) opened the new decade, and is one of the earliest to flower in any season. The blooms are golden, with a red flush, on long stems suitable for cutting, and there is a convenient lack of thorns. This one is strongly scented.

There must be many roses that, for unexplained reasons, are neglected outside their countries of origin. One of these is 'Chrysler Imperial' (Lammerts, 1952), a dark-red rose of considerable merit, popular in the US, Canada and Australia but less well known in the UK, despite its rich fragrance. 'Tiffany' (Lindquist, 1954) is another favourite rose in the US, although it is not easily obtainable in the UK. Its pink-blended flowers on long stems suitable for cutting contrast well with the dark green foliage and are strongly scented. 'Rose Gaujard', introduced by Gaujard in 1957, has a wider international reputation and was awarded the UK National Rose Society's Gold Medal in 1958. The flowers are carmine with a silver reverse, but the blooms are sometimes irregularly formed, which makes it more of a garden than a show rose.

Some heretics have been known to prefer 'Garden Party' (Swim, 1959) – another rose more popular in the US, Japan and Australia than in Europe – to 'Peace'. The large flowers are ivory in the centre touched, like those of 'Peace', with pink. 'Beautée' (Meilland, 1953) carries elegant apricot-to-creamy-orange blooms on a $2\frac{1}{2}$ foot (75 cm) bush with dark-bluish-green foliage. This is a fragrantly scented rose and can be placed in the front of the bed where admirers can stoop to enjoy its fragrance.

'Wendy Cussons' (Gregory, 1959) is in many ways an ideal rose for the garden, for bouquets and for rose shows. It is strongly scented and has carried off gold medals in the UK, Rome and The Hague. The flowers, however, are of a somewhat sharp mid-red and are therefore best placed in a solus position.

The 1960s opened with 'Piccadilly', from McGredy, which won gold medals in Rome and Madrid, and certificates of merit in the UK, and has been called the finest scarlet bicolour ever raised, the flowers being a fiery red with golden reverse. Early- and long-flowering if not long-lasting, this has nevertheless failed to catch on in the US where it might be vulnerable to fading under strong sun or to mildew in areas of heavy rainfall.

The blooms of 'King's Ransom' (Morey, 1961) resemble the gold coins in which the ransom would have to be paid. They are fadeless and on long stems – no faults here.

'Chicago Peace' (Johnston, 1962) was a SPORT from 'Peace' and has flowers as large as the original but with the colours reversed, i.e. central pink with yellow reverses. It has not got much scent, but it is good for the flower vase. 'Super Star' (Tantau, 1960) is known to Americans as 'Tropicana'. This is a luminous orange-vermilion rose that has been given top awards on both sides of the Atlantic despite the need to watch for mildew.

A great year for large-flowered bush roses was 1963. 'Uncle Walter' (McGredy) bears velvety bright red flowers that do not 'blue'; however, the plant is not for the small rosebed. It was named for Walter Johnston, who married Ivy McGredy and became the uncle of Sam MCGREDY IV. 'Papa Meilland' (Meilland) has flowers of the deepest crim-

Ladies botanizing in the 1830s, with tulips and hyacinths ahead of the rose season.

son, veined and shaded with black – attractions that have led rosarians to plant it in Japan, Canada and the US, as well as in the UK. It still features strongly in the Meilland-Richardier list where its colours are described as 'purplish velvet shot with crimson and with bluish black lights'; it is strongly fragrant. 'Pascali', introduced by the breeder Louis Lens of Wavre Notre Dame les Malines in Belgium, could be called 'nurseryman's white'; it is indeed white but has a hint of parchment in the centre. Its petals of substance make this rose a long-laster, both in the garden and in the flower vase. It has won the 'Golden Rose of The Hague' award and has been honoured in the US and Britain to a degree that is unusual for a white rose.

'Mister Lincoln' (Swim & Weeks, 1964) is another really dark red rose, said to be more vigorous than 'Papa Meilland' and more resistant to mildew than 'Josephine Bruce'. It is well scented and will not fade into blue.

'Mainzer Fastnacht' ('Shrove Tuesday in Mainz') is the original name under which TANTAU introduced this rose in 1964 – and it is a far more apt one than the name 'Blue Moon' by which it is more generally known. Large and shaped like full moons the flowers may be, but they have been more accurately described as silvery lilac or just plain mauve. However, it is still in regular demand as an unusual 'once in a blue moon' rose.

'Blessings' (Gregory, 1968) is a large-flowered pink rose that is exceptionally floriferous. It was awarded a gold medal in Baden-Baden in the year of its debut. 'Fragrant Cloud' (Tantau, 1965) is renowned for its scent, and has won the UK National Rose Society's Gold Medal and an award of merit from the Royal Horticultural Society. It bears geranium-red flowers in great profusion. Some doubts have been expressed as to whether it still retains the vigour of the original stock.

The large-flowered roses of the 1970s have been established long enough to be reliable, yet not so long that they are in danger of losing their qualities of resistance. Here, as above, space allows only a small selection of the many popular varieties. All are worth considering and most, within national limitations, are widely stocked.

Certainly 'First Prize', raised by Boerner in 1970, cannot be left out. The deep rose-pink, urn-shaped buds with their silvery reverses can be up to 4 inches (10 cm) long, and the foliage is strong, the stems long. In the nine years following its introduction, 'First Prize' scored more points in American rose shows than any other large-flowered rose. It is also to be found in Australia, Japan and India, but apparently not in the UK.

'National Trust' (McGredy, 1970) is almost but not quite an all-British flower. It is a floriferous bedding rose with bright, long-lasting red flowers, which stand up well to the weather. 'Sunblest', another rose of the same year by Tantau, has fairly large yellow blooms, and no faults. 'Red Devil' ('Coeur d'Amour') (Dickson, 1970) yields a profusion of wonderful blooms just perfect for showing – but it is too delicate to be left out in the rain.

'Troika' ('Royal Dane') (Poulsen, 1972), with coppery-orange-pink blooms, deserves to be better known, for it seems immune from BLACKSPOT, die-back and other diseases from which roses of this coloration often suffer. 'Adolf Horstmann' (Kordes, 1972) is another orange-yellow-pink of medium height and no defects except a lack of scent.

'Just Joey' (Cant, 1972) is a sensational coppery-orange-pink, frilly-petalled rose with a lighter band near the wavy edges. The blooms are large, and appear in abundance even in the autumn, standing up well to rain. It has some scent, too, and like 'Troika' deserves far more recognition than it has received. 'Cheshire Life', (Fryer, 1972) is a distinctively coloured, orange-vermilion rose with substantial dark foliage.

'Alec's Red' (Cocker, 1970) has inherited some of the talent of its parent, 'Fragrant Cloud', and won the Royal National Rose Society's Edland Medal for fragrance. Its profusion of cherry-red flowers and its dark glossy foliage have won it popularity on both sides of the Atlantic, especially in Canada.

It is worth making a special journey to see 'Alpine Sunset' (Cant, 1974). The blooms are variously described as light peach-yellow, or creamy yellow and peach, but the gold and fire of a sunset compel the beholder to stop and look again. It is also well-scented.

'Medallion' (Warriner, 1973), the American 'Rose of the Year' for that year, is a 4–6 foot (1.2–1.8 m) shrub with vast 7-inch (18 cm) flowers of apricot shaded pink, with up to forty-five blooms visible at any one time. 'Red Masterpiece', from the same breeder, was also American 'Rose of the Year', in 1974. Its dark-red-to-almost-black blooms are made up of thirty-five to forty petals of substance that need their fair share of sun if they are to unspiral with freedom.

'Silver Jubilee' (Cocker, 1978) carried off the RNRS President's International Trophy and Gold Medal in that year, and in 1985 it was voted by breeders to be the best large-flowered bush rose in a poll organized by the *Sunday Times* (London), and was awarded the James Mason medal, given to the modern rose that has given particular pleasure to rose lovers. It is a modest 2½ foot (75 cm) plant with beautifully formed flowers of pink shaded with apricot and cream, carried in abundance throughout the season. It is healthy and excellent for bedding, but less so for cutting; it has some scent. 'Dutch Gold', a Wisbech Plant Co. product of 1978, is a reliable non-fading yellow rose, backed up by durable foliage and good scent.

It would be premature to assess colour trends among the new large-flowered roses during the 1980s – if only because the 1980 American 'Rose of the Year' turned out to be a white variety named 'Honor', with satiny petals and dark olive foliage. This was introduced in that year by Warriner.

'Sunbright' (Warriner, 1984) shared the 'Rose of the Year' honours of that year with still another Warriner rose, 'Grand Masterpiece' – a red rose of impressive stature and flower quality. 'Sunbright', which also won bronze medals in Japan and in Baden-Baden, has urn-shaped buds, and medium-size, well-shaped yellow blooms that are impervious to extremes of heat and cold. The foliage is dark green, and there is some scent.

From these few examples, it would seem that no great departures were taking place during the early 1980s from the mainstream of development in the field of large-flowered roses. However, the struggle for improvement continues, and the rose raisers' aim is, as in the past, to raise roses of striking colours that are impervious to the weather, fragrant, resistant to diseases, self-cleansing, long-flowering and long-lasting, with blooms on stems long enough to support large, perfectly formed show flowers.

The future of the large-flowered roses clearly depends on whether the rate of progress in this field is sufficient to attract new sales to new rosarians year after year.

Large-scale rose production in Britain

Wholesale rose nurseries, though not so large in Britain as some in the US, are, nevertheless, the backbone of the UK rose industry.

An organization such as Wharton Nurseries at Harleston in Norfolk, which specializes in sales to garden centres, will grow more than 1.25 million bushes, with 300,000 sold bare-root to retail nurserymen, as well as more than 500,000 bush, climbing, shrub and standard roses in containers and pots plus another quarter of a million grafted or micropropagated miniature roses. At Wharton's, a minimum order of 500 plants is required for some roses, and a £500 order secures free carriage to most of England and about half of Wales.

November-to-March is high season for retail sales for bare-root roses, but root-wrapped roses, bagged in moist sphagnum peat, are sold from early October until March (with a peak from October through December) and are displayed outdoors in all-weather display packs. Container roses, which of course can be planted in the ground at any time of the year, enjoy their best sales from March to June inclusive, when many of them are in flower. April-to-September is the high season for miniature roses.

Wholesale rose nurseries undertake large-scale promotional orders for customers who want special packs, as well as the promotion of SPONSORED ROSES – for example, in the case of the 'Glenfiddich' rose, the 'Typhoo Tea' rose or the *'Family Circle'* rose. Landscape contractors, local authorities and mail-order companies are other big buyers. Roses are also regularly exported from Britain to the Netherlands, France, West Germany, Denmark, Finland, Switzerland and Canada.

At Wharton's, some 40 acres of UNDERSTOCKS are planted every year, each plant having a two-year cycle. These rootstocks are planted as one-year seedlings; this is done mechanically, two rows at a time. A machine with the brandname 'Super Prefer' clears the hole that the stock is to occupy, gathers the rose in a rubber clip and deposits it in place. The soil is settled round the plant by a ridging plough behind the planter. Three planters can plant up to 150,000 rootstocks in a day.

In June or July, the understock will be budded with one of the 200 or more varieties offered by the nursery. Parts of this operation are also mechanized. In the first stage, a de-ridging machine hoes away the earth from around the spot on the understock that is to receive the bud. This is followed by a blast of compressed air delivered from the pipes of the de-ridging machine as it passes along each row.

The opening on the stem of the understock that is to receive the bud (*see* BUDDING) is cut by hand, as are the flowering stems from the varieties that are to provide the buds (the flower at the end of the stem confirms that the shoot is true to type). These stems are taken in bundles to a workshed where they are cut to a uniform length of about 10 inches (25 cm) and the foliage taken off by hand. (A part of each leaf stalk is left in place to provide a convenient 'handle' for the budders.)

The budding teams are supplied by the understock preparation staff with 10-inch (25 cm) scions, which they stow in miniature 'golf-bag' cannisters strapped to their legs. On arriving at the row to be budded, the budder takes out one of the scions and removes the thorns with his knife, inserts the bud in the understock, cuts off any excess and folds the loosened bark of the understock over the bud. He then places a wrapping round the bud and secures the ends of it with twin prongs. The binding is perishable, and will disappear by the time the bud has 'taken'. If the budded rose variety is to be grown on, the foliage of the understock will be cut away in two stages so that the rose is not left at any time without some greenery. Otherwise, the understock will continue to grow and the bud will remain dormant.

The roses are also lifted mechanically by a machine that undercuts the roots. Before this, however, the roses are first 'topped' mechanically to allow the lifting machine to have full access. After lifting, plants are bundled mechanically in the field before being taken to the packhouse.

In the packhouse, a band-saw is used to cut the stems of the bundles to the required length. The roses are graded to well above the requirements of the British Standards Association, and automatically re-tied, some in groups of ten, others individually for root-wrapping. A conveyor system feeds bare-root plants to the packing areas that are also kept supplied with moist peat direct from a peat mixing and wetting machine. After tying, the roses are labelled with the variety name, description and planting advice.

Bush, climbing or standard roses on a 3-foot (1 m) rugosa stock can all be supplied in floppy or rigid pots filled with slow-release fertilizer that gives them a prolonged shelf-life. Compost-mixing and potting – like planting – can be carried out with the help of machines, one of which delivers a stream of potting compost on to the potting area. Seven hundred pots can be filled in one hour.

Some varieties of bush, climbing, shrub, standard and hedging roses are offered with a guarantee that they have been potted and settled in for at least three months prior to dispatch. One of the roses recommended for hedging or ground cover is a variety from Japan identified as 'Keitoli/Ferdi'; it bears a profusion of near-single deep-pink flowers, and grows to around $6\frac{1}{2}$ feet (2 m) height and width.

It has been found to be more satisfactory to supply miniature roses that have been budded in the fields rather than grown on their own roots from cuttings. The miniatures are supplied either bare-root or in pots, and can be one of a number of types: standards, bushes, ground-cover roses and climbers.

Layering

Rose plants, and particularly those with arching shoots, can be propagated by layering – that is, by pegging down shoots and inducing them to grow fresh roots in the soil, in the same way that brambles (unfortunately) do of their own accord. Layering can help gardeners to grow the kind of rose hedge they seem to greatly prefer.

The ground where the new root is to be formed is broken up into a fine consistency to give the new root proper access to the elements it needs for growth. The leaves from the lower three-quarters of the shoot that is to be layered are then removed. The shoot is bent down and a mark is made at the point where it touches the ground. Ideally this should be close to and below a bud. The stem is then cut upwards and halfway through at this point, and a split is thus formed with a projecting 'tongue' from which the new

Layering a rose tree by making a 'tongue' (left) *and pegging down. From* Popular Gardening, *c. 1895.*

root will eventually grow. This tongue should be inserted in a hole about 4 inches (10 cm) deep, with sand sprinkled over the bottom to allow drainage; some hormone powder sprinkled on to the 'tongue' will help. The hole is then filled up and the earth pressed down, leaving the tongue pushed down vertically into the soil. The branch is then pegged down or weighed down with a heavy stone so that it remains 2 to 3 inches (5–7.5 cm) below ground level. The end of the shoot is supported by a small stake to prevent it from moving and disturbing the rooting process, and to encourage the new plant to grow upright.

Fresh growth on the 'new' shoot is the surest sign that the layered root has 'taken', and when thoroughly established, it can be severed from the parent plant if it is to be transplanted.

Linnaeus and the rose

The system of botanical classification of Carl Linnaeus (1707–78) distinguished one class of plants from another according to the number of stamens to be found in the flower. Plants within each class were then differentiated according to the number of styles and the position of the ovary.

The rose was placed in Class XII – Icosandria – that is, among plants with flowers having twenty or more stamens. Within that class, he put the rose among the Polygynia – that is, those having many ovaries. Linnaeus also noted that the stamens were inserted in the calyx and not in the receptacle (*see* ANATOMY OF THE ROSE).

Although Linnaeus must have had first-hand knowledge of the rose, his identification of Rosa species was based, in the main, on *Pinax theatri botanici* by the Swiss botanist Caspar Bauhin. This was first published in 1623, but Linnaeus worked from the later edition of 1671, which contained many fine plates. He also compared Bauhin's descriptions to the dried specimens in the herbarium of Joachim Burser (1583–1639), who had been a pupil of Bauhin's. Burser's herbarium, which had been providentially seized and retained by the Swedish army as war booty during the Danish campaign of 1657/8, comprised twenty-three volumes, arranged according to Bauhin's system of classification, which incidentally was based on naturalistic criteria more in tune with modern thinking than with the Linnaean system.

Rosa carolina was identified by Linnaeus from Dillenius's weighty (17 lb) treatise *Hortus elthamensis* (1732), which included the plants growing in James Sherard's garden in Eltham, a suburb of London.

See also SPECIES ROSES.

Lyrics, the rose in

The word 'rose' is manna to the lyricist – a musical sound with romantic associations, a word meant to be sung, one that is easily enunciated and eminently scannable, with at least 100 permissible rhymes.

This may help to explain why roses have been so indiscriminately used, and why the music of the songs in which they feature is so often superior to the lyrics of which they form part. However, one well-known ballad, though extremely sentimental, must have been written by someone who loved roses for themselves.

Thomas Moore (1779–1852), the Irish poet, at one time held the unusual position of Admiralty Registrar in Bermuda, but he is most remembered for having (at the insistence of another friend and the poet's publisher) burned Byron's memoirs. Publication of *A Selection of Irish Melodies* (with music by Sir John Stevenson) between 1808 and 1834 won him acclaim as the lyricist of his native country, although his best-known composition is not limited to Ireland, or to any other land. A semi-double 'Parson's Pink China' flowering in the grounds of Jenkinstown House, County Kilkenny, inspired Moore to write these lines:

> 'Tis the last rose of summer,
> Left blooming alone;
> All her lovely companions
> Are faded and gone.
> No flower of her kindred,
> No rosebud, is nigh
> To reflect her blushes
> Or give sigh for sigh.
>
> I'll not leave thee, thou lone one,
> To pine on the stem.
> Since the lovely are sleeping,
> Go, sleep thou with them;
> Thus kindly I scatter
> Thy leaves o'er the bed
> Where thy mates of the garden
> Lie senseless and dead.
>
> So, soon may I follow
> When friendships decay,
> And from love's shining circle
> The gems drop away!
> When true hearts lie wither'd
> And fond ones are flown,
> Oh – who would inhabit
> This bleak world alone?

The 'Rose of Tralee' is both a person and a rose. At the annual Festival of Kerry held in Tralee, the county capital, a contest takes place to decide who will be the year's 'Rose of Tralee'. Preliminary competitions to select nominees for the honour from among girls of Irish ancestry are held in centres in the UK, US, Canada, Australia and Ireland. A 'rose of Tralee' memorial can be seen in the town, and the roses surrounding it were originally provided by Sam MCGREDY, who introduced his 'Rose of Tralee', a mid-pink cluster-flowered variety, in 1964.

The song 'The Rose of Tralee' was composed by William Pembroke Mulchinock (1820–64) who lived at Cloghers House, Ballymullen,, on the outskirts of the town. The original 'Rose' was Mary O'Sullivan, a young woman who served in a Tralee hat shop. Mulchinock fell deeply in love with her, but, he overestimated his powers of persuasion: the real Mary rejected his advances and married a policeman instead.

The pale moon was rising above the green mountain,
The sun was declining beneath the blue sea,
When I strayed with my love to the pure crystal fountain,
That stands in the beautiful vale of Tralee.
She was lovely and fair as the rose of the summer,
Yet 'twas not her beauty alone that won me,
Oh no, 'twas the truth in her eye ever dawning,
That made me love Mary, the Rose of Tralee.

The cool shades of evening their mantle were spreading,
And Mary, all smiling, was listening to me,
The moon through the valley her pale rays was shedding,
When I won the heart of the Rose of Tralee.
Though lovely and fair as the rose of the summer,
Yet 'twas not her beauty alone that won me,
Oh no, 'twas the truth in her eye ever dawning,
That made me love Mary, the Rose of Tralee.

One of the best-known rose songs from the stage is 'Only a Rose' from the operetta *The Vagabond King*, a romantic play set in Paris in the days of the 15th-century Louis XI and first presented in New York on 21 September 1925. The lyrics for 'Only a Rose' were written by Brian Hooker and W. H. Post and presented the rose in a brief eight lines as a token of enduring devotion. The music, because it was composed by Charles Rudolf Friml, is somewhat more memorable. He was born in 1879 in Prague, studied under Dvořak and travelled as accompanist to the violinist Jan Kubelik on his European tours. Friml's popular success as a composer was achieved in the US with other songs such as 'Indian Love Call' and 'Donkey Serenade'.

Still in the States, we have Frank Lebby Stanton (1857–1927) who for more than forty years wrote a poem a day for the newspaper, the *Atlanta Constitution*. At least one of his efforts has survived:

Sweetes' li'l' feller –
Everybody knows;
Dunno what ter call 'im
But he's mighty lak' a rose!

This is another example of a song in which the music will probably outlive the lyric – at least as long as the recording of gifted pianist Art Tatum's solo adaptation is still played.

And finally we have 'The Yellow Rose of Texas'.

While there is some doubt about the origins of the song, the explanation that appears to have been accepted by the Dallas Area Historical Rose Group is that of the writer Charles Rogers, who linked the 'Yellow Rose of Texas' to a beautiful mulatto woman named Emily who was not a slave but was indentured as a servant to Captain James Morgan, and was for convenience's sake known as Emily Morgan. When the American settlers in Texas declared their independence from Mexico in 1836, an expedition led by the Mexican general, Lopez de Santa Anna, was sent to bring them to heel. Emily was captured and Santa Anna carried her off, making her share his tent.

Emily, loyal to her former employer, got word to Sam Houston, the leader of the main Texan forces, to warn him of Santa Anna's movements, and she used her charms to prevent the Mexican from leaving his tent to lead his troops. With this aid, the settlers won the battle of San Jacinto, and the Texans won their freedom. Emily was treated as a heroine and praised in song, first in one written by an unknown author which mentions her by name, and later in another in which she was called 'The Yellow Rose of Texas'.

Professor Martha Anne Turner of Sam Houston State University at Huntsville, Texas, has made a special study of the origin of this folk song. In an article in the *Journal of the American Studies Association of Texas*, in 1970, she mentions an early hand-written version of the song in the A. Henry Moss papers in the archives of the University of Texas at Austin. This appears to have been delivered to a Mr E. G. Jones early in the first administration of Sam Houston as President of the Republic of Texas – that is, soon after the battle of San Jacinto. The lyric is almost identical with the current 20th-century version. The first verse begins:

There's a Yellow Rose in Texas
That I'm going to see.
No other darky knows her,
No one – only me . . .

According to Professor Turner, the first publication was registered in New York in 1858 and the cover stated that the song and chorus were composed and arranged expressly for 'Charles H. Brown and J.K.' (I am grateful to John Wheat of the University of Texas at Austin for drawing my attention to this source.)

However, David Ewen in his book *All the Years of American Music* puts the earliest publication date of 'The Yellow Rose of Texas' as 1853, its author being identified as 'J.K.' According to Ewen, the song was later used in the American Civil War as a Confederate marching song, both in its original form and in variations. One of these was 'The Song of the Texas Rangers', and another version gave an account of the disastrous Tennessee campaign of 1864. The 20th-century adaptation, attributed to Don George, was published in 1955.

Over a period of nearly 150 years, the state of Texas has not designated any particular variety of rose as the 'Yellow Rose of Texas', nor would there appear to be any connection between the 'Yellow Rose of Texas' and *Rosa harisonii*, a double-yellow rose of the Pimpinellifoliae family (first found in a New York City garden), although the Prince Nursery of Flushing, New York was distributing it widely across the United States as early as 1830.

The *Yellow Rose Magazine* is published for the Dallas Area Historical Rose Group by James Harrison, 2119 Oak Brook, Richardson, Texas 75081.

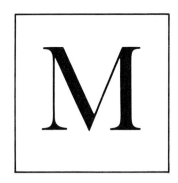

McGredy dynasty, the

Sam McGredy I was already fifty years old in 1880 when he decided to open a nursery at Portadown, Co. Armagh, Northern Ireland, with his son, Sam II, as helper. For a time, the nursery specialized in show pansies and apple trees for the orchards of County Armagh, but during the 1890s McGredy and his son started growing roses obtained from other nurserymen, and towards the end of the century, Sam McGredy II began breeding his own. In 1905 he decided to show a few of his roses at the National Rose Show in London, and at this, his first attempt, he won a gold medal with his pink HYBRID TEA ROSE 'Countess of Gosford'. Sam McGredy I died in 1903 and so did not live to see his son's triumph. The nursery continued to prosper, and McGredy roses such as 'Mrs Henry Morse' and 'Mrs Charles Lamplough' appeared regularly in the honours lists. Sam McGredy II died in 1926, leaving the business to his son Sam McGredy III, then aged twenty-nine. Soon afterwards, 'Margaret McGredy', a carmine and yellow rose and a distant relative of 'Peace', appeared as a tribute to Sam's widow. 'Mrs Sam McGredy', named for Sam III's wife and a very different rose, with scarlet, copper and orange blooms, was launched in 1929 and won a gold medal. 'McGredy's Yellow' (1930) was another gold-medal winner and was formally introduced three years later. Sam McGredy III died unexpectedly in 1934 at the age of thirty-eight, leaving a son, Sam IV, aged only two. Luckily, the late Sam's sister Ivy was married to Walter Johnston who proved able to manage the nursery until Sam McGredy IV came of age. When that happened, 'Uncle Walter' called him over one morning and handed him the keys of the glasshouses, saying, 'Now it's all yours.' At that time, Sam knew little about horticulture and nothing at all about roses.

During his minority, World War II had intervened and much of the rose stock had had to be burned. It needed dedication to replace it and throw out the chrysanthemums that had usurped much of the glasshouse space in the meantime. Until the 1950s the McGredy breeding programme had concentrated on large-flowered roses, but young McGredy quickly came to the conclusion that the breeding strain they had been using since the 1930s had since become played out; in any case, cluster-flowered

roses, despite their relatively insignificant flowers, were the plants of the future. 'Orangeade' (1959) was the first gold medal success to come from the new regime. McGredy was also successful with SPONSORED ROSES, and among these was 'Daily Sketch', a cluster-flowered rose with pink petals reverse white, which took a gold medal. 'Paddy McGredy', named for Sam's sister, won the President's International Trophy in 1969. In the meantime, 'Evelyn Fison' (1963) kept the pot boiling with another gold medal, and 'Elizabeth of Glamis' won the President's International Trophy and the Clay Vase for fragrance in 1964. Two climbers, 'Schoolgirl' (1964) and 'Handel' with cream blooms flushed rose, were the first McGredy roses to enjoy the protection (in Britain) of the then newly passed Plants and Seeds Act. The 'Mullard Jubilee', referred to under 'Sponsored roses', was introduced in 1969.

All the while, Sam was thinking of the wider market of the United States. However, it was difficult in the damp Irish climate to grow varieties that would suit the much drier and warmer conditions prevailing in many parts of the US; in addition, County Armagh had become one of the areas most affected by the new troubles in Northern Ireland. Sam, who had made several visits to New Zealand, then decided that this was a better place in which to grow roses, and in 1972, he took the plunge and travelled out there, taking his breeding stock with him.

Since then, a string of striking cluster-flowered roses have continued to spring from his nursery near Auckland. 'Matangi' (1974) – bright orange-red with a white eye – won the President's International Trophy, and 'Trumpeter', another cluster-flowered orange-red, was introduced the same year.

'Sue Lawley' (1980), a deep-pink cluster-flowered rose with a white centre and white edging, is in the relatively new hand-painted tradition. 'Regensberg', with an equally striking pink-and-white pattern, is more of a PATIO ROSE, while 'Snow Carpet' is a leading GROUND-COVER ROSE, though it is also obtainable as a miniature standard.

Maiden rose trees/bushes

A maiden rose plant is one in its first season following budding. Most of the roses on show at nurseries are maidens. They usually flower later than older roses of the same variety, a point to be borne in mind when planning a visit.

Meilland family, the

The present members of the Meilland family are the latest five generations of French rose growers – best known as progenitors of the LARGE-FLOWERED ROSE 'Peace'. The definitive work on the Meilland family, on which much of the following entry is based, is Antonia Ridge's *For Love of a Rose*, which should be consulted for a very much fuller account of this sector of rosarian history.

Antoine Meilland, born at Chamboeuf near St Etienne in 1884, was apprenticed at the age of eleven to a firm of tree growers at St Galmier, a mineral-water source in the Loire Valley. After working there for four years, he joined the Lyon rose nursery of François Dubreuil, who had himself married the daughter of a spare-time rose grower, Joseph Rambaux. In 1909, Antoine married Dubreuil's only child, a daughter, Claudia, and in due course, he succeeded to his father-in-law's business.

During World War I, Antoine (who had already been nicknamed 'Papa' Meilland) was called up for military service and a large part of the rose nursery had to be turned over to vegetable production, with only a selection of the best varieties of roses remaining. Claudia was forced to manage the nursery and look after her home, young son and elderly father all on her own, with only a handcart for transport. Moreover, when Antoine Meilland returned from the war, he found that, because the nursery had become absorbed into an industrial zone, there was no room to expand. He therefore decided, in 1923, to move to a new 5 acre (2 hectare) site at Tassin, in the countryside to the west of Lyon. Three years later, he was joined in the business by his son Francis, who left school at fourteen and began specializing from 1929 onwards in the hybridization of roses.

Francis was encouraged by another breeder, Charles Mallerin, who brought his work to the notice of Robert Pyle of the Conard–Pyle Company, the American rose growers of West Grove, Pennsylvania. Pyle visited the Meilland nursery at Tassin in 1932 and was so impressed that he signed a contract agreeing to market new Meilland roses in the United States and to pay the Meillands a percentage of the profits as a royalty. Francis Meilland visited the US in 1935, and was fascinated by the American method by which rose bushes could be stored with their roots bare, providing that the temperature and moisture of the atmosphere were automatically controlled. He later built his own rose warehouse on the same lines to allow for winter storage. From this year too, the Meilland rose catalogues were considerably improved, with American style, colour photographs and captions.

Francis Meilland achieved an early international success in 1937 with a new deep-yellow rose marketed in the United States under the name 'Golden State'. In 1939 he married Louisette Paolino, the daughter of Francesco Paolino, a rose grower of Calabrian parentage whose nursery at Cap d'Antibes he had visited and stayed as a guest. Before World War II, he was able to show French and foreign visitors the first flowers of a rose as yet unnamed but known as '3–35–40' – the third specimen of the 40th combination tried in 1935. Meilland had been hoping for a copper-coloured rose with resistant foliage and winter hardiness, but instead, he got a rose of a delicate pale yellow with cerise edging to the petals.

In November 1942, southern France was as yet unoccupied by Hitler's army and the US still kept a consul in Lyon – George Whittinghill, himself a rose lover. When the Second Front and an allied invasion became a probability, the Germans marched in and the consul had to leave, but before he did, Whittinghill got in touch with his rose-growing friends, the Meillands. He would take a small parcel, weighing no more than half a kilo, to friends in the US if it got to him within two hours. And so the scions of 3-35-40 crossed the Atlantic in safety. Other samples of 3-35-40 had already been sent to Germany and Italy, but it was not until 1945 that the Meillands learned that all three consignments had been safely delivered, and had provided splendid roses.

Those in France had been christened 'Madame Antoine Meilland' (in memory of Claudia); in Germany, 'Gloria Dei'; in Italy, 'Gioia' ('Joy'); and in the United States, 'Peace' – an appropriate name because it was launched there at the end of World War II. During the conference that saw the birth of the United Nations in San Francisco, Pyle, by offering the bellboys of the hotel a dollar for each rose delivered, was able to see that every delegate found a rose named 'Peace' in his bedroom. With each rose was a message: 'This rose was christened "Peace" at the Pacific Rose Society convention in Pasadena [California] on the day Berlin fell. We hope the "Peace" rose will influence men's thoughts for everlasting world peace.'

The royalties from 'Peace' made a fortune for the Meillands, and the success of the rose made it clear to them that they had to make a choice between concentrating on production rose-growing or on the search for new breeds; they had neither the time nor the energy to give proper attention to both at once. A compromise was reached in which half the Meilland business at Tassin was sold in 1947 to Francisque Richardier, a prominent rose grower in the Lyon area, leaving the Meillands free to concentrate on new varieties. From then on, Meilland rose hybridizing activities were transferred to Cap d'Antibes, near the Paolino family home, where the climate was more favourable to rapid growth by the seedlings, both out of doors and in greenhouses.

Francis Meilland also performed two other valuable services for rose breeders across the world. He succeeded in securing a French patent for one of his hybrids – 'Meilland Rouge' – until then, a form of protection only available in the United States; there the rose was marketed as 'Happiness'. Rose growers in many other countries have since succeeded in securing a system of legal REGISTRATION for their new hybrids to save them from being 'pirated' by unscrupulous nurserymen. In addition, Francis Meilland was instrumental in 1950 in establishing 'Universal Rose Selection', an international organisation of growers designed to supervise the production and marketing of new rose hybrids by members. As a result, it now became possible for new varieties to be tested worldwide by growers in varying climates and soils before being offered, as truly reliable hybrids, to the public.

Francis Meilland died in 1958, but his son Alain took over his responsibilities in the Universal Rose Selection organization, and his daughter Michèle married into the Richardier family and thus became closely involved in the Établissement Meilland–Richardier at Tassin.

Many successful roses have come from the Meilland gardens since the war. One such is 'Michelle [*sic*] Meilland' (1945), listed by David Austin in his *Handbook of Roses* as 'slender, amber-orange buds opening gracefully to coppery-pink. A very beautiful rose that is free-flowering, robust, and disease-resistant. A little fragrance.' The year 1953 saw 'Bettina' with yellow flowers veined with bronze and copper tints. 'Baccara', a deep-red, long-stemmed rose grown extensively in greenhouses for the cut-flower trade, followed in 1954. 'Grace de Monaco' with very fragrant deep rose-pink flowers and 'Soraya' with flame-coloured petals suffused with deeper reds both appeared in 1956. Other successes have been 'Fantan' with large double bowl-shaped flowers of a rare burnt orange colour, and 'Pink Peace', both launched in 1959 and therefore undoubtedly still Francis Meilland's own creations. 'Papa Meilland', introduced in 1963 and still going strong twenty years later, has much fragrance and offers exemplary dark crimson flowers to succeeding generations of rose growers.

Since coming under the management of Alain Meilland, the company has remained at the forefront of rose production in more than one respect. 'Orange Sunblaze' (sometimes 'Sunblaze' or 'Orange Meillandina', 1980) is one of the new range of PATIO ROSES; 'Darling Flame' (1971), with orange-red blooms, is an outstanding MINIATURE; and 'Swany' (1979), another miniature, closely covers the ground with sprays of white flowers. 'Meiflorol Pareo', a multi-coloured red and orange 'coals of fire' rose raised by Madame Louisette Meilland, won the Gold Medal at the BAGATELLE competition in 1985.

Meiosis

Some knowledge of meiosis is essential if the mechanics of rose inheritance are to be understood. Meiosis is the process leading to the formation of a plant's sex cells, as distinct from the formation of its somatic, or body cells, the latter (called MITOSIS) giving rise to leaves and other vegetal growth. The sex cells are of two kinds: the 'male' gametes that will develop into pollen cells; and the 'female' gametes that will provide the ovules.

'Male' and 'female' will eventually unite together to form the seed of a new plant, but since that one seed must contain no more CHROMOSOMES than in each of the cells of its parents, each of the two gametes that are to form the

future seed must contribute no more than half the number of chromosomes for the seed. Thus normal vegetal cells of a typical rose will contain no fewer than seven pairs of chromosomes (or fourteen), but the gametes will each need only seven chromosomes each – not seven pairs each.

The process by which cells of the rose containing seven pairs of chromosomes are reduced to the specialized sex cells containing only half as many is known as meiosis. The following is a drastically shortened account of what occurs.

1 The members of the normal seven pairs of chromosomes in the cell where the reduction is to take place match up opposite one another in a formation resembling two separate chains.
2 These chromosome chains, one of which will have been inherited from its female parent and the other from the male, are attracted to each other and can be seen to lie alongside each other.
3 The two chains wind round each other, breaking and rejoining in parts so that some male elements are exchanged for female, and vice versa. This process is known as 'crossing over'.
4 The two reconstituted chains begin to separate, and it becomes clear that, during the crossing over, each chromosome has divided into two halves known as *chromatids*, and that some chromosomes consist of a male chromatid paired with a female.
5 When crossing over has been completed, the two chains move away from one another and are drawn to opposite poles of the cell.
6 A division is taking place that, for the sake of simplicity, we will assume to be occurring on a horizontal plane. In other words, the two chains are divided from one another at the 'equator' by a membrane separating the northern hemisphere from the southern. Thus, while the total number of chromosomes remains the same, the number of cells has doubled and the number of chromosomes per cell has been halved.
7 A second division follows, this time on a 'vertical' plane, but now both the chromosomes and the cell nucleus divide.
8 At the end of these two divisions, there would be four cells, each with seven chromosomes only – sex cells waiting to fertilize or be fertilized by others like them.

Inevitably, however, the process of meiosis does not always go without a hitch. The number of chromosomes in the sex cell of a plant is known as the *haploid number* – seven in the case of the genus Rosa – and the vegetal cells of a normal rose carrying seven *pairs* of chromosomes are said to be *diploid*; one with fourteen pairs is a *tetraploid*, and so on up to an *octoploid* with twenty-eight pairs. However, if a normal diploid rose succeeds in hybridizing with a rose having twice as many chromosomes (as often happens), the vegetal cells of their offspring will have seven plus fourteen, or twenty-one, chromosomes – in fact, it is a *triploid*, with three times the basic haploid number. For triploids, the chances of successful meoisis are greatly reduced because of the difficulties, during the first stage of meiosis, of pairing the odd number of chromosomes coming from one parent with the (often) even number offered by the other. Thus many triploids prove to be sterile, and a disappointment to the rose breeder.

See also MENDEL'S LAWS.

Mendel's Laws

The genetic principles that came to be known as Mendel's Laws, and which are of considerable relevance to rose hybridizers, were first put forward in 1865 by Gregor Mendel, Abbot of St Thomas's Monastery at Brno, a Czechoslovakian city that then lay within the Austro-Hungarian Empire. Mendel began his experiments in the monastery garden in 1856, using the domestic pea as a model, and continued them for nine years before publishing the results. Their significance was overlooked and his work remained practically unknown until 1899, when a paper setting out his findings came into the hands of William Bateson, a biologist, who read it on the train while on his way to an international conference on hybridization arranged by the Royal Horticultural Society. Thus rosarians who had shared so much enthusiasm for hybridization remained in ignorance of Mendel's work until the 20th century.

Mendel had noted that certain individual characteristics recurred on an 'either/or' basis (e.g. peas were *either* round *or* wrinkled) and that, when hybridization took place between two pure-breeding strains, these opposing characteristics were passed on to succeeding generations according to certain fixed ratios. For example, when a plant that produced only round peas was hybridized with one that produced only wrinkled peas, the resulting first generation – known to geneticists as F_1 – would be composed of plants yielding only round peas, leading Mendel to conclude that roundness was, in this case, a dominant characteristic, and wrinkledness a recessive one.

However, Mendel discovered, if each F_1 plant was fertilized only from itself and the resulting peas were then sown, the recessive characteristic would reappear in the peas of the second (F_2) generation plants. Twenty-five per cent of the peas from the F_2 plants would be wrinkled, and these, if also segregated and sown, would produce plants yielding only wrinkled peas. Another 25 per cent of the peas from the F_2 plants would be round and, if sown, would produce plants yielding only round peas. The remaining 50 per cent would also be round, but the plants produced from these peas would give rise to a new generation having the same mixed composition as their own.

The validity of Mendel's principles is subject to three conditions:

1. that the two original parents are of a pure strain.
2. that the characteristics chosen are mutually exclusive.
3. that each parent passes on the characteristics with equal frequency.

They do not therefore hold good in cases where the ratios between dominants and recessives are distorted during the 'crossing over' process that takes place during MEIOSIS (*see* MUTATION), or in cases where inherited characteristics depend on a combination of several genes.

See also CHROMOSOMES.

A bouquet of centifolia roses.

Micropropagation of roses

Micropropagation – often referred to as tissue culture, or cultivation *in vitro* – can guarantee the grower a rapidly generated abundance of plants that are virus-free, and therefore suitable for export to countries with restrictions that virtually prohibit the import of conventionally grown rose plants.

The *in vitro* technique ('in glass', i.e. in a test-tube or culture dish) was originally devised for plants such as orchids where conventional methods can be costly and time-consuming, or for species such as lilies that are particularly susceptible to virus attacks. However, since in the great majority of cases *in vitro* cultivation also guarantees the identical reproduction of the parent plant, it is now used commercially by rose growers for MINIATURES and GROUNDCOVER ROSES, where a large spread of identical plants is called for, and also with some success for LARGE-FLOWERED and cluster-flowered roses. The work can be carried out all year round, allowing exports to flow during the off-season from the northern hemisphere to the southern. There is a saving, too, on the acreage that might otherwise have to be devoted to growing UNDERSTOCKS.

The French family firm of Georges Delbard, which celebrated its 50th anniversary in 1985, was one of the first to specialize in micropropagation, and now grows all its large-flowered rose varieties by this method. Trials on potatoes and dahlias had already been carried out in France by G.

Morel and Claude Martin of the Institut National de Recherches Agronomiques, Dijon, and towards the end of the 1970s, Georges and his three sons resolved to apply the technique to roses, a decision that encouraged the multinational Moët-Hennessy conglomerate to finance the necessary expansion. The *in vitro* cultivation now takes place under licence at the firm's laboratory at Commentry in the Auvergne where Georges Delbard lives. In 1985, the Moët-Hennessy group took over the US firm Armstrong Roses, and installed Henri Delbard, President of Delbard International, as chairman of its board of directors.

The Delbard family is convinced that roses grown *in vitro* produce more flowers and repeat more rapidly than the same varieties when grown on understocks. A single cutting can be expected to yield four-to-six shoots after four weeks' cultivation *in vitro* and, if used purely for propagation, can give rise to several hundred thousand plants a year – or, alternatively, can turn into a perfectly formed micro-plant, roots and all, in three to five weeks.

Micropropagation became a possibility when it was discovered that a single cell of a plant can contain all the factors needed to give rise to another whole plant. Complete roses could thus be grown from single cells taken from parent plants, normally from the shoots growing from the axils of their leaves since they are thought to be the most typical of the parent.

In order to maintain a virus-free strain, cultivation *in vitro* must be carried out under laboratory conditions in a sterile chamber. The parent plant itself is sanitized at some cost, often under government supervision, and the cutting cleansed with a 10 per cent solution of sodium hypochlorite. Jars and other equipment are sterilized in an autoclave (a kind of pressure cooker).

The medium used to nourish the cuttings is usually a closely guarded secret, but mixtures containing a round dozen of inorganic feed chemicals together with vitamin supplements are sold commercially in powder form. These are then added to a solution of glucose or sucrose. This nutrient mixture is stabilized in a supporting jelly formed by dissolving crystals of agar (derived from an Asian species of seaweed) in boiling water; agar is especially suitable as a supporting medium because it is resistant to attacks from almost all micro-organisms. After the medium has been mixed and sterilized, it is poured into the flasks or trays where cultivation is to take place.

The cutting taken from the parent plant may originally have been 1 to 2 inches (2.5–5 cm) long, but will have been cut down to perhaps $\frac{1}{4}$ to $\frac{1}{2}$ inch (0.60–1.2 cm) before being implanted in the medium. The unformed cells at the tip, known as the *meristem*, form the vital growing sector from which the new rose will be formed.

The plant is then grown in temperatures of 64–77°F (18 –25°C) under fluorite broad-spectrum lighting for twelve-to-fourteen hours a day. After a few days, there should be signs of growth. If there are side shoots, these can be removed in due course and used for further propagation. If no side shoots appear but the stem lengthens, it can be cut

at the nodes (the points from which leaves arise) and each new growth can in turn be propagated. Thus, in theory, the number of new plants can increase very rapidly, and their numbers will be limited only by the staff available to handle them.

The type of growth in the plants can be controlled to some extent by hormones added to the growing medium. Cytokinin promotes branching and discourages rooting, whereas auxin encourages rooting. A cutting without a viable root structure can be transferred to a medium containing more auxin; and a plant deficient in branches is moved to a medium containing added cytokinin.

As soon as the roots have grown out and the leaves are greened with chlorophyll, the plants will be hardened off gradually. They can then be treated like normal cuttings.

In the meantime, however, several prickings out and replantings would have been needed, and it is clear that the work of micropropagation is labour-intensive and calls for a skilled and highly trained staff, with correspondingly high salaries. Micropropagated roses also need considerable attention (and greenhouse space) during the weaning period. At a time when rose prices are low and new varieties are increasingly resistant to viruses, the average producer may well hesitate before forsaking his or her rose field for the laboratory.

Mildew

There is not one sort of mildew but many – such as apple mildew, peach mildew, strawberry mildew and American gooseberry mildew – but that which most concerns rosarians in their outdoor gardens is known as 'powdery mildew' and even sometimes as 'rose mildew'. If left undisturbed, it will wreck not only the chances of good summer flowers, but will affect the autumn crop and even the constitution of the whole plant.

The life cycle of this parasite comprises three stages. In the first, a greyish-white mould appears on the upper and lower surfaces of the leaves causing them to curl and shrivel. The mould is produced by the finely interwoven threads that form the *mycelium*, or body, of the fungus, and which exude an enzyme allowing the fungus to attack and penetrate the cell walls of the host plant to procure nourishment. In the next, reproductive stage, oval-shaped bodies known as *conidia* are formed at the tips of the mycelium threads, and on maturity, these float on to other leaves and stems, where they germinate and produce filaments of their own. This process continues through several weeks of the summer, thus spreading the infection far and wide.

As autumn approaches, the third stage occurs: new spores are produced within the host tissues and are encased in rounded capsules (eight spores to each capsule) that are both water-tight and frost-proof. During the winter, these fall to the ground with the rose leaves and remain there until the warmth of the sun causes the casings to burst, freeing the spores, which float upwards on to the new leaves to begin another life cycle. This is the time – before the appearance of mildew spots – when the spores are at their most vulnerable.

The experts have appropriately named this fungus *Sphaerotheca pannosa* – the first word referring to the spherical capsule and the second to the withered rose leaf that results.

Systemic remedies that are absorbed through the leaves into the system of the plant are the quickest and most effective counter-measure to powdery mildew. Benomyl (Benlate), triforine (Roseclear) and bupirimate triforine (Nimrod T) are three examples available in the UK. Trials have shown that adding a non-ionic wetter to the spray increases the efficiency of these. One other effective preparation – Dinocap – can be bought in powder form and can be dispensed on small areas by a hand puffer.

Apart from these anti-mildew sprays, other precautions can also be taken. Avoid those varieties of roses that are more prone to powdery mildew than others; many good breeders display warnings of this in their lists but they are too often shunned by the hopeful. Plants that have plenty of air and sun, and good drainage, are less likely to succumb.

Downy mildew (*Peronospora sparsa Berk.*), sometimes called black mildew, takes the form of dark purplish spots on the upper surface of the leaf, and in the corresponding areas beneath, tufts of greyish mould can be detected. This form of mildew is mainly a greenhouse complaint, and is encouraged by the extra humidity that occurs when high daytime temperatures are followed by cold nights – especially if ventilation is inadequate. In such conditions, infection can spread very rapidly, and in severe cases, whole leaves are shed. Sprays with a sulphur content have proved successful in combating attack, but prevention is better than cure, for flowering may be delayed even in roses that are not severely affected. Consequently, many gardeners prefer to use a systemic product such as Nimrod T.

Minden Rose, the

The Minden Rose commemorates the gallant and successful action fought during the Seven Years' War by British troops under Ferdinand of Brunswick, when they routed a larger French army on 1 August 1759 near the town of Minden in northwest Germany. British soldiers who were following up the retreating French units are said to have passed through a rose garden, where they picked roses and wore them in their helmets as battle honours.

The XXth Foot, the Lancashire Fusiliers hold an annual all-day celebration of the event. At reveille, the Corps of Drums play the 'Minden March' through the battalion lines, finishing in front of the officers' mess. The Regimental Colour is trooped in the morning, with the Colonel of the Regiment taking the salute. As well as a dinner for the rank and file and one in the sergeants' mess, a mess dinner is held at which the table is decorated with roses and the 'Minden Toast' is drunk by the officers, each of whom wears two roses.

Later, when the bandmaster has entertained, the port circulated and the waiters withdrawn, the president orders the mess sergeant to place a 'Minden Regiment' – a rose floating in champagne in a bowl – in front of each officer who has joined the Regiment since the previous year's celebrations. These officers then rise and, standing on their chairs, eat the roses and drink the champagne, remaining in place until all the roses and the champagne have been consumed – a feat that few accomplish without asking permission to leave the table afterwards. A similar, if less elaborate, ritual is followed by all battalions of the Suffolk Regiment. In both cases, only red and yellow roses are used, these being the regimental colours. However, to have been flowering on 1 August, the roses would probably have been autumn damasks with, quite probably, flowers of a clear pink.

Miniature roses

The need for roses that can be grown in window boxes, hanging baskets, in troughs on balconies and, under certain conditions, even indoors has grown with the number of city dwellers. The miniature rose in its many different forms not only meets these requirements but, as a small-scale replica of something larger, possesses the same kind of attraction for gardeners that others find in model railways or dolls' houses. There are now more than 300 different varieties to choose from.

As understood in Britain, the typical miniature rose has flowers of little more than 2 inches (5 cm) in diameter. The ROYAL NATIONAL ROSE SOCIETY rates as 'small' those less than 1 inch (2.5 cm) across; 'medium' as being 1-1$\frac{1}{2}$ inches (2.5–4 cm); 'fairly large' as 1$\frac{1}{2}$-1$\frac{3}{4}$ inches (4–4.5 cm); 'large' as 1$\frac{3}{4}$-2 inches (4.5–5 cm); and 'very large' as over 2 inches (5 cm). The leaves of miniatures should be small and the stems thin, with both in proportion to the size of the bush. The internodes (distances on the stem between one leafstalk and the next) should also be small.

The height of the bush is also classified according to that which appears natural to it. 'Very short' miniatures grow naturally to less than 6 inches (15 cm); 'short' miniatures to about 9 inches (23 cm); 'medium' to about 12 inches (30 cm); 'medium-to-tall' about 15 inches (38 cm); and 'tall' to 18 inches (46 cm) or more. A plant readily growing to more than 18 inches is not regarded as a typical miniature rose.

The size and spread of any given variety of miniature will vary according to whether it has been grown on its own roots or budded or grafted on to an understock, and this should be considered when ordering.

In the UK, breeders of miniatures aim to produce roses that resemble very small LARGE-FLOWERED ROSES, or cluster-flowered roses (which most miniatures do) or CHINA ROSES (not to be confused with those known as DWARF chinas). When a rose is of miniature dimensions but nevertheless shows characteristics of a class or species other than the above, then it is not considered to be a typical miniature. Only those varieties officially classsed as miniatures can be entered as such for the Royal National Rose Society competitions.

Thus the old days are passing when a miniature rose was either a curiosity (like a Venus's fly trap) or an alternative to the pelargonium or the chrysanthemum. The miniature is becoming a favourite with rosarians – collectors and hobbyists – on both sides of the Atlantic.

At the beginning of the 1970s, there were only three sources selling miniature roses in the United States, but today there are forty or more specialists, and the number of breeders has increased from two to more than two dozen. The number of miniatures sold there has risen from less than half a million plants in 1970 to several million, and whereas, at the outset, a mere 10 per cent were bought by members of rose societies, the figure has since risen to 25 per cent.

In the US, it is possible to buy 20-inch (50 cm) standards ('rose trees') with varieties budded on to suitable understocks, as well as smaller 'trees' likely to appeal to Japanese bonsai miniature garden enthusiasts. Miniature ramblers are grown for ground cover, for use as trellis roses and for trailing from hanging baskets. In addition, some are marketed as climbing SPORTS of well-known miniature bush varieties.

Because so many varieties are being introduced, both the AMERICAN ROSE SOCIETY and ALL-AMERICA ROSE SELECTIONS have begun testing programmes for miniatures. The American Rose Society carries out two-year trials on seven sites, and grades miniatures from '0' to '5' each year. Leading varieties achieve officially recognized Awards of Excellence. All-America Rose Selections has included miniatures in their trials since 1982.

The history of miniature roses

The miniature rose can be traced back to a China rose, *Rosa chinensis minima*, a cultivated variety that has never been found in the wild. It is thought that Chinese nurserymen achieved the reduction in size partly by seed selection, but also through cultivating the plants in small containers and without enriched soil.

The variety was first described and illustrated in *Curtis's Botanical Magazine* in 1815 as *Rosa semperflorens minima*, or 'Miss Lawrance's Rose'. An English botanist, Robert Sweet, referring to the illustration, commented that the rose had been brought to London from the island of Mauritius in 1810 – the year that the island was first occupied by British forces. He did not, however, claim to have imported it himself, and the name of the introducer remains undisclosed. John Sims, at that time editor of the *Botanical Magazine*, was uncertain whether the rose should be regarded as a separate species or as a variety, and the issue was not settled until 1894, when Andreas Voss's description of *Rosa chinensis* var. *minima* was officially accepted.

Throughout the early part of the 19th century, it continued to be referred to as 'Miss Lawrance's Rose' in deference to Mary Lawrance, whose work *A Collection of Roses from Nature*, containing ninety hand-coloured etchings of roses, appeared between 1796 and 1799. Catherine Gore,

in *The Book of Roses, or The Rose Fancier's Manual* (1838), mentions a dozen varieties, including: the 'Single Lawrance Rose', 3 to 6 inches (7.5–15 cm) high; the 'Dwarf Lawrance Rose', 2 to 5 inches (5–13 cm) high; the 'Laurencéana [*sic*] Mouche', 3 to 4 inches (7.5–10 cm) high; as well as the 'Caprice des Dames', rose-coloured, 5 to 6 inches (13–15 cm) high. Another variety, 'Gloire des Lawranceanas', was dark crimson. However, there is no record of whether Miss Lawrance ever painted any of the roses associated with her name.

These miniature roses retained their popularity at least until the 1860s, when they were eclipsed by the POLYANTHAS. For half a century they were more or less forgotten, until interest in them began to revive during World War I, when Dr Roulet, a surgeon in the Swiss Army, noticed a minute rose growing in a window box in the village of Mauborget, a summer resort and winter sports centre overlooking Lake Neuchâtel. The plant was a mere 2 inches (5 cm) tall, and the diminutive bush was covered with small blooms. Roulet told the famous Geneva nurseryman Henri Correvon about his find. The rose, he said, had grown in the same window box for more than a century and bloomed continuously throughout the season. Correvon went to look at this phenomenon but found that, unfortunately, a serious fire had occurred at the village, and there was not a rose to be seen. However, one of the villagers recalled that a similar rose was to be found growing at Onnens, a village about five miles away. Correvon and Roulet visited Onnens together, and Roulet managed to get a slip of the plant from which Correvon was able to propagate hundreds of replicas, and launch it internationally in 1922. He called the plant *Rosa roulettii* after his friend. It is still treated as an 'honorary' species, and is normally referred to as '*Rosa roulettii (Rosa chinensis minima)*'.

Correvon thought that it was quite different from the 'Lawrance Rose' that he already grew in his own garden, and had a smaller habit than REDOUTÉ's dwarf *R. indica pumila*. He surmised that the rose might have been transplanted to Mauborget from the nearby garden of the great botanist Augustin Pyramus de Candolle (1778–1841), who had made a special study of rose species and had indeed described what he called *R. indica humilis* – 'the humble rose from India' – in his work *Prodomus*. This was clearly a larger plant than *R. roulettii*, but Correvon concluded that the roses at Onnens and Mauborget were so much smaller because they had been grown in pots with the soil unchanged for many years.

R. roulettii is also close to but not the equivalent of the rose 'Pom-pom de Paris', a variety popular in the 19th century as a pot flower. The latter is summer-flowering only, whereas Correvon was able to gather roses from 'his' plant one Christmas.

The arrival of *R. roulettii* spurred European breeders into action. The Spanish hybridizer Pedro Dot Martinez crossed it with various large-flowered and cluster-flowered roses as far back as the 1930s, and in 1935 he was able to launch 'Baby Goldstar', which, despite its blooms in excess of 2 inches (5 cm), is still classed as a miniature, and a popular one at that. This was a cross between *R. roulettii* and 'Eduardo Toda', a rose not now in general cultivation. 'Perla de Alcanada' (also known as 'Pearl of Canada', 'Baby Crimson' and 'Wheatcroft's Baby Crimson') is another Dot rose introduced in 1944 and still going strong. 'Perla de Montserrat, a deep-pink short rose of about 9 inches (23 cm), launched the following year, was a hybrid of 'Cécile Brunner' and *R. roulettii*. The buds of this variety have the perfect miniature high-peaked look of the large-flowered garden roses. 'Para Ti' ('Pour Toi'), a pure white miniature, came in 1946; 'Rosina', a yellow, in 1951; and 'Pixie Rose', dark pink, in 1961. All three of these Dot roses are still popular. 'Si', one of the smallest miniatures with pink flowers of $\frac{1}{2}$ inch (1.25 cm) or less, is another Dot production.

The late Jan de Vink of the Netherlands was the other early European pioneer in the world of miniature roses. His 'Cinderella' (1953), pinky white, 'Simple Simon' (1955), pink, and 'Red Imp' (1951) are still good sellers. His first introduction, 'Tom Thumb' – also known as 'Peon' – launched in the mid-1930s and the first miniature to be patented in the US, was the result of a cross between *R. roulettii* and De Ruiter's orange-red cluster-flowered rose 'Gloria Mundi'. Like the Dot miniatures, this was taken up by Robert Pyle of the American-based Conard–Pyle Company (*see* MEILLAND FAMILY), since when the class of miniatures has never looked back.

In the United States, Ralph Moore of Visalia, California, Harmon Saville in Rowley, Massachusetts (whose company, Nor-East Miniature Roses, is described as the largest retail source of miniatures in the world and the largest wholesale source in the US), Ernest Schwartz in Maryland and Ernest Williams in Dallas have all helped to give the US a head start in this field.

Ralph Moore's Sequoia Nursery has produced three miniature recurrent-flowering MOSS ROSES: 'Kara' (1972), pink; 'Dresden Doll' (1977), pink; 'Strawberry Swirl' (1978), red-and-white striped; as well as 'Lemon Delight' (1978). His unmossed specialities include: 'Green Ice' (1971) and 'Green Diamond' (1975), which have been described as lime green; 'Mr Bluebird' (1960), lavender-blue; and 'Sweet Chariot' (1985), double, lavender-purple, fragrant and suitable for hanging baskets, as is 'Red Cascade' (1976). The American Rose Society award-winning 'Stars and Stripes' (sometimes known as 'Stars 'n Stripes'), which is a miniature version of *R. gallica versicolor*, is another moss rose.

Roses, all scented, from the same nursery include: 'Little Buckaroo' (1956), deep red; 'Little Flirt' (1961), red and yellow but not all that little; 'New Penny' (1962), good for forcing into early flower; 'Yellow Doll' (1962), almost universally cherished; 'Rise 'n Shine' (alias 'Golden Sunblaze', 1977); 'Copy Cat' (1985), with finely shaped mid-pink blooms; 'Jack Pot' (1985), which opens like a beautiful yellow tulip; and 'Earthquake' (1983), which has all the red and orange streaks of a live volcano. In addition, there are climbing miniatures, and, indeed, a practically continuous flow of a new miniature roses comes from the Sequoia Nursery.

'Black Jade' (Benardella), a high-centred, near-black red rose, 'Single Bliss' (Saville), a red-blend single, and 'Winsome' (Saville) with lilac-lavender blooms good enough to cut, have all been introduced by Harmon Saville's Nor-East Miniature Roses of Rowley, Mass., and all have won awards of excellence from the American Rose Society.

The Meilland–Richardier company, which represents Moore in France, has also produced some winners of its own, such as 'Cri-Cri' (1958), with mid-coral-salmon-pink double flowers; 'Starina' (1965), internationally famous with shapely orange-red flowers; 'Mimi' (1965), mid-pink and reminiscent of an old-fashioned rose; 'Darling Flame' (1971), rich orange; 'Minijet' (1977), rich pink and noticeably fragrant; and 'Yellow Sunblaze' (1980), winner of a Royal National Rose Society award. The latter is one of the 10–12 inch (25–30 cm) high group marketed collectively as the 'Meillandinas': they include 'Pink Meillandina', 'Air France Meillandina' (with rose-coloured petals edged with carmine), and an almost single-flowered 'White Meillandina'.

Other famous hybridizers have made their own contributions. KORDES has been successful with 'Bonny' (1974), a mid-pink. TANTAU has provided the outsized 'Baby Masquerade' (1956) – no relation to the full-sized cluster-flowered 'Masquerade', but a colour-changer none the less, from yellow to pink and then to red. In 1980, MCGREDY introduced a white creeping rose appropriately named 'Snow Carpet'. In the UK, HARKNESS has introduced 'Anna Ford', an orange-red, and Mattock has launched the deep-yellow miniature, 'Gold Pin' (1974). 'Angela Rippon' (1978), mid-pink, and 'Mini-Metro' (1979), also known as 'Finstar' and 'Rufin', and an orange-blend, RNRS award winner, are both from De Ruiter.

The appearance of so many specialized types of miniature roses makes it likely that new classes of them will soon appear; for example, there could be show competitions for 'decorative miniatures' and specimen blooms. It has also been proposed that the smallest varieties should be termed 'micro-minis'. Ralph Moore has suggested that the larger miniatures might be designated as 'sweetheart roses', and the American Miniature Rose Growers' Association has decided on the designation 'sweetheart-size miniatures'. PATIO ROSES, the term used by POULSEN Roses of Denmark, might, however, be a more specific, if less romantic description.

'Compacta roses' was the title given to a group of miniature cluster-flowered roses introduced by De Ruiter in the 1950s and named after Walt Disney's Seven Dwarfs. The 'pigmy' roses, also developed in the 1950s in the US by Gene Boerner of JACKSON & PERKINS, were somewhat larger than the compactas and showed more resemblance to the habit and bloom structure of the large-flowered roses. 'Pygmy', on the other hand, is a miniature orange-red rose introduced by Poulsen in 1977.

Cultivation

Miniature roses can be grown from SEEDS, from CUTTINGS, from BUDDING or GRAFTING to UNDERSTOCKS, or by MICROPROPOGATION. Grafting is favoured by some commercial growers since it allows them to produce a smaller plant that can be ready for sale within a year. Budded plants are bigger, and take two years to develop from start to finish.

Breeders (including amateurs) who intend to grow their plants from seed often obtain supplies from crosses between miniatures and full-size garden roses, and in such cases, it has been found advantageous to choose the larger of the two roses as the seed parent and the miniature as the pollen parent. This method ensures more hips with more seeds in each, and a better life-expectancy, than a cross made the other way round. (*See* HYBRIDIZING ROSES.)

After cleaning and dusting with fungicide and rooting hormone, the seeds can be planted directly in seed-trays (known as 'flats' in the US) in a mixture of milled sphagnum moss, vermiculite and perlite rock globules. As with larger roses, the seeds first have to be stratified (*see* SEEDS). Charles Fitch, whose work *The Complete Book of Miniature Roses* (1977) is a classic, recommends placing the newly planted seeds, tray and all, in the plastic bag and then into a refrigerator for not less than four weeks and not more than six, at a temperature of around 39°F (4°C). When the tray is taken out and transferred to a warmer environment of 64–70°F (18–21°C), the seeds will begin to germinate, and they will be ready for potting after about three months.

The majority of miniature roses in the larger nurseries are grown on their own roots from cuttings. These can be planted directly into small flower pots, and will root well if the light and the air circulation are good and the water supply plentiful. In areas where the sun is particularly strong and the plants are grown in the open, water can be misted on them non-stop until the cuttings have rooted, and in these conditions, they will prosper even if they are in direct sunlight for hours at a time. In other cases, however, cuttings are grown in static greenhouses, or in ones that can be rolled away on rails, as happens at the Meilland experimental nursery for miniatures at Cannet-des-Maures, on the Côte d'Azur. Whichever method is used, the plants need to be acclimatized gradually to the conditions they will subsequently experience.

In Britain, some of the miniatures sold in pots will have been budded on to understocks and grown in rose fields in the open, though others will be on their own roots.

Grafted miniatures are usually sold in rigid pots of about 3½ inches (9 cm) in diameter. They can be left in a cold frame until the season of severe frost begins, and can be forced to flower in the early spring, as explained more fully in the section headed POTS. After the roses have flowered, the pots should be placed out of doors for a few weeks in the late autumn to give them the period of dormancy that they would miss if they remained in a greenhouse all year. Alternatively, they may be planted out of doors and then sold the following autumn as open ground

bushes. Grafted miniatures are, understandably, more expensive than those that have been budded.

Bare-root miniatures can be potted and then taken at once out of doors. As with all containers in which roses are grown, the pot should contain a layer of crocks or fine shingle at the bottom to ensure drainage; a specialized potting mixture is then added. When PLANTING the rose, the same precautions are taken as with larger roses.

The advantage of keeping miniatures in their POTS instead of planting them in the ground is that the grower has the option of bringing the plants indoors in the winter without the trouble of digging out the roots. In general, however, miniature roses are commendably hardy, and can winter in pots buried in a border, in a rock garden or in tubs or stone troughs on a patio. 'Weeper' varieties are equally attractive when hanging from baskets or over a dry wall or garden terrace.

In hard winters, precautions against frost are the same as would be taken for larger roses: the plants are earthed up or the area covered with pine branches or sacking. However, if small containers are used, particularly on an outside windowsill, the roses are likely to need extra protection in winter to prevent the frost from reaching the roots. A simple way of insuring against this is to place the pot inside a larger one with a layer of sacking (or some other suitable filling) in between the two. Hanging baskets, like pots above ground, can be brought in under cover in times of heavy frost.

Miniature roses will grow splendidly indoors provided that four requirements are met: light, air, warmth and moisture (humidity). The light, essential for vigorous stems, may come from a large well-washed window with a view of the sky, or from daylight lamps, in which case an indoor garden lighting specialist should be consulted. The air may come from an open (or badly fitting) window, or from a fan turned on automatically at intervals. A maximum temperature of 70°F (21°C) by day and a minimum of 61°F (16°C) at night should not present too much difficulty in most houses. Maximum–minimum thermometers allow anxious rosarians to reassure themselves that these limits have not been exceeded.

Humidity of not less than 40 per cent around the plant should be the aim, and the simplest way of achieving this is to make a habit of using a hand-operated mister. This can be supplemented by standing the plants over trays of water or, in the case of pots, over saucers duly topped up. Saucers for attachment to hanging baskets can be bought, and filling them is easier and safer than trying to water the earth around the plants themselves, with the risk of splashing furniture and electrical fittings. The ornamental wooden logs in which miniature roses are sometimes planted allow moisture to be lost through evaporation, and so do standard clay flower pots. If used, these should be lined with impervious material. Experts can tell at once if the plant in an untreated clay pot needs water: they can judge by lifting the pot – if it's light, it needs water – or they tap the pot with a coin, and if it rings hollow, they top up.

Right: Rosa muscosa, *the moss rose, from the Chelsea Physick Garden, London.*

Below: Rosa moschata, *the musk rose, and an iris from* La clef des champs *by Jacques le Moyne de Morgues, published in 1586 and dedicated to his patron, Lady Mary Sidney.*

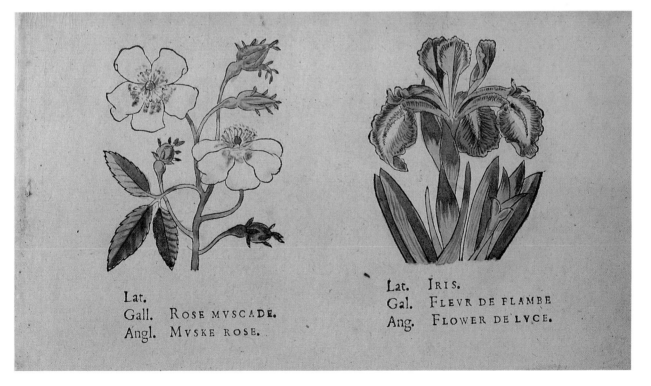

Lat.
Gall. ROSE MVSCADE.
Angl. MVSKE ROSE.

Lat. IRIS.
Gal. FLEVR DE FLAMBE
Ang. FLOWER DE LVCE.

Redouté's Rosa noisettiana ('Le rosier de Philippe Noisette')
appeared in 1821 in the artist's masterwork, Les roses, *and is one
of the most successful of his rose portraits.*

Pierre-Joseph Redouté's Rosa indica, *from* Les roses *(1817)*.

The Perfume Makers, *by Rudolph Ernst (1854–1932).*
The roses are centifolias.

Surface evaporation can be reduced by mulching or covering the earth with plastic sheeting after watering. A product known as Hydrogel can be incorporated in the soil; it retains water and releases it gradually as the soil begins to dry out.

After the winter-flowering season is over, the plants can be taken out of doors, at first in a cold frame and later in the open. In the autumn, they can be repotted if necessary and brought back under cover.

Mitosis

This is the process by which the young vegetal cells of plants such as the rose increase their numbers. Each cell and the CHROMOSOMES within it divide into two parts, forming two daughter cells, which in time grow to normal size. Thus the number of cells is doubled. Mitosis ceases when the plant – or one of its parts – reaches maturity.

See also MEIOSIS.

Mogul emperors and the rose

Six Mogul emperors reigned, between 1526 and 1707, over an area stretching from the Bay of Bengal in the east to the Arabian Gulf in the west. Their numerous rose gardens were based on the traditional Persian *charbagh* (a garden divided into four parts), and were enclosed within four walls, each wall being pierced by a single door. Open water, fast-flowing streams and cascades were special features, and the rose was often chosen as the ideal shrub for edging the waters.

Babur, the first Mogul emperor, planted roses matched with narcissi in his garden at Agra. The emperor Djihanguir who ruled the empire from 1605–28, established gardens at Udaipur, Agra, Shalimar, Srinagar (Kashmir) and Lahore, in which roses were a speciality. The emperor's marriage to thirty-four-year-old Nour-Djihan ('the light of the world'), a Persian, ensured his special interest in roses, and both the summer garden in Kashmir and at Shah Dara – the 'Garden of Delight' – five miles north of Lahore, were as famous for their roses as Samarkand for its tulips or Kabul for its violets.

For a full account of these gardens, and the roses in them, see C. M. Villiers Stuart's *The Gardens of the Great Mughals*.

See also ATTAR OF ROSES.

Moss roses

Moss roses are those that have stalks, sepals and sometimes leaves that carry small globe-shaped glands containing fragrant resinous oils, and the stems of which are noticeably bristly. The mossy character of these roses and the scent that they impart to the hands when touched strongly appealed to Victorian women.

Moss roses are generally regarded as offshoots of the cabbage rose (ROSA CENTIFOLIA) and are typed as *R. centifolia muscosa*. Fréard du Castel of Bayeux in Normandy said, in his *L'école du jardinier fleuriste* (1746), that they had been grown in Carcassonne in the south as far back as 1696, although it is hard to reconcile this with the fact that no French writers of the 17th century mention the existence of the cabbage rose in Provence. Philip Miller, whose *Gardener's Dictionary* is referred to in HISTORY OF THE ROSE, said that he saw one at Leyden in 1727 in the garden of Dr Hermann Boerhaave, who kindly gave him a slip of it for the Chelsea Physic Garden. Boerhaave had included it seven years earlier in the list of plants growing in the Leyden Botanical Garden.

The original moss rose was pink, but there have since been a number of interesting varieties, including the white rose painted by REDOUTÉ and named by Thory as *R. centifolia muscosa alba*, or 'Shailer's White Moss'. It is still grown under this name, but is also sometimes billed as 'White Bath' or 'Clifton Moss'. 'Nuits de Young' is a compact upright plant with small, dark metallic maroon-purple blooms, lit with a few bright yellow anthers. 'William Lobb', equally striking in its way, has large clusters of purple-magenta flowers, with pale mauve reverses fading to grey. This is a lanky plant that ideally needs a wall, hedge, pillar or some other support if it is to appear at its best. 'Capitaine John Ingram' also shows flowers of dark crimson with lighter reverses on the petals, but with rather less mossing.

Two well-loved crimson mosses are 'Madame de la Roche-Lambert' (1851), the flowers of which have a dash of purple and often appear intermittently through to the autumn, and 'Henri Martin' (1863), with semi-double flowers and light green mossing, named by the French nurseryman Jules Laffay after the French historian, not the Impressionist painter. Laffay made a speciality of moss roses in the mid-19th century, as David Austin does today in England.

'Louis Gimard' has true centifolia Brussels-sprout buds that open to flat, tightly packed blooms of cerise veined with mauve. 'Général Kléber' (1856), a Robert introduction, is well-mossed and has large blooms of mauvish pink.

The original *R. centifolia muscosa*, the common moss rose, is otherwise known as the 'Old Pink Moss', though the luxuriant mossing is closer to red than pink. Its intense fragrance makes this one of the best of the breed. 'Gloire des Mousseux' (Laffay, 1852) is similar but larger.

Three other pink mosses have some claims to REMONTANCY. 'Jeanne de Montfort', large enough to rank as a shrub, sometimes shows a second crop of flowers in the autumn. 'Mousseline', alias 'Alfred de Dalmas', is somewhat more dependable, and 'Soupert et Notting' has been habitually listed among the perpetuals. 'Gabrielle Noyelle', 'Golden Moss' and 'Robert Leopold' are mossed SHRUB ROSES with yellowish flowers. Of these last three, 'Gabrielle Noyelle' (Buatois, 1933) is the most repetitive.

'Blanche Moreau' (Moreau–Robert, 1880) is thickly clothed with brown moss that contrasts agreeably with the cluster of large white blossoms. It is an autumn damask hybrid and remontant; the scent is only moderate and not as good as the earlier bright rose-coloured 'Madame Moreau' (Moreau–Robert) of 1872, which is also remontant.

'Salet' (Lacharme, 1854) is a fine rosy colour and is the most reliably remontant of the mosses. Patricia Wiley of Roses of Yesterday and Today, writing about this rose in her catalogue, recalled that the Revd A. Foster-Melliar, one of the great Victorian rose fanciers, declared: 'The real odour of musk is to be found only in "Salet".'

Among the more modern mosses, 'Goldmoss' and 'Rougemoss' (both Moore, 1972) are fully remontant cluster-flowered bushes and deserve wider recognition than they have so far received.

Finally, there is *R. centifolia cristata*, which is not a true moss but is looked on as such because the long fringes of the calyx decorating the bud take on a mossy appearance; this has suggested to some that 'Chapeau de Napoleon' would be a suitable name for it. The original plant, with pleasing pink blooms, was discovered in 1820 growing as a seedling in the crack of a ruin in the Swiss town of Fribourg. Since all the resulting flowers were the same, it was not a SPORT from a normal *R. centifolia*, but a self-perpetuating variety from an escaped seed probably carried to Fribourg by a bird.

See also MINIATURE ROSES.

Mulching

The word 'mulch', derived from the adjective *melsh* meaning 'soft', has a respectable ancestry going back to the late 17th century. Two centuries later, however, the English rosarian Gertrude Jekyll had her reservations about the practice of mulching rosebeds with coverings of straw, leaves and the like: the birds, as she rightly said, were sure to scratch up the material and scatter it over the grass and paths.

None the less, mulching is still with us, (1) to suppress weeds, and (2) to ensure that the soil of the rosebed does not dry out in summer or become frost-bound in winter. A rag-bag of materials can be used, ranging from home-made compost and peat to hop or mushroom manure; 'bagasse' – crushed and shredded sugar cane, ground corn cobs and sawdust – is used locally in the United States. Pine and larch bark chippings, which give an elegant show-biz appearance to the bed, are sold in Britain by the Forestry Commission. They are heat-treated or stored under special conditions before delivery in order to extract the volatile oils present in fresh bark, which have been found to inhibit growth of roses.

'Soft' leaves, such as those from beech, hazel and hawthorn, are also good material. Hard-ribbed leaves from the plane, the field maple or the ash should be rejected as they rot too slowly and so do not add their quota of humus to the soil. Rose leaves and leaves from close relatives of the rose such as the apple and pear should be put aside and burned as they often harbour pests and diseases to which roses are subject.

Lawn mowings can be used for mulching during the summer, provided that they are free of grass-seed and the remains of any weed-killing agent. If applied too thickly, they tend to heat up and should therefore be kept well away from the stems of rose bushes.

Animal manure – rarely available in cities – is best applied in the spring when the roots are newly awakened and ready to benefit from it, rather than in the autumn when they would be less receptive.

Except when grass mowings or animal manure is used, mulching is best carried out in early autumn before the soil has lost its summer heat. Any dressings, fertilizer or spray should be applied to the soil before the mulch is laid down. Some mulches deprive roses of nitrogen, which should therefore be included in the feed. The layer of mulch can be 2–6 inches (5–15 cm) deep, depending on the bulkiness of the material selected, but whatever product is chosen, first-time users are likely to find that the amount they need to cover a small rosebed can prove surprisingly large.

Musk roses

According to the explorer Richard Hakluyt (*c.* 1552–1616): 'The artichowe was brought in the time of King Henry the Eight, and in later times was procured out of Italy the Muske Rose Plant.'

John Gerard, writing in 1596, described the 'Great Muske Rose' and two smaller plants, a single and a double. The 'Muske Rose', he wrote, has very sharp prickles, 'long leaves smooth and shining' and flowers 'of a white colour', adding that 'the Muske Rose flowereth in Autumne or the fall of the leafe; the rest floure when the Damask and the red Rose [i.e. the GALLICA] do.' Neither in this respect nor in fragrance or in the shape of the leaflets did Gerard distinguish between the normal-sized hedge-high 'Muske' rose and the three-times larger 'Great Muske Rose'.

However, as Graham Stuart Thomas has pointed out, John Ray, in his *Historia plantarum* published less than a century after Gerard's *Herball*, noted an important difference between '*R. moschata minor*', which flowered no earlier than the end of the summer or the beginning of autumn, and '*R. moschata major*', which he did not consider to be a true musk since it flowered in June.

Nevertheless, the June-flowering 'musk', often climbing as high as 30–50 feet (9–15 m), persisted in gardens – notably the Cambridge Botanical Garden and the Royal Botanical Gardens at Kew – and understandably, as the old musk rose, which apparently was more tender, became less frequently seen, the larger plant was assumed to be *the* musk rose. There was, however, one feature, that helped to assure the faithful that, quite distinct from the summer-flowering 'musk', there must be a real musk rose about somewhere: reliable botanists, in contradiction to Gerard, had repeatedly described the autumn-flowering musk rose as having downy oval leaflets, whereas those of the June-flowering variety at Cambridge and Kew were 'long' and 'smooth'.

It needed the persistence of Graham Stuart Thomas to

discover that the true musk rose had been cultivated by Canon ELLACOMBE at Bitton in Somerset, and that Ellacombe had given a cutting to the eminent gardener E. A. Bowles (1865–1924), who had recorded in one of his books, *My Garden in Summer*, that the cutting had been planted against a wall at Myddleton House in Enfield, outside London. Thomas decided to take a chance, and in August 1936, nine years after Bowles' death, he asked for permission to visit Myddleton House to see if, perhaps, the autumn-flowering musk rose was still to be found there. His search was successful: the original single-flowered musk rose as described by Johannes Herrmann in 1762 was blooming there. However, the story had a twist in the tail: all Thomas's first buddings from the Myddleton House rose produced double flowers.

Several other questions remain as yet unanswered. In 1822, seeds were brought to England of a rose that had been found some years earlier growing on a southern slope of the Himalayas in Nepal. It was very close to 'R. moschata major' except that the leaves were narrower, longer and hairy. Named *R. brownii* (later *R. brunonii*), it is sometimes known, like various other white roses, as the 'Snowbush'. At the same time, new evidence was emerging which showed that the two *R. moschata* plants that most people had assumed to be natives of Spain, North Africa and Madeira might have been the naturalized offsprings of cultivated roses brought at least part of the way from Asia into Europe by the Moors. French rosarians accordingly adopted *R. brunonii* as the real musk rose, even though it was summer-flowering.

This leaves open the question of whether the original autumn-flowering musk rose was a species on its own or merely a scaled-down variety of 'R. moschata major' and flowered later because it was more tender.

In any case, both large and small musk roses are members of the Synstylae group, so called because their styles tend to grow together into a single column. It is generally believed that the musk perfume is dispensed from these and not, as with most other roses, from the petals. This explains why the scent of musk roses carries over longer distances than that of most other roses.

At the same time as the musk roses got their name, the substance known as *musk*, which was used as a base for perfumes, was obtained from a gland of the Asian vegetarian musk deer and had a delicate fragrance. Later, however, as genuine musk became harder to find, coarser substitutes derived from the carnivorous civet cat were used. No doubt it was musk roses with the former fragrance that so greatly impressed Shakespeare as a fitting accompaniment to Titania's sleep in *A Midsummer Night's Dream* – but one cannot be sure that the musk rose would have been found growing wild on a bank where wild thyme, oxlips, woodbine, eglantine and violets were also to be seen! The play was set near Athens but, in Shakespeare's description of this typically English habitat, *R. arvensis*, the fragrant field rose, seems a better fit.

Apart from *R. brunonii*, there are a number of SPECIES ROSES allied to the musk roses. These include: the white *R. anemoneflora* discovered by Robert Fortune in a garden in Shanghai in 1844; *R. helenae*, also white, first cultivated in 1907; *R. filipes*, a magnificent, hardy, fragrant pillar rose, the best-known variety of which is 'Kiftsgate' (1954). This last, in common with *R. longicuspis*, comes from western China and flowers after most of the other musk roses. *R. sinowilsonii*, found in china by E. H. Wilson and introduced in 1904, is hardier than *R. longicuspis* and distinguished from it by its red-brown angled shoots and its magnificent leaves, sometimes more than 12 inches (30 cm) long, dark green above and purplish-brown beneath. It is a respectable climber to 15 feet (4.5 m) but, unfortunately, is not widely cultivated. *R. dupontii*, with milk-white petals, is thought to be a cross between *R. moschata* and *R. gallica*, but unlike the autumn DAMASK, which is supposed to have arisen from a similar cross, it flowers only in the summer.

See also HYBRID MUSKS.

Mutation

Mutation means – to biologists – the kind of change that can lead to the appearance of a new species (of rose, for instance). It is an accident, if you like, that can occur during the 'crossing over' stage of the MEIOSIS process, and results in a rearrangement of the genes of the sex cells from which the seeds will develop.

The accident can take various forms. Thus the chains of CHROMOSOMES on which the genes are carried can be disrupted, so that one chain ends up with an extra link and more genes, and the other has fewer. A link may also be turned back on itself, thus breaking up the sequence in which the genes are normally arranged. In addition, the normal cell walls may be defective in some way so that, in effect, no cell division takes place. If the sex cell resulting from the accident can nevertheless mate or be mated successfully, then the result is a new species. A mutation rose is thus distinct from a SPORT rose, which is generally taken to mean a plant showing abnormality (for example, in its structure or flower coloration) but which can be propagated by budding and which, in other respects, retains the normal characteristics of its species.

Mutations can be induced artificially either by irradiation or with the aid of the drug *colchicine*. In the latter, the chromosome count of a sterile hybrid can be doubled artificially by applying the drug to the meristem (growth point) of young seedlings. The drug interferes with the process of MITOSIS in such a way that cells, instead of splitting into two daughter cells each with the same number of chromosomes as the mother cell, remain undivided but with the chromosome count doubled.

Irradiation has been used on the rose 'Queen Elizabeth' to produce an orange-red mutant named 'Paula' which, however, is not to be seen in the AMERICAN ROSE SOCIETY's *Handbook for Selecting Roses*. Gamma rays have also been used on the buds of the rose 'Pink Parfait' and on the wild rose, *R. montezumae*, so far with no sensational results.

Naming roses

The principles that are to be followed when naming plants – including roses – are set out (and periodically revised) in the *International Code of Botanical Nomenclature*. A similar code for cultivated plants was issued in 1954, with revisions in 1969 and 1980.

In particular, hybrids are represented by the sign 'x'. Thus the Latin name of 'Hume's Blush Tea-scented China' rose, a hybrid of two species *R. chinensis* and *R. gigantea*, is usually written *R. chinensis* x *gigantea*. The two names can be placed either in alphabetical order or with the name of the seed parent first and that of the pollen parent second, but in a scientific paper, the author should make clear which system is being followed.

When a plant of one genus is hybridized with one of another genus, the two generic names are run together. Thus *Hulthemia persica* hybridized with the rose 'Trier' leads to x *Hulthemosa* 'Trier'.

The term 'cultivar', meaning cultivated variety (abbreviated as 'cv.'), is distinct from the botanical category *varietas*, which represents a naturally occurring type of lesser degree than a species. *Varietas* is shortened to 'var.' and the name of the variety is printed in italics – for example, *Rosa canina* var. *inermis*. Cultivars, on the other hand, are distinguished from the botanical name by being printed in Roman type, and between single quotation marks or, in the absence of quotation marks, by the prefix 'cv.' (e.g. *Rosa filipes* 'Kiftsgate', or *Rosa filipes* cv. Kiftsgate).

It is also recommended that certain types of names should *not* be chosen for cultivars:
*Names consisting of numerals, abbreviations or arbitrary sequences of letters; these would be hard to remember.
*Names containing an initial article – e.g. 'The Duke of Wellington' – as there would soon be too many 'the's. However, 'The Wife of Bath' is acceptable since her title is otherwise incomplete, and likewise 'La France'.
*Names derived from proper names containing abbreviations, except for the abbreviation 'Mrs' in English. Thus 'Mount Everest' (not 'Mt Everest') and 'Harry Wheatcroft' (not 'H. Wheatcroft'). The correct version leaves no doubt about where it should be sought in an alphabetical index.

*Names containing forms of address, unless required by national custom. The latter allows 'Frau', 'Madame', 'Mrs', 'Señora' and equivalents in other languages for married women, but 'Fräulein', 'Mademoiselle', 'Senorita', 'Miss', 'Mister', 'Herr' and 'Monsieur' are considered unnecessary because they confer little distinction and would add to the difficulties of tracking them down in an alphabetical index.
*Excessively long names, such as 'Madame Soledad de Ampuera de Leguizamon' (a rose of 1928), are inconvenient. Oddly enough, they are seldom proposed for roses that are likely to succeed.
*Names claiming supremacy for a cultivar which may be overtaken by later introductions – e.g. 'First to Flower'.
It is hoped that breeders will also avoid giving roses names that could be confused with other similar names – as, for example, 'Helen' or 'Hélène', and 'Catherine' or 'Katherine', etc.

In an ideal world, the name of a cultivar would not subsequently be translated from one language to another, but where this occurs, the translated name is treated as the original name in a different form and the date of its introduction is given as that of the original. Christian names should also be left in peace, and so 'Franz' should not be changed to 'Francis', 'Karl' to 'Charles' or 'Georges' to 'George'.

Each cultivar should have only one REGISTERED name by which it is internationally known. However, it can have one or more legitimate synonyms that are more suited to the country in which it is being marketed.

National Rose Show, the first

Many accounts have been given of Britain's first National Rose Show. This one is taken from the 15th edition (1896) of *A Book about Roses* by S. Reynolds HOLE, Dean of Rochester, who acted as secretary and supervisor of the show.

We secured the services of the Coldstream band – a mistake, because their admirable music was too loud for indoor enjoyment. We advertised freely. We placarded the walls of London with gorgeous and gigantic posters. And then the great day came.

The late Mr John Edwards, who gave us from the first most important help, and who was the best man I ever saw in the practical arrangements of a flower-show, appeared, soon after daybreak, on the scene. He found the hall crowded with chairs and benches, just as it was left after a concert the night before. Early as it was, he had his staff with him – carpenters and others; and when I arrived with my roses, after a journey of 120 miles [presumably from Caunton, near Newark] at 5.30 a.m. the long tables were almost ready for the green baize.

Then came the covered vans which had travelled through the summer night from the grand gardens of Hertfordshire, and the 'four-wheelers' with green boxes piled upon their roofs, from the railway stations. And then the usual confusion which attends the operation of 'staging' – exhibitors preferring their 'own selection' to the places duly assigned to them, running against each other or pressing round Mr Edwards with their boxes as though they had something to sell . . . He, however, was quite master of the situation, and upon his directions, clearly and firmly given, their followed order and peace.

And there followed a scene, beautiful exceedingly. I feel no shame in confessing that when the Hall was cleared, and I looked from the gallery upon the three long tables, and the platform beneath the great organ, flowing with the choicest roses of the world, the cisterns of my heart overflowed.

'Half the nurseries of England,' as Dr Lindley wrote [soon afterwards in *The Gardener's Chronicle*], 'poured their treasures into St James's Hall,' adding that there was an 'infinite variety of form, colour and odour which belonged to the field of roses spread before the visitors'. 'At the sides,' Dr Lindley continued, 'were crowds of bunches daintily set off by beds of moss; in the middle rose pyramids, baskets and bouquets; in one place, solitary blossoms boldly confronted their clustering rivals; in another, glass screens guarded some precious gems; and in another, groups of unprotected beauties set in defiance of the heated atmosphere of the Hall.' There were glorious collections, large and lovely, from Cheshunt and Colchester, Hertfordshire and Hereford, Exeter and Slough . . .

Then the censors reported their verdicts; the prize cards were placed by the prize-roses; and then came the momentous question: Would the public endorse our experiment? Would the public appreciate our show? There was a deficiency of £100 in our funds, for the expenses of the exhibition were £300; and as a matter of both feeling and finance I stood by the entrance as the clock struck two, anxiously to watch the issue. No longer solicitude. More than fifty shillings – I humbly apologise – more than fifty intelligent and good-looking individuals were waiting for admission; and these were followed by continuous comers, until the Hall was full. A gentleman, who earnestly asked my pardon for having placed his foot on mine, seemed perplexed to hear how much I liked it, and evidently thought that my friends were culpable in allowing me to be at large. Great, indeed, was my gladness in *seeing* those visitors, more than 2,000 in number – but far greater in hearing their hearty words of surprise and admiration . . .

At the close of the exhibition, it was my happy privilege to distribute the thirty-six silver cups which had been specially designed for the occasion and were, I need hardly say, prettily and profusely engraved with roses.

The winners were – (of nurserymen) Messrs Paul of Cheshunt,

Mr Cranston of Hereford, Mr CANT OF COLCHESTER, Mr Francis of Hertford, Mr Turner of Slough and Mr Hollamby of Tunbridge Wells.

The amateur winners came from as far afield as Yeovil, Thorpe Malsor (Northants) and Shottesham in Suffolk; three out of the twelve were clergymen. Dean Hole, in addition to acting as secretary and supervisor, won two cups for his roses.

The second National Rose Show was held the following year at the Hanover Square rooms, the former site not being available, but the rooms were too small and the third show moved to the Crystal Palace where the attendance figure rose to 16,000. The fourth National Rose Show was held under the auspices of the Royal Horticultural Society in their gardens at South Kensington, for the Dean was engaged at the time in 'a correspondence which occupied all my time, upon a subject which occupied all my thought – a subject more precious, more lovely even than roses – I was going to be married in May.' Thereafter the rose found herself in mixed company and languished for a while until, in 1876, the National Rose Society, later the ROYAL NATIONAL ROSE SOCIETY, was founded.

National Rose Society
See ROYAL NATIONAL ROSE SOCIETY.

New Zealand, the rose in
New Zealand's first rose, a crimson China, was planted at Oihi by one of the group of women accompanying the Revd Samuel Marsden on the brig *Active*, captained by Thomas Hansen, after they had landed on Christmas Day, 1814 at Rangihoua on the northeast coast of North Island near the Bay of Islands. In a land stretching more than 900 miles from north to south, with wide variations in climates, the visitors had happened on a subtropical area where dormancy is more or less irrelevant. Eight years later, cuttings of the same rose were planted round the veranda of the Kemp homestead at the head of Kerikeri inlet nearby, and the roses were still to be seen there more than a century and a half later.

The National Rose Society of New Zealand was founded in Auckland in 1931, 'to implant the rose in the Hearts and Gardens of the People'. Its first National Convention was held in Palmerston North in 1947, and an international trials ground, with the 'Gold Star of the Pacific' as its top award, was established there in 1969. Two years later, Hamilton was the site for New Zealand's First International Rose Convention, which witnessed the establishment of the WORLD FEDERATION OF ROSE SOCIETIES.

Since then, Sam MCGREDY IV, who had already visited New Zealand several times, has transferred himself and his rose interests from Northern Ireland to Castor Bay, Auckland, where his roses – including 'Dublin Bay' (1976), a deep-red rambler, 'Kapai' (1977), an orange-red cluster-flowered rose, and 'Snowball' (1985), a white miniature – have continued to delight and inspire New Zealand growers.

Rose lovers will want to see the Lady Norwood Rose Garden in the Botanic Gardens of Wellington as well as Cobham Drive, Hamilton; Mona Vale, Christchurch; City Centre, Invercargill; the Parnell Rose Garden at Auckland; and the New Zealand International Trial Grounds at Palmerston North.

Rosa moschata, *the musk rose, one of the parents of the noisette roses, from H. C. Andrews'* A Monograph of the Genus Rosa *(1805).*

Noisette roses

The origins of the noisette roses are described in the section on CHINA ROSES, and the climbing noisettes are included with CLIMBERS. *See also* UNITED STATES and HISTORY OF THE ROSE.

The original 'Blush Noisette' with pale lilac-pink flowers is still grown on both sides of the Atlantic, often as a shrub.

Nurserymen's English

'Nurserymen's English' is the language that growers employ, and for rosarians who are not botanists, it provides a useful exposé of the differences between one variety of rose and the next.

Nurserymen's English often infers and suggests far more than it says, and the speculative reader can sometimes deduce the nurseryman's private opinions from the general adjectives that he or she uses to describe a particu-

lar rose. Such adjectives range through the spectrum from indifference on the one hand to enthusiasm on the other. For instance, the word 'favourite' – which often appears in the phrase 'a popular garden favourite' – can be a species of faint praise meaning: 'Many people, but not necessarily myself, like this variety, which, however, is far too frequently seen.' The nurseryman may also have his (or her) reservations about a rose he/she describes as 'unusual' or 'interesting'; other epithets such as 'charming' or 'pretty' are inserted where nothing more specific is at hand.

'Appealing' is one more subjective and imprecise encomium, but it is seldom employed by good nurserymen unless the customer is likely to assent to it. 'Superb', 'exquisite', 'outstanding' and 'a rose of distinction' are all terms that, while often applicable to a number of particular roses, cannot, for obvious reasons, be used in any one catalogue as frequently as perhaps they should be; they have to be reserved for a highly select minority. Such descriptions can therefore usually be accepted as reliable.

When dealing with growth and habit, the conscientious breeder faces a dilemma. No one wants to buy a spindly or weedy plant, yet if a rose is described as 'a vigorous grower', the smallholder may fear that a single rose bush will take over the whole of his rose patch. Equally, a rose of 'compact growth', though pleasing in appearance, may leave the floor of the rose garden bare, so that additional plants will have to be bought to cover it.

THORNS are another problem. The phrase 'well armed with thorns' could suggest a handsome, virile and ornamental rose bush of the kind that will defeat the neighbour's cat, but it could equally be a bush that is difficult to prune, with stems that are well-nigh impossible to accommodate in a vase.

COLOUR, in so far as it can be accurately defined at all, lends itself to varying interpretations. Thus, 'white, lightly shaded with pink' could suggest to one rose fancier a fine and delicate bloom, whereas another amateur would visualize and recoil from petals indecisively smudged. Blooms said to be 'flushed' or 'suffused' may present an attractive appearance to some, but will disappoint others looking for a more finite contrast. 'Glowing', 'intense', 'vivid' and 'brilliant' are clear enough in their meanings, but do they, perhaps, refer to a rose that will stare the beholder out of countenance – when he would prefer something less obtrusive?

SCENT is the most elusive attribute of the rose since it is the hardest to describe. Most nurserymen confine themselves to assaying its strength, by means of adjectives ranging from 'fragrant' through 'highly scented' and 'a wealth of perfume' to 'heady'. Their experience tells them that what smells sweet to one person may be cloying to the next.

In these circumstances, therefore, the most reliable translation of nurserymen's English is to be derived from close contact with the nurseryman himself, and the customer should take the earliest opportunity of establishing a genuine *entente* before a single rose plant is ordered.

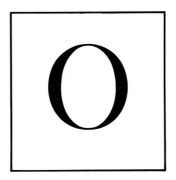

'Old' roses

Many writers treat as 'old' roses those that were most written about and painted before the early part of the 19th century, when the arrival of the CHINA ROSES and other newly imported species led to extensive hybridization and a flood of new varieties. The habit and flowering shape of these 'old' roses, familiar to us from flower portraits on canvas and in print, seem to blend well with traditional furniture, period houses and old garden walls, and in the garden, their soft colours mix well with one another.

The AMERICAN ROSE SOCIETY resolved in 1966 to define an 'old' rose as one that belongs to a group that existed before 1867, and to include with them newer hybrids with features linking them to the 'old' groups – for example, the 'new' roses bred in the 20th century that, in origin and appearance, are nevertheless clearly linked with 'old' classes such as HYBRID PERPETUALS, TEA ROSES, BOURBONS, MOSS ROSES, etc. The year 1867 was chosen as the watershed, dividing the old from the new, because it saw the introduction of 'La France', the rose that is generally accepted as the first of the HYBRID TEA ROSES (now more rationally known as LARGE-FLOWERED ROSES).

See also CLASSIFICATION OF ROSES (horticultural).

Omar Khayyám: The Rubáiyát and the rose

Nowhere in literature is the rose more closely linked to the pursuit of earthly pleasure than in *The Rubáiyát* of Omar Khayyám. *The Rubáiyát* – from the Persian word *rubais* meaning quatrain, or verse of four lines – is an assembly of stanzas, each of which originally stood on its own until they were translated and linked together by Edward Fitzgerald (1809–83).

The rose features prominently throughout *The Rubáiyát*. For example, it has bloody connotations in Stanza XVIII:

> *I sometimes think that never blows so red*
> *The Rose as where some buried Caesar bled;*
> *   That every Hyacinth the Garden wears*
> *Dropt in her Lap from some once lovely Head.*

The rose constantly reappears to add strength and colour to the poet's words:

> *. . . 'Wine! Wine! Wine!*
> Red *Wine!' – the Nightingale cries to the Rose*
> *That yellow Cheek of hers to incarnadine.*

or:

> *Look to the Rose that blows about us – Lo,*
> *Laughing, she says, 'Into the World I blow;*
> *   At once the silken Tassel of my Purse*
> *Tear, and its Treasure on the Garden throw.'*

and:

> *While the Rose blows along the River Brink,*
> *With old Khayyám the Ruby Vintage drink;*
> *   And when the Angel with his darker Draught*
> *Draws up to thee – take that, and do not shrink.*

Omar Khayyám is said to have told one of his pupils, Kwajah Nizami of Samarkand: 'My tomb shall be on a spot where the north wind may scatter rose petals over it' – and a rose tree was indeed planted over his tomb in Naishapur. The story was carried further by Dr J. G. Baker, who, according to Ellen Willmott in *The Genus Rosa*, related that a hip of this rose was brought home by a Mr Simpson, an artist employed by the *Illustrated London News*, and that the seeds from it were planted in Suffolk on the grave of Edward Fitzgerald.

A damask rose, 'Omar Khayyám', is offered by the well-respected Norfolk (England) rose antiquarian, Peter Beales, and is believed to have been propagated from the rose planted on Edward Fitzgerald's grave. The rose has medium-sized light pink blooms (not, alas, red as in the quatrains), which flower in groups of three or four; they are quartered, with button eyes. The foliage is greyish and downy.

Outsize roses

The most frequently quoted example of an outsize rose – and the one that has earned a place in the *Guinness Book of Records* – is the *Rosa banksiae* now in the garden of the Rose Tree Inn in Tombstone, Arizona, but originally from Scotland, and planted in 1885. Its main stem has a circumference of 3 feet 3 inches (1 m) and a diameter of 12 inches (30 cm). The plant as a whole covers an area of 200 square metres, and 150 people have been known to shelter beneath its branches. Further details of this giant can be found in an article by Percy C. Hunt in the September 1985 issue of *The Rose*, the journal of the Royal National Rose Society.

Patio roses

This is a convenient name – used particularly by POULSEN's of Denmark for low-growing, cluster-flowered roses that can be planted with advantage in restricted places in the 'concrete jungle'. At the Toronto meeting of the WORLD FEDERATION OF ROSE SOCIETIES in 1985, a recommendation was accepted that these roses should be denoted as 'dwarf cluster-flowered roses', but at the time of writing, it remains an open question to what degree this label will appeal to growers, garden centres and customers.

See also MINIATURES.

Penzance roses

In the 1890s Lord Penzance, an English judge and some-time President of the Divorce Court, raised a number of hybrids, using *Rosa eglanteria*, the sweet brier, as the seed parent for fragrance and habit, crossed with pollen from HYBRID PERPETUALS and BOURBONS to add colour and size. The aim was thus to raise hybrid perpetual roses with fragrant foliage.

Today, the best known of these flowers are:
*'Amy Robsart' (1894): deep pink.
*'Anne of Geierstein' (1894): dark red.
*'Flora McIvor' (*c*. 1894): rose-pink single flowers with white centres; slightly scented foliage.
*'Greenmantle' (1895): rose-red, single-flowered, fragrant foliage.
*'Julia Mannering' (1895): pink with darker veins.
*'Meg Merrilies' (1894): vigorous, well armed and suitable for hedging. Both fresh crimson flowers and foliage are scented.
Penzance also made crosses with *R. foetida* and its near relatives. These led to: 'Lord Penzance' (1894), blooms that are mid-fawn tinted pink with lemon-yellow centres, and flowers and dense foliage that are both scented; and 'Lady Penzance' (1894), with single flowers of a coppery salmon pink, with large centres of bright yellow stamens.

Perfumery, the rose in

The way in which rose perfume is prepared differs radically from that used to obtain ATTAR OF ROSES. For one thing, the rose used is not the 'thirty-petalled' DAMASK ROSE that yields attar, but the ordinary pink ROSA CENTIFOLIA, or cabbage rose.

Since the beginning of the 19th century, the main centres of rose perfume production have been in the south of France. Some of the blooms are grown locally but others are cultivated in Morocco where the warmer climate allows an earlier start to the season.

The rose petals are first removed and are steeped in solvent (not water, as in the case of attar). This is then drawn off with the aid of a little warmth and a partial vacuum,

'The perfumier at work', from Johannes Baptista della Porta's Magia naturalis *(Nuremberg, 1715). The first edition of this book, which shows distillation in progress, appeared in Naples in 1558.*

Sorting roses for making perfume in Grasse, France, from the Illustrated London News *(4 April 1891).*

leaving behind a wax residue known to perfumers as the 'concrete'. In this way, the lighter fragrances that would be lost in the heat of distillation are preserved. Alcohol is then used to dissolve out the fragrant oils from the concrete. The resulting product is a brown oil known in the perfumery trade as the 'absolute'.

Synthetic rose perfume has been made for more than a century from compounds such as trichloromethylphenylcarbinol acetate, phenylethilic alcohol, nerol (found in the flowers of the bitter orange) and various other forms of primary alcohols. The intention here is not to discover a cheap substitute for the true rose perfume, but to harmonize two or more existing scents to evoke the unconscious or, better still, by skilful blending to produce a striking new perfume.

One of the most successful moves has been to combine ionones – the chemicals that give the violet its characteristic scent – with rose alcohols. The resulting product is stronger than the original rose, and this change has helped to recapture public favour for 'rose' perfumes.

Houbigant's Idéale, launched in 1900, was the first perfume to include an element (20%) of Bulgarian attar, and four years later, Coty enjoyed a considerable success with Rose Jacqueminot. Rose d'Orsay and a Guerlain Rose perfume followed in 1908.

Since World War I, blended flower perfumes have largely replaced single-flower products. However, even though the rose no longer constitutes a perfume on its own, it is an essential element in such products as Chanel No. 5, Crêpe de Chine, Shalimar, Arpège, Joy, Detchema, Fête, White Linen, Nahema and, no doubt, many others.

Perkins, Dorothy
See RAMBLERS.

Pernetiana roses
Pernetiana roses, the first of which was raised in 1900, answered the need for LARGE-FLOWERED, truly yellow garden roses and, if they are grown less today than formerly, this may be because they are short on scent and are suspected, not always justifiably, of being prone to BLACKSPOT.

Previously, growers had had to rely for yellow on unadulterated *Rosa foetida,* or its double form *R. foetida persiana* – which were essentially wild small-flowered briers – or on *R. hemisphaerica,* the yellow globe-shaped blooms of which often failed to open properly in the English climate, or on the pale – and frail – TEA ROSES.

Joseph Pernet (1858–1928) was the breeder who overcame these limitations. He came from a rose-growing family and joined another one when he married Marie, the daughter of Madame Antoine Ducher who, after her husband's death in 1874, had continued to run her late husband's nursery near Lyon under the name of 'Ducher Veuve' (widow). On his marriage, Pernet took the name Pernet-Ducher (although his sons were to remain as 'Pernet'), and he united the two nurseries.

He seems to have been a much-loved, but impulsive man, and one of those rosarians about whom legends grow in their own lifetime. One story goes that when an eminent rosarian and director of public parks in Paris, J. C. Forestier, suggested that one of the Ducher roses was subject to bleaching, Pernet tore off Forestier's hat and told him, 'You too are fading so then you are no more good!' A more fully authenticated encounter took place in 1912 when a Pernet-Ducher rose with flame-coloured blooms won the prize of £1000 offered by the London *Daily Mail* for the best new rose of the year. It was planned to call it the '*Daily Mail* Rose', but unfortunately, Pernet-Ducher had already promised to name the rose after the wife of a friend, Edouard Herriot, who was to become prime minister of France in 1924, but who was then an almost unknown local politician. Pernet refused to break his promise to his friend, so the rose was called the '*Daily Mail* Rose' in Britain but remained 'Madame Edouard Herriot' to the world at large.

In 1883, Pernet began his attempts to secure a worthwhile hybrid from the pollen of foetida roses, and tried many hundreds of crosses with various HYBRID PERPETUALS but without result. Success came in 1900 with pollen from a Persian yellow and seed from 'Antoine Ducher', a hybrid perpetual with red flowers. The seedling raised was of no consequence, but Pernet-Ducher let it grow. The following year, when he came to examine it, he saw what he had failed to notice before: another seedling had appeared beside the first. This second generation was 'Soleil d'Or', which through 'Rayon d'Or' provided many of the most vividly coloured modern roses – bright yellow, orange and copper.

It has sometimes been said that the introduction of the *R. foetida* strain has been responsible for the occurrence of blackspot in succeeding generations. Some blackspot was already known before the arrival of 'Soleil d'Or', and it was not confined to *R. foetida*. In Lyon, because of the dry climate, it is practically unknown. In any case, most of the early Pernetiana varieties have been absorbed into the mainstream of large-flowered roses and the proneness to blackspot considerably reduced. Those that have it are deservedly dropped by good nurserymen.

The Pernet-Ducher nursery continued to produce excellent roses well into the present century – in particular, 'Souvenir de Claudius Pernet', a beautiful, if tender, true yellow rose with a darker centre, which has imparted its good looks to many other modern large-flowered varieties; it won a gold medal at the BAGATELLE contest. This rose was introduced in 1920 to commemorate Pernet-Ducher's son. Because his regiment remained inactive during the early days of World War I, he had resigned his commission in the French army and joined the ranks; he was mortally wounded soon afterwards. Pernet's other son, Georges, was also killed in action, in 1915, and he too was commemorated with a rose, 'Souvenir de Georges Pernet', which also won a gold medal at the Bagatelle trials. But Pernet-Ducher himself never really recovered.

In 1924, he wrote to his old friend Raymond Gaujard in Rome, asking him to send his twenty-two-year-old son Jean to help in his hybridization programme. After three months of working together, Pernet-Ducher offered to pass on his breeding establishment, at that time only a couple of acres in extent, to Jean. Joseph Pernet-Ducher died four years later. It has sometimes been stated that Jean Gaujard became Pernet-Ducher's son-in-law, but in fact, Gaujard married a young woman from Lyon who had no connection with the Pernet-Ducher family.)

Jean Gaujard, in turn, has produced many fine roses – in particular, 'Rose Gaujard' (1958), cherry red with silvery-white reverse, which won an RNRS gold medal that year and an RHS award of merit.

The name of the nursery remained unchanged until 1955, when – now greatly extended in size – it became Roseraies Gaujard. Gaujard's headquarters are now at Feyzin near Lyon, slightly to the south of Venissieux on the left bank of the Rhône.

See also SPONSORED ROSES.

Pillar roses

These are roses that are encouraged to twine round pillars of marble, other types of stone or wood. For this purpose, a cone-shaped evergreen tree or the trunk of a pine tree with the branches cut down to stumps are both particularly suitable. The roses themselves should be capable of producing long flexible canes, without too many branches. Among the old-fashioned roses, 'Tour de Malakoff' and 'William Lobb' – both mauve – are recommended, as well as 'Jeanne de Montfort' (medium pink), 'Madame Isaac Pereire' and 'Madame Ernst Calvat' (both deep pink BOURBONS) and 'Madame Plantier', a white rose of undeclared parentage. Among the moderns, Climbing 'Bettina', an orange blend, and Climbing 'Sonia Meilland', both from the MEILLAND nursery, are worth consideration, and in the United States, the floriferous scarlet 'Blaze' and the sensationally duo-coloured 'Piñata' are in the front row.

Planting

Planting must be planned well in advance since the number of roses or rootstocks ordered from the nurseryman must accord with the space available to receive them. In addition, many of the most popular varieties of roses are advertised on a 'while stocks last' basis – that is, customers who fail to order in June are likely to be disappointed in November.

Ordinary SHRUB ROSES will need 18 inches (45 cm) of space, STANDARDS about double as much, and RAMBLERS and large shrubs an amount varying with their habit. In the United States, it is usual to allow more space between roses in areas where the climate allows a longer growing season. The prudent gardener marks out the required spaces in advance. It is a mistake to plant a rose less than 2 feet (0.60 m) from a wall, because walls tend to shut out much of the rain and they also sometimes prevent what falls from draining away. The SOIL of the rosebed will also require preparing in advance if the new arrivals are to prosper.

Planting can be carried out at almost any time between November and March inclusive, unless the ground has become waterlogged or frostbound. In this case the operation must be postponed and the roses put into STORAGE until conditions improve.

On the appointed day, the roses are taken out of store and prepared for planting, if this was not already attended to when they first arrived. In particular, any damaged roots are cut off above the wound, and vertical tap roots, which promote the wrong kind of growth, are severed. Horizontal roots are trimmed if they exceed their allotted space. All broken stems and SNAGS are removed at the same time, together with any suspect leaves.

It is important that the roots should not be allowed to dry out at any time. The plants are therefore taken out of store one by one, and not left lying about *en masse* during the planting operation, exposed to the sun and wind. If the root hairs appear dry, they should be given a thorough soaking in water before planting.

The shape of the hole in which the rose is to be set will vary with the disposition of its roots. If they have grown out radially like the spokes of a wheel, the stock will be planted in the centre of a circular hole with the floor of the hole slightly raised in the centre to give improved drainage, although this will not occur unless the soil around has been allowed to get sufficiently dry. If, as frequently happens, most of the roots of the rose plant have grown mainly from only one side of the stock, they will need to be fanned out in a hole of that shape, and the foot of the stock placed close to the 'hasp' of the 'fan'. In this case, good drainage is promoted if the floor of the hole slopes away from the stock towards the edges of the 'fan'. For the average shrub rose, this might mean a hole that is 3–4 inches (7.5–10 cm) deep at the shallow end near the stock, and 8–9 inches (20–23 cm) deep towards the edges of the 'fan'. In addition, the new plants will have the best chance of standing up to the wind if their main roots are set so as to point away from the direction from which the prevailing wind in the area blows.

In the case of bush roses, the original point of union between the bud and the stock should be placed level with or at most 1 inch (2.5 cm) below ground level. With standards, there is much to be said for planting at the depth (shown by the earth-ring on the stock) at which it has been previously growing. It is probably best to drive in the stakes, which will support the standards during their lives, before each rose is planted, placing them on the sides of the plants from which the prevailing wind blows. When fully driven home, the top of the supports should barely reach the heads of the growth at the top of the standards. The stocks are then secured to them in several places. Growers in the past used tarred string over bands of sacking tied round the stock to prevent chafing by the string, but garden shops of today sell ready-made ties for standard roses, which can be expanded as the plants grow.

Successful rose growers take the trouble to see that the root fibres of their rose plants are in close contact with the finely crumbled earth that they carry in a bag and sprinkle both above and below the roots while planting. As they fill up the hole, they press down the soil, at first gently by hand and then, as the hole fills up, equally gently with their full weight, working inwards from the edges of the hole. They also find it worthwhile to make an inspection from time to time to make sure the soil has not dried out and that the plant is firmly established and has not been loosened by the wind.

Poetry, the rose in

Only a few of the many poetic tributes to the rose can be mentioned here, and in these circumstances, particular attention has to be paid to some less familiar examples.

The distinction between the rose in poetry and the ROSE IN LYRICS is finely drawn, but 'poetry' is taken here to mean lines not specifically written for setting to music or at least not indissolubly linked with a song.

For non-classicists, it was probably Chaucer who, in his rhyming translation of the ROMAN DE LA ROSE, established the rose garden in England as a rendezvous for the poet as well as for the romantic, but in France, literary historians cite Pierre de Ronsard (1524–85) as the first poet to do justice to the rose. For example:

> La rose est l'honneur d'un pourpris,
> La rose est des fleurs la plus belle,
> Et dessus toutes a le pris:
> C'est pour cela que je l'appelle
> La violette de Cypris.

Justifiably, a beautiful pink-flowered climbing rose was raised and introduced in 1985 by MEILLAND to commemorate the 400th anniversary of De Ronsard's death.

Much earlier, in Italy, the true source of the Renaissance, Dante had written about the rose, in the new Italian that was to supersede the Latin of the traditional literati. The rose appears in *The Divine Comedy (La divina commedia)* – in Paradise, naturally:

> Nel giallo della rosa sempiterna
> Che si dilata, rigrada, e ridole
> Odor di lode al Sol, che sempre verna,
> Qual'è colui, che tace e dicer vuole,
> Mi trasse Beatrice . . .

A free translation might read:

Into the yellow anthers of the rose eternal – the rose that expands by degrees and yields perfumes in praise of the sun, the source of eternal spring – Beatrice, silent, though wanting to speak, drew me . . .

A less symbolic, and more carnal approach than Dante's to Beatrice, is seen in English poems about the rose. However, clearly not all those who wrote about the flower were rosarians.

Thus in Edmund Spenser's 'Shepheardes Calender' (1579), we read for the month of April:

Upon her head a cremosin coronet
With damaske roses and daffadillies set;
Bay leaves betweene, and primroses greene,
Embellish the sweete violet.

We should perhaps simply accept the effusions of poets whose devotion to the rose is less than total and they have no regard for flowering seasons. Even Shakespeare, the greatest of English poets, makes more than sixty references to the rose.

However, the true rosarian is entitled to be somewhat disappointed in respect of two of the most frequently quoted poems about roses. The first of these, 'To the Virgins, to Make Much of Time', by Robert Herrick (1591–1674), though set to music by an accomplished contemporary Henry Lawes (1596–1662), is today more often read than sung. The poem begins:

Gather ye rosebuds while ye may,
Old time is still a-flying:
And this same flower that smiles to-day,
To-morrow will be dying . . .

The remaining three verses were, however, addressed more directly 'to the virgins', and the rose is not mentioned again.

A second disappointment (for rosarians) came much later, in the poem by Robert Burns (1759–96), whose opening couplet ran:

O, my Luve's like a red red rose
That's newly sprung in June . . .

Burns, like Herrick, neglected the rose for the remainder of his poem.

Returning for a moment to the days of the English Civil War, we find poets of different persuasions praising the rose after their fashion. One of them, Edmund Waller (1606–87), seems to have served both Royalists and Parliamentarians at various times, but he showed more devotion to the rose than Herrick when he sent his own message to a reluctant beauty.

Go, lovely Rose!
Tell her, that wastes her time and me,
That now she knows,
When I resemble her to thee,
How sweet and fair she seems to be.

John Milton (1608–74), a Parliamentarian and a contemporary of Waller, named the sight of the rose as one of the pleasures he missed most keenly after he had become blind at the age of forty-four:

With the year
Seasons return, but not to me returns
Day or the sweet approach of ev'n or morn
Or sight of vernal bloom or summer's rose.

The century that followed the Civil War and the Restoration was that of the Hanoverian Kings, of Lancelot 'Capability' Brown (1715–83) who designed the grounds of many of Britain's finest estates, and of William Kent

(1684–1748), progenitor of the romantic element in garden design. In this era, William Shenstone (1714–63) occupied a unique position in that he was both a poet and a celebrated landscape gardener. A contemporary of Samuel Johnson at Pembroke College, Oxford, he studied poetry there, and afterwards published numerous poetical works. He also spent much time and money turning his estate – The Leasowes, west of Birmingham – into 'the perfect landskip garden', and his approach to roses, in both poetry and gardening, was prophetic of the wild garden to come, more than a century later:

And bid Arcadia bloom around:
Whether we fringe the sloping hill
Or smooth below the verdant mead,
Whether we break the falling rill,
Or through meandering mazes lead,
Or in the horrid bramble's room
Bid careless groups of roses bloom.

In the Victorian era, during which the MOSS ROSE was distorted to represent the image of the ideally bashful maiden, it was predictable that some references to the rose, and indeed to other garden plants, would sometimes include a moral. However, few could have stated a credo more succinctly than Thomas Edward Brown (1830–97) when he wrote:

A garden is a lovesome thing, God wot!
Rose plot,
Fringed pool,
Ferned grot –
The veriest school
Of peace; and yet the fool
Contends that God is not –
Not God! in gardens! when the eve is cool?
Nay, but I have a sign;
'Tis very sure God walks in mine.

Victorian society was also greatly preoccupied with the subject of death. This topic was not new, nor its linking with the ephemeral rose, as can be seen in these lines by George Herbert (1593–1633), poet and priest, who had perhaps a premonition of his own early death when he wrote of the impermanence of beauty:

Sweet Rose, whose hue angry and brave
Bids the rash gazer wipe his eye,
Thy root is ever in its grave,
And thou must die.

In their attitudes to roses, two 19th-century poets showed the difference between the 'old' Victorians and the 'new'. Matthew Arnold (1822–88), mourning for a friend, wrote:

Strew on her roses, roses,
And never a spray of yew.
In quiet she reposes:
Ah! would that I did too.

Christina Rossetti (1830–94), sister of Dante Gabriel, thought differently: in a poem, composed for singing but hardly a lyric, she wrote:

When I am dead, my dearest,
Sing no sad songs for me;
Plant thou no roses at my head,
Nor shady cypress tree:
Be the green grass above me
With showers and dewdrops wet;
And if thou wilt, remember,
and if thou wilt, forget . . .

Much attention to the rose was drawn by Edward Fitz-gerald (1809–83) in his translation of *The Rubáiyát* of OMAR KHAYYÁM, and this is dealt with under that heading.

Poets of the 20th century seem to have paid less attention to the rose than to their own psychological, social or even political problems, and where the rose is specified, particularly in the works of T. S. Eliot, the references are usually tangential and the meanings often obscure. Few examples are to be found today of the kind of descriptive poems in which the rose could be expected to feature, and fewer still of these are of a sentimental nature.

In lyrics and ballads, however, the rose continues to flourish.

Pollen

Pollen is gold-dust to the rose hybridizer. The pollen grains of rose blooms and other similar flowers are produced within the anthers attached to the tops of the stamens (*see* ANATOMY OF THE ROSE), and are released when the anthers split. Each fully developed pollen grain is a spore (similar to those seen on ferns) and contains three cells. Two of these are sperm cells, and the third gives rise to a hollow vegetal shoot, known as the pollen tube, through which the two sperm cells will eventually reach and fertilize an embryo.

The pollen grains are, by one means or another, deposited on and retained by the receptive stigmas of a suitable flower; some roses, particularly those in northern latitudes where beetles and other insect visitors are scarce, have been found to be self-pollinating. If conditions are favourable, the point of the pollen tube penetrates one of the stigmas of that flower, and grows downwards within the style towards the ovule, thus allowing the two sperm cells to penetrate the ovary sac.

One of the sperm cells fertilizes the ovule, which can then develop into the seed, and the other sperm cell combines with its opposite number in the embryo sac to form the endosperm, from which the seed draws its nourishment during the early stages of its development. The secrets of this double-fertilization process remained undiscovered until 1830.

Pollen grains are enclosed in a substance of unusual strength and durability, and some are known to have deteriorated little during periods lasting millions of years. They are less perishable than wood, leaves or seeds, and are often the best source of clues about the past. This high survival rate makes pollen grains the most widely distributed and readily available form of fossil within the vegetable kingdom. Moreover, the shape and structure of some grains are sufficiently distinctive to proclaim from which family or even from which species the pollen originated. Unfortunately, however, ancient roses seldom grew on the type of soil most favourable to the preservation of pollen granules, and so far, palaeontologists have had to rely on leaves, prickles and pieces of stem, which are far less reliable guides to the identity of the original rose.

Many roses are prolific pollen growers. Anyone with sufficient patience to count the stamens of *Rosa bracteata*, which Lord Macartney brought back from China in 1795 (*see* CHINA ROSES), will be able to confirm that their numbers sometimes rise as high as 400, with the numbers of pollen grains being equally vast.

See also HYBRIDIZING ROSES.

Polyanthas

The polyanthas and polypom roses of the 19th century are important historically because they were the ancestors of the modern FLORIBUNDA (cluster-flowered) roses. Their development was the response by breeders to the demand for massed colour, irrespective of the beauty of the individual blooms.

Polypom was itself a hybrid word, the latter syllable referring to the 'pom-poms' or small round bobbles used to decorate the fringes of curtains and the tops of children's (or sailors') hats. *Polyantha*, meaning 'many-flowered', was used in error as a name for the species that had already been named *Rosa multiflora*.

Around 1860, seeds of the wild species of *R. multiflora* were first sent from Japan to Jean Sisely by his son, and found their way to the Guillot nursery near Lyon. They were single white flowers, and thus quite different from the pink garden varieties that had previously been received from the Far East from 1804 onwards. Jean-Baptiste Guillot grew the seeds of this white species and crossed the seedlings with POLLEN from dwarf forms of *R. chinensis*, which had been raised by Colville of Chelsea in 1805 and was known at that time as the 'Fairy Rose' or as *R. lawranceana*.

In the first generation of Guillot's seedlings, the dominant element of *R. multiflora* prevailed: the roses flowered only in the summer and were climbers at heart. However, in the second generation, the recessive REMONTANT character came to the fore and yielded two DWARF ROSES – one pure white, the other pink and white – a few inches high, which flowered continuously throughout the season. They were the first polypoms, and Guillot called the white one 'Ma Pâquerette' ('My Daisy') and the pinker variety 'Mignonette' ('Sweetheart'). Each showed about thirty double blooms on a diminutive bush. 'Pâquerette' was shown in Lyon in 1873 and marketed two years later, but 'Mignonette' was held in reserve until 1881.

Strictly speaking, since the term *polyantha* had been used as a synonym for *R. multiflora*, it should not be used to describe any other cluster-flowered roses. However, the French, who were the pioneers in the development of these roses, thought otherwise and have been generally supported. Guillot's 'Gloire des Polyantha' appeared in 1887, and from then on, the term became more and more frequently used.

The earliest varieties of polypoms had been based on open pollinated crosses between *R. multiflora* and *R. chinensis*, but already in 1881, 'Cécile Brunner', and in 1883 'Perle d'Or', showed that TEA ROSES had been added to the equation. Gradually the polyanthas became more and more remote from the original *R. multiflora* x *R. chinensis* cross.

It is at this point that we can begin to distinguish between the polyantha roses proper – low-growing (up to 18 inches, 45 cm), compact and bushy, with small double, almost scentless flowers presented in close pyramidal clusters throughout the summer – and the hybrid polyanthas, which had a different inflorescence and plant structure showing the influence of species other than *R. multiflora* and *R. chinensis* (for instance, *R. wichuraiana* and *R. sempervirens* as well as NOISETTES and other hybrids).

Attempts to improve the polyanthas continued up to and including the 1930s, but these experiments were largely unsuccessful. For example, breeders who increased the influence of *R. moschata* (the MUSK ROSE) in hybrid polyanthas found that this reduced the length of the flowering season, and the addition of more lively colours increased the risk of BLACKSPOT. Consequently, polyanthas have now been surpassed by the floribundas and few are grown today.

'Little White Pet' of 1879 is still available, and is floriferous and remontant, but almost scentless. 'Mevrouw Nathalie Nypels' (1919) is, like the foregoing, low-growing, to about 2 feet (0.60 m), pink-flowered and remontant, with some scent and is also to be found in nurseries here and there.

It is also worth recalling that two dwarf polyanthas – 'Gloria Mundi' (De Ruiter, 1929) and 'Paul Crampel' (Kersbergen, 1930) – were the first two roses to show the brilliant 'day-glo' orange-scarlet COLOURS due to pelargonidin, a compound that gives pelargoniums their brilliant colours but which had never previously been detected in roses.

Portland roses

Portland roses were greatly prized by gardeners of the early 19th century for their brilliant scarlet blooms. They were thought to be hybrids of 'Slater's Crimson China' (*Rosa chinensis semperflorens*, see CHINA ROSES) and a variety of the autumn damask (*R. damascena bifera*) that was known in France as 'La Rose des Quatre Saisons'. At least three varieties of these were commercially grown in France for use by florists, even before the French Revolution. One of these, painted by REDOUTÉ as *R. bifera pumila* – 'Le Petit Quatre Saisons' – was a pygmy pink, clustered, double-petalled pom-pom, featured by a Parisian florist named Noël. A pink form of the full-size 'Quatre Saisons' was grown by André Dupont in the Jardin du Luxembourg, and there was also a darker form that the essayist Montaigne had been astonished to see growing in the open in

Italy in 1580 and of which he had brought back a plant for his own garden in France (*see* DAMASK ROSES). It was known as *R. paestana* (a reference to Virgil's *Georgics; see* HISTORY OF THE ROSE), and this type must be considered the most probable ancestor of the Portlands.

This is all at variance with an account accepted by many rosarians. According to this, in about 1800 this rose was brought directly from Italy to England by the Duchess of Portland, who was said to have been an enthusiastic gardener. In Britain, it was crossed with 'Slater's Crimson China', and then sent by the Duchess to André Dupont who, at about that time, would have been establishing JOSEPHINE's rose garden at La Malmaison. However, a member of the Cavendish–Bentinck family has since declared that the Duchess showed no particular interest in roses, or indeed in any form of gardening, and thus a more likely explanation is that the rose was indeed imported into England, crossed there and then sent on to France, but the dispatcher was more probably the Lee & Kennedy nursery, which is known to have supplied roses to La Malmaison. The suggestion that the rose should be named after the Duchess would have been made to Dupont probably by Kennedy, not because the Duchess was a rosarian, but because she was the wife of the 3rd Duke of Portland, twice Prime Minister of Britain and one of William Pitt's closest associates. The Duke could have been influential in persuading Pitt to give John Kennedy the *laissez-passer* that allowed him to take roses to La Malmaison without hindrance from the British navy.

The Portland rose was bred intensively in France, but because of the laws of hybrid inheritance (*see* MENDEL'S LAWS), only a proportion were found to be truly REMONTANT. Nevertheless, one seedling raised in 1812 (probably a cross with a GALLICA ROSE) showed unusual qualities, with large, fragrant, semi-double, vividly coloured flowers produced almost throughout the whole season. The Comte de Lélieur, who had retained the position of superintendent at the royal gardens at Saint Cloud, was content to let the new discovery be called 'Rose de Lélieur'. However, at the insistence of the Comtesse du Cayla after the reinstatement of Louis XVIII, it was renamed 'Rose du Roi' in 1816, and was distributed by Charles Souchet who succeeded Lélieur at Saint Cloud. It was introduced in England as 'Lee's Crimson Perpetual' (1819), certainly a parent of memorable HYBRID PERPETUALS if not the first of the line.

Today, one of the most favoured Portlands is a small remontant SHRUB ROSE, the 'Comte de Chambord' (1860), the blooms of which are strongly scented, deep-pink, flat and crowded with petals reflexed at the edges. Because of their flower shape, some of the Portlands are now regarded as Portland damasks.

Portland Rose Festival

Ever since lines of 'Madame Caroline Testout' roses were planted along its sidewalks, Portland, the largest city in the state of Oregon, has been known as the 'City of Roses'. The climate and soil are ideal for rose growing, and the

Portland Rose Society was founded in 1887, shortly before the debut of 'Madame Testout'.

The city-wide rose festival was first held in 1907 and has since developed into the most important civic event of the year, lasting for three weeks. Held as early as the first week in June, it opens with the selection and coronation of the new 'Queen of Rosaria' and continues with the Society's rose show and other events such as a starlight parade, cart-racing and a Golden Rose ski classic, plus the Grand Floral Parade rivalled only by the Pasadena Tournament of Roses further south in California (*see* ROSE BOWL).

Postage stamps, roses on

At the time of writing, more than 150 different postage stamps from 42 countries have been issued with a rose as the principle feature.

The finest of these are probably the two stamps issued by the United Nations in 1975 to commemorate UN peace-keeping operations, which showed wild roses growing against strands of barbed wire. Like many others, these roses were basically symbolic and not named as any specific species or variety.

Bulgaria, Hungary and Switzerland have all produced particularly large numbers of 'rose stamps'. Since the end of World War II, the Bulgarian Postal Services have issued nineteen different rose stamps, including a set of eight in 1962 showing red, pink and yellow LARGE-FLOWERED ROSES. Since 1958, Hungary has issued fourteen different rose stamps, including one triangular, two diamond-shaped and, in 1962, a set of six large-flowered rose stamps, designed to encourage rose culture. Switzerland, among fourteen rose stamps issued since 1945, produced a set of four stamps in 1975 that illustrated large-flowered roses.

Rosa canina (the dog rose), being a single-petalled rose and therefore easily reproduced on a small scale, has been used as a model by Austria, Bulgaria, Liechtenstein, Romania, San Marino, the USSR and Yugoslavia. *R. acicularis* has been used by both Canada and Mongolia as particularly suitable to their more northerly climates.

In 1964, the United Kingdom issued a stamp featuring *R. canina* to celebrate the 10th International Botanical Conference in Edinburgh, and in 1976 the UK Post Office issued four rose stamps to celebrate the centenary of the ROYAL NATIONAL ROSE SOCIETY: 'Elizabeth of Glamis' (cluster-flowered rose; 8½p); 'Grandpa Dickson' (large-flowered mid-yellow rose; 10p); '*Rosa mundi*' (*R. gallica versicolor*, 11p); and *R. eglanteria* (sweet brier; 13p).

In 1971, New Zealand issued three stamps to commemorate the meeting held there of the WORLD FEDERATION OF ROSE SOCIETIES. The roses chosen were 'Tiffany' (2 cents), 'Peace' (5 cents) and 'Chrysler Imperial' (8 cents) – all large-flowered roses. These were followed by a number of others in 1976.

Denmark has featured 'The Queen of Denmark' ('Königin von Dänemarck', but in Denmark itself 'Dronningen af Danmark'), a vivid carmine ALBA ROSE of 1826.

A collection of rose stamps is kept at the National Post Office Museum at King Edward Street, London EC1A 1LP.

Pot-pourri

'Pot-pourri' is the French term, adopted by the British in the early years of the 17th century, for drying rose petals to preserve their scent, but the practice was already current in Britain towards the end of the 16th century and, no doubt, much earlier elsewhere.

The most frequently quoted example of an early pot-pourri appears in Sir Hugh Platt's *Delights for Ladies*, which was published in 1594. Platt was the son of a wealthy London brewer, but his own talents lay in the direction of mechanical invention and scientific agriculture, his chief work on gardening, *Floraes paradise* appearing in 1608. He also looked into and wrote about the best ways of dyeing hair. Platt's recipe for pot-pourri was:

You must in rose-time make choice of such roses as are neither in bud, nor full blowne which you must specially cull and chuse from the rest, then take sand and drie it thoroughly well, and having shallow boxes, make first an even lay of sand, upon which lay your rose-leaves [i.e. petals] one by one (so as none of them touch other).

Set this box in some warme, sunny place in a hot sunny day (and commonly in two hot sunny dayes they will be thorow dry) and thus you may have rose-leaves and other flowers to lay about your basons, windows, etc., all the winter long.

The modern method of making pot-pourri differs in several respects from that advocated by Sir Hugh. In the first place, the petals are spread out on wire trays or muslin rather than on sand; this speeds up the drying process, making it unnecessary to hasten the process by exposing the petals to the heat of the sun (which drives away some of the essential oils). There is now also a trend favouring the use of spices not readily available in Platt's time, as well as lavender, rosemary and other well-scented herbs.

Gertrude Jekyll, who never believed in doing things half-heartedly, made her pot-pourri once every two years – in 100 kilo (228 lb) lots. The roses, which must not have been rained on since bud stage, were picked six or seven bushes at a time; the petals were removed in the house and rammed down into cylindrical stone jars with layers of salt between. They were taken out of the jars some two months later and then mixed with spices and turned into a tub. The whole operation involved a team of three or four persons.

One modern recipe calls for eight cupfuls of dry rose petals – centifolias and damasks (particularly *R. 'kazanlik'*) are especially suitable – to which are added:

*2 tablespoons of dried mace
*2 tablespoons of ground cloves
*2 tablespoons of ground nutmeg
*2 tablespoons of allspice
*⅔ cup of orris-root powder (as a 'fixer')
*1 stick of cinnamon (crushed) or its equivalent in powder
*5 drops of rose oil, unless the rose petals are very strongly scented (which they should be)

The dried petals are laid in a large open bowl with the spices and ¾ cup of coarse salt scattered over them. The bowl is then set in a dry airy place and stirred every day. When thoroughly mixed and dried – probably after ten days – the mixture can be placed in decorative bowls or bagged into sachets.

Petals of flowers other than roses are often added as a zest or to improve the appearance of the mixture.

Pots and other containers, growing roses in

LARGE-FLOWERED ROSES growing to 3 feet (0.90 m), as well as cluster-flowered roses and MINIATURES are frequently sold in various types of containers for growing outdoors. There is also an increasing demand for them from flat dwellers with balconies, as well as from amateurs who like the idea of bedding-in a rose while it is actually flowering. Such roses can be grown on their own roots, but nearly all will have been field-BUDDED or, in the case of miniatures, possibly GRAFTED, or grown from CUTTINGS to produce smaller plants in a shorter time. These last two will be sold in pots of about 3 inches (8 cm), whereas the field-budded plants will be in containers of 5¼–8½ pints (3–5 litres).

Wise buyers always seek an assurance that the roses of their choice have been grown in the containers in which they are sold, and are not ones that have been bought elsewhere and thrust into pots with some of their roots chopped off to make a good fit. Therefore, roots projecting through the base of a pot (in moderation) can be a good sign.

However, it is the fortunate possessor of a greenhouse who gains most benefit from growing roses in pots, because with careful management a display of one rose or another can be enjoyed almost throughout the year. Varieties, some of which are too tender to be left out of doors, can be grown, and blooms that would fail to open fully if subjected to normal rainfall, can be seen at their best when

protected in a frame or greenhouse. If the plants that have been bought in pots from the nursery are on their own roots (i.e. they have not been budded on to stocks), they can be repotted in the spring and left to grow in the open until the autumn frosts. The aim should be to encourage the formation of a limited number of shoots with really firm ripe wood.

As the plants grow, the enthusiastic amateur will transfer them during the season to larger pots to give adequate room for the roots. In every case, the normal precaution is taken of placing a piece of broken crock over the hole at the base of the flower pot to make sure that the drain hole does not become blocked with earth; a turf of peat on top of the crock will give an added assurance against blockage. The pot should stand on an inverted saucer or other platform that will still allow water to drain away but will prevent the roots of the rose from becoming anchored in the ground – or worms from entering the pot from below. Commercial nurseries cover the ground with material that allows water to drain away but prevents weeds from growing. Some growers prefer to 'plunge' the pots into the earth, which at least prevents them from being blown or knocked over.

A final pruning should be given in the autumn, when some of the vertical shoots can also be gently bent down and staked in order to encourage lateral growth and so obtain a well-balanced, rounded plant. The more tender plants should be taken to a sheltered spot as winter approaches.

Roses on their own roots that have not been bought in pots from the nursery but are to be taken from the grower's own garden can be lifted in the early autumn and potted. They are then placed in a cold frame, at first closed and later opened slightly. The hardier roses should be in the frame for only a few days, after which they can then be taken out and left in the open. The more sensitive varieties

Two stages in pruning a pot-grown rose to produce a well-shaped flowering specimen, from Popular Gardening (c. 1895).

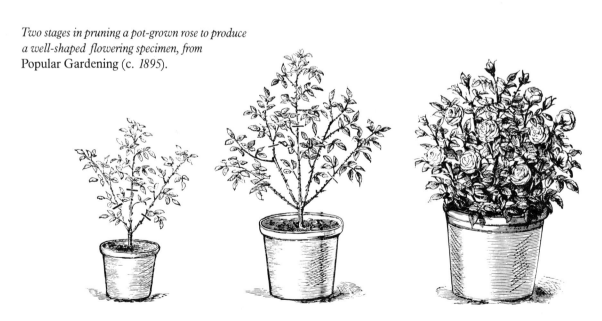

Redouté described this rose as Rosa eglanteria, *but it has the straight,
unequal prickles, sharp sepals and deep yellow colouring of* R. foetida, *the Austrian brier,
so called because specimens introduced to Western Europe in 1583 came via Austria. It is native to Asia Minor
and an area stretching to the western Himalayas.*

Rosa gallica versicolor *('Rosa mundi'). This particular portrait*
by Redouté, not included in Les roses, *shows two expanded blooms, whereas*
the earlier portrait had but one, poised above a rather inelegantly
truncated stalk.

will overwinter in the frame or in some other sheltered spot. This method ensures that all these roses will all flower at their normal times.

However, roses that are REMONTANT can be induced to flower in pots out of doors from November to January by cutting down the main shoots at the end of the summer, and sheltering the plants in a cold frame from October onwards. The glass of the frame is kept open except in damp weather, and straw mats are laid on top during a frost. In severe weather, the plants can be brought into the greenhouse. After flowering, the remontant roses remain in the cold frame. In early spring, they will be repotted, pruned and returned to the open, where they will flower again in July. They may also need repotting in the autumn. Roses that have been brought into an unheated greenhouse early in December and kept there can, however, be expected to flower in May at the latest.

Roses that have been budded on to UNDERSTOCKS in the garden during the summer can be lifted and potted later in the autumn, when the bud is dormant. They will flower earlier under glass than those on their own roots.

Many growers like to grow an understock in a pot and bud the chosen variety on to it there. In this case, the understock cuttings – often of *Rosa rugosa* – are taken during November and are left to root out of doors for a year. If the budding is to take place in the pot, rooted cuttings are potted the following November, and placed in a cold frame or airy greenhouse. They are returned to the open in April and are budded in the normal way in July. For the next three months, the plants are kept in partial shade and without too much water, in order to hold back the growth of the bud. In early autumn, the roses that are to be brought into flower during the winter months are taken to the greenhouse and the understock cut down to a point just above the bud. The greenhouse is heated during January and February to much the same heat that the rose might expect if it were out of doors in March to May – that is, about 50°F (10°C) by day, rising gradually to 65°F (18°C). After blooming, the 'summer-flowering' roses are taken out in early spring and placed in a sunny but sheltered position.

Stocks that have been budded in July can be lifted in September and forced in their first season, although these first-season plants are unlikely to show any blooms before the middle of March. Plants on their own roots that have been taken from the ground should be allowed to grow for a year – or, better still, two – before forcing.

The remontant roses in the greenhouse will flower a second time, in April or May, if their shoots are first cut back to two or three eyes. They, too, are gradually hardened off after flowering, and repotted if necessary before being returned once more to the open. Despite having been forced, they would flower again in the early autumn, but this will probably reduce the number and quality of flowers to come in the following spring. Consequently, the autumn flower buds are usually rubbed off as soon as they appear.

Smaller roses, including miniatures, are often grown by nurseries in the US from cuttings placed in fibres of basalt rock, known commercially as 'rockwool' (also called vermiculite). A litre of rockwool weighs only about $3\frac{1}{2}$ oz (100 g), but will hold as much as $10\frac{1}{2}$ oz (300 g) of water, the rest of the bulk being largely air. This combination of lightness, air and water is highly favourable to the formation of roots.

Small cuttings can be planted about $1\frac{1}{4}$ inches (3 cm) from each other on sheets of rockwool, measuring about 39 by $7\frac{3}{4}$ inches (1 m × 20 cm) and $2\frac{3}{4}$ inches (7 cm) thick, in rows 3 inches (7.5 cm) apart. In the greenhouse, the temperature is kept at 64°F (18°C), or rather more than is needed for CUT ROSES. Rooting takes place within six weeks, after which the roses can be grown on in containers of 3 inches (7.5 cm) in diameter.

Development is rapid, and plentiful watering and feeding are required. When roses are grown on rockwool out of doors, a slow-releasing fertilizer can be used, and the pot, hanging basket or trough can be covered with plastic sheeting to prevent the rapid evaporation that would otherwise take place.

See also MICROPROPAGATION.

Poulsen family, the

Dorus T. Poulsen, first in the line of famous Danish rose breeders, set up his nursery on the then outskirts of Copenhagen in 1878. He first specialized in asparagus and strawberries and then in beets, cabbage and swedes, before turning to garden shrubs, herbaceous plants and so to roses. In 1925, he handed over his business, which had expanded to include a nursery at Kvistgaard, to his three sons – Dines, Poul and Svend – of whom all had worked with him for more than a decade.

Dines Poulsen had studied rose culture in Germany under PETER LAMBERT as well as in England, and he was the first of the family to achieve international success. His roses – in particular, 'Ellen Poulsen' (1912), pink; and 'Rödhätte' ('Red Riding Hood', 1911) – were low-growing large-flowered POLYANTHAS capable of giving a good show of blooms during the short Scandinavian flowering season.

During World War I, Dines turned over the hybridization programme of Poulsen Roses to his youngest brother Svend, who produced new varieties such as 'Else Poulsen' (pink) and 'Kirsten Poulsen' (mid-red), both introduced in 1924. They, too, were low-growing cluster-flowered roses with large blooms, and because there was then nothing quite like them, they became generically known among nurserymen as 'Poulsen roses'. (The term FLORIBUNDA was coined later in the US.) Svend Poulsen's son, Niels D. Poulsen, was also to prove to be a successful breeder. He introduced 'Chinatown', the outstanding yellow-flowered SHRUB ROSE that won the ROYAL NATIONAL ROSE SOCIETY's Gold Medal in 1962, and also launched 'Pernille Poulsen' (1965), a pink cluster-flowered rose; 'Troika' (1972), a large-flowered orange rose; and 'Bellevue' (Jarlina, 1976), a large-flowered pink.

In 1953, there was a reorganization of the firm. Svend

Poulsen and Harriet Poulsen, widow of Dines, took over at Kvistgaard, which had become the main Poulsen nursery, and in 1963 Niels D. Poulsen became a partner in the firm, along with Harriet Poulsen's grandchildren. In the years following the oil crisis of 1973, fuel costs rose phenomenally, and most rose growers went through difficult, if not hard, times. In 1976, two years before the firm's centenary, another reorganization took place. Following a period of illness, Niels retired, and Pernille, his eldest daughter, took over the breeding programme, with her husband Mogens Olesen as managing director. The business was formed into a limited company – Poulsen Roses Aps – with a nursery at Fredensborg, near to the summer residence of the Danish monarch.

The firm now specializes in three types of roses, all suited to the smaller rose gardens of today. Their 'Parade' roses (forced pot roses), often classed as MINIATURES, sell particularly well in Denmark where pot plants have always been popular: annual sales of 'Teeny Weeny', a pink 'Parade' rose of 1982, have exceeded a quarter of a million. Poulsen's GROUND-COVER ROSES are used as AMENITY ROSES in parks and around public buildings. 'Pink Bells', 'Red Bells' and 'White Bells' caused a sensation when they appeared in the UK in 1983, and one of their latest ground-cover roses has been named 'Caterpillar'. PATIO ROSES (one size larger than miniatures) include 'Evita' and 'Texas'.

In the more traditional sectors, 'Lakeland Princess' ('Poulak'), alias 'Vintage Wine', is a successful red-blend large-flowered climber, and there are two large-flowered shrub roses: 'Ingrid Bergman' and 'Modern Art', both awarded gold medals at shows in Europe in 1984.

Printed portraits of the rose

Here, we are considering reproduced portraits of the rose, and not those made directly by the artist on to canvas, vellum, porcelain, plaster, mortar, stained glass, or in the form of designs for textiles, tapestry, wallpaper and the like, since these are reviewed in the section on ART.

The early reproductions of portraits of the rose were of extremely poor quality. Before the advent of printing, which occurred in the West at the end of the 15th century, the only method of circulating flower portraits was to copy them by hand, but most of these were both second-hand and second rate since the drawings were derived, not from life, but from earlier drawings. These had themselves been handed on from one generation to the next since the 6th century AD, when an illustrated edition of Pedanius Dioscorides' great work *De materia medica* appeared. As a result, botanical representation had deteriorated to the point where the flowers shown were almost unrecognizable symbols. Those that could be attributed to existing species were drawn mainly for apothecaries, to enable them to distinguish between plants known as *'officinalis'*, which could be safely used in medical prescriptions, and others that might be ineffective or even poisonous.

No roses were known to be poisonous, so there was no reason to distinguish one variety from another. All were easily represented by conventional, quasi-heraldic designs, and this remained the general position until well into the 16th century, when plants were first studied for their structure as well as for their medicinal virtues.

The first printed pictures of the rose were executed as woodcuts. The illustrations were cut into small blocks of wood and then inserted into the *forme*, or body, of the type and printed simultaneously with it. One artist would provide the original drawing on paper or vellum; this would have to be copied (possibly by a second artist) on to the wooden block; a third person, a craftsman, would then be needed to cut away from the wooden block all those areas that were not to appear black in the final print. A mistake by any one of the team could mar the total effect, which was often stilted and lifeless. Thus, an early printed representation of the sweet brier in William Turner's *New Herball*, completed in 1568, has been described as unrecognizable, and there is little that is commendable in the portraits of the rose in Gerard's *Herball* (even in the 1633 edition) or in Parkinson's *Paradisi* (*see* HISTORY OF THE ROSE).

Two developments brought about a change in this lamentable situation. The first was the growing interest in the study of plants as plants and not as mere adjuncts to the medicine chest.

The second development was the gradual changeover from the woodcut to the more durable and finer copper plate, which could be either engraved or etched, two distinct processes. Engravers use a handtool known as a *burin* to plough a furrow in the copper plate for each line that is to appear in the printed drawing. The plate is later inked over and wiped clean except for the ink that remains in the furrows, which will be transferred to the paper when a roller presses it against the copper plate. Engraved prints are clear and decisive, but the burin, since it has to be pressed forward in order to do its work, is a difficult and exhausting tool to use, and expensive mistakes can easily occur. One of the earliest and most sumptuous albums of engravings is the *Florilegium* of Emanuel Sweerts, published in 1612; however, the quality of the engravings is variable and, overall, not very high.

In the etching process, the plate is not engraved. Instead, the whole of the plate is first covered by an acid-resistant coating, and then the design to be printed is drawn on the plate with a needle or similar tool, which removes the protective coating from those areas that are to show up in the final product. The plate is then placed in an acid bath and left there until the unprotected areas have been sufficiently 'eaten away'. The plate is then wiped clean and inked, as for engraving. Both processes allow plants to be shown in fine detail, and the inked portions of the paper, having been pressed into the furrows of the plate, stand out (for better or worse) in sharp relief. This is particularly the case in the work of GEORG DIONYSIUS EHRET, who in many cases engraved or etched his own work.

Designs etched or engraved on copper plates (loosely known as *intaglio work*) could not be printed simultaneously with letterpress, in which the text is inked from letters in relief, as on a typewriter, but in the case of the rose, this was an advantage, as it encouraged the use of separate coloured inks for illustrations.

The great era of flower painting, and thus of botanical printing, opened in the 18th century when new plants began to flood in from India, China and America, and wealthy private patrons were willing to pay for individual portraits of their hothouse treasures. In this context, the rose was not overlooked and considerable attention was paid towards the end of the century to the new roses arriving from China.

A number of advances in the techniques used for etching and engraving were made during the 18th century, and these added to the attractions of colour printing off copper plates. These refinements made it possible to reproduce the soft washes of watercolours so essential to true representations of the rose. Thus in the mezzotint process, the whole copper plate is first roughened with a toothed tool known as a 'rocker'. The burring is then scraped off the areas that are to appear white, leaving untouched the napped areas that will be printed in black. Intermediate tones can be obtained by lightly burnishing the remaining burring.

The aquatint process was a sequel to the normal etching process. The plate, after normal etching, is coated all over with grains of an acid-resistant powdered resin, which, when gently heated, adheres to the plate. The resin is then removed from the areas to be treated, and a suitable acid is applied. Because of the presence of the grains on the frontiers separating black areas from white, the contrasts are less pronounced and closer to those of a watercolour.

The refinement that made most difference to the portraits of the rose came with advent of stippling, a technique that can be used equally well with etchings or engravings. In both cases, the lines normally drawn or engraved on the plate are replaced with 'dots', i.e. very fine depressions made with a needle or sharply pointed *roulette*, a spur-like wheel. Varying the depth of the depressions gives the artist a far more definite control over the finished plate than can be obtained by other methods, and the shallow stippling dots allow some of the ink to 'wash over' under the pressure of printing, with highly gratifying results. Miss Mary Lawrance used stippling, although in a somewhat heavy-handed way, in the ninety plates of her monograph *A Collection of Roses from Nature*, which appeared from 1796 to 1799 and was the first illustrated monograph to be devoted exclusively to the rose. REDOUTÉ, during his months in England, learned the technique of stippling from Francesco Bartolozzi, and employed it very effectively by applying several different coloured inks to separate areas of the same plate, using them simultaneously in a single imprint. In other cases, a print with several colours was achieved on the same plate by changing the colours between imprints or by using a separate replica plate for each colour to be printed.

The invention of lithography by Aloys Senefelder in the last years of the 18th century gave a further impetus to flower portraiture. The design to be lithographed is drawn on a thick slab of stone with greasy ink or with a greasy crayon and then chemically 'fixed'. The stone is then dampened and a roller coated with greasy ink passed over it. The ink is repelled by the damp areas of the stone and adheres only to the greasy design already drawn. Paper is then laid on the stone and pressed down so that the inked design is transferred on to it. Later, roughened zinc plates were used instead of the stone slabs.

The principle advantage of the lithograph is that, since it is produced from a design *drawn* by the artist, it *looks* like an artist's drawing in a way seldom achieved in an engraving or etching. And since there is little wear on the stone slab or zinc plate, many copies can be produced cheaply and quickly without much deterioration.

Before the era of photographic colour printing, coloured lithographs were produced by making a separate drawing on stone or zinc for each colour used. Redouté himself turned to lithography in the last years of his life but was dissatisfied with the results. Walter Fitch (1817–92), probably the most productive and successful botanical illustrator of the 19th century and unique in his ability to transform dried herbarium specimens into living plants, was his own lithographer, and used the technique for portraying the rose – though all too seldom.

Most of the illustrations of roses appearing in nursery catalogues today are colour photographs taken either of an artist's painting or of the rose itself. The former is often preferable to the botanist and plant fancier alike, since the artist is able to emphasize selective details often glossed over in a photograph.

Provence roses

See ROSA CENTIFOLIA. The connection between Provence roses and the Provence region of southern France appears conjectural, since the centifolias seem to have first been cultivated intensively in the Netherlands.

Provins, the Rose of

The ancient fortified town of Provins, 55 miles (90 km) southeast of Paris, can be seen from afar across the flat fields of wheat and sugar beet for which it is the natural market centre. The Roman emperor Probus (AD 276–82) accorded it the privilege of cultivating the vine, which had been forbidden in Gaul since the days of Domitian, two centuries before. However, Provins eventually became better known for its roses than for its wine.

In the 11th century, the town came into the possession of the counts of Champagne. Count Thibault IV (1201–53) – '*Le Chansonnier*' – of Champagne, Blois and Chartres, who also inherited the Kingdom of Navarre, is the man usually credited with endowing Provins with its rose, which he is said to have brought back – presumably in the form of hips – from the Seventh Crusade. The rose was a semi-double form of *Rosa gallica*, found in the wild in many parts of Europe. It kept its fragrance so well that it was adopted as the 'apothecaries' rose' and given the Latin name of *R. gallica officinalis* (*see* GALLICA ROSES).

155

In 1310, the citizens of Provins offered *dried* roses to the Archbishop of Sens on the occasion of his visit, which seems to confirm the fact that we are dealing here with the apothecaries' rose, the fragrance of which improves with drying, and not, as has sometimes been suggested, with *R. damascena*, the fragrance of which deteriorates when dried. In any case, the DAMASK ROSE, which flourished in Roman times, seems to have been lost to Europe and not recovered until long after the Crusades.

The link, if any, between the Rose of Provins and England was established when Edmund 'Crouchback', 1st Earl of Lancaster (1245–96), who already bore a rose in his coat of arms, married Blanche, the widow of Henri le Gros, the Chansonnier's son. While in Provins, Edmund, according to the French historian Opoix, modified his own personal emblem to represent the local rose, but the supporting evidence for this statement has not been forthcoming and the connection between the two roses was probably coincidental.

More recently, Provins has become instrumental in promoting '*La route des roses*', a scenic tourist route along Route Nationale 19 that takes in plantings, notably at Villecresnes, Grisy Suisnes and Guignes-Rabutin.

See also ROSA CENTIFOLIA.

Pruning

Left to its own devices, a rose bush increases by means of vigorous new shoots that spring out, often from the base of the plant. This growth is at the expense of the older branches in the centre, which become twiggy at the extremities and eventually die off.

The aim of the pruner is, therefore, to hasten the departure of the older branches, thus concentrating the energies of the plant on fresh growth, while at the same time admitting air and light into the centre of the rose bush.

Pruning becomes less of a mystery if certain common-sense principles are borne in mind:

1. With all roses, dead or damaged wood in which pests could flourish is removed. To make sure that only live wood remains, examine the pith at the place where the cut has been made. If it is white, the operation has been successful; if not, more wood will have to be cut off. However, a distinction must be made at the outset between two types of rose bushes, namely:

(a) those that flower on shoots that grow after the end of the previous season's flowering. In this case, only the shoots that have already flowered can be pruned, and this can be carried out in the summer as soon as flowering has ceased.

(b) those that flower on shoots grown from buds in the same season. These roses are pruned in the winter by cutting off the upper parts of the stems so that the buds that are left can produce really vigorous shoots. We will deal first with this second type of rose.

2. Roses make their new stem growth almost entirely from the few buds at the top of stems; consequently, if the stems are left unpruned, they will become top heavy above and spindly and bare beneath. MAIDEN bushes particularly need to be pruned more severely than established plants to ensure that the main growth starts from the base of the plant.

3. Pruning the stems of rose plants keeps the leaves and flowers near to their main source of supply: the roots. Furthermore, the shorter the stem, the less risk there is that it will unsettle the roots by 'rocking' them in high winds, or that the stems will break off altogether in a gale.

4. In general, the weaker plants require the hardest pruning; the more vigorous the plants, the less attention they need. It was probably this thought that led Wilhelm KORDES, the famous rose raiser and hybridist, to declare:

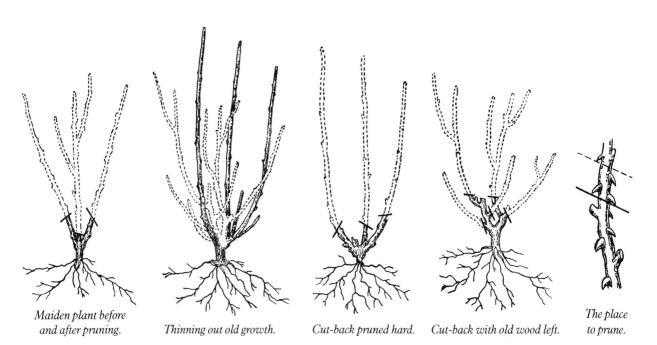

Maiden plant before and after pruning.   *Thinning out old growth.*   *Cut-back pruned hard.*   *Cut-back with old wood left.*   *The place to prune.*

'*Der schrechliste der schrechen ist der gärtner mit seine schere*' (The horror of horrors is the gardener with his secateurs).

5. When established, large-flowered and cluster-flowered roses commonly found in rosebeds, which flower on wood grown during the same season in which the flowers appear, can be cut down during the winter period when the plants are dormant. They should be pruned to perhaps five buds, or eyes, from the ground – leaving about 8–10 inches (20–25 cm) of stem.

6. This winter pruning operation can be carried out at any convenient time from January to March, since the roses will not be wasting energy during these months on unproductive growth. Getting out the secateurs or pruning knife too early will expose the ends of the cut stems to ice and frost, possibly damaging them and opening a way for enemies to gain an entry before the spring sap can seal the wound. On the other hand, leaving matters until late could involve the plant in wasting energy on superfluous growth that will be lost during the pruning. Roses in a mild southern climate can be pruned earlier than those further north; late frosts can strike anywhere, but there is no point in delaying pruning if the plant is about to shoot anyway. William Paul, in *The Rose Garden* (1848), rightly distinguished between those roses that he called 'excitable', which should not be pruned too early – 'the Chinese, Noisette, Bourbon and Tea-scented' – and others, such as PROVENCE, MOSS and ALBA roses, which are seldom provoked by pruning early in the dormancy period.

7. Plants that are expected to yield blooms for exhibition need more severe pruning than those grown for general display in the garden. Lighter pruning means doing it earlier, which will result in more flowers but smaller blooms.

8. Cluster-flowered BUSH ROSES are usually pruned down to three to four eyes in their first season. Thereafter the basal shoots are pruned lightly – cut perhaps by a third – while the remainder are shortened to the first strong eye below the flowers. This system may be varied to keep the bush in balance.

9. Standard ('tree') roses cannot be pruned as severely as bush roses, because their food supplies have to travel further up the long UNDERSTOCK. However, the general principle is the same: the older shoots are cut back rather than the newer. It is also important to preserve the general shape of the head.

10. CLIMBING ROSES need little pruning except for some of the side shoots. Many of them flower on laterals from wood grown the previous season, and if this wood is cut off during the December pruning operations, there will be no flowers the following summer. In any case, more flowers will be obtained by training climbers to grow horizontally than by any amount of pruning. However, where a climber has got out of hand and is bare-legged below, some of the principal branches should be cut back hard to promote new growth.

11. Most RAMBLERS flower on the side branches of the wood grown the previous year and should therefore be pruned with caution, although new sappy growth may

Pyramidal pruning, finished.

safely be cut back but only as far as and no further than the beginning of the ripe wood. (To find out if the wood is 'ripe', test the prickles by running over them gently with the thumb; if they can be detached crisply, the wood is ripe.) In some plants, the new wood springs from the base; in others, it grows as laterals from the main stems. If the new canes are long, they may need to be tied to prevent them thrashing about in the winter gales. If the rose is summer-flowering only and not REMONTANT, and no display of hips is looked for, some pruning may be carried out in the summer as soon as flowering has ceased, in those branches that are not expected to flower again.

12. Weeping STANDARD ROSES can be treated in much the same way as ramblers.

13. SPECIES ROSES usually flower on the wood of the previous year, and sometimes on the wood of the year before that. The main aim here should be to preserve the informal habit of the plant. Dead canes, however, should be cut out, even if this means bringing them out in pieces.

14. Large SHRUB ROSES need little attention except to balance the plant and the cutting out of dead wood where seen.

15. MINIATURE ROSES need little pruning except where old branches have to be removed.

The techniques of pruning are equally straightforward:

1. Use sharp secateurs. Don't employ them on branches too thick for them – or on bamboo canes – and have them sharpened or, if this is impossible, discard them if they cease to give a clean cut.

2. Cut on a slant and not at right angles to the stem. This should be done above, but not too far above, a bud that is pointing outwards if outward growth is required (or inward if inward growth is needed).

3. Gather up and burn the prunings in case they harbour pests.

Quality standards

'Quality standards' – specifying the number, length and diameter of various types of roses sold to and supplied by growers – are in force in several countries, including the United States, the United Kingdom and the Federal Republic of Germany. In Britain, details are given in Document BS 3936 (Part II), obtainable from the British Standards Institution (Lindford Wood, Milford Keynes MK14 6LE). Since, at the time of writing, this costs £7.00, the average gardener will instead want to have a look at Michael Gibson's summation in his book *Growing Roses*.

Only one grade for each of the various types of roses is recognized in the UK, but the US standards give an idea of the comparative differences to be expected between the main types of roses. There, large-flowered roses and GRANDIFLORAS rated as Grade 1 are expected to have a minimum of three strong canes, at least two of which should be 18 inches (45 cm) long. Grade 1 cluster-flowered FLORIBUNDAS should have canes 15 inches (38 cm) long, while POLYANTHAS call for a minimum of four canes of at least 12 inches (30 cm). Climbers are rated Grade 1 if they have at least three canes 24 inches (60 cm) long. Roses in Grade 1½ – known in the trade as 'halves' – include large-flowered roses and grandifloras having two canes of 15 inches (38 cm), floribundas with two canes of 14 inches (35 cm), and climbers with canes of 18 inches (45 cm); no other roses are included in this grade. In Grade 2, only large-flowered roses, grandifloras and climbers will qualify if they have two canes of 12 inches (30 cm).

Quartered roses

Theophrastus (*see* HISTORY OF THE ROSE) was probably the first observer to comment on quartered roses. When referring to the 100-petalled roses said to grow on Mount Pangaeus near Philippi, he wrote: 'The inner petals are very small (the way in which they are produced being such that some are outside, some inside).'

More precisely, quartering is to be seen in 'old-fashioned' chalice-shaped rose blooms with a superabundance of petals that form several small and distinct whorls within the body of the flower. The whorls are usually – but not invariably – four in number, one in each quarter.

Shirley Hibberd, who edited *The Gardener's Magazine* from 1861 to 1890 and wrote many entertaining and influential works on gardening topics, spoke for his contemporaries when he wrote: 'The quartered rose is generally objectionable and can be recognized as admissible in a show class only because, in spite of our rules and harsh empiricism, very many quartered roses are so lovely that we would sooner burn and forget our rules than lose these roses.'

Before the 19th century, quartering in the centre of a rose was seen as an attractive feature because of the gradual revelation that accompanied the opening of the bloom – a revelation that was completed only when the flower was fully open. Today, however, we like to see the high-peaked individual blooms of the large-flowered classes only half-to-three-quarters open. Those who show roses describe this as the 'perfect stage' as distinct from the later 'full-bloom' stage – which is thus less than perfect.

Queen Mary's rose garden

The rose garden most easily accessible to central Londoners appears in older guidebooks as the 'Inner Circle Garden', Regent's Park, but since 1935, it has been known as Queen Mary's Garden. From 1840, the Inner Circle site had been leased by the Crown to the Royal Botanic Society, but when the lease expired in 1932, the Society's Winter Garden and various other buildings were pulled down with a view to merging the site with the rest of the park. However, partly because of the Great Depression of the Thirties, a number of rose growers had excellent stocks of roses on hand, and the British Rose Growers' Association persuaded the Office of Works to start a rose garden there, with plants presented by them. In 1935, King George V, knowing his wife's particular interest in roses, gave his permission for it to be known as 'Queen Mary's Garden'.

The garden now contains some ninety individually numbered, closely planted beds of roses, as well as tall pillars with rope swags between, along which ramblers and climbers are trained. The impressive display of some of the most famous varieties is worth visiting in a mild autumn as late as the first week of November.

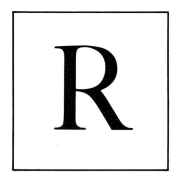

Ramblers

These are roses with long arching canes, not compact enough to rank as SHRUBS nor rigid enough to be classed as CLIMBERS. They flower on shoots sent up after flowering has finished in the previous year, thus differing from the stiffer climbers. Those mentioned here are garden varieties, as distinct from SPECIES ramblers and some of the hybrids very closely linked to them, which are described under WILD ROSES.

The light-pink 'Dorothy Perkins' is probably the best known of all ramblers. Most books give the date of appearance as 1901; however, the Nickerson Cup awarded to the JACKSON & PERKINS company by the NATIONAL ROSE SOCIETY for the white 'Dorothy Perkins' – 'the best climbing rose blooming in clusters' – is dated 1908. According to Jackson & Perkins' Susan Funk (December 1984):

About thirteen years ago, some effort was made to find out who Dorothy Perkins was by talking with some Jackson & Perkins employees who had been with the company for thirty years or more. [It was found that] Dorothy Perkins, for whom the rose was named, was the daughter of George Perkins, and granddaughter of Charles Perkins, founder of the company. Inasmuch as George Perkins was born in 1870 and graduated from college in 1892, and named the 'Dorothy Perkins' rose in 1908, we feel fairly safe in assuming that his daughter was still very young at the time the rose was named for her. In 1971, Miss Perkins (then Mrs Esterbrook) was said to be living in Philadelphia, Pennsylvania.

There is also a red, dating from 1909 and marketed as 'Excelsa', that is popular in both the UK and Australia. Ramblers of this kind should not be grown on walls, where they are likely to be exposed to damp without getting the airing they need.

The year 1909 also saw the arrival of thornless rambler 'Veilchenblau', which at times comes near, but not very near, to being a 'blue' rose. It bears large clusters of white-centred, semi-double, purple-violet flowers fading through bluish-lilac to mauvish-grey, and it can stretch to 15 feet (4.5 m). The blooms of 'Violette' (1921, which in other respects is a similar rose, are more definitely purple and would contrast well with anything pink in the same bed.

The virtue of 'Albéric Barbier', a much older, turn-of-the-century rose, is that it is almost evergreen and so can be used to screen an ugly fence without the risk that the eyesore will become exposed in winter. Its flowers are creamy white to yellow. 'François Juranville', also from Barbier, is almost as popular, and has deep rose, flat, double-flowers packed with petals and a fresh fragrance that has been compared to that of an apple. Peter Beales, the 'old' rose specialist nurseryman, reckons that this rose is far superior to the more commonly seen 'Albertine'.

'Dr W. van Fleet' (1910) is a large-flowered rambler that has won lasting popularity for its hardiness and the fact that its pink-tinged white flowers are on stems long enough for cutting. 'American Pillar', launched by Dr van Fleet in 1902, has single flowers of bright pink. It makes a fine show but lacks the mystique of fragrance.

'Emily Gray', a rose of 1918, is sometimes classed as a climber rather than a rambler. The flowers come in clusters and are parchment to golden yellow and well-scented. It is probably hardy since, otherwise, it would not be so popular.

'Turner's Crimson Rambler', derived from *Rosa multiflora*, had a chequered career before it was introduced in 1893. It was found in a garden in Japan by Robert Smith, an engineer who was then a professor at the University of Tokyo, and it was known there as the 'cherry rose'. Smith sent it to Scotland to Thomas Jenner, a friend, who named it 'The Engineer' and passed it on to J. Gilbert who, after propagating it in quantity, showed it at the Royal Horticultural Society in 1890. Turner's Nursery at Slough then bought the sole rights and marketed it in 1893. 'Crimson Shower', introduced by Norman in 1951, is, however, much preferred.

Four excellent, either REMONTANT or continuously flowering BOURBON shrub roses may be conveniently mentioned here, as they sprawl somewhat and are the better for support. 'Louise Odier' (1851) has bright rose-pink, beautifully circular blooms. 'La Reine Victoria' (1872), like the last, is a vigorous grower and tends to produce its delicate lilac-pink blooms almost out of reach. (As Graham Thomas has pointed out, the 'La' in the name should really be omitted; *see* NAMING ROSES.) Its pale pink SPORT, 'Madame Pierre Oger', is often grown but it is not immune to MILDEW or BLACKSPOT. 'Madame Ernst Calvat' (1888), the fourth rose in this group, is the most vigorous of them all and can even be used as a hedge. The flowers, which appear almost continuously from June to September, are pale pink with darker reverses. This is probably a sport of 'Madame Isaac Periere'.

Redouté, Pierre-Joseph

Pierre-Joseph Redouté (1759–1840), the most famous of all the artists who have sought over the centuries to glorify the rose, was born in St Hubert, which, until it was transferred to Belgium in 1831, formed part of the Duchy of Luxembourg. He came from an artistic family and was trained in his father's studio. At the age of thirteen he was sent to earn his living as best he might as a travelling painter of portraits, religious scenes or whatever other subjects people wanted to pay to have painted.

His elder brother Antoine-Ferdinand was already employed as a theatrical designer in Paris, and in 1782, Pierre-Joseph worked with him in the preparation of stage scenery for the new Italian Theatre in the Rue Louvois. However, he was irresistibly attracted to flowers and spent his spare time painting them, seeking subjects in the Jardin du Roi. There, his style and ability attracted the attention of a dealer named Chereau who had some of his paintings engraved and showed them to a wealthy magistrate and enthusiastic botanist, Charles Louis L'Héritier de Brutelle. L'Héritier provided Redouté not only with work but also with the botanical knowledge without which no artist can produce flower paintings that are accurate as well as desirable. As a result, Redouté was able to contribute more than fifty illustrations for L'Héritier's work *Stirpes novae* (1784–5), about newly discovered plants. When L'Héritier decided, during a visit to England in 1786, to prepare a further work on the rare plants grown at Kew, he sent for Redouté, and the two shared rooms in London on Poland Street, near to Carnaby Market and to the house of Sir Joseph Banks, who put his library at their disposal.

L'Héritier and his protégé spent fifteen months in London, and when they returned to France, Redouté was recommended for, and given, the honorary appointment of 'Artist to the Cabinet' of Queen Marie Antoinette. Despite this connection with the palace and with L'Héritier, who was also a known royalist, Redouté's 'foreign' Flemish accent set him apart, and as he lived only for painting, he was untroubled by the storms of the Revolution. In 1792, he was appointed to the post of draughtsman in the Academy of Sciences, and when this body was merged into the Museum of Natural History in the following year, Redouté was allowed to provide drawings on vellum of new plants to add to the sixty-four volumes of drawings that had come from the royal library. In 1796 Redouté and his family were allowed to move into official accommodation in the Louvre.

His connection with JOSEPHINE Bonaparte seems to have come about, once again, through L'Héritier, who introduced him to the plantsman Jacques-Martin Cels, whose nursery was at Montrouge. Redouté's first commission was to paint some floral portraits for Josephine's boudoir at La Malmaison, and his brother decorated the walls. During one of his visits to Cels' garden, Redouté encountered Étienne-Pierre Ventenat, the botanist, who was at that time gathering material for a book on Cels' rarities (two were eventually published between 1800 and 1808). Redouté was asked to illustrate Cels' plants in the same way that he had already portrayed the rarities of Kew, and when Josephine heard of this, she insisted that a similar work must be prepared covering the plants in her garden at La Malmaison. The result was *Plantes cultivées dans le jardin de Malmaison*, which appeared in two volumes published in 1803 and 1804.

A further volume of rare plants at La Malmaison and at the Château de Navarre, illustrated by Redouté but with text by Bonplan, appeared between 1813 and 1817. Mimosas, melaleucas and many other strange and beautiful plants were featured – but no roses. However, at the same time, Redouté had been engaged on another work that, though not on roses, gave him the mastery of perspective that was to give his rose portraits their unique quality. The work was the *Plantarum historia succulentarum*, which dealt with thick-leaved and ultra-spiny plants that, by their very nature, could not be preserved within the pages of a dried-plant herbarium, and which could be convincingly represented in illustrations only if the perspective and lighting were exactly right. This work continued to appear in parts from 1798 to 1829. Redouté was equally successful with *Les liliacées*, published in eight volumes between 1802 and 1816, and, in a less ambitious way, with his illustrations to Rousseau's *Lettres elementaries sur la botanique*, published in 1805.

With his new-found prosperity, Redouté was able, in 1805, to take over and adapt a small farmhouse with a garden at Fleury, near the Forest of Meudon. It lay about $7\frac{1}{2}$ miles (12 km) from Paris and 5 miles (8 km) south of La Malmaison. (Previously, while working for Josephine, he had occupied a modest house on the border of the Malmaison estate.) In Paris, he rented rooms in the Hôtel Mirabeau, and installed studios and printing machinery for draughtsmen and engravers – though in many cases, and particularly so with cacti, he undertook the engravings himself.

Redouté had painted few roses during his time at La Malmaison, but he had nevertheless thought for some years of publishing a book devoted entirely to them. A suitable collaborator lived near him in the country: Antoine-Claude Thory, whose garden was at Bellevue, a kilometre or two away from Fleury. Thory was, like L'Héritier, an able botanist, and he was also connected with the law; as clerk to the criminal court at Le Châtelet in Paris, he had once signed a warrant for the arrest of Marat and, for some years after Marat's assassination in 1793, had had to live in obscurity. Under Napoleon he had been rehabilitated, and was appointed Deputy Mayor of the newly created Ier arrondissement of Paris, the prestigious area bordering on the Tuileries and the Rue de Rivoli.

However, the roses that Redouté wished to paint and Thory to describe did not come readily to hand. Those at

La Malmaison had died, disappeared or become unidentifiable after Josephine's death in 1815; Cels had died in 1806 and Ventenat in 1808; and Redouté had to look for subjects in the public gardens of Paris and Sèvres, in nurseries such as those of Cugnot at Sèvres, Jean-Paul Vibert at Chennevières-sur-Marne, Amédée le Pelletier in Mesnil-le-Montant, and in those of amateurs such as the Duke of Orleans at Neuilly, and M. le Dru, the Mayor of Fontenay-des-Roses. Redouté, himself now a rosarian, raised some varieties in his own garden at Fleury, including the hybrid *Rosa pimpinellifolia* x *R. glauca*, which was then known as *R. redutea*, and a semi-double of *R. eglanteria*. Redouté had also taken a cutting and grown the 'purple' *R. gallica* that had come to La Malmaison in 1810 from the Van Eeden nursery in Haarlem, and Redouté's specimen thus survived the destruction of the original plant. In addition, he found the apple-hipped *R. villosa* for himself in the woods near Meudon, *R. andegavensis* and the Rose of Anjou in hedges on the boundary of General Montcera's estate, and his daughter Josephine discovered *R. tomentosa* close to La Faisanderie, nearer to Paris than it had ever been found before.

However, despite such improvisations, *Les roses*, published in thirty instalments between 1817 and 1824 and subsequently bound in three volumes, accomplished everything that its authors could have wished. The large-folio edition, limited to 500 copies, was printed on vellum and contained a double set of 169 prints, one in colour and the other in black and white; a second folio edition in three volumes, but with only 160 plates, was published in Paris by Panckoucke between 1824 and 1826; and a third edition in octavo, but with 181 plates, appeared in 1828–30. The rose portraits, all in pure watercolours, were exquisitely painted, and the perspective and highlighting that Redouté had used so effectively for succulent plants was repeated here in such a way that the roses appeared to float in mid-air, entirely divorced from any earthly backdrop. Some 170 of the species and varieties that had been grown at La Malmaison were eventually included, and the first edition was dedicated to Redouté's new patroness, Marie-Caroline-Ferdinand-Louise of Naples, Duchesse de Berry, who later married the son of Charles X of France.

Three other illustrated monographs on the rose had already been wholly or partly completed: Mary Lawrance's *A Collection of Roses from Nature*, which came out in parts between 1796 and 1799; *Roses* (in German) by Dr C. G. Rössig, which was published from 1801 onwards; and *A Monograph of the Genus Rosa* by Henry C. Andrews, which appeared in two volumes, the first in 1805 and the other in 1828. However, because of his artistic mastery of the subject and the sheer scale of the enterprise, Redouté had nothing to fear from these competitors.

In 1978, a folio-size *Commentary* was produced to celebrate the publication of the first complete facsimile edition of *Les roses*, which took the form of a symposium and contained both a full list of the synonyms for Redouté's roses and a critical analysis Redouté's original three volumes by the late Baronesse Gisèle de la Roche. Only minor faults were discovered – for instance, in the illustration of *R. pimpinellifolia mariaeburgensis*, in which glands were shown on one pedicel but not on another, and in that of *R. pendulina*, for which Thory's text specified stiff hairs on the pedicels and receptacles, whereas the illustration showed none. In fact, one of the encouraging facts to be learned from the *Commentary* is that nearly half the species and varieties shown in *Les roses* are still grown more than 150 years later.

Redouté's reputation shone even more brightly after the appearance of *Les roses*. In 1822 he was appointed to be one of the two Maîtres de Dessin at the Museum of Natural History, and the thirty lectures that he was obliged to give proved to be extremely popular. He also continued to give private lessons. One of his pupils was Hortense, Josephine's daughter, married to Napoleon's brother Louis who had been King of Holland from 1806 to 1810; he also taught the Duchesse de Berry, to whom *Les roses* had been dedicated. Madame Adelaide d'Orleans, sister of King Louis-Philippe, was another pupil, as were her two elder daughters, Princesse Louise, who afterwards became Queen of Belgium, and her younger sister, Princesse Marie. Redouté was also appointed official artist to the niece of Marie Antoinette and the Duchesse de Berry's aunt, Marie Amelie, who became Queen of France in 1830 and eventually followed her husband Louis-Philippe into exile in 1848. He had already given lessons to Napoleon's second wife, the Austrian Archduchess Marie Louise, while she was still in France. We are told that Redouté's appearance was unprepossessing and that he had the hands of a mason rather than of an artist, but he evidently possessed considerable charm. In 1825, Redouté and a number of other artists, including Ingres and Sir Thomas Lawrence, were made members of the *Légion d'honneur*.

Books continued to appear. The years between 1827 and 1833 saw the publication of *Choix des plus belles fleurs*, in which butterflies and fruit were included as well as blooms. In 1835, a *Collection des jolies petites fleurs* – from Europe and other parts of the world – appeared, and in 1836 there was *Choix de soixante roses* – dedicated to Louise, Queen of Belgium. This contained new portraits and was not a reprint of former work, but only three out of the four projected parts seem to have appeared. His last work – *Choix de roses* – was dedicated to the family of Louis-Philippe and consisted of four folio illustrations. It was published in 1843, three years after the artist's death, under the title *Bouquet royal*.

Redouté continued to work right up to the end. He had to, as for many years he had lived well beyond his means. To make ends meet, he was obliged to sell the originals of *Les roses* to Charles X for 30,000 francs, and to part with his silver and furniture as well. His final project, conceived in his eightieth year, was to be a giant picture, a magnificent tribute to flowers in which other artists, each with their own speciality, be it architecture or the representation of human figures, would participate, and which would be funded by the Ministry of the Interior (for by now Redouté had exhausted his list of royal patrons) for a fee of 12,000 francs. The suggestion had been put to the minster by Redouté's daughter, Josephine, who seems to have carried out secretarial duties for her father during his last years. However, one afternoon when he came in from his walk, Redouté saw that an official letter for his daughter had arrived from the Ministry, and he opened it impatiently. It was signed personally by the minister Charles de Remusat and, in a few words, said that his budget did not allow him to entertain Redouté's proposal. That evening while examining the structure of a white lily that a pupil had brought him, Redouté suffered a severe stroke, and he died the following day.

Some observers may wonder whether the artist had found it difficult to work so closely first with Josephine, then with her supplanter Marie Louise, and subsequently with the rulers who followed Napoleon. However, as one of his biographers, Roger Madol, has pointed out, Redouté's immortality rests on the fact that, throughout the years, he remained faithful to one queen who never went out of fashion: the rose.

Registration of rose varieties

In 1955, the 14th International Horticultural Congress at Scheveningen (Netherlands) established the International Registration Authority for Roses (IRAR), which is administered by the AMERICAN ROSE SOCIETY (P.O. Box 30,000, Shreveport, Louisiana 71130). The IRAR seeks to ensure that each named variety of rose on sale will have been duly registered in its country of origin, and that the name under which it is proposed to market it is not already in use in any of the other nations subscribing to the Authority.

The name of a variety that is registered with a national authority and the IRAR is known as the 'genetic' name, and is backed in all countries that have ratified the International Convention for the Protection of New Varieties of Plants. Once cleared with the IRAR, a patent can be applied for, provided that the application is made within one year. A local trade name can be used to suit an individual country, provided that it is clearly linked to the genetic name; in this case, both names are legally protected. Thus one well-known large flowered rose is known internationally under its genetic name 'Tanorstar', but it also carries the trade name of 'Tropicana' in the US and 'Super Star' in Europe.

US law permits the holder of a patent not only to stop infringements of his or her rights but to collect damages in compensation. The names of roses in US catalogues often include carry the letters PAF, which means 'patent applied for', PP ('patent pending'), or PRR, which stands for 'patent rights reserved' and means that the breeder is considering making an application.

The American Rose Society supplies official information for the series known as *Modern Roses* (published by the McFarland Company and sold through the ARS), which places on record each new registered variety, the breeder,

the year of introduction and its class, together with its parentage, if known, and a brief description.

Occasionally, a rose with an apt, commercially desirable trade name will fail to sell well, and in this case, the breeder may wish to use the same trade name for another rose, but if he does so, he will have to link it to a different genetic name. In countries where no patent laws operate or where the patenting procedure is likely to be unduly protracted or costly, it is possible to register a name as a 'trademark', in which case no other grower will be entitled to sell a rose with the same name. In this case, however, the rose variety as such is not protected, and it would be possible for rival growers to sell the same variety of rose provided that it it was marketed under a different trade name. In such countries, both the American Rose Society and the ROYAL NATIONAL ROSE SOCIETY cooperate with a Geneva-based organization known, for short, as CIOPORA – the Communauté Internationale des Obtenteurs de Plantes Ornementales de Reproduction Asexuée (International Community of Breeders of Asexually Produced Ornamentals.)

The earliest legislation to protect the rights of hybridizers over the roses that they had developed was the US Plant Patent Act of 1930. This allowed the 'inventor' of a new rose variety to collect royalties from anyone producing it by vegetative means (e.g. from cuttings, buds or, as became possible later, from tissue) for a period of seventeen years. To be valid, application for a patent must be made within a year of the introduction of the variety, having first been described in a catalogue or journal or actually marketed. The fact that the US had taken the lead in promoting a registration system made it logical to establish the IRAR in that country.

In Britain, the protection of rose breeders' varieties stems from the Plant Variety and Seeds Act of 1964, elaborated in the Plant Breeders' Rights (Roses) Scheme of 1965, and a number of amendments. Originally the protection for rose varieties lasted for fifteen years with the option of a further five years, but now, in accordance with the international convention, the licence has an automatic life of twenty years – provided that the application fee, test fee and renewal fees are promptly paid. Details of varieties to which licences have been granted appear in the *Plant Varieties and Seeds Gazette*, published by Her Majesty's Stationery Office. Licences are issued by and a booklet on plant breeders' rights is obtainable from the Controller, Plant Variety Rights Office, White House Lane, Huntingdon Road, Cambridge CB3 0LF.

Remontant

Although this word was ferried over the Channel from France to Britain during the 1880s, it has since achieved acceptance as an English word. The *Concise Oxford Dictionary* defines it as: '(Rose) blooming more than once a year.' Remontant flowering – that is, two or more separate bursts – is to be distinguished from 'continuous' or 'perpetual' flowering.

Some breeders refer in their catalogues to roses that

flower 'repeatedly' or to varieties of which the flowering is 'recurrent', but many true rosarians cling to 'remontant'. The word retains its original meaning in French, though it is applied to all plants that flower repeatedly and not to the rose alone.

Ringelreihen.

Ringe, ringe, reihe!
Sind der Kinder dreie,

A German version of 'Ring-a-ring o' roses'.

Ring-a-ring o' roses

Ring-a-ring o' roses,
A pocketful of posies,
A-tishoo, a-tishoo,
We all fall down.

It has been suggested, with some plausability – though, alas, without documentary proof and in face of some contradictory evidence – that this jingle, like many another nursery rhyme, was engendered by a social or political disaster: in this case, an epidemic of the plague and possibly the Great Plague of 1665, when London lost a sixth of its population.

The 'roses' refer to the *petechiae*, round red spots that appeared over the swollen lymph tissue, known as buboes, which were characteristic of plague, one extremely infectious form of which – pneumonic plague – is spread by coughing and sneezing, thus 'a-tishoo'.

Robin's pincushion

This is a whimsical name for the rose gall. It is also known (with greater reason) as the 'sweet brier sponge', for this

growth is often to be seen on this species in the wild and occasionally in the garden, where it occurs on *Rosa glauca*.

The fiery manifestation is due to the attentions of a gall wasp (*Cynips rosae*), which lays its eggs within a stem, at the same time injecting a stimulant that impels the rose to produce the moss-like deformity. Later, legless larvae are to be found in cells within the gall. Little harm is done to the rose bush – unless, of course, the gall is carelessly removed.

The rose gall is occasionally known as the 'bedeguar gall' from the Persian word meaning 'wind-brought'.

Rockrose

This is a Mediterranean 'family', but not of roses. The most showy are the Cistus shrubs to be seen in Greece, Cyprus, Crete, Portugal, the Canaries and other haunts of the package holidaymaker. Gardeners are more familiar with the smaller rockroses, the Helianthemums, which are sometimes all too successful in the well-drained rockery. They are undershrubs with five-petal flowers but without a thorn or hip to be seen. In the wild, they prefer limestone or chalky soils, not at all to the taste of the rose.

Roman de la rose, Le

This 13th-century allegorical poem, written by Guillaume de Lorris, with additions by Jean de Meung, told the story of a lover in a dream world searching in a fantasy garden for the perfect rose – or perhaps for the perfect woman. Sweet Idleness ('la bel Oiseuse') opens the gate to let him enter and he is greeted there by Bialacoil (*bel accueil*, i.e. 'Welcome'). We are introduced to 'good' characters such as Good Hope, Sweet Thought, Sweet Longing and Sweet Speaking, and 'bad' ones such as Felony, False-Semblance, Covetess and Jealousy. The roses that most pleased the visitor were 'redde' with upright stalks and 'knoppes' (buds) and a scent so strong that he felt as if embalmed.

Le roman de la rose was soon translated into English rhyming couplets as *The Romaunt of the Rose*, and it is generally agreed that the first 1670 lines, known to Middle English scholars as 'Fragment A', were the work of Geoffrey Chaucer.

Roots, growing roses on their own

All roses that are MICROPROPAGATED *in vitro* and those raised by modern large-scale nurseries from CUTTINGS are, of course, grown on their own roots, and it can reasonably be claimed that these methods avoid not only the inconvenience of SUCKERS but also the variations that can occur when a rose of one variety is BUDDED to the UNDERSTOCK of another.

Much the same conclusion was reached by William Robinson, who wrote in his *English Flower Garden* (14th edition, 1926):

The queen of flowers, fair as it is, would be much more at home with all if one could get rid of certain drawbacks. The common idea that roses can only be grown in heavy clay soil, if carried out, would exclude them from a large area of our country where light, sandy and calcareous soils prevail. If we can get roses on their own roots, we can grow them well in such soils – in some cases, better. The trade practice of grafting all roses from various climates on the native dog rose is a source of infinite trouble to rose growers. Some do well on the stock, though in the end suckers will prevail, some kinds flower badly, and some die.

For years I have grown many hundreds of roses in my flower garden and also in open plots, and found that quite half the tea and China roses did badly, or perished, if worked on the brier, the most vigorous of wild roses. The old summer-flowering roses of European origin did well on the brier; the trouble arose from attempting to put the roses of Chinese origin on our native stock. I had at first no choice but to use the plants sold to me by the trade, and so I lost years in trying to overcome the difficulty.

Rosa centifolia.

Rosa centifolia

The French do not claim this as the rose of PROVENCE, although it is now much cultivated there. Instead, they have politely called this *'rosier à cent feuilles'* (rose of 100 petals), while the English more prosaically named it the 'cabbage rose' because of its globular shape and its petals, reversed around the base of the flower. Theophrastus (*see* HISTORY OF THE ROSE) heard of some growing in the mountains above Phillippi in northern Greece, but these may have been double forms of *Rosa damascena*. No other Greek or Latin writers – including Pliny, who flattered himself that his works were fully comprehensive – mentioned a 100-petalled rose or any other that resembles the modern cabbage rose.

What we have today is a spreading rose plant measuring about 6 by 4 feet (1.8 × 1.2 m), with large, broad, greyish, wrinkled leaflets and unequal hooked prickles, larger near the base of the plant. The flowers are bright pink, but the large outer petals fade rapidly in strong sunlight and only the smaller petals near the centre of the bloom retain their vivid colour. The profusion of petals is such that the stamens are crowded out and the plant is usually regarded as sterile, though it can be artificially hybridized if the petals are removed. The flowers droop and are best examined – and their scent enjoyed – from beneath as they hang down from long arching branches; it will then be seen that the flower is not quite closed up but has an opening like a brandy glass or an old-fashioned glass lampshade. With only a little exaggeration, H. C. Andrews wrote, in his monograph on this rose (1805–28):

This is the most fragrant of all roses, and therefore particularly desirable, for although it cannot be ranked among the rare, it is nevertheless one of the most beautiful. Its sweetness joined with the abundance of its blossom has rendered it an object of culture for the purpose of destruction [i.e. for making perfume] as it yields a much greater quantity of scented water than any other rose.

R. centifolia needs to be kept under close control. Its habit is lax and sprawling and gardeners who are sparing with the secateurs will find themselves left with a gaunt gibbet of a plant instead of a nice compact bush.

The cabbage rose of today seems to have first appeared towards the end of the 16th century. In Gerard's *Herball*, it is shown as '*Rosa Hollandica* or Batava, the Great Holland Rose, commonly called the great Province Rose', and Gerard notes that the flowers are 'in shape and colour like the Damaske rose, but greater and more double, insomuch that the yellow chives in the middle are hard to be seene'. Surprisingly, he goes on to say that this rose is 'of a reasonable good smell, but not ful so sweet as the Common Damaske Rose.' He may have smelled it on a cold day (*see* SCENT). Gerard's nomenclature suggests that the plant was linked with Holland rather than with PROVENCE or PROVINS, and it seems possible that, at least in this case, 'Province' was linked with the establishment of the United Provinces of the Netherlands in 1579, and with the fact that *R. centifolia* appeared in Holland for the first time because it had been newly created there by skilful horticulturalists, subsequent examination of the chromosomes of *R. centifolia* having suggested that it is a hybrid derived from several other species. The four most likely ancestors would be *R. gallica*, *R. phoenicia* (the two that are thought to have given rise to the summer-flowering DAMASK), plus *R. canina* and *R. moschata*, which with *R. gallica* launched the autumn-flowering damask – a powerful combination.

The *R. centifolia* was the rose most beloved of 17th-century Dutch artists (*see* ART, THE ROSE IN) and, according to Antoine-Claude Thory, who wrote the text for REDOUTÉ's

Les roses, 100 different varieties of *R. centifolia* were cultivated in Holland alone. Many of these would still be grown today if the plants were more strongly upright. However, a centifolia has to have a support if its nodding blooms are to be fully appreciated by the rosarian beneath.

Redouté's *R. centifolia bullata*, sometimes known as the 'lettuce-leaved rose' because of its outsize puckered leaves, is still grown as a CURIOSITY. The same is true of *R. centifolia cristata* – usually known as the crested moss – which has a crest of fringed sepals, the arrangement of which in the bud stage are said to resemble Napoleon's three-cornered hat. Only the tips and edges of the sepals are fringed – a feature that distinguishes it from the MOSS ROSES proper. This variety exemplifies more distinctly than any of the other centifolias a riddle dating from the Middle Ages, which invited the listener to guess which family was described in the quatrain:

> *Five brothers of one house are we,*
> *All in a single family.*
> *Two have beards and two have none,*
> *And only half a beard has one.*

These lines refer to the arrangement of the sepals in the bud stage, when two have both edges exposed and are therefore capable of growing beards; two other sepals have both edges enclosed and therefore cannot grow beards; and the fifth sepal, of necessity, has only one edge exposed, and can therefore grow only half a beard.

'Fantin-Latour', named after Henri Fantin-Latour, the 19th-century Romantic painter (particularly of flowers), is a latecomer appearing first in 1900. Its blooms are exquisitely shaped and of surpassing beauty.

The *R. centifolia pomponia*, otherwise known as the 'De Meaux Rose' (1789), is a smaller version of the normal centifolia and bears small flat flowers shaped like the pompoms that are used on curtains. The De Meaux roses preceded the MINIATURES derived later from *Rosa chinensis* var. *minima*, and can be either pink or white. 'Petite de Hollande', on the other hand, is a true, scaled-down centifolia, with globe-shaped flowers unlike those of the pom-poms.

Robert le Diable became Duke of Normandy in 1028, but we have no record of when the centifolia rose named after him was first grown. The lurid violet, cerise and scarlet of its petals suggest that there may be an element of GALLICA in the pedigree. It needs the support of a hedge or wall if it is to be seen at its best.

'The Bishop' is another centifolia for which the date of introduction is unknown. It has rosette-shaped flowers of mixed magenta, purple and cerise, which again suggests a gallica trace. In certain conditions, this rose is said to show blue lights more strongly than any other (*see* COLOUR). 'Tour de Malakoff', a larger, more sprawling version of 'The Bishop', is also described in the section on colour.

'Unique Blanche' is a white variety discovered by chance, in 1775, by a nurseryman when he was riding past a garden by a mill in which 'an elderly female' named Richmond lived, in either Needham Market, Suffolk, or Needham, Norfolk (depending on which writer is relating the story). More confusion has arisen over the nurseryman's name: H. C. Andrews in *Roses* (1805–28) gives it as Greenwood, of Little Chelsea Nursery, but the Revd Joseph Pemberton among others gives the credit to Daniel Grimwood whose nurseries at that time covered some forty acres in the St Mary Abbots area of Kensington in London. Greenwood (or Grimwood) is said to have bought the whole plant for £5 and to have followed this up with a presentation silver cup for the 'elderly female'. The rose may have been introduced to the public in 1777.

Other varieties of centifolias include: 'Pompon de Bourgogne', in various shades of pink; 'Variegata', alias 'Village Maid' (white, striped lilac pink); and 'La Noblesse', a late flowerer.

Rosarian

Some might consider this a pretentious designation for the amateur rose grower. The French generally use the word *rosiériste*, and the name of one of the original HYBRID PERPETUAL roses is 'Gloire des Rosomanes'. 'Rosaholic' would be the nearest suitable English equivalent of this.

True rosarians, according to Edward Bunyard, are ones who know the roses in their gardens as the shepherd knows the individual sheep in his flock, or the huntsman the hounds in his pack. However, more stringent qualifications were suggested by the Revd A. Foster-Melliar in his *Book of the Rose*, originally published in 1894:

> The man of business, who rises at daybreak to attend to his roses before his day's work in the town; who is quite prepared if necessary to go out with a good lantern on a November night to seize a favourable condition of soil for planting at once some newly arrived standards or dwarfs; and who later in the winter will turn out in the snow after dark to give some little extra protection that may be required for his beds; that is the sort of man for me, and for the rose as well.

'Rhodologist' has been suggested as a descriptive term for someone more interested in the botany of the rose than in its cultivation.

Rosary

Originally this word denoted a rosarium, or rose garden, and thus in medieval times, in a symbolic sense, an abode of spiritual beauty and purity. A Latin verse attributed to St Bernard (1091–1153) suggests that the link between the rose and prayers to the Virgin Mary already existed in the 12th century:

> *Ave, salve, gaude, vale*
> *A Maria, non vernale*
> *Sed de Rosis spiritale*
> *Tibi plecto nunc crinale*
> *De Rosarum flosculis*

of which a free translation might be:

> Hail and flourish, rejoice and be strong,
> O Mary, no springtime wreath of rosebuds do I entwine
> but, for you, from the roses, a spiritual one.

The use of the rosary as an aid to prayer was officially approved in 1216 by Pope Innocent III, just after the Albigensian Crusade, ostensibly against heresy in southern France (but it was also not unrelated to greed and political manoeuvring), and just before the Fifth Crusade in Palestine. The early rosaries were made up of rose petals, strung together and, later, rose hips may have been used instead. By the end of the 16th century, a more formal symbolic association between the rose and the Virgin Mary was proclaimed in a book of prayer entitled *The Rosary of Our Lady*.

The modern rosary is a series of prayers consisting of fifteen decades of 'Aves', each decade being preceded by a Paternoster and followed by a Gloria. The rosary chain is therefore made up of fifteen sets of ten beads, each set of ten being separated from the next by one larger bead – an arrangement that enables the devout to keep a tally of their devotions.

See also SAINTS AND THE ROSE.

Rose

In its cautious assessment, the *Oxford English Dictionary* classes the word 'rose' as being current in Old English – that is, before the middle of the 12th century – but rosarians can point to its use at an earlier time. For example, according to Canon ELLACOMBE the 10th-century ecclesiastic, Aelfric, included the word in a glossary that he compiled.

At that time, the rose had already been cultivated by the Arabs for centuries and before this by the Greeks who, it seems, originally coined the word. The same word was spread by the Romans over large parts of France, Germany and the Netherlands, and probably by the French across the Channel.

Rose Bowl, The

The Rose Bowl is the classic post-season football championship held between two teams from various colleges and universities across the United States. It is the concluding event of the Tournament of Roses festival held annually on New Year's Day in Pasadena, California, 10 miles (16 km) northeast of Los Angeles. The championship was first held in 1902 and again in 1916, since when it has been an annual event. The present Rose Bowl stadium, holding about 100,000, was inaugurated in 1922.

Before any football is played, however, the Tournament of Roses parade travels through the city. This is probably the most elaborate in the world, with a vast number of floats, entirely covered with flowers (not necessarily roses), all vying for prizes, as well as dozens of marching bands and celebrities. It is televised across the United States, and is now an obligatory part of every American's New Year's Day celebrations.

Rose gardens, a selection of internationally famous

The selection of rose gardens that follows is part of a list that could be extended almost indefinitely. Others are mentioned in sections devoted to individual countries: e.g. AUS-TRALIA, BERMUDA, CANADA, ISRAEL, JAPAN, NEW ZEALAND, ZIMBABWE.

Austria The best-known rose gardens are at Baden near Vienna, but others are to be found in the capital itself in the Donau Park, and also at Linz in upper (western) Austria.

Czechoslovakia The Rosarium of the Czechoslovak Academy of Sciences at Pruhonice, near Prague, was established in 1963, and is open to the public; it contains about 1000 varieties of roses, including some from early Czechoslovak breeders, together with a collection of roses raised in the USSR.

The Rosa Klub of Bohemia and Moravia has been instrumental in developing a rosarium at Olomouc, a town in central Czechoslovakia, where international horticultural exhibitions are held. Official rose trials are held each year at Hradec Králové.

Denmark The main rose garden in the capital at Valby Park (between the suburb of Valby and the continuation of the South Harbour) is run by the Corporation of the city of Copenhagen with support from the POULSEN nursery. The beds are arranged in the form of a large horseshoe.

France The two most famous rose gardens – CHATEAU DE BAGATELLE in the Bois de Boulogne, and the ROSERAIE DE L'HAY-LES-ROSE near Bourg-la-Reine – are discussed in separate entries. The Parc de Tête d'Or, in Lyon, lies at the confluence of the Rhône and Saone rivers. Its Roseraie Paysagère Nouvelle is, as its name implies, delightfully informal, with rustic bridges, stepping stones across the grass, a stream, a fountain and a raised pergola. There is also a botanical rose garden and a rose-trials ground, and it is also the headquarters of the French society Les Amis des Roses.

Further details of French municipal gardens and others are to be found in *Guide des Parcs et Jardins de France* (Editions Princesse, 55 Quai des Grands Augustins, Paris 6).

Germany, East (German Democratic Republic) The Sangerhausen Rosarium, 40 miles (64 km) north of Weimar (and a mere 12 miles, 19 km, from Eisleben, birthplace of Martin Luther) is the setting for a collection of up to 6500 varieties of roses – including 400 HYBRID PERPETUALS divided into ten groups. The beds are arranged in an informal overlapping design in between winding labyrinthine paths, and are set off by two lily ponds and some willow trees and, at one end, by an outcrop of rock. PETER LAMBERT helped to launch the garden, which was formally opened in 1903 under the auspices of the VEREIN DEUTSCHER ROSENFREUNDE (Association of German Friends of Roses). SPECIES ROSES are arranged together in a double hedge, and there are 130 *Rosa gallica* varieties. The garden contains a statue to the honour of Professor Ewald Gnau (1853–1943), nicknamed the 'Rosenvater' (Father of the Rose).

Germany, West (Federal Republic of Germany) *See* VEREIN DEUTSCHER ROSENFREUNDE.

India The finest rose-growing areas are in the north and west of the country. Chandigarh – redesigned after the partition of India as the future capital of the Punjab, by the

Swiss-born architect Le Corbusier – likes to be known as the 'City of Roses'. Its Zakir Rose Garden, which opened in 1968, covers some thirty acres.

Comprehensive displays of roses are also to be seen at the All-India rose shows organized by the Rose Society of India (founded in 1958) in grounds adjoining the Safdarjung Tomb in New Delhi: in December for large-flowered roses, and in March for the cluster-flowered varieties. The gardens of the society itself cover about three acres in the diplomatic sector of the capital.

Those unable to travel so far can see two locally produced Indian hybrid roses on postage STAMPS. These are: 'Mrinalini' (IARI [Indian Agricultural Research Institute], 1974), a large-flowered light pink; and 'Suganda' (Bhattacharji, 1964), also a large-flowered variety with mid-red blooms.

The influence of the MOGUL EMPERORS in the design of gardens in India and on rose growing is described separately.

Italy   The Rosarium at the Villa Reale at Monza, about 10 miles (16 km) north of Milan, contains about 5000 roses of 1000 varieties and is the headquarters of the Italian Rose Society.

The Roseto di Roma is sited in a natural amphitheatre on the Monte Aventino between the Circo Massimo and the Tiber. Four thousand bushes in groups of five are crowned with a magnificent backdrop of CLIMBING ROSES. Other commendable displays of roses are to be seen at Cavriglia, between Florence and Arezzo, and in the villa Grimaldi Park at Nervi, near Genova.

The Netherlands   Westbroekpark in The Hague – setting of an annual international rose competition (*see* INTERNATIONAL ROSE TRIALS AND AWARDS) – was opened in the 1920s, but a rosarium was not added until 1961. Its style is especially agreeable in as much as it has paths, the beds being set in the midst of lawns on which visitors are permitted to walk. Another point of interest is that the rosebeds are arranged in three sectors: the first with oblong beds only, the second with square beds only, and the third with triangular beds only. All, however, comprise the same area – 16 square metres, with, in the case of bush roses, the same number of plants (77) in each – an arrangement that makes it possible to compare the overall effects of different varieties *en masse*. Some 20,000 plants representing 350 varieties are shown. Shrub roses, climbers and miniatures are grouped in smaller numbers.

The rosarium in Amstel Park, Amsterdam is on a smaller scale. (*See also* AALSMEER.)

Northern Ireland   The Sir Thomas and Lady Dixon Park in the outskirts of Belfast is the setting for the North of Ireland annual INTERNATIONAL ROSE TRIALS, and contains an 11-acre rose garden with 20,000 roses. The park was presented to the Belfast Corporation in 1959, and the first roses were planted there in 1964/5, with encouragement from Sam MCGREDY, Pat DICKSON, the newly formed Rose Society of Northern Ireland and the present City of Belfast Parks Director, Craig Wallace. Belfast Rose Week was inaugurated in 1975 to involve the public more closely with the rose trials.

Spain   Although the rose is cherished widely in Spain, and beautiful rose gardens are to be found, for example, in Córdoba, Granada, Valencia and Seville (where the Parque de los Principes de Espania was opened in 1976), the most impressive display of roses is to be found in the Rosaleda del Parque del Oeste in Madrid, which lies to the north of the former royal palace near the road from Madrid to La Coruña. A splendid 'balcony' view is obtained from the Paseo de Rosales above the garden (the name has nothing to do with roses, but commemorates the Spanish artist Eduardo Rosales [1836–73] who specialized in painting scenes from history).

Switzerland   Geneva, at the southwest extremity of the country, is the setting for one of the world's most famous rose gardens, known as the Parc de la Grange, where an international rose competition is held. It lies on the south side of Lake Leman off the Quai Gustave Ador, not far from the floral clock and from that magnificently plumed jet of water that rises so far into the air that it can easily be distinguished from aircraft as they prepare to land several miles away. The site was presented to the City of Geneva in 1917 by William Favre. It is octagonal in shape, and on three levels, with pergolas, fountains and pools joined to one another by steps. About 12,000 rose plants are kept, in 200 varieties.

Other notable Swiss rose gardens are at Lausanne, at La Vallée de la Jeunesse, originally a feature of the Swiss National Exhibition of 1964; and at Berne, where a terrace rose garden is approached by going through the old town and across the bridge at the end of it – leaving the famous bears and their dens to the right. Lugano also has two rose gardens – the Parco Tassino and the Parco Ciani – and Rapperswil, on the Lake of Zurich, has three.

Rose growing in Switzerland is very much a family business. The Hauser family at Vaumarcus, near Neuchâtel, and the Wyss family at Zuchwil in the canton of Solothurn have both grown roses for more than a century, and the Woodtli nursery at Ostermundigen near Berne and the Huber nursery at Dottikon in the Aarg canton are both third-generation concerns.

See also GESELLSCHAFT SCHWEIZERISCHER ROSENFREUNDE.

United Kingdom   Gardens showing roses that have undergone trials at the headquarters of the ROYAL NATIONAL ROSE SOCIETY are listed under that heading. QUEEN MARY'S GARDEN, in Regent's Park in London, is also described in a separate item. Other rose gardens are to be found in the list published by the National Trust and available in most public libraries. There are also two annual lists of private gardens open to the public on certain days for charity, issued by the National Gardens Scheme Charitable Trust and the Scotland Gardens Scheme, and both obtainable from bookshops.

One National Trust garden of special interest is at Mottisfont Abbey, $4\frac{1}{2}$ miles (7 km) northwest of Romsey, Hampshire. It is a former 12th-century Augustinian priory and contains a walled garden well stocked with old-fashioned roses. Sissinghurst Castle in Kent (also managed by the National Trust) is the perfect background for a variety of roses, old and new – stage-managed by that great gardener, the late Vita Sackville-West.

Other 'old' roses are to be seen in profusion at Humphrey Brooke's Lime Kiln Rosarium, at Claydon, 3 miles (4.8 km) north of Ipswich, which is open on certain days in aid of charity. The Heritage Garden at Mannington Hall, 18 miles (29 km) north of Norwich, has a series of period rose gardens, each containing the appropriate historic roses. The nursery owned by Peter Beales, an outstanding authority on old-fashioned rose varieties, is nearby at Attleborough.

Roses are also to be seen in quantity at the Royal Botanic Gardens at Kew as well as at the Royal Horticultural Society's garden at Wisley.

In Scotland, Aberdeen has paid special honours to the rose in Duthie Park where all paths lead upwards to the 'Rose Mountain', where 38,000 roses are to be seen in a mass plantation. Aberdeen is also the headquarters of the famous COCKER nursery.

United States See list of public rose gardens under ALL-AMERICA ROSE SELECTIONS.

Rose Growers' Association

This represents all sides of the British rose-growing industry, from small selling units to companies with an international market. It also publishes the guide *Find that Rose*, which lists rose varieties currently on offer and where these are obtainable.

Each year, following trials, members choose a new variety to be designated 'ROSE OF THE YEAR'.

The address is: The Rose Growers' Association (Secretary: Angela Pawsey), 303 Mile End Road, Colchester, Essex CO4 5EA.

Rose of Jericho, the

Like the ROCKROSE and the Rose of Sharon, this is not a rose. The name refers to a small annual plant – *Anastatica hierochuntina* – of the Crucifer, or cabbage, family, which flourishes in the desert areas of southwest Asia and northeast Africa. The leaves near the root form a rosette, which even when completely shrivelled by drought will uncurl again if moistened. For this reason, it is sometimes called the 'resurrection plant' or the 'rose of the Virgin'.

See also BIBLE, ROSES IN THE.

Rosen Kavalier, Der

In Richard Strauss's lavish waltz-spectacular – for which 112 instruments are needed – the Cavalier (or Knight) of the Rose was the young Count Octavian who was deputed by the Princess von Werdenberg (whose lover he has been) to convey a proposal on behalf of the bucolic Baron Ochs von Lerchenau to the youthful Sophie von Faninal. As a symbolic pledge from the suitor, Octavian carried with him a silver rose. However, instead of acting as a mere mes-

senger, he fell in love with and won Sophie. The libretto, by Hugo von Hofmannsthal, tells the bittersweet story of the Princess who, as an older woman, knows that she will not be able to hold Octavian for ever.

Der Rosen Kavalier was first performed in Dresden in 1911.

Roseroot

Here is a plant that, botanically speaking, has nothing to do with roses. It is a fleshy succulent belonging to the Sedum, or stonecrop, genus and found at sea level in Arctic Europe, Asia, North America and on mountains as far south as the Pyrenees, the Italian Alps, northern Greece, Japan and New Mexico. The name 'roseroot' was given to the plant because its roots, when cut, yield a scent reminiscent of rosewater.

Rose of Sharon, the

See BIBLE, ROSES IN THE.

Rosette

Although 'rosette' is the French diminutive for 'rose', rosarians seldom make use of it, perhaps because it is not exclusive to the rose but is also associated with other flowers such as the lotus and the chrysanthemum. A yellow-blended TEA-ROSE, 'Rosette Delizy', was introduced by the French nurseryman Paul Nabonnand in 1922. Otherwise, even MINIATURE ROSE specialists seem to have avoided it.

The word has, however, been used since the beginning of the 19th century to describe a bunch or knot of ribbons arranged in rose-fashion, which are used as decoration on the animals at horse and dog shows. Botanists use the word to describe a rose-like arrangement of basal leaves, and to architects, 'rosette' signifies any decoration resembling a rose, including even a ROSE WINDOW.

Rose windows

The appearance of rose windows in the cathedrals of Europe from the 10th century onwards is both a tribute to the rose and to their builders who, as they learned more about the management of strains and stresses, realized that less solid masonry was needed than they had thought was required to support the fabric of a cathedral; larger windows, giving more light, could be introduced without the risk of structural collapse. Consequently, a mere tracery of stonework was all that was needed to hold the precious stained glass in place. The original model for the rose window may have been Romanesque or even Gallo-Roman, but they eventually featured not only on the façades of cathedrals but also at the top of Gothic lancet windows.

There is a touch of pedantry among those who refer to these adornments as 'rosette windows', or even as 'wheel

Right: The south rose window of Notre Dame in Paris. The structure of the window dates from the 13th century and some of the glass from as early as the 11th.

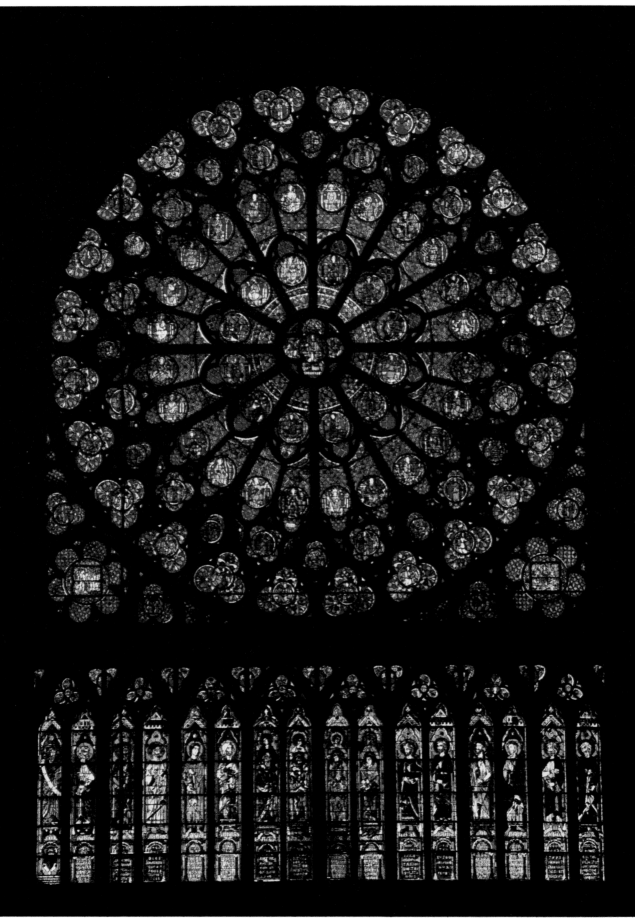

La conclusion du rommant

A cabbage rose, Rosa centifolia bullata, *from Pierre-Joseph*
Redouté's Les roses *(1817).*

Left: *Illustration from a Flemish edition of* Le roman de la rose (c. *1500),*
showing the lover attaining the rose.

windows' on the grounds that many of them are endowed with twelve 'spokes' instead of the mere five more appropriate to the rose.

The main impetus came from France, where rose windows (known there simply as *'la rose'*) are to be seen in the cathedrals of, for example, Chartres, Rouen, Rheims, Beauvais, Amiens and Notre Dame de Paris, where the rose window leading to the cloisters is far larger – nearly 43 feet (13 m) across – than the better-known rose window on the façade.

Some good examples of rose windows are to be seen in England at the cathedrals at Durham and at Lincoln, where the 13th-century window in the north transept is known as the 'Dean's Eye' and its companion in the south transept as the 'Bishop's Eye'.

Rosewood

No rose plant could provide the lustrous purplish-brown wood with a black grain that decorates some of our most delicate cabinetry. Instead, rosewood comes principally from two members of the vetch family: *Dalbergia nigra*, known in Brazil as the jacaranda tree; and its cousin in Honduras, *Dalbergia stevensoni*.

Rose of the Year (ROTY)

The 'Rose of the Year' (ROTY for short) trials in Britain are organized by the ROSE GROWERS' ASSOCIATION, together with the BRITISH ASSOCIATION OF ROSE BREEDERS, to provide better roses and make them easily obtainable, through cooperation between growers and breeders. The object of the trials – unlike those held by the ROYAL NATIONAL ROSE SOCIETY – is to discover the new variety most likely to be acceptable to the public at large (an attribute not always possessed by gold medallist roses) and to choose the most suitable name for it. (One breeder wished to call his winning rose 'Money Maker' because it reminded him of a successful tomato of that name, but peaceful persuasion was used to induce him to change it.)

The trials are supervised by a panel made up of three members of BARB and three of the Rose Growers' Association. Six widely scattered nurseries (nine from 1986 on) act as testing stations, and up to fifty judges may participate – although no one is invited to judge roses in which he or she has an interest. The roses are judged as MAIDENS after first flowering and again at the end of the season, with the proviso that they must also be distinguishing themselves in the trials held by the Royal National Rose Society. Foreign breeders are encouraged to compete.

Winners in recent years have been: for 1982, 'Mountbatten', a cluster-flowered yellow shrub rose by HARKNESS; for

1983, 'Beautiful Britain', a cluster-flowered red by DICKSON; for 1984, 'Amber Queen', a cluster-flowered apricot blend by Harkness; for 1985, 'Polar Star' (synonym 'Polarstern'), a large-flowered white rose from TANTAU; and for 1986, a Dickson rose not immediately given a tradename.

Rosicrucians

The Society of Rosicrucians was reputedly founded by Valentine Andrea, using the pseudonym Christian Rosenkreutz ('cross of roses'), in the 15th century, but remained a secret society until 1614. It aimed at the moral regeneration of the world, but its members claimed also to have the power to transmute metals, and to prolong human life. The Society still exists today, and its emblem is a cross decorated with roses.

Rosier de Madame Husson, Le

De Maupassant's famous account of the rise and fall of Madame Husson's rose-king deserves to be printed in full (and would if space allowed), but its significance for rosarians arises from De Maupassant's use of the tradition observed in a number of small French municipalities – especially Nanterre (now engulfed in Paris) – of awarding a citation and a purse of money to the young girl (thereafter known as *la rosière*) whose piety and conduct during the year most amply merited the honour. De Maupassant chose the Norman town of Gisors as his setting, and the local doctor as the narrator of this tale of an affront suffered by its respectable citizens.

The unworthy episode occurred when Madame Husson, the guardian of civic morals, decided that Gisors must set an example like Nanterre and choose and fête its own *rosière*. Unfortunately, however, no young woman could be found in Gisors whose reputation was beyond suspicion and Madame Husson allowed herself to be persuaded to accept instead a male *rosier*: Isidore, assistant to Virginie the fruiterer, who blushed at the very sight of a skirt and whose virginity had become the talk of the town. On the day appointed for the citation, Isidore was decked out in a virgin-white suit and was placed next to Madame Husson at the municipal banquet held on the ramparts, where the mayor handed him a handsome purse containing 500 gold francs and a savings book and clasped him to his bosom. However, the rich food, and the wine that went with it, so bemused Isidore that, after the feast was over, he caught the next stage coach to Paris, went on a spree lasting a whole week, and turned into an incurable alcoholic.

Royal National Rose Society

The National Rose Society – the forerunner of the Royal National Rose Society – sprang from a suggestion made at a rose show at Reigate that the Brockham (Surrey) rose show, founded by the Revd A. Cheels in 1868, might be extended to become a new national rose show. The proposal was welcomed by John Cranston, the Hereford nurseryman, and he decided to call a meeting to establish not only a new annual national rose show (which would really be a

Left: The Madonna of the rose bower. *This painting, treasured in the church of St Martin, Colmar, France, was executed by Martin Schongauer in 1473, by which time the rose had become fully acceptable as an adjunct to sanctity and a symbol of virtue.*

continuation of a series that had languished) but also a National Rose Society. The Society was launched at a meeting held at the Horticultural Club in London in 1876, and held its first show the following year, in the St James's Hall, Piccadilly. Dean HOLE, who had done so much to organize the first NATIONAL ROSE SHOW in 1858, was elected President, and remained so until his death in 1904.

The circumstances were favourable. For the first time, the extended and improved railway services made it possible to bring new varieties of roses in fresh condition to distant venues where they would be admired and coveted, and a growing demand for rose plants was to be expected from thousands of amateur gardeners. Nevertheless, up to the turn of the century, breeders, with few exceptions, continued to devote most of their efforts to providing roses for the show bench rather than for the wider public, and some were less than cooperative. One of these, Henry Bennett, incurred the wrath of the Society when, on two occasions, he preferred to sell roses for which he had won NRS awards exclusively in the American market. (The story of Bennett's quarrels with the Society are engagingly recounted in Jack Harkness's *The Makers of Heavenly Roses.*) Because of this attitude, during the first twenty-five years or so of its existence the membership of the Society remained fairly constant at between 500 and 900.

It needed campaigning writers of the calibre of William Robinson and Gertrude Jekyll to persuade the average sparetime gardener that the new REMONTANT rose varieties would not monopolize an entire garden, but were worth their place in the herbaceous border alongside other favourites as COMPATIBLE PLANTS. Once this concept had been accepted as self-evident, the effects were dramatic, with the Society's membership figures shooting up. In 1902, the National Rose Society issued its *List of Varieties*, which for the first time allowed amateurs to choose reliably named plants with predictable performance. A handbook on the then mysterious (to the amateur) art of pruning followed in 1905, and that miniature classic, *The Enemies of the Rose*, appeared three years later.

In its early days, the National Rose Society held its shows in the Crystal Palace, that wondrous construction of glass and iron designed for the Great Exhibition of 1851 by the gardener-*in-excelsis* Joseph Paxton. But Upper Norwood, the suburb of London to which the Crystal Palace had been moved from its original station in Hyde Park, was felt to be too remote, and in 1901, Temple Gardens, adjoining the north bank of the Thames, was chosen instead. Three years later the venue was changed again to the Inner Circle of Regent's Park. (This site was leased from 1840–1932 to the now defunct Royal Botanic Society and would be transformed later into what became known as QUEEN MARY'S ROSE GARDEN.) In 1905, the Society held its first autumn show, at the Royal Horticultural Society Hall in

Vincent Square, Westminster – indirect evidence of the number of remontant and autumn-flowering varieties then on offer.

By this time, the membership had reached some 6000, but the Society remained an informal organization until 1915 when, for the first time, it acquired its own offices. Its original trial grounds were set up in 1937 near Haywards Heath in Sussex, on land next to the garden of Courtney Page, the secretary of the Society from 1917 until his death in 1947, when it became necessary to look for a new trial ground. This was established near St Albans, first at Oaklands and then, in 1960, at a new headquarters at Bone Hill, bought for the modest price of £20,000. The tile-hung country house of soft red brick, built nearly a century ago, makes the perfect background for roses old and new. By 1965 – the year when, at the Queen's command, the Society earned the right to add 'Royal' to its name – membership had reached the 100,000 mark and had grown too large to be managed by any small, closely knit clique. Specialist committees were set up and are now in charge of particular branches of the Society's activities, such as exhibitions, publications and the management of the rose gardens.

The Society's rose gardens at Bone Hill cover some 12 acres, two-thirds of which came with the original 1960 purchase, while the remainder were bought in 1964. They are open every year from mid-June until the end of September, and show many different kinds of roses in different backgrounds. There are roses, including MINIATURES, in small beds. There are beds with roses alongside other garden flowers, all chosen to give the bed a comprehensive flowering programme. There are bush roses, cluster-flowered roses, and climbers and ramblers covering pergolas, walls and the brickwork of the headquarters. There are roses around a pool, hedges and displays of wild roses, and finally there are the trial beds in which the roses of the future are tested. The trials last for a period of three years, and there are usually about 500 varieties from growers in different parts of the world undergoing trials at any given time. (*See* INTERNATIONAL ROSE TRIALS AND AWARDS.)

Award-winning roses are shown not only at Bone Hill but also at display gardens in Saughton Park, Edinburgh; Pollock Park, Glasgow; Roath Park, Cardiff; Harlow Carr Gardens, Harrogate; Borough Park, Redcar; Vivary Park, Taunton; and at Norwich, Nottingham and Southport.

The Society also holds four rose shows each year – in spring and autumn at the Royal Horticultural Society at Vincent Square, London, in early July at St Albans and a week later in the north at Holker Park, Cumbria.

Members of RNRS can make use of the Society's specialist library of books, and can hire films and slides, and those with experience of exhibiting can apply to qualify as judges.

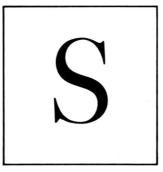

Saints and the rose

As well as the Virgin Mary (*see* ROSARY), four saints are also particularly associated with the rose:

St Cecilia, Virgin, Martyr and Patron Saint of Music. She was a Roman Christian who was being pressured to marry a non-Christian named Valerian. Although the marriage ceremony was performed, Cecilia insisted that it should not be consummated, declaring that she was under the protection of an angel who would avenge the loss of her virginity. Valerian said he would respect her wishes if she would show him the angel. 'If you will believe in the one true God and receive the water of baptism, then you will see the angel,' Cecilia replied. Valerian consented to be baptized and Cecilia sent him to Bishop Urban who received him into the Christian church. When Valerian got back, he saw an angel who stood beside Cecilia and held two chaplets of roses and lilies, which he placed on their heads. She was supposedly martyred in AD 176. St Cecilia's feast is celebrated on 22 November, but according to *Butler's Lives of the Saints*, neither the date of her martyrdom nor the details of the above legend have been authenticated.

St Dorothea of Caesaria. Like St Cecilia a virgin martyr, she perished about AD 303 at the time of the Diocletian persecution. Like many other Christians, she had been offered the choice of marriage to a non-Christian or death. She refused marriage, and when two women of loose morals were sent to suborn her, she converted them to Christianity. On the road to her execution, a young lawyer named Theophilus mockingly asked her to send him some fruit and roses from the Garden of Paradise to which she said she would be going, and she promised that she would. On reaching the appointed place, she knelt down and prayed and was then executed. Suddenly an Angel appeared, bearing a basket containing three apples and three roses. Theophilus tasted the fruit, was converted, baptized, and himself later suffered martyrdom. St Dorothea's name day is celebrated on 6 February.

St Rita of Cascia. She was born in 1381 near Spoleto in central Italy. Following the deaths of her husband and two sons, she entered an Augustinian convent and acquired a reputation for sanctity through the severe penances to which she submitted during her novitiate. On her deathbed in 1457, she asked a visitor to bring her roses from the garden at Roccaporena where she had lived as a child. Her name day is 22 May.

St Bernadette of Lourdes. St Bernadette (1844–79) is doubly linked to the rose. When the Virgin Mary first appeared to

---

The rose also symbolized 'saintliness' in general, even if the saint in question was not particularly linked to the flower. Here, Saint Elizabeth of Hungary is shown with a bouquet of centifolia roses gathered up in her robe.

Bernadette, the young girl noticed that roses wreathed the feet of the Holy Mother. Later, the site of the healing spring of Lourdes was disclosed to Bernadette when the apparition of the Virgin emerged through the screen of wild roses that had hitherto concealed the entrance to the miracle-working cave.

Other saints, even if their connections with the rose (if any) are obscure, are, nevertheless, commemorated in roses:

*'St Alban': a cluster-flowered mid-red HARKNESS rose of 1978 – inspired, perhaps, by the proximity of the town of St Albans to the Harkness nursery.

*'St Boniface': a cluster-flowered, orange-red KORDES rose of 1980.

*'St Exupéry': a large-flowered mauve rose from Delbard-Chabert, introduced in 1961.

*'St Helena': a mid-pink, cluster-flowered rose of 1983 from CANTS.

*'St Ingebert': a large-flowered, pale yellow LAMBERT rose of 1926.

*'St Nicholas': a pink damask of 1950, from Hilling.

*'St Quentin': a large-flowered rose from Kriloff, apparently not officially registered.

*'St Victor': a large-flowered mid-red rose introduced by Croix in 1979.

*'St Mark': 'St Mark's Rose' is a synonym for *Rosa virginiana plena*, also known as the *Rose d'amour*, said to have been cultivated in Europe as early as 1768.

Scent

Scent, they say, provides the rose with its soul. Certainly it is through the medium of its scent that the rose speaks most directly to its admirers – and thus, indirectly, to those who are admired. Florists are conscious of a belief among their customers – and it may be a well-founded one – that roses that possess the most fragrance are those that last longest.

There is, of course, no single rose scent, but many different ones, as can be seen in some of the leading rose catalogues. Thus, among the SPECIES ROSES, *Rosa pimpinellifolia* (the delicate little burnet rose that grows so often near the coast in Britain) provides a fragrance that resembles lily of the valley. *R. bracteata*, the Macartney rose, is thought to smell of apricots; *R. primula* has long been nicknamed the 'incense rose' because of the fragrance of its foliage. *R. longicuspis*, that popular climber, is said to dispense the odour of bananas, and *R. banksiae* the fragrance of violets. The old climbing tea rose 'Maréchal Niel' has the scent of raspberries and so has 'Madame Bravy', one of the progenitors of the first HYBRID TEA (large-flowered) roses.

Among RAMBLERS, both 'Belle Amour' and 'Constance Spry' are credited with a myrrh-like fragrance. 'Fritz Nobis', one of the modern SHRUB ROSES, offers (though not too importunately) a clove scent; and 'Grüss an Teplitz' carries the fragrance of the *épicerie*. The 'Königin van Dänemarck', a superb form of *R. alba* with many (some

would say, too many) petals, gives forth a rose scent of unalloyed sweetness, while 'Roseraie de l'Hay', a purple-flowered shrub rose, and a derivative of *R. rugosa*, recalls the delights of sugared almonds. The fragrance of ROSA CENTIFOLIA is fit for a sachet in a trousseau drawer; that of the DAMASKS for the romance of a summer's evening; and the delicate perfume of the CHINA ROSE for the morning boudoir. Other scents, including green apples, anisette, clover, bay rum, hyacinth, woodland moss, orris, geranium and wine, have been detected here and there among roses.

It has to be said, however, that these descriptions are necessarily approximate, and by no means easily recognizable by the uninitiated. Neville F. Miller, in a valuable article published in the *American Rose Annual* of 1962, reported that twenty-five different elemental odours were found in 170 varieties of roses tested in the Hershey Rose Gardens in Pennsylvania. The seven most common of these, occurring either singly or in combination, were rose (as typified by the Kazanlŭk variety used for ATTAR OF ROSES), nasturtium, orris, violets, apple, lemon and clove. The synthetic makeup of five of these seven is fairly well known, but the rose and the apple scents have elements that defied the efforts of the analysts of the day to reproduce them satisfactorily.

The average layperson who trusts to his or her nose is in much the same difficulty as the analyst because, very often, the perfume under assessment contains more than one element. Sometimes 'rose' is combined with 'nasturtium', but at other times, it is combined with 'lemon', 'geranium', 'clove' or 'orris'. Or perhaps 'orris' is combined with 'raspberry', and 'violet' with 'clove' or 'lemon'.

Another difficulty arises from the fact that the fragrance coming from a flower may, if concentrated, have a distinctly different smell from the same perfume if diluted. To confirm the truth of this, one has only to experience the difference between the odour at the mouth of a scent bottle and the effect produced by the same perfume when a spray is used.

Fragrance is generated by volatile liquids that evaporate rapidly – rather as though they were on the boil – at ordinary atmospheric temperatures, and some with lighter molecular weights are more volatile (i.e. vaporize more freely at a given temperature) than others. Consequently the proportions of the various elements that provide a complex fragrance cannot be relied upon to remain constant. In cold weather, only the more volatile elements of a complex perfume will be detectable, but as the temperature rises, other, less volatile, elements will come to the fore.

Eugene Boerner, the famous US hybridist for the JACKSON & PERKINS nurseries, had his own way of answering anyone who alleged that one of his best roses 'had no scent'. He would take off his hat, balance the rose on the top of his head and replace his hat; after a few minutes, he would take out the flower and offer it to the accuser for a sniff. He found that this procedure usually settled the argument . . . and it was so much quicker than taking the flower back indoors, where roses often have a different fragrance.

A country flower show, drawn by Arthur Hopkins for The
Graphic *(1894). It is almost certainly a deeply scented rose that
has brought the lady to her knees.*

The chemical processes by which the rose produces its
perfume are highly complex, and only a simplified outline
can be given here. In the first place, carbon extracted by
the plant from carbon dioxide in the atmosphere is combined with hydrogen to form a starch that is stored in the
leaves of the plant. The starch in turn is reconverted by a
chemical process into glucose and then into glucosides,
which are of many different compositions. These, in turn,
decompose, rather as in wine-making, into various alcohols
that can then be oxidized to produce still more volatile
compounds known collectively as aldehydes, and it is these
that produce the fragrance.

In most cases, rose perfume is dispensed from the petals
and is at its best in newly opened flowers. It follows that
roses with double flowers are usually more fragrant than
single-petalled species and, since one petal protects the
next, are likely to retain their fragrance for a longer period
than the single-flowered roses. Usually, red-petalled roses
carry more fragrance than others and are commercially
more popular. White and yellow roses have lighter, fainter
fragrances.

Some roses – particularly MOSS ROSES and the sweet
brier – exude perfume from 'glands', small vessels carried
at the tips of bristles or hairs on the leaves or stem. However, in the case of the MUSK ROSES, the scent is believed to
issue from the styles (which are fused into a single column)
rather than from the petals. The scent of the musk roses is
said to carry further through the air than any other – as
well it might, for the styles would probably be a better
form of transmitter than the petals.

Most rosarians must have noticed that, as the flowers of
a rose begin to age, its fragrance changes. This could be
because the more volatile elements of a compound fragrance escape first, while the heavier elements, having less
opportunity for doing so, are left until last. On the other
hand, the production of scent may fall off once the rose
has been pollinated, having fulfilled its main aim of
attracting the pollinators. These are points to be taken into
consideration by those who judge such matters.

The connoisseurs of scent hope for warm days for it is
then that the process of converting the neutral glycosides
into odoriferous alcohols and aldehydes is speeded up. The
warmth from the sun helps in this process, but light is also
a stimulus, and it is at dawn that the rose begins to shoot,
and the petals to unfurl (if they are still in bud), and to
open wider if they are that far developed; on dull days
there is less activity. Naturally, visitors to rose gardens also
hope that there is no hither-and-thither wind to interfere
with their appreciation of the fragrance there.

It is also generally agreed that roses are at their best

after a shower of rain. One explanation could be that roses, like the countryside in general, are refreshed when it rains, and spring back into action after it; or perhaps rain washes the air free of the dust and pollen that can interfere with our appreciation of the rose's fragrance. Fragrance probably remains longer in the atmosphere when the humidity is high: this could also help to explain why so many rosarians have written of the delights of smelling their roses before the sun rises and dries the air.

Next: the human element. The sense of smell comes into play when the chemical vapours already discussed stimulate – or perhaps even assault – the nerve endings of the inner nose, the sensitive palate in the roof of the mouth and, to some extent, the membranes around the eye sockets, which few people take into account unless they happen to be standing the wrong side of a bonfire. Tastes as well as sensitivities vary, and an odour that appeals to one connoisseur will disappoint or even repel another. Many rosarians of the past have written off *R. foetida*, the Austrian brier, and its coppery cousin, saying that they have an unpleasant smell, but more recently the word has been getting round that their odour is more akin to that of linseed oil.

It is also hard to assess the various forms of fragrance accurately enough for one rose to be compared with another. Perhaps in the near future some rosarian will invent a breathalyzer that can measure the strength of rose perfume, but until then we have to rely on subjective criteria such as 'scent just detectable', 'faintly scented', 'slightly scented', 'well-scented', 'strongly scented', 'very strongly scented', 'extremely strongly scented' and 'supremely scented'.

Whether the ideal rose perfume can ever be found remains open to question. Changes in fashion and the psychological atmosphere that gives rise to them make any success impermanent. A century ago, when it was thought desirable for women to be coy and on the defensive, the most appropriate perfume was considered that of the violet. However, today, when women all-rounders are as good as or better than men, a more active perhaps strident perfume is more appropriate, in keeping with the sharper colours of the modern rose.

Breeding for scent alone, when so many other features – hardiness, flower structure, length of flowering season and so on – have to be considered first, is a risk no rose breeder would willingly take. If the resulting hybrid shows outstanding qualities of fragrance, so much the better, but this is a bonus that can be hoped for rather than expected. And meanwhile, the great PERFUMERY firms make capital out of the rose, by combining its fragrance with that of many other seductively smelling plants, just as thoughtful gardeners can do in their own gardens.

Sealand Nurseries Ltd

The history of Sealand Nurseries, one of the largest rose production and breeding centres in the UK, is closely connected with the name of Arthur K. Bulley, the first of the great 20th-century patrons of plant-collecting expeditions.

Bulley, the penultimate of the fourteen children of Samuel Bulley, a Liverpool cotton broker, developed an interest in natural history while still a schoolboy at Marlborough, and after joining the family firm, he took up gardening as a hobby. It was Bulley who, in 1904, sent out George Forrest to Yunnan on his first expedition, and he also recruited Frank Kingdon-Ward, then in Shanghai, to take up plant collecting, and sent him off on his first foray in 1911.

Bulley's private garden was on the Sands-of-Dee in the Ness area of Cheshire, and when he found expenses mounting, he decided to use part of it as a commercial nursery, which he set up under the name of Bees Ltd. The company soon outgrew the gardens at Ness, and moved to a new site at nearby Sealand, about 4 miles (6.4 km) west of Chester. However, all Sealand plants are still trademarked 'Bees of Chester'.

Today, occupying 270 acres of ground and more than 2 acres of glass, Sealand grows $1\frac{1}{2}$ million roses a year in over 100 varieties, and has had the distinction of winning two gold medals at the Chelsea flower Show every year for seventeen consecutive years: 1969–85.

Seeds, propagation of roses by

No one but the most enthusiastic amateur will have enough patience to sow a rose seed and wait for it to grow into a rose bush. It can take as long as eighteen months for the seed to germinate, and, in many cases, seeds don't breed true to the parents, because of the unknown indiscretions in the plant's ancestry. Furthermore, even when breeding from species, there is always the risk that, despite the normal precautions, the stigmas of the parent rose may have been somehow mated with pollen from an alien rose, so the family tree is flawed and a bastard rose is bred.

The time-scale is much shorter and the chances of success greater if the seed (which amateurs, if they like to experiment, can obtain by HYBRIDIZATION) is allowed to develop only as far as the seedling stage before being BUDDED on to a suitable rootstock. In this case, seedlings will be budded in July on UNDERSTOCKS that have been planted the previous February. The stock will be headed (cut) back early the following year, and the plant will flower that summer, after which (in the case of a nursery) it can be lifted and offered for sale in the autumn. Some breeders prefer to wait until the seedling has produced a flower or even a hip so that they can decide which seedlings show the most promise. Other growers argue that seedling flowers are not a reliable indication of the colour and shape of the blooms of the mature plant, and prefer to dismember the seedling as soon as it has grown some wood, and bud all the eyes, whether of flowers or not, on to a reliable rootstock.

William Paul in *The Rose Garden* (1848) put it this way:

I have seen seedlings of the Bourbon and Chinese Roses [flowering] when little more than a month old. This, however, should be prevented rather than encouraged. The flowers may be white, they may be red, and this is the absolute amount of knowledge to be gained from them.

Both schools would agree that it is quicker and safer to grow seeds individually in pots, under glass, than out of doors.

Strictly speaking, we are dealing here, not with the seed alone but with the *achene*, the dry outer-covering that encloses the seed itself. The HIPS that contain the achenes should be picked as soon as they are ripe – before they begin to soften up. The standard practice used to be to bury the whole hips in sand, but the current method, followed more than sixty years ago by the Revd Joseph Pemberton, is to liberate the achenes from the hip at once –perhaps with the help of a kitchen blender.

The main problem when growing roses from seed is that most rose hips contain an inhibitor known as abscisic acid (ABA for short) which prevents them from developing until the passing of the wintry conditions that they would meet with in their natural habitat. This period of dormancy varies considerably – from weeks to months and even to years. Under natural conditions, continuous cold encourages the production of GIBERELLIC ACID (GA3), which counteracts the influence of ABA and promotes germination. However, this is a gradual process, and the aim of the rose breeder is to shorten the dormancy period as much as possible, by means of artificial chilling.

It has been found that this is best accomplished by first placing the achenes in moist vermiculite (*see* POTS AND OTHER CONTAINERS, GROWING ROSES IN), in a temperature of 68–79°F (20–26°C), before commencing the artificial chilling process. If no greenhouse is handy, a domestic airing cupboard can be pressed into service. Perhaps because the achenes are deposited in a stratum of vermiculite, this process is sometimes known as 'stratification'.

In preparation for the warming-up, the achenes are washed in water, to which breeders often add a suitable fungicide. It has been said that those achenes that float on the surface of the washing water are probably infertile and should be discarded, but buoyancy or non-buoyancy is more likely to be due to the presence or absence of air cavities than to any other cause. The seeds of at least one species – *Rosa palustris* – float naturally and the fact that a seed sinks does not guarantee its fertility.

The object of placing the achenes in moist vermiculite under heat is to soften the walls that, partly because of the pressure they exert, prevent the seed inside from expanding or even breathing. As the walls become softer, water can permeate into the interior of the achene, dissolving out some of the inhibitor and allowing some contact with the outside world. The vermiculite in which the achenes are placed consists of mica – plates of magnesium and iron silicates – which can absorb large quantities of water. Horticultural vermiculite should be used and not the builder's variety, which sometimes contains undesirable chemicals. The vermiculite should be soaked and then drained before the achenes are placed in it. The aim should be to keep the achenes in an atmosphere of saturated water vapour. If the vermiculite starts to dry out, it should be watered, provided that the excess water can drain off. Perforated plastic bags resting on seed trays are often used.

This warming-up period can last from four to six weeks, according to the dormancy period to be expected of the rose in question. If any achenes are seen to be germinating, they can be removed and, if caught sufficiently early, will probably survive if transferred at once to a growing medium.

The chilling process that follows the warming-up stage likewise varies according to the dormancy of the variety, with two months being the average length of time. In winter, chilling can take place outdoors either in a cold frame or a garden shed protected from the frost, or it can be carried out indoors at a temperature a little above freezing – say, 41°F (5°C). Small plastic containers suited to the restricted space inside a domestic refrigerator can be used, provided that there is air space above the achenes. They should not be allowed to dry out nor should they become water-logged.

The medium in which the achenes are placed during the chilling process will depend on the method chosen for their development. Some breeders treat the chilling as a distinct and separate operation, in which case, the achenes can remain in vermiculite or milled sphagnum moss until the chilling process has been completed, when they are transplanted to a medium in which they can germinate and grow on. Others prefer the achenes to be chilled, germinated and grown on in the same medium, but this method calls for more space and for special care in choosing the compost in which the seedlings will be grown.

Another procedure, simpler for the amateur, is to place the achenes in seed compost in pots or seed boxes and harden them off right away. The achenes should be covered to a depth of at least $\frac{1}{2}$ inch (1.5 cm) – some breeders say up to 2 inches (5 cm) – and should be positioned safely out of reach of the most enterprising mouse or bird. They can be brought indoors if the weather becomes really severe. Dampness stimulates growth provided that the drainage is good, and dryness inhibits it; but the soil should not be allowed to become caked through overwatering.

Germination of the seedlings is carried out in temperatures of 54–61°F (12–16°C), and development at 64–68°F (18–20°C).

The appearance of two kidney-shaped 'seed leaves', known as *cotyledons*, perhaps three weeks after the end of the chilling process, indicates that the seed has germinated. At this stage, the plant is at its most vulnerable, and strenuous efforts must be made, if the seed is cultivated under glass, to protect it from woodlice, APHIDS, spider mites and various kinds of MILDEW, all of which are usually more virulent under glass than in the open. Seedlings from hips collected in the autumn will probably have sprouted in February or March, and can be removed from the greenhouse and planted out in April.

If no artificial aids have been employed, there could, in the case of long dormancy species such as *Rosa canina*, be a wait of eighteen months from the time the achenes have been planted out of doors until germination occurs.

Sherlock Holmes and the rose

A MOSS ROSE that he was carrying served to concentrate the thoughts of the great detective on higher things, even though at that time he was being called on to solve the case that came to be known as 'The Naval Treaty' in *The Memoirs of Sherlock Holmes* by Sir Arthur Conan Doyle (1894). 'Our highest assurance of the goodness of Providence,' Holmes speculated,

seems to me to rest in the flowers. All other things, our desires, our food, are really necessary for our existence in the first instance. But this rose is an extra. Its smell and its colour are an embellishment of life, not a condition of it. It is only goodness which gives extras, and so I say again that we have much to hope for from the flowers.

(The above is based on a note contributed anonymously to *The Rose Annual* of 1971.)

Showing roses

The gardens of devoted rose exhibitors are distinct from other rose gardens. Their roses are placed further apart, so that each can reach maximum perfection. Their rose garden has fewer flowers because those not wanted for the next rose show will have been disbudded long before they can open, and the few varieties that are there are not necessarily the ones that make the best showing in the garden. Several examples of each variety will have been planted so that, if one is not in good form, a substitute may be ready to hand. Often they are delicate, hard to grow, and given to yielding a few very beautiful blooms rather than the displays that gladden the heart of the average rosarian. The flowering season may also be shorter there, if it is timed to coincide with particular competitions (though it has to be said that, today, really dedicated rosarians who show roses can enter shows right through the summer to the 1st of September).

Nevertheless rose shows help to encourage the faint-hearted; they raise horticultural standards; and they serve to introduce new varieties of roses to those who might not otherwise have had occasion to see them. It is worth remembering that, in the UK, the Royal National Rose Society organizes, as well as its well-known shows, competitions for those growing fewer than fifty roses (or fifteen in the case of miniatures), for those who have never previously won an award, and for those who have never previously shown roses at one of the Society shows. Thus, while useful hints can be picked up at local flower shows, novices need not hesitate to enter at least one of the Society's events. As soon as it is available, competitors should obtain a schedule giving details of the rose shows for the season. This will give dates and times for the various classes, the numbers of roses and varieties to be shown.

Displaying roses in competitions

Competitions take a number of different forms. There are contests for decorative roses of conventional garden size, arranged in bowls or vases in such a way as to show off the natural growth and foliage of the variety or varieties. There are also 'floral art' FLOWER ARRANGEMENTS – not limited to roses alone – that are often linked to a chosen theme.

Perhaps most keenly fought of all are the contests for exhibition or, as they are called, 'specimen' blooms, which are shown either in bowls or vases, or are set out in shallow trays resting inside wooden 'boxes'. These trays are perforated at regular intervals with 1-inch (2.5 cm) holes into which metal or plastic 'test-tubes', flanged at the top, are placed. The tubes are filled with water, and a rose is placed into each. A stiff wire holder can be introduced into the tube to hold the stems of the roses upright. The surface of the tray, except for the holes, is usually covered with green fabric.

'English' boxes (provided by the ROYAL NATIONAL ROSE SOCIETY, which allows no others to be used) are built to hold six roses and are placed alongside one another when displays of twelve or twenty-four blooms are to be shown. The standard box for six roses is 18 inches (45 cm) from front to back, 4 inches (10 cm) deep in front, $6\frac{1}{2}$ inches (16.5 cm) at the rear and $11\frac{3}{4}$ inches (30 cm) wide; the box for MINIATURES measures $6\frac{3}{4}$ inches (17 cm) from front to back, 2 inches (5 cm) deep in front, $3\frac{1}{2}$ inches (9.5 cm) at the rear and $4\frac{1}{2}$ inches (11.5 cm) wide. The 'American' box, favoured by the Federation of International Rose Exhibitors in the US, takes nine roses, including at least two cultivars, arranged in a 3×3 geometrical pattern. This can take the form of a St George's Cross, a St Andrew's Cross, a square with another colour in the centre or horizontal, vertical or diagonal stripes. This box is 16 inches (40 cm) square (6 inches [15 cm] square for miniatures). No boxes are used in Australia, and indeed, some rosarians question whether they should be used anywhere because this method of display leaves the viewer in doubt as to the carriage and foliage of the rose.

Bowls and vases are normally supplied by the organizers, and are of uniform size for any given event. However, competitors should measure the sizes of the bowls they are given to make sure that they are the ones specified for the event in which they are interested.

The number of stems to be shown in a bowl or vase will be specified in the schedule. For example, the number of stems to be shown in a 10-inch (25 cm) vase might be six in the case of specimen blooms, or nine in the case of LARGE-FLOWERED ROSES – with a maximum of three flowers per stem. As a rough guide, it may be assumed that the total height of the exhibit will be $1\frac{1}{2}$ times that of the vase in which the rose or roses are standing. Narrow vases taking one rose only are sometimes used, and contests for the best single large-flowered rose shown in a vase, one bloom to a stem, are the most popular and prestige-winning in the US. Wedging placed in the neck of the vase to hold the flower upright is seldom permitted there, but a 'lid' of thin rubber pierced by the stalk of the rose is sometimes used.

Bowls, too, vary in size from perhaps 7 to 10 inches (18–25 cm), and a 10-inch bowl might take as many as eighteen stems with six or more varieties in the bowl. The trend in the US appears to be towards more and more contests for miniature roses and less interest (at shows) in cluster-flowered varieties.

When arranging a vase or bowl, the exhibitor hopes above all to create a design that is well-balanced both in regard to the size and colour of the roses and the length of the stems on which they are carried. Some bowls are 'all-round' bowls, to be viewed by the judge from any angle; others are 'frontal' bowls, to be looked at only from the front.

Preparation

Preparations for a rose show can begin a year in advance, since it is then that exhibitors will be planting the varieties they plan to show. Once the new season has started, stems from which they hope to get specimen blooms of exhibition quality will be disbudded – that is, buds are taken off the shoot, which if allowed to develop would produce several inferior blooms instead of the single superb flower that is required.

Since it rarely happens that rose shows are held on sites conveniently close to where the roses have been grown, a great deal depends on the precautions that have been taken to see that the roses are presented in good condition and remain so until seen by the judge. Many books have been written on the best methods of accomplishing this, and only an outline can be given here of the methods used.

Obviously, roses will have to be brought on or held back according to the prevailing weather. Heat and sun will bring on the flowers, causing them to open earlier than they would have in cool weather under grey skies. Roses can be held back (and protected from the rain) by the application of conical waterproof hoods, which are clipped to bamboo canes and can be raised, lowered or removed by opening up the clips; the stem carrying the bloom that is to be protected is, in turn, secured to the bamboo cane. Hoods may have to be clipped on and taken off several times a day if the weather is unsettled.

Another precaution to be taken before the selected rose is picked is that of 'tying it' – that is, holding in the petals except for the outer row by circling them with a strand of soft wool (but only if the petals are dry). This gives a higher-peaked bloom but brings with it the risk of the flower opening all too rapidly when the wool is finally removed. The wool will probably have to be loosened and retied every day if the petals are not to show a mark where they have been constricted. Clearly the exact timing of the whole operation depends on the type of rose that is to be shown. As a rule, roses with petals of substance open more slowly than those with delicate flimsy petals, and double roses take longer to unfold than single.

Just before the show

Some contests include prizes for large-flowered (hybrid tea) roses in three stages of development: in the bud stage (showing full colour with one or two petals beginning to unfurl above an opening calyx); in the 'perfect' stage,

when the flower is half-to-three-quarters open, with the petals symmetrically arranged giving a circular outline and regularly surrounding an upright, well-formed centre; and in the 'full bloom' stage, when the rose is fully open with the petals symmetrically arranged within a circular outline (the stamens, if exposed, should also be fresh and of good colour). A contest of this kind gives exhibitors an easier choice – if they have enough roses from which to choose.

Two or three days before the date of the show, a selection has to be made of the roses that are to be shown and of the substitutes that will take their place in case of accidents. The roses in the 'substitute' team should, if anything, be in a slightly less-advanced condition than the first team of blooms.

The roses are best cut at the time of day when they are temporarily dormant – that is, between first light and 7.00 a.m. or in the cool of the previous evening. Many exhibitors believe that the evening before the show is the right time to cut, as this gives plenty of scope for the roses to be properly examined and prepared. The rose stems should be cut obliquely so that, when placed in water, only the point of the stem rests on the bottom of the container.

Each stem is name-tagged as it is cut and should be placed immediately up to the neck (but no further) in a bucket of water, for if left in the air, even for a short time, the cells of the stem harden, making it more difficult for the plant to drink. As each bucket is filled, the roses can be taken to a cool and shaded staging area where they can be finally reviewed. At this point, some rosarians add a dose

The Royal Horticultural Society's show at Temple Gardens in 1901, drawn by Frank Craig for The Graphic. *Here, the roses are the big draw.*

of a proprietary 'reviver' marketed in the UK as 'Chrysal' and as 'Floralite' in the US; others rely on any soft drink that contains sugar (but no more than 2 per cent of the total content) and carbonated water, adding to this some form of bactericide. After their foliage has been cleaned, blooms and sprays can be wrapped and placed in the refrigerator or even the freezer in extreme cases.

The problem of getting roses to a show in good condition has never proved easy – even for experienced exhibitors. William Paul had this to say in *The Rose Garden*, published in 1848:

If the distance be great, the plants should be packed for travelling the day before. All is bustle and anxiety. A light spring-van is the best vehicle for their conveyance, the space in which, from twelve to eighteen large plants will fully occupy . . . In packing, each plant should stand clear of the other, and all free from contact with the sides of the van. Between the pots, moss or sawdust should be *tightly* pressed, at least half their depth to keep from shifting. A light tilt [awning] must go over the van, to exclude sun, rain, or dust, the last of which, by the bye, is not always easy to do. But all is ready, and there is nothing like being at the place of exhibition in time. A careful person ought to accompany them, as the pace at which they travel should be a steady walking one. Attention, John! From home to the place of exhibition, *all* depends on you. You must neither trot, gallop, nor canter. If you do, the consequences will be disastrous. Put your horse to his easiest walking pace, having reckoned up beforehand the time he will require for the journey.

Today, in the case of decoration roses, which are shown as long sprays, the roses will probably be taken to the show packed in crates. They should travel dry in these, because the appearance of the petals will be spoiled if they are rubbed at all while damp. Some experts put the roses in plastic sleeves closed at each end with rubber bands to conserve moisture and prevent 'drying out', and crushed ice is occasionally used at the base of the stems.

Various methods have been devised for transporting roses to shows with their stalks in water – either in plastic bottles held in crates used for milk or wine bottles or in a home-made container. The latter consists of a wooden framework about 12 inches (30 cm) high, shaped like a box with a floor, corner posts and top rails but no side panels. The framework is fitted with a false bottom in which holes have been drilled about 6 inches (15 cm) apart into which 'test-tubes' are fitted. The tubes are secured at the top to battens or canes slotted into vertical holes in the top rails, and are then filled with water and the roses placed in them. A look round an average pharmacist will suggest various types of plastic or aluminium containers that will serve as test-tubes. Alternatively, the rose stems can be inserted into cylinders of 'Oasis', the absorbent foam used in flower arrangements, which will hold them firmly while supplying them with water.

At the show
On arrival, the stems of those roses that have been transported out of water should be cut afresh, plunged into water up to their necks and left in a dark, cool, still room to recover. It has been calculated that a rose loses water six times faster in a temperature of 77°F (25°C) than it does when the air is cooled to 43°F (6°C) – in other words, one day at 77°F equals six days at 43°F. Those roses that have travelled while in water should be topped up on arrival and placed on the ground, which is usually a cooler spot than the showbench itself, and the lid of the box can be propped open an inch or two to allow some air to circulate. However, it is a mistake to start arranging the displays too much in advance of judging.

If the competition rules allow rose blooms to be supported with wire (not the case in the US), this operation is carried out at the first convenient opportunity. Florist's rose-wire is inserted into the seed chamber of the rose, and the bloom is held in an upright position while the wire is wound discreetly round the stalk and cut, or the wire can be drawn along the stem and then the stem and the wire are bound together with finer wire.

When arranging a box of blooms, it is usual to place the largest blooms in the 'top' (i.e. back row), the medium-size blooms in the middle and the smaller ones in front, which masks the disparity in size. Where there is a choice, each row should begin with a rose of a different colour and no two roses of the same colour should be placed next to each other. Good yellow roses are scarcer than pinks and reds, and if one is available, it will probably be placed as an 'eye-catcher' in a middle position. For harmony's sake, 'soft' colours should be placed next to 'sharp' colours.

The blooms can then be 'rehearsed' before the competitor has to leave the hall to allow judging to begin. Any wool ties must be removed and the rose 'dressed'. The more the inner petals show, the more extra colour there is to the rose and the larger the size of the blooms. If, despite this treatment, the rose has not opened sufficiently, it can been encouraged to do so by the insertion of pellets of foam or cotton wool; the rose is then coaxed into opening still further, and the petals to reverse, by the gentle persuasion of a camel's hair brush. However, all the pellets have to be removed before the roses are judged, and in any case, a rose that appears not to have opened naturally loses points, as does a rose from which a damaged petal has been removed – unless this has been done so skilfully that it escapes the judges' notice. The foliage of the rose must be clean, and not artificially glossed with egg white, clear glue, oil, milk, etc. The leaflets must face the right way and the bloom must look directly at the judge. Experienced exhibitors are not afraid to make last-minute changes and put in one of their 'reserve' roses if a member of the original selection appears to be wilting.

In the case of decorative roses and floral art arrangements, some space must be left in the display to allow for the possibility that, in the heat of the hall, some of the blooms may wish to spread. For roses that may have to be arranged and perhaps rearranged, exhibitors will need a sharp knife for removing foliage and thorns, secateurs for recutting stems, a small jug and funnel (or, for miniatures, a syringe) for topping up with water, florist's wire of various thicknesses, scissors for trimming the petals, pliers for cutting wire, and a small 'puffer' as used by photographers for blowing dust off their lenses. In flower arrangements, the stems of lupins, delphiniums and foxgloves are often used as fillers in vases; experts warn against using reeds or lonicera, which apparently inhibit roses from taking their fair share of water. In the case of decoration roses, Oasis, available in bricks or cylinders, is commonly used as a base for holding rose stems in position. It is important, once having placed a stem in Oasis, not to withdraw it from its original position, because doing so may cut off the rose from its water supply. Other hints when using Oasis: don't compress the wet foam or air may get in; make sure that the stem is closely surrounded by the foam; water from time to time, making sure that the water can get through to the bottom of the vase, bowl, etc.

Apart from the style in which the roses are arranged, the judges will be influenced by the carriage of the flowers, their beauty and abundance, and their quality.

Labels indicating the event for which the exhibit is entered and the names of the varieties shown can be prepared in advance, but it is as well to bring some spare cards and a waterproof marking pencil just in case of accidents.

See also FLORISTS AND THE ROSE, JUDGING ROSES.

Shrub roses

Botanically, all roses are shrubs in so far as they show a permanent woody growth, and 'shrub roses', one might think, are those roses that are too large for the average flowerbed. However, it is as well to bear in mind that, to serious rosarians, the term 'shrub' has a special significance. To them, shrub roses are those that are neither CLIMBERS, nor RAMBLERS, nor MINIATURES, nor cluster-flowered roses nor the LARGE-FLOWERED ROSES formerly designated as HYBRID TEAS.

In this sense, they are variable in size, with 'tall' specimens over 9 feet (3 m) and 'very tall' ones that are loftier still. The 'short' ones can be 2 feet (1.8 m) high or less and can thus be grown in pots or tubs; these technically remain shrub roses so long as they do not have the habit and characteristics of miniature roses. Some climbers and ramblers can also be trained as shrubs and vice versa, but here we will only be dealing with large shrubs.

The spread of a shrub rose is variable, too, with some growing as wide as they are tall, or even wider. Thus some of the larger varieties are excellent for hedging, but equally impressive as specimen plants where there is enough space to display them properly. In some countries of continental Europe, the name 'park rose' has unfortunately been bestowed upon these larger shrub roses. Their popularity in Britain increased considerably towards the close of the 19th century, when 'natural' and 'wild' gardens of the kind recommended by William Robinson and his disciple Gertrude Jekyll came into fashion.

At that time, too, when many new species and hybrids were appearing, attempts were made to link the new varie-

ties of shrub rose with one or other of the traditional groups that already existed. Because the decision as to which group a new variety belonged lay at the discretion of the individual breeder, there were many anomalies. Today, in the CLASSIFICATION agreed by the WORLD FEDERATION OF ROSE SOCIETIES, shrub roses are classified under three main headings: (1) shrubs that can be identified with the old shrub roses of tradition; (2) modern shrub roses introduced more or less since the turn of the century (these are subdivided into shrub roses that are REMONTANT, and those that are not); and (3) wild shrub roses.

It is worth taking particular care when choosing a shrub rose, especially if it is to occupy a solus position in the garden. Hardiness, remontancy and large flowers are indispensible, as is resistance to disease, since MILDEW and BLACKSPOT are harder to deal with on plants that cannot be reached without a step-ladder. Blooms that open freely without 'BALLING' and petals that will stand up to rain, yet will drop off after flowering, are especially desirable in such specimen plants. However, few shrubs have all the necessary qualities, and remontancy has therefore been given priority in the selection that follows. (Some shrubs that are closely connected with 'old' wild roses, such as *Rosa pimpinellifolia*, and which are not assuredly remontant, are described separately in the section dealing with WILD ROSES.)

One of the classics among shrub roses – and Edward VII's favourite rose – is 'Frau Karl Druschki', since acclaimed as the 'Snow Queen' and as 'White American Beauty'. Introduced in 1901, and named in honour of the wife of the then president of the VEREIN DEUTSCHER ROSENFREUNDE, the pure white double flowers (and how rare purity is among white roses) are carried on an upright bush that can rise to 10 feet (3 m). It is, alas, scentless, but is produced remontantly.

'Commandant Beaurepaire', the flowers of which are striped with pinks, carmines, purple and white, is a unique shrub and worth including even though it is not invariably remontant. Despite its late introduction and the fact that one of its parents was the hybrid tea rose 'Madame Caroline Testout', this is included among the 'old' shrubs, since its other parent was the HYBRID PERPETUAL, 'Merveille de Lyon'.

They say that old soldiers never die and 'General Jacqueminot', now a veteran of more than 125 years, is still going strong. He is a hybrid perpetual in every sense since his lineage can be traced in many of the modern roses. 'General Jack', as he is sometimes disrespectfully called, makes a splendid shrub, with large, crimson, well-scented flowers, and is remontant.

'Fellemberg' with cupped pink-to-crimson flowers is often billed as a climbing CHINA ROSE, but left to itself, it will show cascades of continuous bloom on arching rambler stems. The merits of 'Madame Isaac Periere' are sung in the section on BOURBON ROSES, as are those of 'Comte de Chambord' in the entry dealing with PORTLAND ROSES.

Outstanding shrub roses of the 'modern' era include

'Uncle Walter', which is popular in the UK, West Germany and Australia. It is a tall large-flowered rose with dark crimson, peaked flowers. 'Angelina' (Cocker, 1975) is another shrub rose with a strong touch of hybrid tea (and some *R. pimpinellifolia*); it is remontant, with flowers of light carmine.

Other fine modern shrubs are of the cluster-flowered FLORIBUNDA types. 'Chinatown' (Poulsen, 1963), with large, well-scented, clear yellow flowers, won the Royal Horticultural Society's Gold Medal in 1962. 'Fountain' (Tantau, 1971) has modern peaked flowers, some clustered, others singly, all dark crimson and scented; it flowers almost continuously.

'Golden Wings' (Shepherd, 1956) is a pimpinellifolia derivative, but remontant nevertheless, and prodigal with its clusters of light yellow flowers, deeper at the centre. It has received the Royal Horticultural Society's Award of Merit.

The name 'Nevada' is not quite right for this rose, which is creamy rather than snowy; it is only semi-remontant and moderately scented. However, the flowers – 4 inches (10 cm) across and nearly single – and the profusion with which they are displayed have earned it a reputation as one of the finest of all shrub roses. It was the result of a cross between a relative of *R. moyesii* and 'La Giralda', which in turn was derived from 'Frau Karl Druschki' x 'Madame Édouard Herriot', so something rather special could have been predicted. It was raised in 1927 by Pedro Dot Martinez from the Spanish city of Barcelona.

'Cerise Bouquet' (Kordes, 1958) has won warm praise for its clusters of fragrant crimson-pink flowers and greyish foliage. Although classed as a shrub, it needs some support to stand upright, and it is an exception to this list since it is not remontant.

It is debatable whether 'Dorothy Wheatcroft' (Tantau, 1960) should be included here. It is a gaunt leggy plant that needs covering at the base with a 'footstool' of lavender or rosemary to hide her bare shins. There is little scent, but the startlingly well-structured, vivid clusters of orange-red double blooms won it the Royal National Rose Society's Gold Medal in 1961.

'Fred Loads' (Holmes, 1967), which won the same gold medal six years later, is also a scarlet-orange rose, and like 'Dorothy Wheatcroft', which was one of its parents, is especially good for cutting. It was raised by the same amateur breeder as 'Sally Holmes', another outstanding shrub rose with clusters of ivory flowers faintly tinged with an evanescent pink.

This last is one of the HYBRID MUSKS that form a large group within the shrub class. One of the best of these is 'Buff Beauty' (Pemberton, 1922), which has large, double, scented blooms of light apricot; the growth is thick enough to make a hedge, and remontant. 'Moonlight' (1913) was one of Pemberton's earlier hybrid musk successes, and won the RNRS's Gold Medal in the year of its launching. Its clustered flowers are pale primrose, semi-double and well-scented.

'Penelope' (1924), with hundreds of flowers changing from salmon to pink, earned a RNRS Gold Medal for Pemberton and can be used as a hedge. 'Cornelia' was the first really outstanding hybrid musk rose to have been developed by Pemberton, and shows large clusters of small, strawberry-coloured pom-pom flowers. 'Ballerina' came from Pemberton's nursery in 1937, three years after his death. It had single pink blooms in large clusters and, perhaps because of this, was classed as a hybrid musk. Its parentage is unknown, and Michael Gibson in *Growing Roses* suggests that it contains a strong element of POLYANTHA.

In the 1930s, Wilhelm KORDES introduced a number of remontant shrub roses by crossing hybrid musks with large-flowered roses. These include 'Wilhelm' (1934) – marketed as 'Skyrocket' in the US – showing large dark red flowers with violet shading, and 'Hamburg' (1935) with vivid red blooms. Post World War II varieties include: 'Berlin' (1949), with orange scarlet flowers; 'Nymphenburg' (1954), with pink-orange flowers; 'Ilse Haberland' (1956), with rose and yellow colouring; 'Bischofsstadt Paderborn' (1964), vermilion and suited to its alternative name of 'Fire-pillar'.

There remain those shrub roses that are linked closely with wild roses but which are also remontant. In this respect, *R. rugosa* is the most important source. The finest of the rugosa shrubs is probably 'Roseraie de l'Hay', introduced in 1902 by Cochet-Cochet (the 'echo' in the name was introduced when Charles Cochet married a Cochet cousin), but Graham Stuart Thomas has indicated that it may actually have been grown a year earlier by Gravereaux (*see* L'HAY, ROSERAIE DE). The lavish 4½-inch (11 cm), dark purple flowers are richly scented, and have a complement of luxurious, bright green foliage. It is good for a hedge, too. 'Pink Grootendorst' (1923) has abundant clusters of small pink flowers, with fringed petals.

There are a number of other good *R. rugosa* shrub rose varieties. 'Frau Dagmar Hartopp' (alias 'Frau Dagmar Hastrup'), introduced by a Hastrup in 1914, has light pink flowers. The flowers of 'Harvest Home' (1980) are somewhat more mauve. The white form, *R. rugosa alba*, is also highly commended. Both red and white flower fairly continuously. *R. rugosa alba* 'Pax' (1918), with creamy-white flowers and amber stamens, is too lax-growthed for some.

In the case of shrub roses, particular attention should be paid to the descriptions for growth given in the *Rose Directory* published by the Royal National Rose Society, which distinguishes between plants which are: 'normal' (having a width about one-third of the height); 'fairly wide' (one-half of the height); 'wide' (about two-thirds of the height); and 'very wide' (as broad or broader than the height).

See also MOSS ROSES and ALBA ROSES.

Single and double roses

The ultimate in single roses is represented by the four-petalled *Rosa sericea* and its near cousin *R. omeiensis*. At the other end of the scale, we have the ROSA CENTIFOLIA – which are sometimes described as 'very double'. Many roses fall somewhere between the two extremes.

The ROYAL NATIONAL ROSE SOCIETY, however, saves us from uncertainty, and tells us where we may draw the line. It recognizes seven degrees of fullness, namely:

Single	4 to 7 petals
Semi-double	8 to 14 petals
Not full	15 to 19 petals
Moderately full	20 to 24 petals
Fairly full	25 to 29 petals
Full	30 to 40 petals
Very full	Over 40 petals

Size of flower

The rose sizes recognized by the ROYAL NATIONAL ROSE SOCIETY are:

Very small	less than 1 inch (2.5 cm) diameter
Small	1 to 1½ inches (2.5–4 cm)
Rather small	2 inches (5 cm)
Medium	3 inches (7.5 cm)
Fairly large	4 inches (10 cm)
Large	6 inches (15 cm)
Very large	7 inches (18 cm)
Extremely large	more than 7 inches (18 cm)

The above measurements apply to LARGE-FLOWERED ROSES (HYBRID TEAS), cluster-flowered roses, FLORIBUNDAS, SHRUB ROSES and CLIMBERS, but not to MINIATURES, which are measured as follows:

Small	less than 1 inch (2.5 cm)
Medium	1–1½ inches (2.5–4 cm)
Fairly large	1½–1¾ inches (4–4.2 cm)
Large	1–2 inches (4.2–5 cm)
Very large	over 2 inches (5 cm)

Snags

A snag, in rose parlance, is the unattractive and superfluous stump that remains when the pruning cut on a stem has not been made sufficiently close to the source.

Leaving a snag encourages 'die-back', with an attendant risk that the dead portion of the branch will attract one or other of the ENEMIES OF THE ROSE.

Soil

Although some roses, particularly the HYBRID PERPETUALS and some WILD ROSES such as *Rosa pimpinellifolia* and *R. moyesii*, can be grown successfully on chalk and limestone, it seems generally agreed that roses do best on a soil that is slightly acid.

The degree of acidity in soil is indicated by what is known as its pH number. Neutral soil has a pH number of 7; alkaline soil has a higher number; and acid soil a lower one. The rose takes kindly to soil that, when tested using an inexpensive apparatus available at most garden centres, shows a pH value of 6.0 or 6.5. If the pH value is much

below this, the addition of calcium nitrate or potassium nitrate to the soil will help to reduce the acidity. Iron sulphate, ammonium nitrate and ammonium sulphate are also used to reduce alkalinity, as are peat and leaf-mould. Only in extreme cases should it be necessary to import special soil to suit the rose.

Clay is not, as is sometimes thought, an ideal soil for roses. It holds water in wet weather when it should not, and lets it run away too quickly during a drought. It can, however, be improved in a number of ways: with humus (compost or other decayed vegetable matter), calcium sulphate, coarse peat moss, sphagnum moss or old-fashioned farmyard manure (well-rotted, not fresh). Magnesium is usually added in liquid form as magnesium sulphate; bonemeal or superphosphate are the best sources of phosphate.

Roses will not flourish in soil that is not properly drained. An excellent way of testing garden soil is to dig a hole 18 inches (45 cm) deep and fill it with water. If it drains away in a couple of hours, there is no need to worry. If water remains, it may still be possible to improve the drainage by breaking up the subsoil.

Roses should not be planted in soil previously used for growing other roses. For reasons not fully understood, such soil is said to be 'rose-sick', and must be dug up and replaced by other soil if a new rose is to be planted. For safety's sake, an area measuring 2 feet (0.60 m) each way should be excavated.

See also SOIL DEFICIENCIES, SIGNS OF.

Soil deficiencies, signs of

Abnormally coloured leaves can point to a shortage of elements needed by the rose:

Colour	*Deficiency*
Abnormally dark green	Calcium or boron shortage
Predominantly pale yellow	Iron shortage
Pale yellow only in the centre	Magnesium shortage
Pale yellow between green veins	Manganese shortage
Turning yellow first at veins	Oxygen shortage through waterlogged roots
Brown at edges with shoots unusually red	Potash shortage
Young shoots yellow	Nitrogen shortage

Ordinary garden centre test kits can determine whether the soil contains enough potash, nitrogen and phosphorus, but not the smaller trace elements. Remedies are on sale for all the above complaints, except in the case of poorly drained rosebeds, which may have to be abandoned in favour of a drier site.

See also SOIL.

Species roses

Most people believe they know what the word 'species' means – until they come to define it, particularly in the case of roses. LINNAEUS, when dealing with roses in his *Species plantarum*, wrote:

Species of roses are distinguished with difficulty, and are determined with even more difficulty. It seems to me that Nature may have mixed together several of them or, by chance, formed several out of one. Hence he who looks at a handful finds it easier to tell them apart than anyone who examines a larger number.

Linnaeus originally succeeded in defining a dozen species of roses, but later added three more, and dropped one, leaving fourteen in the third edition of *Species plantarum*, the last to be published in his lifetime.

Today, though the number of rose species has been put as high as 250, the problem of defining which is and which is not a species has become, if anything, more difficult.

The accepted definition of a species is: A group of inter-breeding individuals with so many features in common that they form a distinct and generally recognizable group. However, roses do not conform to these criteria. Some are known to be capable of self-pollination and therefore may not always interbreed. Others do interbreed, have many features in common and appear to make up a distinct and generally recognizable group, but are nevertheless believed to be hybrids formed, as Linnaeus suspected, from other species. The evidence for this comes from the CHROMOSOME count, and from the discrepancies between the numbers of chromosomes coming from the 'male' parent and those from the 'female' parent.

A typical case is that of the 'White Rose of York'. This was formerly designated as *Rosa alba*, but is now classed as a hybrid of *R. canina* and *R. damascena*, and should be (but rarely is) denoted as *R. x alba* to indicate its hybrid origin. It is not known whether the original cross-breeding took place in the wild or in a garden. Similarly, DAMASK ROSES were formerly regarded as botanical species, but the sum-mer-flowering damask is now recognized as a hybrid of *R. gallica* and *R. phoenicia;* and the autumn-flowering damask is seen as a cross between *R. gallica* and *R. moschata.* Never-theless historic hybrids such as these – and *R. centifolia* – are treated as species even though there is no evidence that they have ever bred in the wild.

See also WILD ROSES.

Sponsored roses

Sponsorship – the arrangement that allows the rose breeder to supplement his or her income, and the sponsor to publi-cize his, her or its name – must be beneficial if it provides a profit for nurseries that might otherwise make none.

An early success was scored by Pernet-Ducher of Lyon when he was approached in the late 1880s by Madame Caroline Testout, a fashionable couturier with showrooms in London and Paris. A native of Grenoble who had bought her silks in Lyon and so became enthralled by the city's roses, she asked Pernet-Ducher outright to name a rose for her. He suggested that she should choose one of his available varieties, but was dismayed when she selected what he thought was a rose without a future; he did not want to have to produce it in quantity with his name at-tached to it, even indirectly. It had been sown in January 1888 and flowered the same year, but Pernet-Ducher

feared that the blooms might fail to open well. In the event, he left it alone, and the following year the flowers were more than satisfactory. Madame Testout had been right after all, and this vigorous rose with outsize flowers of sil-very pink with deeper centres was introduced at her salons in 1890, is still grown on both sides of the Atlantic and, in particular, is a special feature of the rose city of Portland, Oregon (*see* PORTLAND ROSE FESTIVAL).

The amounts paid by commercial sponsors to breeders is usually a closely guarded secret, but it varies according to the number of roses involved, the type of service to be pro-vided by the breeder, the amount to be spent by the spon-sor on promotion and the long-term prospects of the rose itself. For example, the Mullard Company paid Sam MCGREDY £10,000 in 1970 for the right to call one of his roses the 'Mullard Jubilee' rose, but that was a very special flower, winning gold medals from the ROYAL NATIONAL ROSE SOCIETY and INTERNATIONAL TRIALS in Belfast and The Hague.

Today, the going rate for a first-class variety, such as the red rose grown to commemorate the 200th anniversary of the London *Times* in 1985 (it won both a gold medal and the President's International Trophy at the Royal National Rose Society's contests), would not be less than £30,000, and the ensuing demand makes it possible to offer a rose at £3.50 a plant, which might otherwise have fetched perhaps only half as much.

The same would be true of DICKSON's pale yellow rose marketed in Europe and three other continents as 'Peau-douce', after the disposable nappy firm, although in this case the promotion seems to have been particularly lavish.

A breeder has, however, to balance the amount offered by the sponsor – whose name may have only a purely national (rather than international) significance – against the very much larger six-figure royalties that can be earned by a rose that is not only good in itself but has a name with trans-world sales appeal.

Apart from sponsorships in which a commercial enter-prise is involved, roses are often named for personalities (some professional, some not), in circumstances where no money passes in either direction. The Royal family would clearly be included in the second of these categories. Or, to take another example, glasshouse men had been familiar since 1979 with an excellent pale-pink cut-flower rose known as 'Flamingo', codenamed 'Korflug'. When Reimer KORDES decided in 1984 to market this as an outdoor garden rose, the Bonn (West Germany) Central Gardening Society requested him to name it 'Margaret Thatcher'. An appro-priate ceremony took place at Number Ten, Downing Street, and the representative of the German Horticultural Association stressed that the naming was another expres-sion of Anglo-German friendship and very close coopera-tion in the horticultural field.

The cluster-flowered rose 'Hiroshima's Children' ('Harkmark') (Harkness, 1985), which has flowers like 'Peace' on a smaller scale, was named at the request of a visitor to the HARKNESS nursery, who asked if he could be provided with a rose for presentation to the Mayor of

Hiroshima in 1985, the 40th anniversary of the first atomic bomb, as a symbol of healing and reconciliation.

Usually, if not always, when a rose is named for a stage, television or other personality, no money passes either way, it being assumed that each side stands to gain from the arrangement. In the UK, SEALAND NURSERIES have specialized in this branch of promotion with success. For example, many of their customers did not wait to see the LARGE-FLOWERED pink-blend rose named in 1984 after the Olympic and World skating champions, Jane Torvill and Christopher Dean, before ordering it.

Sport
A spontaneous development in which one part or feature is untypical of the rest of the plant. The special characteristic of a sport can be propagated vegetatively – for example, by BUDDING – but not through SEED, a limitation that distinguishes it from a species MUTATION.

Standard roses
'Few things have had a worse influence on the flower garden than the standard rose,' wrote William Robinson in *The English Flower Garden* (1883).

Grown throughout Europe and Britain by millions, it is seen usually in a wretched state, and yet there is something about it which prevents us from seeing its bad effect in the garden, and its evil influence on the cultivation of the rose, for we now and then see a fine and even a picturesque standard, when the rose suits the stock it is grafted on, and the soil suits each; but this does not often happen.

To Henry Bennett, the 19th-century begetter of HYBRID TEA roses, standards were 'broomsticks', yet no one who has not seen the roses of the BAGATELLE should underestimate the effectiveness of standards as a contrast to bush roses.

Standard roses are those of which the leaves and flowers spring from the top of a straight and leafless rootstock. The standard rose is propagated by BUDDING a scion of the cultivated variety on to an UNDERSTOCK of a species such as *Rosa canina* or *R. rugosa* – the stock being as important as the flowers it is to carry. For a 'standard' standard, the stock is usually 3 feet 3 inches (1 m) to 3 feet 6 inches (1.1 m) high. The stocks of 'weeping' standards in which the branches droop downwards, are usually 5 feet (1.5 m) high, and half-standards approximately 2 feet (0.60 m). LARGE-FLOWERED ROSES – formerly HYBRID TEAS – and FLORIBUNDAS provide most of the standard and half-standard varieties, but RAMBLERS are best for weeping standards.

Both standards and weeping standards, and even half-standards, need support from a stake, which should be either cedar or other wood treated with an anti-rot preservative. The stake should be substantial – measuring at least 1 by 1½ inches (2.5 × 4 cm) – and should carry several of the modern figure-of-eight adjustable ties.

The first standards were imported to Britain from France by Lee & Kennedy from André Dupont (*see* JOSEPHINE AND HER ROSES AT LA MALMAISON) in about 1800. It is

A standard ('tree') rose: the ideal formation – and no supporting stake!

now possible to bud standard roses to give blooms in two different colours, e.g. apricot and pink, or even as a tricolour. These, too, originally came from a French nursery.

Storage of rose plants
Commercial rose growers who are able to control the temperature and humidity of their storage houses find it possible to keep rose roots, bare and unplanted, for an almost indefinite period. Amateurs, however, have to use more rough-and-ready methods when they get roses from the nursery that can't be planted immediately.

If the ground is frost-bound or waterlogged at the time the parcel arrives, it will be in order to leave the roses untouched in their packing for up to a week. If, at the end of this period, it is still unsafe to plant, the package may be opened with great care and the roots moistened. The plants, still in their bundle, can then go into a plastic bag, bucket or a carton from the supermarket filled with damp peat, and kept in a frost-proof but unheated room or shed.

If further delays occur, the roses can be taken out, the roots moistened if necessary and then temporarily heeled in – that is, placed side by side in a shallow v-shaped trench with the stocks supported by one side of it. The trench, which should be placed in a sheltered part of the garden, is then filled in with earth that is trodden down firmly. It is as well to make sure that the original earthmarks on the stems are not obliterated during this operation. The tops of the plants are protected against frost with branches or sacking.

Planting should be carried out as soon as possible.

Suckers

These are growths from the original UNDERSTOCK on to which the cultivated variety of rose has already been BUDDED. In other words, it is an attempt by the foster parent – possibly a brier – to mount a takeover bid at the expense of the rose that the gardener is trying to cultivate.

It is comparatively easy to detect suckers that appear on the straight stock of a standard rose, because it is obvious that they should not be there. If small enough, they can be rubbed off by hand – a far better procedure than cutting them out with a knife, with the attendant risk of wounding the stem by removing bark as well.

Suckers starting from the stems of shrub roses are less easily distinguishable from the main body of the plant but can often be recognized by the disparate colour of the wood or the colour and shape of the thorns (if any) or by the presence or absence of typical brier bristles. Furthermore, suckers usually thicken as they grow away from the stem; genuine shoots become thinner.

In the case of suspect shoots starting from or near the roots, it is important to make the diagnosis as early as possible. If the shoots are still small, a sharp tug may remove them. Otherwise, they will have to be cut off as near to the root as possible or even with part of the root. Cutting them off at ground level will leave the rump more vigorous than before.

Symbol, the rose as a

To the Greeks and Romans of classical times, the rose symbolized the high life, joyous celebrations, dissipation – perhaps even decadence (*see* HISTORY OF THE ROSE) – and it was the emblem of Venus, Goddess of Love. However, AD 312 marked a watershed: in this year, Constantine the Great, then emperor of the Western Empire, was converted to Christianity, and under the authority of the Roman Catholic Church, the rose eventually became an invitation to righteousness rather than an adjunct to pleasure.

As early as the 6th century, Bishop Medardus of Noyon, to the north of Paris, is reported as having blessed a rose festival and to have used the occasion to present a wreath of roses and twenty gold crowns as a dowry to the most virtuous maiden in his diocese – a foretaste of LE ROSIER DE MADAME HUSSON as well as of the GOLDEN ROSE.

A close association was soon established between the rose and the Virgin Mary (*see* ROSARY). In the following poem, probably dating from the 13th or early 14th century, the Holy Mother is assigned the role not merely of the flower but of the whole rose bush:

The rosebud is displayed as the symbol of health on the dress and in the hair of the lady chosen to advertise Beecham's Pills in the Illustrated London News *(1892). A report by the British Medical Association, published in 1909, said that the pills contained only aloes, powdered soap and powdered ginger, and that the ingredients of a box of fifty-six pills would cost only a twelfth of their sale price of $1\frac{1}{2}$ pence, but the advertising was nevertheless highly effective.*

> *Of a rose, a lovely rose,*
> *Of a rose, a lovely rose,*
> *Of a rose is al myn song.*
>
> *Lestynt lordynges, both elde and yinge,*
> *How this rose began to sprynge,*
> *Swych a rose to myn lykynge*
> *In all this world ne knowe I non.*
>
> *The aungil cam fro hevene tour,*
> *To grete Marye with gret honour,*
> *And seide sche schuld bere the flour,*
> *That schulde breke the fendes bond.*

In the secular world, the rose has persistently symbolized the maiden protecting her virginity with thorns. However, in many other examples, she is also portrayed as the embodiment of a beauty that is transient and perishable. Edmund Spenser (*c.* 1552–99) was to combine both images when he wrote:

> *Ah! see, whose fayre thing doest faine to see*
> *In springing floure the image of thy day!*
> *Ah! see the Virgin Rose, how sweetly shee*
> *Doth first press foorth with bashful modestee,*
> *That fairer seems the lesse ye see her may.*
> *Lo! see soone after how more bold and free*
> *Her bared bosome she doth broad displaye.*
> *Lo! see soone after, how she fades and falls away.*

In the traditional 'language of flowers', various roses came to have quite specific symbolic meanings. For example, according to *Brewer's Dictionary of Phrase and Fable*, the Burgundy rose (a small-flowered variety of *R. centifolia*) signified simplicity and beauty; the CHINA ROSE, grace or beauty ever fresh; the dog rose *(R. canina)*, pleasure mixed with pain; a faded rose, 'beauty is fleeting'; the MOSS ROSE, voluptuous love; the MUSK ROSE, capricious beauty; the PROVENCE ROSE, 'my heart is in flames'; a white rosebud, 'too young to love'; a spray full of white rosebuds, secrecy; a wreath of roses, beauty and virtue rewarded; and a yellow rose, infidelity.

From the days of the Crusades – 1096 onwards – when it became usual for each of the leaders of the various private armies to have his own coat of arms, the rose became involved in both politics and, since coats of arms later became hereditary, in HERALDRY. Traditionally, the 'Red Rose of Lancaster', which was to feature so prominently in stories of the Wars of the Roses (1455–85), was supposed to have been derived from the ROSE OF PROVINS, but the weight of evidence suggests that Edmund 'Crouchback', 1st Earl of Lancaster, had already adopted a red rose as his emblem long before he went to Provins. Lancaster's mother, Eleanor of Provence, the wife of Henry III (1207–72), had already adopted the white rose as her personal symbol, and this descended through Edward II, Edward III and the latter's youngest son Edmund, Duke of York, to Richard, Duke of York, leader of the Yorkists in the opening stages of the war. Thus the scene in Shakespeare's *Henry VI, Part I* (II, iv) in which the two sides chose their emblems during a quarrel in the Temple gardens in London, has no historical foundation. No doubt if the Yorkists in the field wished to wear a white rose, they had to make do with *Rosa arvensis*, the field rose, or with the white form of *R. canina*, rather than the semi-double form of *R. alba*, the variety more appropriate to royalty. The white rose placed in the centre of a golden sun was adopted by Edward IV in 1461 following the Yorkist victory at Mortimer's Cross, as memorialized in the lines of Shakespeare's *Richard III:* 'Now is the Winter of our discontent made glorious Summer by the *Sun* of York.' This rose-in-sun symbol later appeared (1465) on a gold coin that bore the name 'rose noble'.

The 'Tudor rose', adopted at the end of the Wars of the Roses as a badge of reconciliation between the two sides, consists of a double rose with an outer ring of red petals and a centre of white ones. The so-called 'York and Lancaster rose' is a hybrid DAMASK ROSE in which some of the white petals are suffused or blotched with pink, an untidy blossom far removed from the ordered simplicity of the Tudor device. According to Roy Shepherd, it was first described by the Spanish botanist, Nicholas Monardes, in 1551, sixty-six years after the end of the Wars of the Roses.

The political life of the rose did not, of course, begin or end with the Wars of the Roses. Even in Roman times, the rose bower or enclosed rose garden was traditionally a place in which confidential matters were discussed. In private houses, where the rose was as much an ornament indoors as in the garden and guests would sit with roses on the table or painted or embossed on the ceiling above, it was understood that nothing said among friends *sub rosa* ('under the rose') should be the noised abroad. In time, this convention was extended to include conspiracies, and the white rose (a fully double one as distinct from the Yorkist semi-double) became a token of recognition among Jacobite conspirators of the 18th century who wished to turn out the Hanoverian kings and bring back the Stuarts. In addition, in the 16th century, a picture of a rose was placed over confessionals, to emphasize the confidentiality of the matters confessed.

The rose has also been widely adopted as an emblem without genealogical or armorial significance by nations, provincial states and municipalities (*see also* POSTAGE STAMPS, ROSES ON). The rose is England's national emblem as it also is of Czechoslovakia, Honduras, IRAN, Poland and Romania. Among English cities that include a rose in their civic crests are Cambridge, Carlisle, Derby, Eastbourne, Leicester, Lowestoft, Morecambe, Newark, Oldham, Southampton and Westminster (London). The Lancashire County Council and the West and North Yorkshire authorities have also, predictably, chosen roses to decorate their insignia.

Elsewhere, the presence of a rose on a crest, etc. may be taken as an indication of national or civic good taste or a hint that there are rose nurseries in the neighbourhood. The *fleur de lys* is the national emblem of France, but the city of Grenoble is one of many that include the rose as part of their crest. The arms of the Finnish Republic show a lion rampant, sword in hand, slashing away in a field of five-petalled blossoms that could be roses – or, possibly, bramble flowers. However, in China, from which so many of the world's most wonderful roses have come, it is not specially honoured.

In the US, the rose has been adopted as the state emblem of Georgia, Iowa, New York and North Dakota, as well as by the District of Columbia, and certainly the observant traveller will find many other telling examples the world over.

See also MINDEN ROSE, ROSE IN POETRY, ROSE IN LYRICS, ROMAN DE LA ROSE.

Tantau, Mathias and family

The Tantau nursery at Uetersen, Holstein, West Germany, with a yearly output of some four million roses and 10,000 square metres of glasshouse space, is a large-scale production centre almost entirely wholesale, as well as the original source of several hundred new rose varieties. It was founded in 1906 as a general nursery, but with an eye to forestry, by Mathias Tantau Sr, the father of the present owner. However, from the end of World War I, Tantau began to specialize in roses, and in the following quarter of a century, he launched some sixty successful varieties including, in the single year 1942–43, 'Tantau's Überraschung' ('Tantau's Surprise'), 'Tantau's Triumph' ('Cinnabar') and 'Käthe Duvigneau', the last-named, a mid-red cluster-flowered rose, being the best known outside Germany. Shortly after, these were followed by 'Silberlachs' ('Silver Salmon'), 'Märchenland' and 'Fanal'.

In 1946, Mathias Tantau Sr handed over the nursery to his son and namesake, and it was during the post-war years that Tantau's roses became truly world famous. 'Garnette' (1951), a deep-red cluster-flowered rose with small, very full flowers that are splendid for cutting, first won acclaim in the US where it was launched by JACKSON & PERKINS before becoming popular in Europe; it grows especially well under glass. In 'Baby Masquerade' ('Baby Carnaval', 1956), Tantau entered the realm of MINIATURES with a rose that now has worldwide appeal.

Among the LARGE-FLOWERED Tantau roses, 'Prima Ballerina', a deep pink, was launched in 1957. 'Superstar' ('Tropicana'), with its sensationally brilliant vermilion colouring, appeared in 1960 and has maintained its popularity, despite the need to take anti-MILDEW precautions, at least in Britain. 'Duftwolke' ('Fragrant Cloud', 'Nuage Parfumé', 1967) set a new standard in modern, scented, large-flowered roses, and 'Landora' ('Sunblest', 1970) with deep yellow blooms is widely used as a bedding rose.

On the continent of Europe, where more flowers are grown under glass than in the UK, Tantau has been successful with 'Belinda' (1971), an orange-blend cluster-flowered rose; 'Magitta' (1981), a ROYAL NATIONAL ROSE SOCIETY medal winner; and the more recent 'Ilseta', 'Perl-Ilseta' and

'Orange Ilseta', the blooms of which will last up to twenty days.

In 1985, Tantau began placing special emphasis on their selection of particularly fragrant large-flowered roses, such as 'Polarstern' ('Polar Star', 1982), white; 'Frohsinn' (1982), peach-yellow; and 'Duftgold' (1981), butter-yellow. 'Polar Star' was voted ROSE OF THE YEAR for 1985 in the ROTY annual poll among British growers.

References to many other Tantau roses will be found elsewhere in this book.

Tea roses

The early history of the tea rose is related with that of the CHINA ROSES, and the resultant climbing forms are included under CLIMBING ROSES.

Most of the shrub tea roses are as delicate as the colours of their flowers but, to judge by nursery catalogues, are still cherished in suitable habitats by devotees both in Europe and the United States. The original progenitors of this class were described as 'tea-scented roses' but intensive hybridization transformed or diluted the original fragrance, and the word 'scented' fell into disuse. The teas in these cases were either from 'Hume's Blush Tea-Scented China', which provided the pink element, or from 'Park's Yellow Tea-scented China', which offered pale yellow. The best cultivars can be credited to crosses between noisettes x teas crossed with pink BOURBONS x teas.

'Adam' (Adam, 1830), sometimes classed as a climber, was one of the earlier introductions, producing light pink, very fragrant flowers. 'Catherine Mermet' (Guillot *fils*, 1869) was highly praised by the great Gertrude Jekyll for its translucent inner petals of pale soft pink and salmon, contrasting with the outer petals of deeper pink to lilac. The peaked centres foreshadowed the modern style of bloom, and the long stalks make this variety good for cutting. It is still obtainable but, we are warned, it hates rain.

The 'Duchesse de Brabant', an unpretentious plant, has tulip-shaped rose-pink blooms, which, Roy Shepherd tells us, were often to be seen in the buttonhole of America's President Franklin D. Roosevelt.

'Maman Cochet' (Cochet, 1893) has that pleasing characteristic of the China roses – colour deepening with age. The petals open pale pink with a darker pink centre, but later the outer petals darken, too, to match the inner. The lemon zone at the base of the petals adds a pleasing gloss.

The blooms of 'Marie van Houtte' (Ducher, 1871) are cream, shaded on the reverse with carmine down to the golden base, and are very double and fragrant – a vigorous and bushy plant, much favoured in the south of France.

'Madame Bravy' is famous for having been one of the assumed parents of 'La France', officially the first of the LARGE-FLOWERED ROSES, formerly known as the HYBRID TEAS. It was first raised by the Guillot nursery of Pont-de-Chervy about 18 miles (29 km) from Lyon, France, in 1844, assigned (under the name 'Danzille') to another Guillot nursery in Lyon in 1846 and introduced as 'Madame Bravy' two years later. The flowers are cream, flushed or streaked with carmine. 'Souvenir d'un Ami' is much admired for the silky nature of its petals, which are pale rose, tinged with salmon, and strongly scented. Some observers feel that 'Frau Karl Druschki' (*see* SHRUB ROSES), often classified as a HYBRID PERPETUAL rose, should come within the tea-rose sector.

'Safrano' (Beauregard, 1839) is perhaps the most sensationally coloured of this tea-rose group. The flowers are a blend of apricot orange changing to creamy-pink parchment, and the plant provides them in abundance.

Among the other tea roses obtainable from specialist nurseries, 'Homère' (pink with white centres) and 'Perle des Jardins' (sulphur-yellow to buff-rose) are said to be hardier-than average. This also applies to the bush form of 'Lady Hillingdon', which Lowe & Shawyer introduced in 1910. The apricot-to-orange flowers have the true tea scent and are framed in grey-green leaflets developed from plum-coloured shoots. The Climbing 'Lady Hillingdon' is equally tough.

'Buy My Sweet Roses', from Thomas Rowlandson's Characteristic Sketches of the Lower Orders *(London, 1820)*.

'Thorns'

Few writers on gardening matters have much to say about thorns: they prefer to ignore them. Academic botanists go still further and have established to their satisfaction that the *prickles* that grown on rosebushes are quite distinct from true *thorns*. Thorns, they tell us, are sharp pointed structures representing a modified branch, as in the blackthorn. The prickle, on the other hand, is a superficial growth arising from the skin cells of the plant and seldom involves more than a few of the underlying cells. They may occur on a branch but can also be present on the stalks of leaves, on the mid-ribs of leaflets, on the flower stalks, on the receptacle and even on the calyx – as, for instance, in *Rosa laevigata*, the Cherokee rose. Thus, to them, every rose is without a thorn, though those who have handled *Rosa sericea pteracantha* or even the more civilized R. CENTIFOLIA will know better.

The 'thorns' on roses do differ from species to species: centifolia prickles are scattered and nearly straight; 'alba' prickles are hooked and scattered; damascena prickles are numerous and dilated at the base; gallica prickles are fewer and softer.

The best-known 'thornless' rose is the BOURBON variety 'Zéphirine Drouhin' (Bizot, 1868). It is semi-double, cerise and fragrant, and can be treated either as a shrub or as a climber. The GALLICA ROSE 'Belle de Crécy' is almost without prickles, as are two WILD ROSES, *R. glauca* and *R. pendulina*.

Truss

This short word – which to the sailor means to secure with rope, to the poulterer the process of preparing a chicken for cooking, to the coiffeur a method of pinning up the hair, to the doctor an appliance to keep the intestines and other organs in place, and to the farmer a bundle of straw or hay – signifies to rose growers any part of the rose plant that projects beyond the leaves – that is, the flowers or flower buds. The word came into use in 1688, when it meant a compact cluster of flowers growing on one stalk.

Understocks

The understocks on which roses are BUDDED are usually given a heat treatment to ensure that they are free of virus, and for this reason, they are grown in commercial nurseries in a separate area known as a stockblock. Canes from the plants are cut in September and cuttings taken from them are planted in the open in November or December. In the larger nurseries, the cuttings are positioned in rows marked out with tarred paper in which holes have been pre-punched at the correct intervals. The paper acts as a MULCH, conserving moisture. The cuttings should have rooted by the following May and can then be budded in July.

The budwood with which the understocks are budded will have been collected the previous December or even later, and placed in cold storage at a temperature slightly below freezing point. If necessary, it can be kept in storage even until the following mid-summer.

If the budded plants are to be grown in one season for cultivation under glass for cut flowers, the top of the understock is broken over by being cut halfway through the stem, between ten and twenty days after budding. This 'breaking over' is carried out mechanically. Later, the top of the understock is completely removed as soon as the budded eye has produced a bloom, and the plant is left to grow on in the field until the end of the year. The work is carried out in two stages, so that the rose is not at any time completely devoid of foliage.

If, on the other hand, the budded understock is to go to a nursery where it will be grown on and sold at the end of the following year, the budded understock will be delivered to the nursery with the bud in a dormant state. In this case, the top growth of the understock will not have been broken over but will have been left untouched, to discourage the bud from developing. The understock is left intact until the January following the budding, when it is replanted, and the twigs at the top mowed off and chopped up so that they do not have to be collected and taken away. The rest of the understock is then cut by hand to a point just above the bud, which then develops into a rose to be sold in the autumn.

Budded understocks for nurseries are sold in sizes that are graded according to the circumference of the root at the point where it becomes fibrous: 4–6 mm, 5–8 mm and 8–12 mm. The middle size is the one that is most often planted.

Understandably, understocks without THORNS are preferred to the armed varieties, but in cases where thorns are present, some planters go to the trouble of disarming their cuttings by rolling them on a rough board without, it is hoped, damaging them in other respects.

Rosa canina, the dog rose in various forms (especially the 'thornless' variety), is popular as an understock with professional breeders for growing in fields, but it is said to be not especially successful on light soils, and sometimes yields smallish plants, unless the bud applied to it has come from a really vigorous parent.

R. coriifolia 'froebelii', another members of the Caninae group, is also extensively used in fields as an understock. It was introduced in 1890 by the Froebel Nursery of Zurich and is known to the trade as 'Laxa', not to be confused with *R. laxa*, a wild rose belonging to the same group as *R. rugosa*, which is also used, but mainly in the US, as an understock for STANDARD ROSES. 'Laxa' is popular in Britain and in the Rhineland, and is grown in quantity in Denmark and the Netherlands as well as in the UK. It throws no suckers and the neck is clean of hairs. It therefore needs no preparation before budding, which is more than can be said for *R. multiflora*, a species used extensively in the US for budding in areas where BLACKSPOT is not to be feared.

For larger plants, *R. eglanteria* and the aforementioned *R. rugosa* are often used as understocks and, if conditions are sufficiently mild, *R. indica major*. The 'Manetti' rose, a pink semi-double form of NOISETTE originally raised from seed by Signor Manetti of the botanic gardens at Monza near Milan, was introduced into England by Signor Crevelli, who recommended it as a stock to Thomas Rivers of Sawbridgeworth around 1835. It is still popular today because of its vigour, which makes for a high success rate and allows it to be budded later than most other varieties. Its roots, too, are shallow, which makes for easy lifting.

United States, the rose in the

The 17th and 18th centuries
Roses got off to a good start in America. Edward Winslow

(1595–1655), one of the original Pilgrim Fathers who landed in Massachusetts in 1620, reported a year later that 'an abundance of roses, white, red, and damask, single but very sweete indeed' had been planted by the settlers. Dr William Blackstone, who came to the colony in 1623 and was the first to live on the future site of Boston, is said to have grown *Rosa pimpinellifolia* either there or at Pawtucket where he moved in 1634 to live in greater privacy while he established his orchard there. John Josselyn, who visited the Plymouth Plantation in 1636 and afterwards wrote a book entitled *New England Rarities Discovered* (published in 1672), mentioned the 'Sweet Bryer and other English Roses' that, he declared, were flourishing there. Such roses were no better than and probably not as good as those that John Gerard had described in his *Herball* nearly fifty years earlier, but they were a link with the home that the colonists had left behind them, probably for ever.

William Penn, when he returned to America in 1699 after a visit to England, brought with him eighteen rose bushes, to which he referred in his *Book of Physics*. However, John Bartram – whose garden above the Schuylkill River in what is now Pennsylvania he opened in 1729 and which is said to be the first truly botanic garden in North America – was more interested in American plants that were dissimilar to those in England (from which he could get seeds to send to his wealthy clients at home) than in English plants for the limited American market. He is supposed to have supplied George Washington with an *R. eglanteria*, but if so, the transaction must have taken place before 1777, the year Bartram died. At that time, the redcoats were threatening to overrun his garden, so it is just possible that the rose was entrusted to Washington for safety.

A survey of the roses grown in Colonial times in Virginia, undertaken by the Colonial Williamsburg Foundation, suggests that about a dozen roses were to be found in gardens there before the end of the 18th century. These included two natives: *R. palustris* from about 1726, and *R. virginiana* from 1762, though this last had been loosely described by Parkinson more than a century earlier in England. The cultivated roses included: *R. canina*, the dog rose; ROSA CENTIFOLIA, the cabbage rose; *R. centifolia muscosa*, the MOSS ROSE; *R. damascena*, the DAMASK ROSE; *R. damascena versicolor*, the 'York and Lancaster rose'; *R. eglanteria*, sweet brier; *R.* GALLICA, the French rose; and *R. gallica versicolor*, known as 'Rosa mundi.' Today these roses can be seen in Colonial Williamsburg in the Governor's Palace Gardens, particularly in the boxwood garden to the west of the main ballroom garden.

On a scale less ambitious than Bartram's, John Clayton (1685–1773), who came to Virginia in 1705 and served for fifty-one years as Clerk of Gloucester County, devoted his attention to studying America's native plants, and assisted the great Dutch botanist, John Frederick Gronovius, in the preparation of his work *Flora virginica*, the 2nd edition of which, using the LINNAEAN system of nomenclature, appeared in 1762. Gronovius, too, included *R. palustris* and

R. virginiana in his identifications, and credited 'Dr D. D. Johannes Claytonus' with having observed them. Meanwhile, Robert Prince had founded the Prince Nursery at Flushing, New York in 1737, and was the first to conduct business on an international scale.

Among the residents of Virginia, Lady Skipwith, with an estate in the Dan River area of southern Virginia, was noted for her enthusiasm for roses. She was the wife of Sir Peyton Skipwith, whose ancestor, Sir Harry, had been knighted by James I. However, during the English Civil War his estates were made forfeit by Cromwell's men as a punishment for raising forces for the king, Charles I, and he was executed together with all but one of his sons. The descendants of this remaining son, seeing no future at home, emigrated to Virginia and prospered there. Lady Skipwith declared that she had a tolerable collection of roses, among which were 'double and single yellow roses' and 'marbled and cabbage rose[s]'. Henry William, the Baron van Stiegel, a glass manufacturer, had by 1733 also acquired a reputation as a collector of rose varieties.

During the American War of Independence, Virginia was in turmoil. The story is told that, when the Redcoats approached Yorktown, General Thomas Nelson (1738–89), one of those who signed the Declaration of Independence and who had bankrupted himself to pay off debts incurred in the service of the colonists, had to remove his family to Offley, near Richmond. His wife took with her, for safety, what came to be known as the 'Offley Rose'. This flower was extensively written about in rosarian literature of the time and, for a while, achieved legendary status, but modern opinion inclines to the view that it was simply a particularly fine specimen of *R. gallica*.

Then there was John Custis, a pugnacious planter, whose widowed daughter-in-law, Martha Dandrige Custis, married George Washington. Custis received plants from England sent by the botanical collector Peter Collinson, John Bartram's patron. It is not clear how much interest Martha Washington took in roses (though a variety of *R. roxburghii* was named after her), but the estate of Mount Vernon on the Potomac river had so many roses on show that, on one occasion, picking them took two whole days. George Washington was certainly interested in garden plants, as his signature (to be seen in a photograph in Ann Leighton's scholarly work *American Gardens in the Eighteenth Century*) appears on the outside cover of a garden catalogue of the day.

The catalogue on which Washington relied was entitled *The Universal Gardener and Botanist, or a General Dictionary of Gardening and Botany Exhibiting in Botanical Arrangement according to the Linnaean System every Tree, Shrub and Herbaceous Plant that merits culture either for use or ornament or curiosity in every department of gardens*. This imposing production had been prepared by 'Thomas Mawe, Gardener to His Grace the Duke of Leeds, and John Abercrombie, Authors of *Every Man his own Gardener* etc.', and it was printed in London. On roses, Abercrombie and Mawe took a conservative line:

The sorts of roses are very numerous and botanists find it very difficult to determine with accuracy which are species and which varieties, as well as which are varieties of the respective species. Linnaeus and some eminent authors are inclined to think that there is only one real species of rose which is *Rosa canina* or Dog Rose of the hedges.

Nevertheless, Mawe and Abercrombie's list include: *R. canina; R. centifolia; R. alba; R. gallica*, together with its variety 'Velvet Rose'; the white damask ; *R. foetida bicolor; R. cinnamomea*, the cinnamon rose; *R. alpina inermis* (now *pendulina*), the alpine rose without thorns; *R. moschata*, 'supposed to be a variety only of the Evergreen MUSK ROSE'; *R. sempervirens;* and *R. villosa*, 'the apple-bearing rose with large single red flowers, large prickly hips as big as little apples. (Pulp has an agreeable acid relish often made into tolerable good sweetmeat).'

Mawe and Abercrombie were an oddly assorted pair, and when the two first met, Abercrombie, the son of a market gardener, declared that Mawe was so powdered and bedaubed with gold lace that he thought he must be in the presence of the Duke of Leeds himself. However, they kept in touch for thirty-eight years.

Like Washington, Thomas Jefferson, who became the third President of the United States, was a gardening man. He exchanged plants with André Thouin, whose influence as cultivator-in-chief at the Jardin des Plantes in Paris had survived the upheavals of the French Revolution and the Napoleonic era that followed. Jefferson had been sent to Paris with John Adams and Benjamin Franklin (another of those who corresponded regularly with Peter Collinson) as one of the plenipotentiaries in the negotiations that led to formal independence from Great Britain in 1783. In 1785, Jefferson succeeded Franklin as Minister in Paris, remaining there until 1789 when Washington recalled him to be Secretary of State. Back home, his garden book entry for 6 July 1791 shows that he ordered thirty roses (three of ten different kinds) from William Prince's nursery, and he is also believed to have been the recipient of the first plant of *R. multibracteata*, which reached him at his Virginia estate, Monticello, in 1799. It should be remembered, however, that on larger estates roses of the day, being non-REMONTANT, were often prized more as shrubs for hedging and for soil stabilization than as adornments to the flowerbed.

On the West Coast, the cultivated rose secured a foothold through the establishment of the Spanish missions, San Diego (founded in 1769) being the first of the original twenty-one. There is evidence that the missionaries introduced *R. damascena bifera*, *R. centifolia*, and (later) *R. banksiae*. However, for the time being, the main developments in rose culture and hybridization occurred in the eastern states.

The 19th century
It was in the United States that the first-ever cross between a 'European' rose and one of the newer CHINA ROSES was made. John Champney, the rice-planter of Charleston, is thought to have used pollen from 'Parsons' Pink China' to fertilize the white MUSK ROSE of Miller. Put in botanical terms, the equation was *(R. chinensis* x *R. gigantea)* x *(R. moschata)* = 'Champney's Pink Cluster Rose'. The new hybrid had the clustered flowers, fragrance and climbing habit of the musk rose, with the semi-double pink flowers of 'Parsons' Pink China'; it soon became locally popular. Graham Thomas puts the date of Champney's hybridizing at about 1802, and it was evidently only some years later that Philippe Noisette succeeded in raising a different generation of 'Champney's Pink Cluster' from seed to give the first NOISETTE rose. Breeders, however, showed little interest until the strain of the original 'Champney's Pink Cluster', raised by the Flushing, New York nursery of William Prince, became more widely known.

It was in the 1820s that two of the first American botanical societies were founded: the one in Pennsylvania in 1827, and the one in Massachusetts in 1829.

William Prince and Samuel and John Feast of Baltimore all began experiments in the first half of the 19th century with *R. setigera*, the prairie rose and the only native American species of climbing habit. One of these, 'Baltimore Belle' (1843) a pale blush rose, was awarded a silver medal by the Horticultural Society of Maryland, and it is still to be found in some nurseries, but Feast's other notable success, 'Queen of the Prairies', with blooms of deep rose stripped with white, seems to have disappeared.

A further American success occurred when a New York attorney and amateur rose breeder, George F. Harison, discovered the merits of a rose that had grown for years in the family garden but had been overlooked. The plants were hardy, and it has since been conjectured that it was a hybrid of two species of the Pimpinellifoliae group. Its blooms appear in early summer and are modest in size, but are nearly double, deep yellow and well-scented. 'Harison's Yellow' is of upright growth, takes little room in the garden and is still to be found in Europe as well as in American nurseries. Harison exchanged his rose with Thomas Hogg, the New York nurseryman, receiving a camellia in return, but Hogg lacked the resources to market it and this task was taken in hand by the Prince nursery in Flushing. It became popular over a wide area of the US despite being nicknamed (unjustifiably) 'The Yellow Rose of Texas' (*see* LYRICS, THE ROSE IN).

The Prince nursery remained in the public eye. In 1846, the *Prince Manual of Roses* by William Robert Prince, great-grandson of the founder, appeared, listing, among other things, 144 varieties of BOURBON ROSES and twenty perpetually flowering MOSS ROSES.

Robert Buist (1802–80), who came from Scotland to America, was another figure of influence in the 19th-century American rose scene. He set up what we would now call a garden centre in Philadelphia in 1828, supplying shrubs, gardening sundries and cut flowers and roses in partnership with Thomas Hibbert, another rose man. After Hibbert's death, Buist retained the name 'Hibbert & Buist' until 1837, when he moved to larger premises. Edith Campbell Schurr, in her introduction to the facsimile edition of Buist's *The Rose Manual*, tells us that the success of Buist's business was such that he had to move twice more, on each occasion to larger premises. *The Rose Manual*, the first edition of which appeared in 1844, was not Buist's only successful book. His *American Flower Garden Directory*, first published in 1832, ran to six editions. Among other classic roses that he introduced in the United States were the white damask 'Madame Hardy' (Hardy, 1832); 'Aimée Vibert' (Vibert, 1828), a white noisette; and Thomas Rivers' 'George the Fourth' (Rivers, 1820), a dark red hybrid China, a rare rose but still obtainable at the time of writing from Lowe's Own Root Nursery, Nashua, New Hampshire.

To some, Buist's writings have an old-fashioned flavour in as much as he refers to 'DWARF ROSES' when he means 'roses suitable for the rosebed' – as distinct from what he called 'STANDARD ROSES', known to Americans as 'tree roses'. However, he was progressive in realizing that women were to be the amateur rose growers of the future.

American nurseries participated whole-heartedly in the development of the HYBRID PERPETUAL class. William Prince's list of 1846 included seventy-four imported varieties, and in 1855 W. B. Osborne in Los Angeles advertised 20,000 rose plants representing 100 different varieties. The famous hybrid perpetual rose 'American Beauty' was also an importation, which arrived in the United States in 1882 and enjoyed an immediate success. It had been raised by a French nurseryman Henri Lédéchaux and was introduced in Europe in 1875 under the name 'Madame Ferdinand Jamain'. The original blooms, still obtainable from leading 'old' rose nurseries in the US, are of intense pink shaded with smoky carmine. In 1925, it was named the official rose of the United States. However, some modern florists have been loath to restrict such a commercially successful name to one variety and, therefore, have attached it to a number of commercial cut-roses of variable quality.

Some local hybridization of hybrid perpetuals did, however, take place about the same time as the arrival of 'American Beauty'. Marshall P. Wilder', with very full blooms of scarlet crimson, was raised by Ellwanger & Barry and introduced in 1884; it is still obtainable.

R. rugosa, which had been known in England from 1796, did not reach the US until nearly 100 years later (1882) and came there direct from Russia, where it had been developed from the wild Siberian form. Its hardiness appealed to American nurserymen, and some enthusiastic hybridization took place, though none of the resulting varieties is listed today.

In 1888, Louis Späth (of the Berlin nursery of which Karl Druschki was at one time manager) sent plants of *R. wichuraiana* to the Arnold Arboretum in Massachusetts who, two years later, distributed them to American nurseries. One of these was the Newport Nursery of Rhode Island, where an employee, Michael Horvath, was alive to the possibilities of this vigorous, strongly scented and semi-evergreen species, and he raised some very promising hybrids.

His success may well have encouraged Dr Walter Van Fleet (who had hitherto been concerned mainly in improving such things as chestnuts, gooseberries, pears and freesias for the US Federal Bureau of the Plant Industry) to turn to roses. One of the trial grounds of the US Department of Agriculture was situated at Glenn Dale between Baltimore and Washington (close to the present-day Godard Space Flight Center), and Dr Van Fleet established his own house and rose garden next to the trial ground. One of his early successes was 'American Pillar' (1902), a rose with *R. wichuraiana*, *R. setigera* and probably a red hybrid perpetual in its parentage. Some years later, he was successful with a cross between *R. wichuraiana* and the apricot tea rose 'Safrano', which gave a shell-pink, large-flowered climber that he called 'Daybreak'. He sold all but one of the plants to the Peter Henderson nursery, where unfortunately all were lost, and Henderson had to return to Dr Van Fleet for a new supply. When these were successfully raised and introduced in 1910, Henderson renamed the rose after the Doctor, and today it remains one of the most popular and reliable varieties in its field.

Another rose used to promote business: 'The Puritan' is not cultivated today, but was presumably a rose of the purest white.

195

The famous 'Max Graf', the cross between *R. rugosa* and *R. wichuraiana*, was discovered in an American garden and introduced 1919 by James H. Bowditch of Pomfret Center, Connecticut. However, we have now moved into the new century and must have one more look at the old.

For most of the 19th century, rosarians and breeders sustained the close links between the rose and the North Atlantic seaboard, an area not exceptionally suited to the rose's constitution. Not even the decline of the Indians in the West, nor the improvement in US agriculture, nor the Gold Rush of 1848–49, which raised the population of California from 12,000 in 1850 to 380,000 in 1860, nor even the joining of the Central Pacific to the Union Pacific railroad in Utah in 1869, which established transcontinental railroad travel, alerted rose growers to the amazing opportunities that lay open to them in the west. As late as 1924, the JACKSON & PERKINS COMPANY, then celebrating its first fifty years, declared that, despite having already set up a rose garden in California, the ones in Newark, New York were located where the best stock could be grown. All this took place before the US film industry (which needed instant sunshine even more than roses) became fully established in Hollywood, and before express delivery of roses by air became a matter of routine.

However, there was one genius who realized clearly enough that there had to be a self-generating US rose industry: the brilliant Henry B. Ellwanger, who died at the age of thirty-two from typhoid, which he contracted while attending a rose show in Boston. In his famous work, *The Rose* (1882), Ellwanger voiced his dissatisfaction with the supremacy, at that time, of British and French varieties of rose (*see* HISTORY OF THE ROSE). In his international overview of the industry, he credited Feast of Baltimore with three good varieties (all introduced in 1843); the Revd James Sprunt of Kenansville, North Carolina, Joshua Pierce of Washington DC and James Pentland of Baltimore each rated two good varieties; and Daniel Boll of New York and Anthony Cook of Baltimore had introduced one each. However, in Ellwanger's view, no American nursery deserved to be placed among the top twenty in the world.

This state of affairs was highly undesirable, according to Ellwanger. 'A drawback to the purchase of new varieties,' he wrote, 'is the knowledge, gained from past experience, that a large number of those sent out as new sorts are not sufficiently distinct from known varieties to prove of any value. This is notably the case with French roses.' One French offering, 'Gloire de Paris', especially provoked him: 'A deceit,' he commented, 'sent out as a new sort; it is but "Anne de Diesbach"' (which was one of his favourites).

The naming and the quality of English roses was more effectively supervised, but here, too, there were pitfalls. Some of the finer roses, he noted, faded badly 'if exposed to our hot sun'. Among hybrid perpetuals, 'Dr Andry' was 'a better rose in England in in this country'. 'Princess Beatrice' (1872), a rose from William Paul & Son, 'fades quickly and is not desirable'. 'S. Reynolds Hole' of the same year is 'shy in the autumn and subject to mildew. A rose of great beauty but not at all adapted to general cultivation.'

However, all was not lost, for, as Ellwanger put it: 'With an extent of territory that gives greater variation of climate and soil than is to be found in any other country, it must be that America will yet produce her share of fine roses.'

General conditions for cultivation

'The history of roses in America has been more or less a question of the survival of the fittest.' These, the opening words in that standard treatise *Roses for All American Climates* (1924) by George C. Thomas, Jr, sums up the problem faced by the amateur rose enthusiast in the US. The differences are immense: in Cape Cod, for instance, which stretches a mere 30 miles (48 km) out to sea, the season for rose growing is six weeks longer than in New England generally.

The distribution of the wild rose species in the United States bears witness to the wide variations in temperature, rainfall and hours of sunlight in different parts of the country. Thus, *Rosa carolina, R. nitida, R. palustris, R. setigera* and *R. virginiana* are all easterners used to the rigours of the Atlantic seaboard, whereas *R. californica, R. nutkana* and *R. woodsii* prefer the less extreme conditions of the west. The pink-flowered *R. acicularis*, the Arctic rose, though not exclusive to the United States, is a star performer, venturing as far north as the Arctic Circle from New Brunswick, Canada to the Bering Strait, and it is still grown in American gardens.

The AMERICAN ROSE SOCIETY divides the country into eighteen regions, partly for administrative reasons, but here we paint with a broader brush, so that, within each area, there will be some variation, particularly in California where coastal and montane climates are juxtaposed, and the soil varies from sand dunes to adobe brick-clay.

In the north, in a band running from Maine in the east, through the Great Lakes states to North Dakota, Montana, Idaho and Washington, growers expect long periods of frost, with the thermometer well below zero. In this region and in some areas further south (especially in the east), measures have to be taken to protect roses through the winter, either by mounding up the earth 6 to 12 inches (15–30 cm) high around them or by removing them to a covered trench; some enthusiasts grow their roses in tubs and move them under cover during the winter. Climbers that are to flower in the following year on wood grown during the current season will clearly need more protection than those that flower on wood grown during the new season. Ramblers are often pegged down and covered with burlap or evergreen boughs.

In this northern region, there is a short growing season and variable rainfall, which, combined with a limited ration of sunshine, adds to the danger of BLACKSPOT. There will probably be some fog near the coast, hence the prudent gardener chooses vigorous growers, resistant to blackspot and capable of profiting from the short summer.

Under these severe conditions, fully double roses, which

open only in response to warm sunshine, are at a discount, as are also those that BALL or become discoloured when it rains. Petals of good substance are needed for protection from the weather, and roses that flower only for a short period are acceptable, since the summer itself is brief. In addition to *R. acicularis*, *R. hugonis* (the yellow pimpernell-type rose), *R. rugosa* and *R. gallica* are hardy enough to pull through, and among the earlier of the 'modern' roses, 'Grüss an Teplitz' is recommended as a reliable red for this area.

The climate of the central region, immediately below the northern band, allows more freedom to the rose grower. There, frosts are not as common, and the summers are prolonged; the rain falls mostly near the coast (where there is also some fog), and the climate is drier inland. Here, varieties that bloom longer, with flowers of substance, come into their own, though, in the damper areas, there is some risk of MILDEW, blackspot and balling.

The choice of roses for growers in this sector is wide, and varieties appear and disappear with surprising rapidity. The latest reliable cultivars, however, are those that have undergone tests at the ALL-AMERICAN ROSE SELECTION trial gardens established in twenty-one states.

The southeastern states in the region south of Virginia and east of the Mississippi have their own problems. Here, the summers are prolonged, and roses with a correspondingly long flowering period are in demand, as are those with a profusion of petals that open slowly and with decorum. Mildew can be a problem near the coasts, and the long sunny days lead to fading the more delicate pinks and cause 'blueing' in some of the reds. Loss of foliage can also be a problem with some varieties.

The southern band across the interior of the country, from Texas to southern California, is the driest and hottest, but there are late frosts too, and roses that are late starters in growth and flowering enjoy an advantage. Those with large blooms and substantial petals are needed to withstand the drought and desert winds, but roses that seek to limit evaporation by shedding their leaves are not acceptable. However, extensive irrigation allows the benefits of almost continuous sunshine and rapid growth to be enjoyed without some of the disadvantages, and Tyler, near the eastern border of Texas, has become one of the world's largest rose production areas.

There remain the coastal northwest and southwest Pacific areas, which run between Oregon and souther California. In the north, the presence of the ocean moderates the temperature; frost is not a problem and there are long, relatively mild summers in between the spring and the autumn rains, which average 60–80 inches (152–203 cm).

In Oregon, the climate is especially suitable for growing the kind of roses that do well in the UK and continental Europe, and travellers from across the Atlantic are likely to meet old friends such as 'Madame Caroline Testout', produced by Pernet-Ducher nearly a century ago, 'Frau Karl Druschki' – almost as old and known in the US as 'Snow Queen' – 'Mermaid', a high-flying, remontant climber, not tolerant of severe winters, and the thornless 'Zéphirine Drouhin'. The city of PORTLAND and its surroundings are the special home of the rose here.

The climate of the southern coastal Pacific region is markedly different and raises special problems for rose enthusiasts. The growing season is a very long one, starting in the New Year and continuing through the spring and summer and far into the autumn. Consequently, roses that do well during the cool periods at the beginning and end of the season are at a disadvantage during the summer, when periods of moderate heat are interspersed with intense heat waves and scorching winds. There is little or no rain during the summer, but the evenings are cold, with winds off the sea and some fog, and growers need to be watchful for signs of mildew, blackspot and balling. However, there are wide differences between some areas close to the sea and others a short distance away in the hills behind.

One has only to read a few issues of the *American Rose* magazine to realize how successfully enthusiastic amateurs all over the US have succeeded in overcoming their difficulties and how successful the All-American Rose Selections organization has been in fostering the 'all-climate' rose.

See also AMERICAN ROSE FOUNDATION, AMERICAN ROSE SOCIETY, ROSE BOWL, WILD ROSES (North America), and GESELLSCHAFT SCHWEIZERISCHER ROSENFREUNDE (for data on rose-growing under alpine conditions).

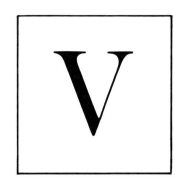

Verein Deutscher Rosenfreunde

The Association of German Friends of Roses was founded in Hamburg in September 1883, and published its first rose journal three years later. Its first independent rose show was held in Trier in 1891, and the Rosarium of Sangerhausen, near Dresden, was set up in 1903.

The VDR survived the turmoil of World War I but was virtually suppressed under the Hitler regime. During World War II, Sangerhausen was overrun by US troops, and, when Germany was divided at the end of the war, the Rosarium passed to East Germany. Permission to re-establish the VDR in the west was withheld by the Occupation Powers till 1949; symbolically, the revival ceremony took place in Hamburg in July of that year.

A trial centre for new rose varieties was established in Baden-Baden in 1951, and the West German Rosarium in Westfalen Park, Dortmund – which, with more than 3000 varieties, holds the largest collection of roses in the Federal Republic – was opened in 1969. The varieties there are arranged according to the countries in which the hybrids were originally bred. The beds are on several different levels, and some are arranged to form an amphitheatre.

Der Rosenbogen ('The Arc of Roses') was established by the VDR in 1964 as a quarterly magazine. The VDR also regularly makes presentations of 5000 roses to the winners of best-kept village competitions in West Germany. Similar presentations of AMENITY and PATIO and balcony roses to well-kept towns and cities are currently envisaged.

Veteran roses

Some climbing roses can undoubtedly outlive some of the buildings that are supposed to support them, but presumptions about the age of roses need to be treated with caution. The magnificent rose at the Alhambra Palace in Granada in southern Spain, which covered one side of the building and displayed a trunk with a diameter of 10 inches (25 cm), was said to have been planted by order of the Spanish king, Charles I, whose first visit to Spain took place in 1517, two years before he was elected emperor of the Holy Roman Empire and took the name Charles V.

This would have credited the rose with a lifespan of more than four centuries. On closer examination, however, the Alhambra rose turned out to be a 'Maréchal Niel', a climbing NOISETTE with the blooms and fragrance of a TEA ROSE, that was launched by the French nurseryman Pradel in 1864. The case of the single form of *Rosa banksiae*, one of the CHINA ROSES, which was said to have grown without flowering for 113 years (from 1796) at Strathay in Scotland, is also unproven.

We are on firmer ground, however, with the '1000-year-old' rose growing against the apse of the cathedral crypt at Hildesheim in West Germany. It has no pretensions to nobility and, according to the Senior Director of the Archives and Library of the City of Hildesheim, is an ordinary hedge rose, of a form intermediate between *R. canina* and *R. dumalis*. (The main differences between the two are that *R. dumalis* has smaller prickles than *R. canina* as well as broader upper stipules and bracts that are broader and often red-tinged, plus sepals that persist at least until the hip is ripe, whereas those of *R. canina* fall before the 'fruit' is ripe.)

The earliest mention of the Hildesheim rose, as attested by the city archivist, occurred in a history of Hildesheim written by Father Georg Elbers (1607–73) and published in 1629, but even at that time, the rose was described as being very old. Earlier records were destroyed in the great fire from which the cathedral suffered in AD 1013, and it may be that, while they perished, the rose did not. It has certainly survived some very severe weather, not to mention the air raid of 22 March 1945, when its shoots were burnt down to 6 feet (1.8 m).

The supposition that the Hildesheim rose is more than 1000 years old, though unsupported by documentary proof, is based on the fact that the Bishopric of Hildesheim was founded, and the original cathedral built and consecrated on the hill where the present one stands, in the year AD 815. The rose of Hildesheim has been thought to have died more than once, but as with any other dog rose, new growth has come from suckers and canes at the side of the plant.

Weeds and weedkilling

Eternal vigilance is the price of freedom from weeds in the rose garden for, as the old saw has it, 'One year's seeding means seven years' weeding.' The hoe is the weapon of instant defence particularly against 'soft' weeds such as chickweed and groundsel, which act as winter refuges for various pests.

Each rosebed incurs its own problems according to its surroundings and the degree of acidity or alkalinity of its soil, but few rose gardeners in the UK will have not met the delicate, almost petal-less pearlwort *(Sagina apetala)*, the almost ubiquitous, blue-jewelled slender speedwell *(Veronica filiformis)*, and the pink and white trumpets of the *Convolvulus arvensis*, the field bindweed. Of these, the last named is far the most persistent and will probably be finally subdued only by repeated application of weedkiller; however, as a temporary measure, it can be greatly discouraged if the growing tips are nipped off by hand. The speedwell, like other small recumbent plants, can be smothered by MULCHING.

Weedkillers with new names and fresh constituents appear with some regularity but need to be used with great caution, and those that kill through the roots of the weeds should not be used at all, unless roses have not yet been planted. Those weedkillers that are absorbed through the leaves of the weeds are best applied at a time when rose foliage is at its minimum and on a windless day.

Couch grass *(Agropyron repens)*, ground elder *(Aegopodium podagraria;* also called goutweed) and the above mentioned bindweed, which can sprout again if the smallest piece of root remains in the ground, should all be tackled individually.

Plants such as docks, dandelions and hogweed, which have parsnip-like tap roots, should be dug up, together with the more shallowly rooted buttercups. Brambles should also be dug up and burned.

Some experiments have been carried out to see whether the growth of some weeds can be inhibited if certain plants, particularly marigolds, are grown near them, but no definite conclusions appear yet to have been reached.

Wild roses

Wild roses and their near hybrids in Britain

Rosa arvensis (the field rose). The white flowers, with styles as long as the stamens and joined together, make this easily recognizable in almost every hedgerow – though it is somewhat scarcer in the north. The stems are rampant, but weak and straggling, shooting earthwards rather than to the heavens. They are green when developed but often purplish as shoots.

The musk-like scent make it likely that this was the 'MUSK ROSE' extolled in Shakespeare's *A Midsummer Night's Dream* and later by Keats. Unfortunately, it is a safe hiding place for rabbits.

See also AYRSHIRE ROSES.

Rosa pimpinellifolia (the burnet or Scotch rose). This rose spreads by suckers, and more or less hugs the ground. The branches are armed with numerous straight prickles intermingled with bristles; the leaves are small and oval; the flowers, which come early in the season, are white and solitary; and the hips round and blackish purple, like large round sloes. It also grows across Europe and parts of Siberia, producing a number of variants, and is merely one of the vast worldwide family known as the Pimpinellifoliae.

The naming of this rose has led to some controversy. In many catalogues, it appears under the pseudonym *R. spinosissima*, which is a very suitable description for a cultivar of its spiny nature. However, *R. spinosissima* is what botanists call a *'nomen nudum'* – that is, no particulars of a plant with this name had ever been put forward and published in the internationally prescribed manner.

No such objection applies to the name *R. pimpinellifolia*, although the justification for the name is somewhat far-fetched. The leaflets of thise rose are said to resemble those of the salad burnet, which, because its fruit resembles a peppercorn, was formerly known as the pimpernell.

'R. spinosissima altaica' is an impressively armed form of the species found in the Altai Mountains of Siberia. It is a large shrub, growing up to 6 feet (1.8 m), and carries single cream-to-ivory blooms; it has been popular with gardeners

from 1820 onwards, and is known in the US as the 'Hardy Cherokee Rose'.

Many garden forms of burnet rose were raised in Scotland in the last century by Robert Brown, a nurseryman of Perth (who later emigrated to America and is buried in Philadelphia), and a few are sold today under indecisive descriptions such as 'Double Blush', 'Marbled Pink', 'Single Red', etc. A few improved forms of the species are also in cultivation, notably 'Andrewsii', a clear pink, and the diminutive 'William III', rich maroon fading to dark pink.

There is also an extensive choice of hybrids. 'Harison's Yellow' (1830), a hybrid of the burnet rose with (probably) *R. foetida*, shows nearly double, vivid sulphur-coloured blooms; 'Stanwell's Perpetual' arose from a chance seedling at Stanwell, Middlesex, and its pedigree is therefore uncertain, but it produces well-filled, fragrant, blush pink flowers which appear almost continuously throughout the summer.

R. x hibernica (light pink) is an early cross between the burnet rose and *R. canina*. 'Golden Wings' (Shepherd 1953), a very good shrub, is another pimpinellifolia hybrid.

However, the most spectacular successes with '*spinosissima*' hybrids are those that have been achieved from 1937 onwards by the KORDES nursery at Sparrieshoop, West Germany. These resulted from crosses between the garden improvement known to nurserymen as *R. spinosissima grandiflora* and various HYBRID TEAS, notably 'Joanna Hill', a vigorous, fragrant rose with apricot blooms:

*'Frühlingsanfang' (literally, 'the beginning of spring', 1950) has large ivory white flowers.

*'Frühlingsduft' ('spring fragrance', 1949) has blooms of lemon yellow flushed with pink.

*'Frühlingsgold' (1937), bred from a more coarsely haired '*spinosissima*', has large golden yellow flowers. 'Maigold', a hybrid of 'Frühlingsgold', can be a climber or a shrub. Its flowers are dark parchment yellow, semi-double and strongly scented. There is occasionally a second crop.

*'Frühlingsmorgen' ('spring morning', 1941) is an outstanding rose with blooms that are rose-pink at the edges and primrose at the centre, with dark maroon stamens.

Other *pimpinellifolia* hybrids from species native to areas outside the UK (e.g. the US and China) are described in the sections dealing with those areas.

Rosa canina (the dog rose). The strongly curved or hooked, broadly based prickles of this rose have earned it its somewhat unattractive name – it sometimes even has a few prickles on the back of the leaves. The flowers are white or pink, the stigmas are conical, and those observers with sufficient patience will note that the sepals usually fall off the hip before it ripens.

Genetically, it is one of the most influential among wild roses, having probably given rise to the ALBA ROSES and to ROSA CENTIFOLIA. A 'thornless' form of *R. canina* has often been used as an UNDERSTOCK for BUDDING but rather less for HYBRIDIZATION because of the irregular pairing that takes place during its MEIOSIS. The hips are usually preferred by birds to those of other wild roses.

There are a number of other species closely related to *R. canina* and native to the UK. *R. dumalis* has sepals that persist on the hips at least until they ripen; its stigmas are flatheaded, and the flowers are on shorter stalks than those of *R. canina*. The leaves of *R. obtusifolia* are ovate or oval and usually pubescent; the prickles are more strongly hooked and more stoutly based. *R. x andersonii* is a natural hybrid between *R. canina* and *R. arvensis*.

R. villosa, literally the 'downy' rose, and its near relatives are also grouped with the dog rose. *R. villosa* grows mainly in the north of Britain and has straight prickles, straight branches that can grow 10 feet (3 m) in a single season, and sepals that stay erect on the hip until it falls or decays. The leaves are dull pale green with a bluish tint and are covered on both sides with short cottony hairs; the flowers are deep pink and the hips globe-shaped. *R. tomentosa* is a near-relative, with both the young stems and the leaflets pale green, and in *R. sherardii*, the leaflets and young shoots are somewhat glaucous.

In *R. stylosa*, which in Britain flowers mainly in the south, the styles are fused into a column shorter than the stamens. This distinguishes it from the Synstylae roses, in which the styles are as long as the stamens, and therefore it is grouped with the Caninae roses.

Finally, there are the sweet briers, which are also grouped botanically with the dog roses. Four of these are native to Britain, and all have hooked prickles and serrate leaves, thickly clothed below with sticky, sweet-scented glands. The best known is the rose generally called *R. eglanteria* in the US and *R. rubiginosa* in Europe – the eglantine or sweet brier, with bright pink flowers and erect stems. (The stems of *R. elliptica* are also erect, but the flowers are scentless.) The confusion of the name has arisen because, in 1760, LINNAEUS gave the name *R. eglanteria* to *R. foetida*. He amended this in 1771 by renaming it *R. rubiginosa*, but forgot that, in 1753, he had recorded the sweet brier as *eglanteria* in his *Species plantarum*. The double rose known as 'Manning's Blush Sweet Brier' is a hybrid of *R. eglanteria*, as are 'Janet's Pride' and 'La Belle Distinguée'.

'Fritz Nobis' (Kordes, 1940), a well-shaped shrub, is another hybrid of *R. eglanteria* and offers soft pink, clove-scented flowers with frilly petals. Although not REMONTANT, it has an unhurried flowering season. 'Sparrieshoop' (1953), so called after the site of the Kordes nursery, is also a sweet brier hybrid. Its blooms are single, pink and remontant.

The two remaining UK species, *R. micrantha* and *R. agrestis*, both have arching stems, but the flowers of *R. agrestis* are of a paler shade of pink and the leaflets wedge-shaped at the base.

R. macrantha, another member of the Caninae group, is thought to be a historic hybrid between *R. canina* x *R. gallica*; its flowers are darker pink, and the leaflets rounded at the base. 'Scintillation' (Austin, Sunningdale, 1966) is a Macrantha hybrid – a spectacular scrambler with blush pink clusters of blooms in midsummer. 'Chianti', also summer-flowering, has purplish maroon flowers.

Some older sweet brier hybrids are described under PENZANCE ROSES. Other wild roses belonging to the Caninae sector and which occur in continental Europe are described below.

Continental European species

Rosa sempervirens (the evergreen rose).   In its native Mediterranean habitat, this is a trailing rose with arching green canes and reddish prickles. The flowers are large, single, pure white, fragrant and displayed in groups of two or three. The species was already known in the UK in 1629 when Parkinson described the leaves as consisting of seven leaflets with the three pairs increasing in size from the lowest upwards. Roy Shepherd has surmised that this species might originally have arisen as a natural hybrid between *R. moschata*, which grows wild in an area to the east of it, and *R. arvensis*, which is to the west and north.

The earliest garden hybrids of *R. sempervirens* came in the 1820s from French nurserymen, and the best known today is probably the rambler 'Felicité et Perpetué', originally grown by Jacques in the château garden of Philippe d'Orléans at Neuilly. Jacques was expecting an addition to the family, and had reserved a rose to be named after the child. When twin girls were born, one rose had to suffice for the two of them, both named after saints. The rose is practically evergreen and therefore useful for screening a fence. The flowers are small and globe-shaped but are presented in large clusters.

R. glauca is a SPECIES ROSE that grows wild on mountains from the Pyrenees to the Balkans. Its single pink flowers, with petals standing free like the sails of a windmill, are shown off by plum-grey foliage, making the present name far more accurate than the old one of *R. rubrifolia*. It is much prized for decoration, as well as for use as a hedge. The hybrid variety 'Carmenette' has larger flowers but less attractive foliage.

R. pomifera – the 'apple-bearer' – is a very close relative of *R. villosa*, the native British species. It can be depended on to produce larger and more spectacular globe-shaped hips, decorative enough in the garden but too bristly for the birds.

R. pendulina, the alpine rose, is native to the mountains of central and southern Europe, and is often grown in gardens. It is the 'rose without a thorn' (one of several) and has flowers of the deepest pink. It is extremely hardy and will survive even in partial shade. The adjective *pendulina* refers to the hips that hang downwards. 'Morlettii', with mauve flowers, is the garden hybrid of this species.

R. gallica and the other GALLICA ROSES are described separately.

This seems to be a convenient place to mention *R. majalis*, which, though its homeland stretches eastward across Asia to Japan, is also found in Sweden, the Baltic states and eastern Europe. As Henry Phillips, in *Sylvia florifera* (1823), put it: 'It is a favourite with our fair sex as it may be worn in the bosom longer than any other rose without fading, whilst its diminutive size and colour together with a pleasant perfume, adapt it well to fill the place of a jeweller's broach.' This dark red rose is really the most typical member of the vast Cinnamomeae family, and was named *Rosa cinnamomea* by Linnaeus until it was discovered that this adjective had already been used for *R. pendulina*, described above. However, *majalis* is a useful description since it reminds the gardener to expect some blooms in May and, in fact, *R. majalis* is sometimes referred to as the 'Whitsun rose'. Some experts have complained of being unable to home in on any traces of cinnamon scent in this rose and have wondered whether the name could have been suggested by the colour of its stems, which are reddish brown. While Linnaeus may have taken this into account, the stems of *R. pendulina* are green, so that whomever originally named the alpine rose *R. cinnamomea* would probably have been influenced more by the scent rather than by the colour of the stems.

North America

As many as 170 species of roses have been identified as native to North America. The following is devoted mainly to those roses which are found fairly frequently over wide areas of the continent, and it is probably most convenient to deal with them according to the geographical regions in which they best flourish.

One species, *Rosa acicularis*, the Arctic rose, appears all along the circumference of the Arctic Circle and knows no frontiers. It is a low shrub with stems that are often densely armed with bristles and flexible prickles, and large, solitary, dark pink flowers. It is one of the earliest to flower, and is found as far south as Wyoming and Colorado. 'Pike's Peak' is the garden hybrid of this species.

R. blanda is, like the preceding, a member of the Cinnamomeae family, and flowers with the melting snows, but it is taller and almost unarmed. The greyish-green leaflets, pale beneath, set off the solitary pale pink flowers. It is an easterner, hardy, and tolerates rocky and even damp terrain.

R. setigera, the prairie rose, is a useful plant that will flourish on almost every kind of soil, and quickly too, so that a 10-foot (3 m) wall will soon be masked and bare ground expeditiously covered with decumbent and arching shoots. The single, deep pink or white flowers, 2 inches (5 cm) across, appear conveniently in late summer when many other species roses are finished, though, as one might expect, there is no autumn repeat. The hips are small but, like the flowers, borne in profusion. Botanically, the plant is interesting, having been described as the only member of the Synstylae group (*see* CLASSIFICATION) found wild in the United States.

Thomas Rivers the nurseryman, whose *Rose Amateur's Guide* was first published in 1837, wrote of prairie roses: 'I will dismiss them with the remark that none of them are worth cultivating.' ELLEN WILLMOTT disagreed, though she admitted that they were 'deficient in scent'. However, at least one undoubted modern authority, Graham Stuart Thomas, in his classic *Shrub Roses of Today* speaks of 'mallow-pink flowers with broad petals, which are very fragrant in spite of numerous statements to the contrary'.

R. setigera is also the only native CLIMBING ROSE in North America and has the additional distinction of being mentioned in Charles Darwin's studies on the movements and habits of climbing plants for being responsive to the stimulus of the highlights and shadows of a trellis. Furthermore, it is unusual for carrying fertile male and female flowers on different plants, so that one bush may have a profusion of hips and another none. Its hybrids are, for the most part, unremarkable.

One would expect to find prairie roses in Illinois, Wisconsin, Iowa and Minnesota, but this species also ranges as far south as Texas and Florida. To the French explorer André Michaux, it seemed so typical that he suggested that it should be called the 'Rose of America'. However, it is on balance an eastern plant and is not seen in a wild state west of the Rockies.

R. nitida is a petite shrub usually less than 3 feet (0.90 m) tall, useful as an undershrub in the in the rose garden, with stems covered with red bristles and dark green glossy leaves. It flourishes in New England and north of the border in Ontario. Catherine Gore wrote that its small cup-shaped deep-red flowers were used in her time by Eskimos for decorating their hair and the seal and reindeer skins that they wore.

R. virginiana is so called because early specimens were brought from that colony to Europe, but in fact it decorates the landscape from Quebec to Georgia and westwards to Missouri. It spreads by means of suckers, and could be considered as a possible ground-cover plant. It displays a profusion of pink flowers, contrasting with the glossy paddle-shaped leaflets that led it in former times to be called *R. lucida*, the 'shining rose'; these turn to brilliant orange in the autumn. The double form, which may be a hybrid, is known as the 'Rose d'Amour'.

Imbricated rose petals overlapping like tiles, from The Gardener's Assistant.

R. carolina, another rose of eastern America, was so named by Linnaeus. It is highly rated as a landscape rose, and was adopted as the state flower of Iowa. The leaves are sharply serrate; the flowers, mainly solitary, are pink. Double forms of this species are to be seen occasionally in gardens. It is a late flowerer.

R. palustris has sometimes been confused with *R. carolina* but, as its name implies, this rose prefers a swampy habitat where some specimens rise above the rushes to a height of 8 feet (2.5 m). The flowers are displayed in small corymbs and are deep pink. They can be found in suitable habitats from Quebec to Florida, and like the preceding species, it is a late flowerer.

R. foliolosa was discovered by Thomas Nutall, an impecunious printer from Liverpool who came to Philadelphia to make his fortune. He explored the Missouri–Mississippi area and joined up with one of John Jacob Astor's fur trading parties while on his way to the Rockies. He found this rose in 1818 in Arkansas, but it also grows wild in Texas and Oklahoma. The flowers are dark cerise on very short stems, but the leaves are the most remarkable feature – there can be as many as eleven narrow leaflets to each leaf stalk. It is a late starter that flowers into September. REDOUTÉ painted a rose similar to this, calling it *R. rapa* because the hips were shaped like turnips; unfortunately, his portrait shows only the flowers.

The central and western area of the US is the home of *R. woodsii*. The wild rose, described by Catherine Gore as growing beside the Mississippi, is undistinguished, but the garden variety, *R. woodsi* 'fendleri', has bright lilac-pink flowers, greyish leaves and shining, globular, bright red hips, which in England, at any rate, are left to the very last even by hungry birds, and so remain to delight the eye. Much the same has been said about the 'fruit' of *R. nutkana*, a rose that straddles the Rocky Mountains, flowering in northern California and along the coast north to Alaska as well as in Wyoming.

R. californica is native to an area running from British Columbia to Baja California and eastward to Nevada. The semi-double variety, *R. californica plena*, is a floriferous and graceful plant, with arching sprays of rich dark pink.

This is a convenient place in which to mention *R. montezumae*, discovered in Mexico by Humboldt in 1825, and thought at the time to be native there. However, now it is considered to be a less thorny variety of *R. eglanteria* and may have been introduced by Spanish missionaries.

R. arkansana occupies the heart of the US, from Kansas northward, and appears over the border in Saskatchewan and Manitoba. Its near relative, *R. suffulta*, shows some remontant characteristics, and both roses are low-growing shrubs with bristly stems and flowers in corymbs, pink in the case of *R. suffulta*, red in that of *R. arkansana*.

R. gymnocarpa, a native of northwest America, is a 3 foot (0.90 m) shrub with paired prickles and pink flowers. It thrives on the fringes and in the clearings of the forests, and is one of the few roses to tolerate shade.

R. pisocarpa, so called because its hips are small and

rounded, suggesting red peas, is another western rose, though it shuns the seaboard, ranging as far north as central Alaska.

Two 'near roses', both native to the North American continent, can be described here. *R. stellata* and *R. minutifolia* are both so unlike conventional roses that they have been placed by themselves in the sub-genus Hesporhodos. The differences lie in the unusual shape of the leaves, in the calyx (shaped like an acorn-cup) and in the hips, which are dry within, and not fleshy.

R. stellata, which grows in the mountains of New Mexico and south of the border in Mexico, is thought to be a relict of pre-Ice Age times, and was discovered only in 1897. It grows to a mere 2 feet (0.60 m) as a shrub, with long, straight, pale yellow prickles, which perhaps led to it being called the 'gooseberry rose'. The leaflets are a mere ½ inch (1.2 cm) long, blunt-ended and wedge-shaped, with just three to a stalk like those of some trefoils. The hips are brownish, pear-shaped and bristly. The flowers are up to 2 inches (5 cm) across (large for the size of the bush) and are of a dullish rose set off by long, narrow, pointed sepals projecting from between the petals in a starry design. A somewhat larger form, *R. stellata mirifica*, known as the 'Sacramento rose', has been in cultivation since 1916.

R. stellata's nearest relative, *R. minutifolia*, grows in a colony some 500 miles (800 km) away, in that long Mexican peninsula known as Baja California. This is a larger shrub than the preceding species, with smaller, white flowers, and greyish-green leaflets with deeply cut, jagged margins. This rose can survive in the driest and most arid soil, but does not seem to have found any takers among rose breeders.

Finally, it is fitting to pay attention to a rose that, although not native to North America, was found growing there and well established by Michaux in 1803. This is *R. laevigata*, the Latin adjective calling attention to its glossy leaves. It is better known as the 'Cherokee rose', a name bestowed on it because, as Michaux discovered, it was a special favourite of the Cherokee Indians in southwest Arkansas. It is a mighty evergreen rose, a rambler–climber with large, white, single flowers and shiny leaflets, three to a stalk. One of the first plants to be sent to Europe from the East India Company's China station, it was described by the English naturalist Leonard Plukenet in 1696. There is no record of Europeans bringing the rose to America, though it is conceivable that it was taken there by one of the Spanish gold-hunting expeditions well before the general westward expansion of the pioneers. It has since been adopted as the official flower of Georgia. It needs a warm wall and lots of space, and in a northern climate, the flowering period is short.

Asia Minor and the Middle East

Many wild roses came to Europe from the area lying between Turkey and Afghanistan, without much note being taken of the fact. One of these was *Rosa phoenicia*, so called because it was introduced to the West in ships coming from ports on the coast of Syria, which formed part of the ancient kingdom of Phoenicia. It is a rose without much presence, rather similar to the MUSK ROSE but less vigorous, and it offers single white flowers in panicles. It is, however, believed to have been one of the original parents of the summer-flowering DAMASK ROSE, and possibly of the HOLY ROSE OF ABYSSINIA.

A second important ancient species, this time from Persia (present-day IRAN), is *R. foetida*, once referred to as the 'Austrian brier', because it first became widely known to Europeans when Clusius brought it from Vienna to Holland in the 16th century. It is a pure yellow, single rose with golden stamens and chocolate-brown wood, but was not used successfully for hybridization until the first quarter of the 19th century. Its SPORT, the 'Austrian copper brier', *R. foetida bicolor*, with petals coppery on the inside and bright yellow on the reverse, also appeared in the 16th century. The double form of the Austrian brier, *R. foetida persiana*, was introduced to Britain in 1837 by Sir Henry Willock, Britain's ambassador in Tehran.

The double yellow rose seen earlier in 17th- and 18th-century flower paintings was a different species: *R. hemisphaerica*, the 'sulphur rose' painted by Redouté, which came originally from western Turkey, where the single form *R. hemisphaerica rapinii* is native. Clusius noticed a replica of *R. hemisphaerica* in a model of a Turkish garden in Vienna and managed to obtain a plant, but growers found that the blooms seldom opened except in persistent sun.

Sir Henry Wotton – poet, diplomat and the originator of the aphorism that 'ambassadors are good men sent abroad to lie on behalf of their country' – was sent in 1614 on a mission to The Hague and, eight years later, was able to procure a plant for the Earl of Holderness. However, like John Gerard's earlier specimen, it failed to prosper. Since then, as William Paul made clear in *The Rose Garden* (1848), other growers have met with more success.

This rose has hooked prickles, which distinguish it from *R. foetida persiana*, the double form of *R. foetida*. The single *R. foetida* crossed with a burnet rose led to the popular hybrid 'Harison's Yellow'. Crossings made with *R. foetida persiana* at the end of the 19th century led to bright yellow LARGE-FLOWERED ROSES.

A very beautiful rose, native to Turkestan, was discovered in central Asia by Olga Fedtschenkoana in 1875. It was classified as a member of the Cinnomomeae family and named for her by Dr Albert Regel of the Imperial Botanical Garden in St Petersburg. *R. fedtschenkoana* is a fairly dense shrub rising to 6 feet (1.8 m) or more, with pinkish prickles, greyish shoots and pale sea-green leaflets. It blooms almost continuously during the summer, so that the red bristly hips are sometimes on show at the same time as the white flowers. Some observers deprecate the SCENT of this rose, but no doubt, as with *R. foetida*, matters improve on a really hot day. It deserves to be grown more widely and probably would be if the name were less of a tongue-twister.

Another species native to Persia and the area to the east is the near-rose known as *Hulthemia persica*. In one of his most striking portraits, Redouté showed its distinctive features: the typical group of rose leaflets are replaced by undivided, unstalked, alternate leaves, and the solitary flowers are lemon yellow blotched in the centre with a ring of dark purplish chocolate, in a manner reminiscent of a ROCKROSE. The hips are covered with a dense thicket of bristles and remain green.

This was another find by the French explorer André Michaux *père* (1746–1803), during his expedition to Iran in 1788. It was grown successfully in Paris by the French nurserymen Jacques-Martin Cels and later at La Malmaison (*see* JOSEPHINE AND HER ROSES AT LA MALMAISON), and imported to England in 1790 by Sir Joseph Banks. It seems to prosper in arid soil, and would probably be reasonably common in the wild but for the fact that it is used in Iran for cattle fodder and for fuel.

In 1836, J. A. Hardy, the curator of the Luxembourg Gardens in Paris, succeeded in raising a cross between *Hulthemia persica* and *R. clinophylla*, a relative of the wild American species *R. laevigata*, and this is still in cultivation. The hybrid is a larger plant than the parent, with lemon-yellow flowers 2 inches (5 cm) across and more prominent markings. However, neither *Hulthemia persica* nor the hybrid *Hulthemosa hardii* are easily raised, and attempts have therefore been made to discover more vigorous natural hybrids. Trials have been carried out, with varying success, with crosses between *Hulthemia persica* and three HYBRID MUSKS ('Ballerina', 'Buff Beauty' and 'Cornelia'), with 'Canary Bird' (a hybrid between *R. hugonis* x *R. xanthina*), with *R. chinensis mutabilis*, with 'Mermaid' (a hybrid of *R. bracteata*), and with *R. rugosa*. In every case, better results were achieved with *Hulthemia* as the seed parent.

However, the first hardy *Hulthemia* hybrid to be launched commercially arrived in 1985 from the HARKNESS nursery, and was named x *Hulthemosa harprier* 'Tigris'. The pollen parent was the white rambler 'Trier', and the resulting flowers are canary yellow with a red eye. 'Euphrates', a rose-coloured counterpart that is not so fully petalled, has also been raised.

The Himalayas and Eastern Asia

Some of the most important wild roses from China – notably *Rosa chinensis*, *R. gigantea* and *R. banksiae* – are described, together with their chief hybrids, in the entry for CHINA ROSES. Other Asian species briefly mentioned there, or by name only, are included below. *R. laevigata*, the 'Cherokee rose', although a native of China's southern provinces, has, however, been adopted so enthusiastically in the United States that it has been included among the wild roses of North America.

Here, we begin with two roses native to the Himalayas for which we are indebted to Nathaniel Wallich, a Danish surgeon who in 1817 was put in charge of the Calcutta garden of the East India Company. He was responsible for sending home *R. macrophylla*, so called because it was con-

sidered to have unusually large leaves (although they by no means qualify for the record book). It is an unusually large shrub, needing plenty of room; enthusiasts ideally need stilts to appreciate the proudly held, deep rose-coloured flowers. Both the species and a variety known as 'doncasteri' are cultivated today in gardens, the latter having smaller flowers but better hips than the original. 'Auguste Roussel' (Barbier, 1913) is an alternative garden variety.

R. sericea is another Himalayan rose that was introduced in 1822, only four years after *R. macrophylla*. It is singular in that the creamy white flowers normally have four petals only instead of the rose's usual five, and the large triangular 'thorns' and bristly shoots give the plant a 'wild' look. It is closely allied to another species from western China – *R. omeiensis* – which has an even fiercer armament of prickles, as well as filmy leaflets, up to seventeen to each stalk. Seen against the sun, the translucent thorns, forming an almost unbroken line, are spectacular. *R. omeiensis* 'pteracatha' is the best variety.

One of the more influential species to leave the Far East is *R. multiflora*, a rose to be admired more for its constitution and breeding qualities than for its beauty. Scent it has, being a member of the Synstylae group (*see* CLASSIFICATION), and Canon ELLACOMBE recorded that he had counted more than 600 flowers on a single TRUSS. As a hedge or windbreak, it can present a formidable barrier, and as an UNDERSTOCK its vigour makes it almost unsurpassable. Although the pyramidal clusters of small white flowers are over in July, and the plant can become uncontrollably large, it is nevertheless the ancestor not only of many good RAMBLERS but of the POLYANTHAS and FLORIBUNDAS.

It was first accurately described in 1784 by Karl Peter Thunberg, chief surgeon at the Dutch East India Company's station on Deshima, Japan, and *R. multiflora* var. *carnea*, a pink variety, was grown in England as early as 1804. A number of other forms, including a thornless one, are cultivated, and the best known of these, which may be a historic hybrid, is *R. multiflora platyphylla*. It is also known as the 'seven sisters rose', supposedly because the colours of the blooms vary with age: In a group of seven (or, for that matter, any other number), the youngest will be of a freshly coloured mauve and the oldest will show only ivory petals. 'De la Grifferaie' (Vibert, 1846) carries double, fragrant magenta flowers on branches that are almost thornless, and it is therefore often used as an understock; it is probably a multiflora hybrid. *R. multiflora watsoniana* is more fully described in the entry devoted to ELLEN WILLMOTT.

R. farreri persetosa (1918) – called the 'threepenny-bit rose' because of its minute flowers – is the garden variety of the original species *R. elegantula*, no longer grown. Its fine leaves turn to crimson and purple in the autumn.

Few roses can show a better display of hips than *R. moyesii*, a native of central and southern China. It was first collected in 1894 but only named twelve years later, in honour of the Revd J. Moyes of the China Inland Mission, who had been host to 'Chinese' Wilson at the time the rose

Rosa setigera, *the 'prairie rose' of America, painted by Alfred Parsons*
for Miss Ellen Willmott's masterly work, The Genus Rosa, *published in 1914.*
The rose is to be found in almost every US state from the Atlantic
to the Rocky Mountains.

Rosa sepium is today known as R. agrestis *and is not sufficiently
common in Britain to merit a vernacular name. It belongs to the same Synstylae group
as* R. canina, *the dog rose, from which it can be distinguished by its smaller leaflets,
narrowed to a wedge-like shape at the base.*

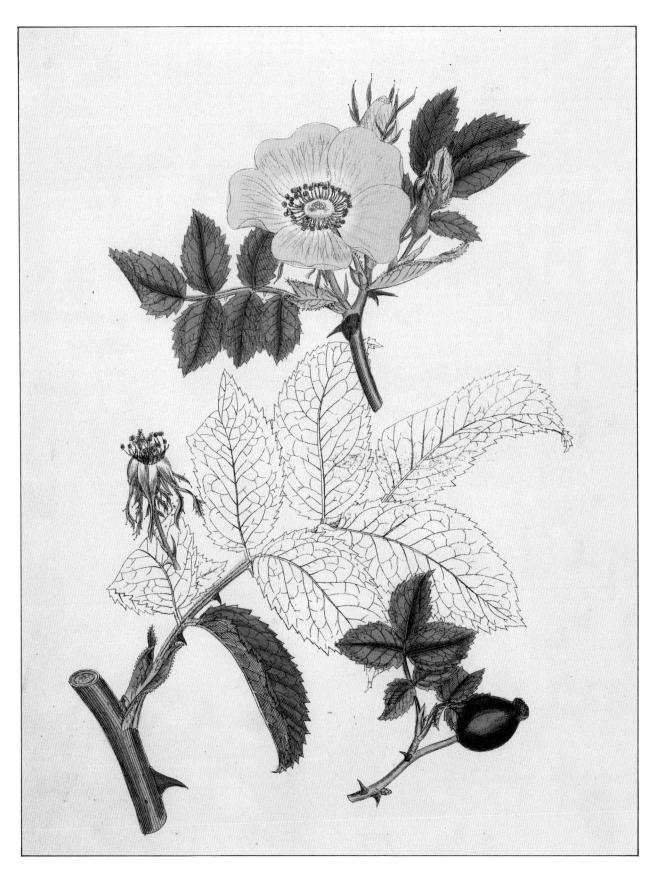

Rosa canina, *the dog rose, so called either because its prickles resemble*
a dog's teeth, or because, like the dog violet, it has little or no scent.
The flower stalks are relatively long – usually more than ⅖ in (1 cm)
– and the flower may be white or pink.

Rosa eglanteria (R. rubiginosa), *the sweet brier, is unusual*
in its scented glandular hairs, and in its bright pink flowers, which secrete nectar
as well as pollen. The leaves are said to smell of apples.

was rediscovered in Szechuan. The original species is a 10–15 foot (3–4.5 m) shrub with single flowers of an intense red, some 2–3 inches (5–7.5 cm) across. It has few prickles, and luxuriant foliage, with up to thirteen leaflets to each stalk. The orange hips are flask-shaped.

Pink, rose-red, and scarlet varieties are grown as well as a crimson hybrid named 'hillieri'. 'Nevada', the magnificent shrub rose with creamy flowers 4 inches (10 cm) across, is a hybrid between one of the *moyesii* varieties and 'La Giralda', a large-flowered rose apparently no longer in cultivation.

Another spectacular display of hips can be looked for from *R. sweginzowii*, a pink-flowered shrub rose from northwest China, of about the same size as *R. moyesii*. The hips are smaller but develop earlier in the season.

Small rounded leaflets stippled against the dark canes suit the modest pink blossoms of *R. multibracteata*, which has curved thorns, large bracts, hundreds of stamens and woolly hips. This is a rose that can be depended on to flower late, but it resents the frost. 'Cerise Bouquet' (Kordes, 1958) is a cross between *R. multibracteata* and 'Crimson Glory'. The vivid carmine-cerise blooms of this impressively large shrub are fragrant, but summer-flowering only. The ancestry of 'Floridora' and the GRANDIFLORA ROSES can also be traced back to *R. multibracteata*. 'Mermaid', a cream-flowered remontant climber (NATIONAL ROSE SOCIETY Gold Medal, 1917), is, however, a hybrid of *R. bracteata*, a different Asian species.

In the 1890s, there were mixed feelings among English rosarians following the arrival of the ground-hugging evergreen *R. wichuraiana* and the profusion of hybrids that followed. As the inveterate campaigner William Robinson wrote in *The English Flower Garden:*

The Wichuraiana roses are based on the beautiful Japanese rose of that name, which is more beautiful than many ramblers raised from it. Some of these cover the earth in many gardens with roses that are little better than brambles. These ramblers have done infinite harm to the culture of roses, and, excepting the few kinds one really enjoys after a thorough trial, would be best abolished.

Today, however, it is the original species which remains in comparative obscurity and the hybrids which flourish.

In its original form, *R. wichuraiana*, a native of Korea, Formosa and eastern China, as well as of Japan, was observed trailing along the banks of a Japanese river in 1861 by Dr Max Ernst Wichura, a German botanist. Specimens of this rose, sweetly scented with yellow buds and creamy white flowers, were sent to Germany but most of them failed there. Twenty years later, the Belgian botanist and rosarian, François Crepin, noticed an unnamed rose from Japan in the Brussels Botanic Garden of which he was the director, recognized it as the rose that Wichura (who had died shortly after returning from Asia) had sent to Berlin, and named it after him. The leaflets are egg-shaped, dark green and glossy, the flowers scented, small, white and arranged in corymbs. Because it flowers later

than most other roses, there are few if any natural hybrids. It was taken up by the nursery of Louis Späth in Berlin, who shipped plants to the Arnold Arboretum at Jamaica Plain, Boston, Massachusetts, and from there, roots were sent to the Royal Botanic Gardens at Kew and to various US nurserymen.

One of the most successful of these was Michael Horvath of the Newport Nursery in Rhode Island, who began by crossing *R. wichuraiana* with 'Cramoisi Superieur' and with 'Pâquerette' to yield hardy large-flowered climbers. Other US nurserymen followed his example – in particular, Dr Walter Van Fleet of Glenn Dale, Maryland; James Farrell of the Hoopes Bros. and Thomas Company, West Chester, Pennsylvania; JACKSON & PERKINS, Newark, New York; and Jackson Dawson of the Arnold Arboretum.

Some of their original cultivars are still grown, notably: 'American Pillar' (Van Fleet, 1902), a cross between *R. wichuraiana* x *R. setigera* x a hybrid perpetual, which is deep pink with white eye; 'Dr W. Van Fleet' (Van Fleet, 1910), double, pink fading to ivory; and, of course, 'Dorothy Perkins', which some would say is queen of the RAMBLERS. There was also 'New Dawn' (Somerset Nurseries, 1930), a continuously flowering sport of 'Dr W. Van Fleet', which can perform either as a shrub or climber; its neat flowers of delicate pink have received high praise. Many hybrid POLYANTHAS, floribundas, and large-flowered bush roses have also benefited from *wichuraiana* influence.

R. luciae, a rose discovered in about 1870, is so similar to *R. wichuraiana* that botanists have concluded that they are really one species. In this case, 'wichuraiana', being the junior of the two names, should be dropped, but as yet, little notice seems to have been taken of this ruling.

The ever-popular coppery-salmon 'Albertine' came from the French nursery of Messrs Barbier et Cie in Orléans, with *R. luciae* as the parent. 'Albéric Barbier' and a number of others came from the same breeder.

R. primula, sometimes called the 'incense rose' because of the fragrance that arises from its young shoots, is to be found as far west as Turkestan. The pale yellow, translucent petals do indeed match those of an English primrose, and the narrow leaflets with as many as fifteen to a leaf stalk add a graceful touch. It has been cultivated since 1910 but was not properly identified until 1936.

The largest leaflets of any rose are thought to belong to *R. sinowilsonii*, the rose named for the English plant-hunter E. H. Wilson, who truly deserved his nickname of 'Chinese' Wilson. This rose grows to 20 feet (6 m) or more, and the 3-inch (7.5 cm) leaflets are saw-toothed along the edges, and the flowers are white.

On the same expedition in 1904, Wilson found *R. longicuspis*, so called because of its unusually long 'thorns'. It is similar to but rather more tender than the previous species. *R. filipes* is not far removed from *R. longicuspis* and, like that rose, a late flowerer. Graham Thomas recalls it growing shoots of 20 feet (6 m) during a season, occupying a base of 100 feet (30.5 m) and climbing to 50 ft (15 m) up a copper beech. The small white flowers are grouped together in corymbs with blooms on stalks as thin as filaments – hence its name.

While on the same early 20th-century expedition, Wilson discovered a fine shrub, *R. willmottiae*. It had branches arching like spouts from a sprinkler, doubly serrate leaflets and mauve flowers, mostly solitary, along the branches. It belongs to the Cinnamomeae family.

R. helenae, introduced in 1907 and named by Wilson for his wife, is another magnificent scrambler with dark green leaves and hemispheres of small creamy flowers, followed by pendant hips. *R. rubus* is similar but more vigorous. The wild type is downy; the garden variety glabrous.

Large prickles are perhaps the most noticeable feature of *R. setipoda*, until the clear pink flowers come in June. They are supported on purplish stalks and a purplish calyx tube, both covered with scented glands. This rose was introduced from central China in 1895, and is still grown in gardens as a tall shrub; the hips are flagon-shaped.

R. soulieana was found in 1896 by Jean André Soulié, a medical missionary, on one of the several forays along the borders of Tibet that he made before falling into the hands of robbers who murdered him. This rose makes a large attractive shrub, with its greyish leaves, orange prickles, creamy yellow flowers and orange hips. It is said to be tender but capable of recovering after being laid low by frostbite.

A fine show of soft pink blossom is to be expected from *R. davidii*, a 10-foot (3 m) shrub introduced from southern China in 1908. It resembles *R. macrophylla*, described above.

R. rugosa, the 'wrinkled rose', is one of the most valuable roses to have come to us from Japan, where it had been noted earlier than the 10th century. It was discovered there by Thunberg (to whom we also owe *R. multiflora*) and described in his *Flora japonica*, published in 1784. The vernacular name for *R. rugosa* was, according to Thunberg, 'Ramasa', which is thought to comprise two words meaning 'beach tomato', which refer to its hips and to its love of the seaside; it is still sometimes called the 'Ramasa rose'. It also flourishes in China, Siberia and Korea.

R. rugosa seems almost immune to the normal complaints of the rose, and its hardiness makes it especially suitable for naturalizing in the wild garden or for planting in city parks. Despite this, when the Lee & Kennedy nursery at Hammersmith, London offered the plants to their customers in 1796, they found few takers because the colour of the Japanese variety, mauve, was unoriginal, and the blooms were somewhat shapeless and short-lived when cut. Today, however, the true colour of the species is taken as being purplish-red, which contrasts very agreeably with the dark, shiny, wrinkled leaves.

The main varieties of *R. rugosa* are white, pink and dark crimson, and some are double. One of the best known of these is 'Frau Dagmar Hastrup' (sometimes 'Hartopp'), the semi-double blooms of which are a true mid-pink. The variety known as 'Hansa' (Schaumt & Vantol, 1905) has double flowers of deep purplish maroon, but there may be

some hybrid blood in them. Those of 'Roseraie de l'Hay' are dark wine-purple with characteristically crumpled petals. This variety from Cochet-Cochet dates back to 1901, and should not be confused with 'Rose à Parfum de l'Hay', which is not a sport of the species but a hybrid of *R. rugosa*, with damascena and 'General Jacqueminot' parentage. It has a reputation for heavenly fragrance but evidently needs a warm climate if it is to oblige. The parentage of a more modern and vastly popular variety 'Scabrosa' (1939) is unknown. It bears flowers up to 5 inches (13 cm) across, mauve-red with pale yellow stamens, and is a typical rugosa that flowers continuously.

Among the more openly declared hybrids, 'Blanc Double de Coubert' (1892), also from Cochet-Cochet, is said to be a cross between *R. rugosa* and 'Sombreuil', which is classified as a climbing tea rose. It has whiter-than-white, crumpled-paper petals, forming a blossom that, despite the title, is only semi-double. *R. fimbriata*, said to be a rugosa derivative, is a modest shrub rose with the fringed petals of a carnation, and small, double, pale pink flowers.

A rugosa cross with 'Gloire de Dijon' led to 'Conrad Ferdinand Meyer', rather leggy and thorny with double, pale pink, fragrant blooms; and a cross with 'General Jacqueminot' led to 'Mrs Anthony Waterer', a bush rose with deep crimson flowers. *R. rugosa* crossed with a polypom named 'Madame Norbert Levavasseur' yielded 'F. J. Grootendorst', also with fringed petals opening almost continuously, but without scent, a defect shared by 'Pink Grootendorst' and 'Grootendorst Supreme'.

There are some excellent *R. rugosa* hybrid PILLAR ROSES – for example, 'Agnes', coming from a cross between *R. rugosa* and *R. foetida persiana*, carried out in Canada and introduced in 1900. It has double, mid-yellow, fragrant flowers. One of the parents of 'Sarah Van Fleet' is surely rugosan, but the other partner is uncertain. Its flowers come early and are large and double, and the growth is thick enough to make a good hedge.

Other remontant shrubs derived from *R. rugosa* include:
*'Carmen' (1907), an early flowerer with semi-double crimson blooms.
*'Dr Eckner' (1931), large, scented, semi-double yellow flowers.
*'Lady Curzon' (1901), large, single, pink flowers.
*'Nova Zembla' (1907), white flowers.
*'Ruskin' (1928), double, crimson, scented flowers.
*'Schneelicht' (1894), single, white flowers.
*'Schneezwerg' (1912). semi-double, white.
*'Vanguard' (1932), fragrant, bronzy-salmon flowers.
There are also rugosas that are sometimes used for GROUND COVER. In 1919, *R. rugosa* was crossed with *R. wichuraiana* to produce 'Max Graf', which possessed the hardiness of *R. rugosa* and decent-sized pink, scented flowers. It is a ground-hugging plant frequently spreading with new roots. Another possible ground-cover rose is the hybrid between *R. rugosa* and *R. arvensis*, known as *R. x paulii;* there is also a pink form, *R. x paulii* 'rosea'. 'Hamburger Phoenix' (1954) and 'Ritter von Barmsted' are two climbers derived

from *R. rugosa* via a Kordesii seedling. In general, it should be said that first- and second-generation rugosa hybrids are the most successful: the more remote the descendants, the less similar in looks, and the less vigorous.

Two brilliant yellow species from China, *R. hugonis* and the early flowering *R. xanthina*, have brightened the garden scene for more than eighty years. Both are members of the Pimpinellifoliae family and have the black hips of their tribe. Frank N. Meyer sent the double form of *R. xanthina* from Peking to the US in 1906, and the single form 'var. *spontanea*' followed two years later from Lushang in the Shantung province. *R. xanthina* was first discovered by the French missionary Armand David; *R. hugonis* was named in honour of 'Father Hugo', the Revd Hugh Scallan. *R. hugonis* crossed with *R. xanthina* produced 'Canary Bird', which has cup-shaped single flowers of intense yellow crowding the branches in early summer. The best-known hybrid of *R. hugonis* is the cross with *R. spinosissima altaica*, known as 'Headleyensis', which is also a fairly large, floriferous shrub with yellow flowers strewn along the branches in late spring. *R. ecae* the brilliant yellow rose native to Afghanistan, is described more fully with the HOLY ROSE OF ABYSSINIA.

R. roxburghii, the 'chestnut rose' and a native of China, has been placed in the separate sub-genus Platyrhodon because of its various peculiarities. It was first noted in 1820 by William Roxburgh (1751–1815), a Scot who arrived in India in 1776 as assistant surgeon to the East India Company and, in 1789, was placed in charge of the company's garden at Calcutta, which was used as a staging post for many of the plants coming out of China. Roxburgh wanted to call the rose *R. microphylla* because of its small, rounded leaflets – as many as fifteen per stalk – but this name had already been used. Roxburgh's rose was a double form that had been discovered in a garden in Canton; the single wild-rose form with 4-inch (10 cm) flowers was not discovered until 1864, forty years after the double had first flowered in England. This cultivated form reached the United States in 1828.

Several features distinguish this species from the conventional rose. The chief of these is the heavily burred 'squashed globe', chestnut-shaped hip, 1 inch (2.5 cm) or more across, which suggested its common name. It is known in the southern states of the US as the 'Chinquapin rose' – a corruption of the Indian name for the dwarf chestnut. The wood is angularly jointed, and the sepals alternately bristly and smooth; a pair of reddish prickles decorate the base of each leaf stem. Both single and double forms are in cultivation. The flowers are normally bright pink, but a number of hybrids with red, or reddish violet, blooms have been raised.

Willmott, Ellen

Ellen Willmott (1858–1934) can be numbered among the outstanding plantswomen – and eccentrics – of the gardening world.

She was the eldest daughter of Frederick Willmott, an able solicitor, who had made a fortune out of property dealing at a time when London was still the commercial centre of the world. In 1876, at the age of forty, he felt rich enough to retire to a country estate in keeping with his means (and social ambitions) and bought a Queen Anne mansion – Warley Place, near Shenfield in Essex – which included a library, music room, winter garden and chapel (for the Willmotts were Roman Catholic). It was surrounded by 33 acres of land, with pleasure grounds to the south, an old walled garden and some ancient fishponds; a vinery and peach-house were built on later. A barouche, a Victorian landau, a pony cart, a brougham and a waggonette allowed the family to travel in style.

Ellen soon took over control of the garden, although at first it was only one of her many interests. She played tennis and badminton, skated, took up turnery (i.e. worked at a lathe), photography and painting, learned to play the violin and the ocarina, sang in a choir and attended garden parties and regimental balls at Warley barracks. Various suitors appeared – for in those days, she was a beauty and is said to have broke more hearts than lances – but they seem to have been discouraged, partly by the fact that the family spent much of the year holidaying abroad in Paris, Brussels, Rome and elsewhere (on one occasion for nine months), and partly because none of her admirers could successfully understudy the authority of her own father. In addition, Ellen herself was more energetic, more talented and intelligent than most of the young men she met.

Dr W. T. Stearn, who wrote an appreciation of her in *The Garden* magazine of June 1979, has surmised that she would have liked to have married George Ainslie High who shared her musical and botanical tastes, but he chose the Indian Forestry Service as his career and selected as his partner a less exacting helpmeet who had entranced him when he was still an undergraduate.

And then there was her garden. In 1882, still in her early twenties, she received permission from her father to set up an alpine garden with money given to her as birthday presents by her godmother, Helen Ann Tasker. This was designed to reproduce several different types of environment in which alpines can grow, and was laid out for her by Backhouse of York, the leading experts in this relatively new branch of gardening.

In 1880, Helen Tasker died, leaving Ellen a fortune of £140,000 – enough, one might have thought, to fulfil her wildest dreams. Frederick Willmott died in 1892 and his wife six years later, and so at the age of forty, Ellen found herself living alone at Warley Place, a wealthy spinster and likely to remain one.

Already in 1889, while her father was still alive, she had bought a second estate at Tresserve, near Aix-les-Bains in French Savoie, and had begun to fill the house with Louis XV furniture and the garden with choice plants from the Henri Correvon's nursery at Geneva. In her desire to achieve perfection, she indulged in bouts of breathtaking extravagance. Many of these and much other fascinating material are to be found in Audrey le Lièvre's definitive biography, *Miss Willmott of Warley Place*, published in 1980.

In 1906, at a time when motoring was still the exception rather than the rule, she bought a large chain-driven French car and hired a black chauffeur from Mozambique and, later, purchased a larger car in case the first broke down. At Warley, the costs mounted, too. The gardening operations were supervised by James Preece, to whom five or so foremen, each with his own speciality, were responsible. There was one foreman for herbaceous plants, another for vegetables and fruit, another for roses, another for chrysanthemums, and Jacob Maurer from Switzerland for the alpines. At one time, the total number of the staff at Warley reached 104 as compared with a mere thirteen kept by her mother, and they all had ceremonial uniforms that included 'boater' hats in green and white straw with a green ribbon, knitted green silk ties and dark blue aprons; these last they were ordered to remove, fold and tuck under their arm whenever they had to cross the road to reach one part of the garden from the other. Spectacular orders were placed: 11,000 rose bushes were planted at Tresserve, and 10,000 camassia bulbs were ordered for naturalizing at Warley.

In 1905, Ellen Willmott bought a third estate, Boccanegra on the Côte d'Azur near Ventimiglia, and maintained it for eighteen years, even though, as with Tresserve, she usually paid it only two short visits a year. Yuccas, bay trees, acacias and many other plants were ordered for Boccanegra from nurseries in Menton, Beaulieu and Cannes.

However, all this needless extravagance was matched by meticulous care for individual plants. Famous nurserymen, including Henri Correvon, and institutions, such as the Arnold Arboretum in Massachusetts and the Royal Botanic Gardens at Kew, sent Ellen Willmott plants that they would have entrusted to no one else. One small plant is particularly associated with her name – the brilliant dark blue plumbago, *Ceratostigma willmottianum*, that offers consolation in so many gardens for the approach of autumn. The famous explorer E. H. 'Chinese' Wilson brought home its seeds from his first expedition to China on behalf of the Arnold Arboretum in 1907, but only two of the original seeds germinated – one in Ellen Willmott's garden and the other in her sister's garden.

Many of her plants, some of which were sold to and shown by other growers, received special awards, and several gained the Royal Horticultural Society's coveted Award of Merit. They included two aethionemas (alpines), a primula, a campanula, a crocus, a dianthus, a narcissus, a nerine, a phlox, a salvia and a syringa. *Rosa willmottiae*, a purplish-flowered species collected by E. H. Wilson in Szechuan, is but one of a dozen or more species, sub-species and varieties of plants that bear or have borne her name or that of Warley.

As might be expected, she was befriended and revered (if not always loved) by the great gardeners of her time – Gertrude Jekyll, William Robinson, Frank Crisp, Dean HOLE and Sir Thomas Hanbury, whom she persuaded to buy sixty acres of land at Wisley to present to the Royal

Horticultural Society for their gardens. She also served on the Society's narcissus and tulip committees.

She was awarded the Royal Horticultural Society's Victoria Medal of Honour, founded to commemorate the 60th anniversary of the Queen's accession and limited to sixty horticulturalists resident in the United Kingdom who were considered deserving of special honour. She was also the first woman member of the Linnean [*sic*] Society.

It was Canon ELLACOMBE who persuaded her to undertake her great work: *The Genus Rosa*. This first appeared in twenty-five parts and, when completed, was published by John Murray (Byron's publisher) in 1914 in two magnificent volumes totalling 552 pages. One hundred and eighty species were identified and described, mostly by John Gilbert Baker, an expert at the Royal Botanic Gardens at Kew. A Royal Academician, Alfred Parsons, was commissioned to paint the flower portraits from which 132 coloured illustrations were reproduced by the chromolithograph process, and although some of these suffered in the process and lack the vitality to be seen in the originals at the Lindley Library in London, they are drawn with an appropriate lightness of touch. Where the portraits do not show hips, these are represented by elegant and meticulously executed line drawings.

It has been said that *The Genus Rosa* relied heavily on the work of A. C. Thory (who provided the commentary for REDOUTÉ's *Les roses*), on Dr John Lindley's *Rosarum monographia* (1820) and on Mary Lawrance's *A Collection of Roses from Nature* (1780–1810), and that a number of roses are put forward as species that should have been regarded as varieties. Some botanists, too, would have liked more about the morphological connections between the species.

But where else would you look for a full description and portrait of 'Rosa watsoniana', with its minute $\frac{1}{2}$-inch (1.2 cm) flowers, pink-white with pointed petals; its sword-like leaflets, pale green with darker veins; and its general habit, suggesting that of a dwarf bamboo rather than a rose? It is of unknown origin and has never been seen in the wild, we learn, but was sent by Edward Rand of Dedham, Massachusetts, to the Arnold Arboretum. It had been found growing in a garden in Albany, New York, and is today regarded as a variety of *Rosa multiflora*.

However successful Ellen Willmott might have been as a rosarian, she was quite unable to manage her own finances. In 1907, only a year after she had had Warley lavishly redecorated and the music room redesigned, a servant's carelessness with a candle led to a fire that devastated the house at Tresserve. It was uninsured and the costs of rebuilding and replacing the furniture with items of even higher quality was formidable. To pay for these expenses, she borrowed £15,000, using Warley Place as security, and though her gardening staff was cut, more borrowing followed. She still hoped to retain all three of her properties, and even accepted paying guests at Warley in order to do so.

However, Tresserve had to be sold in 1921, and Boccanegra two years later. Then she had to sell off jewellery and precious botanical works in order to pay the gardeners' wages at Warley, even though their numbers had been reduced by the military call-ups during World War I. The orchid house there had to be closed, and Ellen herself eventually lived alone with only a single oil stove for heating in the winter.

Ellen Willmott had always valued her privacy, and the grounds of Warley Place were protected not only by a night watchman with a dog, but also by trip wires, designed to loose gunfire if they were disturbed by an intruder. Moreover, perhaps because she was only 5 feet 4 inches (1.62 m) tall, she sometimes carried a loaded revolver in her handbag.

As time went by, she acquired a well-deserved reputation for other eccentricities. She is said to have slept on a bench by St-Martin-in-the-Fields in London while en route to Oxford, to avoid the expense of staying a night in a hotel, and to have passed the night in a police cell in Oxford rather than pay for a night's lodging there when the friends, at whose house she was to have put up, proved to be away.

She had long been accustomed to wearing a 19th-century garden-party hat both inside and outside the house, and to enter her drawingroom wearing her gardening clogs. However, with age, she became more and more casual about her dress, and on one occasion set out to visit Queen Mary (one of several royal gardeners with whom she was on visiting terms) without gloves. From then on, her housekeeper was deputed to see that she never left home on one of her frequent journeys to London without scarf, gloves and a clean handkerchief.

Although autocratic and imperious towards her servants (who were under strict orders never to appear anywhere in the grounds within sight of her windows), she could be charming to those relatives and friends who responded to her enthusiasms. She was, however, never able to conceal her distaste for anyone who was boring or pretentious. With age, she developed a penchant for *bon mot* uttered with a chuckle at the expense of others, and her anecdotes about people of whom she disapproved were often embroidered with an edge of malice. She was a good hater, too, and on one occasion stood outside the entrance to a Royal Horticultural Society show, distributing leaflets attacking the botanist-explorer, Reginald Farrer, who had criticized her friend Sir Frank Crisp for decorating his alpine garden with metal chamoix. She showed great spirit in adversity and was indifferent to the hardships and discomforts that it brought.

Regrets she may have had as her close relations and too many of her friends died, but, as she put it, 'Plants and gardens come before anything else during the day, and after dark I read or write about them.'

Ellen Willmott died suddenly from a heart attack in the early hours of the morning of 27 September 1934. Warley Place was sold and then sold again before the old house was partially demolished with a view to building several new ones on the site. Local authority consent for this plan was, however, not forthcoming, and no construction took place. Thus the skeleton of the house now remains while the grounds have been leased to the Essex Naturalist Trust who care for what is left of Ellen Willmott's stupendous garden.

World Federation of Rose Societies

The objects of the Federation, membership of which is open to all rose societies representing their countries, are:

1. To encourage and facilitate information about and knowledge of the rose between national rose societies.
2. To coordinate the holding of international conventions and exhibitions.
3. To encourage and, where appropriate, sponsor research into problems concerning the rose.
4. To establish common standards for judging new seedling roses.
5. To assist in coordinating the registration of rose names.
6. To establish a uniform system of rose classification.
7. To grant international honours and/or awards.
8. To encourage and advance international cooperation on all other matters concerning the rose.

Conventions have been held in Hamilton, New Zealand (1971), Chicago (1974), Oxford (1976, ROYAL NATIONAL ROSE SOCIETY centenary), Pretoria (1979), Jerusalem (1981), Baden-Baden (1983) and Toronto (1985). In each case, these meetings were hosted by the national rose society of the country concerned.

The 1988 convention is to be held in Australia, and Italy and Northern Ireland are likely candidates for subsequent gatherings. Japan and India are also applicants for future conventions.

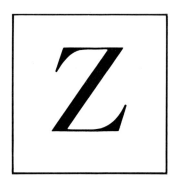

Zimbabwe, the rose in

Since achieving independence, Zimbabwe has built up an export trade in CUT ROSES and, despite various handicaps, exported 485,000 stems to Britain in 1984 – more than double the combined totals from France, Italy, Spain, West Germany and South Africa. The industry got off to a slow start partly because the sanctions imposed on the then Rhodesian government in the early 1960s by the British government prevented the import of new rose varieties. A shortage of shade-cloth and the high cost of glass (and fibre-glass) meant that the roses were grown in the open with blooms too large and stalks too thick for the export market. However, three growers continued production and have since increased their 'take' with well-established varieties such as 'Sonia', 'Baccara', 'Ilona', 'Mercedes' and 'Pascali'.

There is a promising Rose Society of Zimbabwe, which has become a member of the WORLD FEDERATION OF ROSE SOCIETIES.

Amateur growers usually plant and prune their roses at the same time during June and July (equivalent to the Northern Hemisphere's December/January), the best growing area being the 'high field', which has an altitude of around 4000 feet (1220 m) and an annual rainfall of 30 to 40 inches (75–100 cm). However, all their rain falls between November and February leaving a dry gap of at least three months following planting, but given enough water, the first flowers appear in mid-September and are at their best in the first week of October. There is no period of intermission and bush roses continue flowering until the end of June.

Zygote

This is almost, but not quite, the last word in most English dictionaries, but happens to be relevant to the development of the rose as well as that of many other similar plants. It denotes a single germ cell resulting from the union between two reproductive cells, or gametes. A gamete, in turn, is a sexual protoplasmic body that, on joining with another, gives rise to the zygote.

In other words, in this, the closing entry of this book, we are describing the process whereby the true male cell unites with a female egg cell, or ovule, to form the first cell of a future rose. It would be hard to choose a more appropriate place in which to emphasize the everlasting future of the Queen of Flowers.

Such is Love

Ainsi est l'amour

Selected bibliography

Books

ALLEN, MEA, *William Robinson 1838–1935*, Faber & Faber, 1982.

D'ARNEVILLE, MARIE-BLANCHE, *Parcs et jardins sous le premier empire*, Librairie Jules Tallandier, Paris, 1981.

BEALES, PETER, *Early Victorian Roses*, Jarrold, 1977.

——————, *Edwardian Roses*, Jarrold, 1979.

——————, *Georgian and Regency Roses*, Jarrold, 1977.

——————, *Late Victorian Roses*, Jarrold, 1979.

BERMUDA ROSE SOCIETY, *Old Garden Roses in Bermuda*, Bermuda Press, Paget, 1984.

BLACKMORE, STEPHEN and TOOTHILL, ELIZABETH (eds), *Dictionary of Botany*, Penguin, 1984.

BLAIKIE, THOMAS, *Diary of a Scottish Gardener at the French Court*, Routledge, 1931.

BLUNT, WILFRID, *The Art of Botanical Illustration*, Collins, 1950.

BOYLE, THE HON. MRS ('E. V. B.'), *Ros Rosarum*, Elliot Stock, 2nd ed. 1896.

BRIGGS, D. and WALTERS, S. M., *Plant Variations and Evolution*, Weidenfeld & Nicolson, 1969.

BUIST, ROBERT, *The Rose Manual*, Carey & Hart, Philadelphia, 1844; Earl M. Coleman, New York, 1978 (facsimile ed.).

CARPENTER, HUMPHREY and PRICHARD, MARI, *The Oxford Companion to Children's Literature*, Oxford University Press, 1984.

CHARLTON, DON, *Growing and Showing Roses*, David & Charles, 1984.

CLAPHAM, A. R., TUTIN, T. G. and WARBURG, E.F., *Flora of the British Isles*, Cambridge University Press, 1962.

CLEMENTS, JULIA, *The Book of Rose Arrangements*, Batsford, 1984.

ELLACOMBE, CANON HENRY, *In a Gloucestershire Garden*, Edward Arnold, 1895; Century, 1982.

ELLWANGER, H. B., *The Rose*, Dodd, Mead & Co., New York, 1882; Heinemann, 1893.

FAIRBROTHER, F., *Roses*, Penguin, 1963.

FITCH, CHARLES MARDEN, *The Complete Book of Miniature Roses*, Hawthorn Dutton, New York, 1977.

FLETCHER, CYRIL, *Cyril Fletcher's Rose Book*, Collins, 1983.

FLETCHER, HAROLD R., *The Story of the Royal Horticultural Society*, Oxford University Press/Royal Horticultural Society, 1969.

FLETCHER, H. L. V., *The Rose Anthology*, Newnes, 1963.

FOSTER-MELLIAR, THE REVD A. (ROBERTS, THE REVD F. PAGE and MOLYNEUX, HERBERT E., eds), *The Book of the Rose*, Macmillan, 4th ed. 1910.

GENDERS, ROY, *The Rose*, Robert Hale, 1965.

GIBSON, MICHAEL, *Growing Roses*, Croom Helm, London and Canberra; Timber Press, Portland, Oregon, 1984.

GORE, CATHERINE FRANCES, *The Book of the Rose, or The Rose Fancier's Manual*, Henry Colburn, 1838; Heyden & Son, London, and Earl M. Coleman, New York, 1978 (facsimile ed.).

GRAVEREAUX, JULES, *Les roses cultivées à L'Hay en 1902*, Librairies Pierre Cochet, Grisy-Suisnes, 1902.

HARKNESS, JACK, *The Makers of Heavenly Roses*, Souvenir Press, 1985.

HARVEY, N. P., *The Rose in Britain*, Souvenir Press, 1958.

HARVEY-CANT, *Rose Selection and Cultivation*, Garden Book Club, 1951.

HENREY, BLANCHE, *British Botanical and Horticultural Literature before 1800*, Oxford University Press, 1975.

HESSAYON, DR D. G. and WHEATCROFT, HARRY, *Be Your Own Rose Expert*, pan britannica industries, 1965.

HIBBERD, SHIRLEY, *The Rose Book*, Groombridge, 1864, 2nd ed. as *The Amateur's Rose Book*, 1894.

HOLE, S. REYNOLDS, *A Book about Roses*, Edward Arnold, 15th ed. 1896.

INTERNATIONAL COMMISSION FOR THE NOMENCLATURE OF CULTIVATED PLANTS, *International Code of Nomenclature of Cultivated Plants*, Bohn, Scheltema & Holkema, Utrecht, 1980.

JEFFERSON, THOMAS, *Thomas Jefferson's Garden Book*, American Philosophical Society, Philadelphia, 1944.

JEKYLL, GERTRUDE and MAWLEY, EDWARD, *Roses for English Gardens*, George Newnes, 1902; Antique Collectors' Club, 1982.

KEAYS, ETHELYN EMERY, *Old Roses*, Macmillan, New York, 1935; Earl M. Coleman, New York, 1978 (facsimile ed.).

KORDES, WILHELM, *Roses* (trans. N. P. Harvey), Studio Vista, 1964.

KRÜSSMANN, GERD, *Roses*, Timber Press, Portland, Oregon, 1981; Batsford, London, 1982.

LE GRICE, E. B., *Rose Growing Complete*, Faber & Faber, 1965.

LEIGHTON, ANN, *American Gardens in the Eighteenth Century*, Houghton Mifflin, Boston, 1976.

LE LIÈVRE, AUDREY, *Miss Willmott of Warley Place*, Faber & Faber, 1980.

LINDEBOOM, GERRIT, *Herman Boerhaave*, Methuen, 1968.

MCCANN, SEAN, *All the World's Roses*, Frewen, 1974.

MCCLINTOCK, DAVID, *Companion to Flowers*, George Bell, 1966.

MCFARLAND, J. HORACE, *The Rose in America*, Macmillan, New York, 1923.

MCGREDY, SAM and JENNETT, S., *A Family of Roses*, Cassell, 1971.

MCQUOWN, F. R., *Plant Breeding for Gardeners*, Collingridge, 1963.

MATTOCK, MARK, *Roses*, Blandford Press, 1980.

MITCHELL, PETER, *European Flower Painters*, A. & C. Black, 1974.

NATIONAL ASSOCIATION OF FLOWER ARRANGEMENT SOCIETIES, *Handbook of Schedule Definitions*, 1982.

NICOLAS, DR J. H., *A Rose Odyssey*, Doubleday Doran, 1937.

NORTH, C., *Plant Breeding and Genetics in Horticulture*, Horticultural Education Association/Royal Horticultural Society/Macmillan, 1979.

PAL, B. P., *The Rose in India*, Indian Council of Agricultural Research, New Delhi.

PARK, BERTRAM, *The World of Roses*, George S. Harrap, 1962.

PARKER, ERIC, and ROHDE, ELEANOR SINCLAIR, *The Gardener's Week-End Book*, Seeley Service, 1939.

PATERSON, ALLEN, *The History of the Rose*, Collins, 1982.

PAUL, WILLIAM, *The Rose Garden*, Sherwood Gilbert & Piper, 1848; Earl M. Coleman, New York, 1978 (facsimile ed.).

PAVIÈRE, SYDNEY J., *A Dictionary of Flower Painting*, F. Lewis, 1962.

PEMBERTON, THE REVD JOSEPH H., *Roses: Their History, Development and Cultivation*, Longmans Green, 1908, 2nd ed. 1920.

PEREIRE, ANITA and VAN ZUYLEN, GABRIELLE, *Private Gardens of France*, Weidenfeld & Nicolson, 1983.

PIERCY, HAROLD, *The Constance Spry Handbook of Floristry*, Croom Helm, 1984.

PLANT VARIETY RIGHTS OFFICE, *Guide to Plant Breeders' Rights*, 1983.

——————————, *Supplement* (to the above), 1985.

PORTER, SIR ROBERT KER, *Travels in Georgia, Persia, Armenia, etc. 1817–1820*, 1821.

POULSEN, SVEND, *Poulsen on the Rose* (trans. C. Campbell McCallum), MacGibbon & Kee, 1955.

PRINCE, WILLIAM ROBERT, *Prince's Manual of Roses*, A. Clark & Co., New York, 1846; Earl M. Coleman, New York, 1979 (facsimile ed.).

PROCTER, MICHAEL and YEO, PETER. *The Pollination of Flowers*, Collins, 1979.

RAMSBOTTOM, JOHN and WILSON, G. FOX (PARK, BERTRAM hon. ed.), *Enemies of the Rose*, National Rose Society, 1952.

RIDGE, ANTONIA, *For the Love of a Rose*, Faber & Faber, 1963.

——————————, *The Man who Painted Roses*, Faber & Faber, 1974.

RIVERS, THOMAS JR, *The Rose Amateur's Guide*, Longman, Brown, Green & Longmans, 1837, 4th ed. 1846; Earl M. Coleman, New York, 1979 (facsimile ed.).

ROBINSON, WILLIAM, *The English Flower Garden*, John Murray, 1883, 14th ed. 1926.

——————————, *The Wild Garden*, 1870; Century, new ed. 1983.

ROYAL HORTICULTURAL SOCIETY, *The Report of the National Rose Conference held in the Society's Gardens at Chiswick on July 2nd and 3rd 1889*.

SHEPHERD, ROY E., *The History of the Rose*, Macmillan, New York, 1954; Earl M. Coleman, New York, 1978 (facsimile ed.).

SICHEL, EDITH, *The Renaissance*, Williams & Norgate, 1922.

SINGER, MAX, *Dictionnaire des roses* (2 vols), published by author, Paris, 1885.

SITWELL, SACHEVERELL, *Old-Fashioned Flowers*, Country Life, 1939.

SOCIÉTÉ NATIONALE D'HORTICULTURE DE FRANCE, *Les plus belles roses au début du XXᵉ siècle*, Librarie Charles Amat, Paris, 1912.

SPORNE, K. R., *The Morphology of Angiosperms*, Hutchinson, 1974.

STACE, C. A. (ed.), *Hybridization and the Flora of the British Isles*, Academic Press/Botanical Society of the British Isles.

TAKHTAJAN, ARMEN, *Flowering Plants: Origin and Dispersal* (trans. C. Jeffrey), Oliver & Boyd, 1969.

THEOPHRASTUS, *Enquiry into Plants* (trans. Sir Arthur Hort), Heinemann, 1916.

THOMAS, A. S., *Better Roses*, Angus & Robertson, Sydney, revised ed. 1955.

THOMAS, GEORGE C., *Roses for All American Climates*, Macmillan, New York, 1924.

THOMAS, GRAHAM STUART, *Climbing Roses Old and New*, J. M. Dent/Royal Horticultural Society, 1983.

——————————, *Shrub Roses of Today*, J. M. Dent, 1980.

——————————— and HURST, DR C. C., *Old Shrub Roses*, J. M. Dent, 1983.

WELSH, JAMES R., *Fundamentals of Plant Genetics and Breeding*, John Wiley, New York, 1981.

WHEATCROFT, HARRY, *My Life with Roses*, Odhams, 1959.

WILLMOTT, ELLEN, *The Genus Rosa*, John Murray, 1914.

WILLSON, E. J., *James Lee and the Vineyard Nursery, Hammersmith*, Hammersmith Local History Group.

YOUNG, NORMAN (WHYATT, L. A. ed.), *The Complete Rosarian*, Gardeners' Book Club, 1971.

Periodicals

American Rose, American Rose Society.

The Rose, Royal National Rose Society.

Der Rosenbogen, Verein Deutscher Rosenfreunde.

Index

Name Index

Page numbers in *italic* refer to illustrations

Picture credits

The author and publishers wish to thank the following for permission to reproduce photographs:
Bridgeman Art Library/British Library, page 170; Bridgeman Art Library/Chelsea Physick Garden, pages 53 *above*, 131 *above* and 205; Bridgeman Art Library/Christies, pages 18 *below* and 19; Bridgeman Art Library/Lindley Library, RHS, pages 17, 112, 131 *below*, 134 and 171; Bridgeman Art Library/St Martin, Colmar, France, page 172; Bridgeman Art Library/Victoria and Albert Museum, pages 56, 73, 111 and 152; Colefax & Fowler (Interior) Design, page 91; Painton Cowen, page 169; Dickson Nurseries Ltd, page 60; Mary Evans Picture Library, pages 15, 77, 105, 117, 125, 157, 164, 177, 181, 187, 202 and 214; Fine Art Photographs, pages 18 *above*, 20, 54 and 133; Fotomas Index, pages 58 and 114; R. Harkness & Company Ltd, pages 80 and 81; Angelo Hornak, front cover; Mansell Collection, pages 8 *right*, 26, 53 *below*, 70, 84, 87, 88, 90, 97, 107, 163, 174, 206, 207 and 208; Ann Ronan Picture Library, pages 8 *left*, 24, 42, 43, 52, 63, 65, 66, 69, 119, 142, 143, 150, 188, 191 and 195; Arthur Sanderson & Sons Ltd, page 94 and back cover; Sotheby Parke Bernet & Company, pages 92 and 93; Victoria and Albert Museum, page 55; Vision International/photos Angelo Hornak, pages 74 *above*, 132 and 151; Watts & Company Ltd, page 74 *below*; Frederick C.H. Witchell, page 113.

Illustrations on pages 13, 28, 38, 39, 57, 140 and 156 are taken from the Revd Joseph H. Pemberton, *Roses: Their History, Development and Cultivation*, Longmans, Green & Co., 1920.